Notes for a Life

Bryan Forbes

Notes for a Life

Collins   London   1974

William Collins Sons & Co Ltd
London · Glasgow · Sydney · Auckland
Toronto · Johannesburg

First published 1974
© Bryan Forbes Ltd 1974

ISBN 0 00 211567 0

Set in Monotype Garamond
Made and printed in Great Britain by
William Collins Sons & Co Ltd Glasgow

'We are born under a layer of superstition and false ideas; we grow up under it, go on living under it, and say to ourselves that we shall die under it, without ever for one single day of our lives having lived otherwise than in subjection to the ideas of idiots and the customs of savages, which we cannot infringe or even denounce without danger to ourselves. Into this environment we throw our children, who are defenceless or have defences as dangerous for them as the evils of the system. We say that life has always been like this and always will be, over the whole surface of the earth. We try to smile and bear things philosophically, but remain deeply impressed.'

Henry de Montherlant, Essays

'Spare my face, aim at my heart.'

Murat, at his execution

For the women in my life . . .

For my mother, Betty, Ivy Richardson,
Innes Gotto, Sarah, Emma

and once again

For Nanette

with my love.

List of Illustrations

Foreword

To write at all is a sort of arrogance, and to attempt an auto-biography before the age of fifty bloats the conceit.

From the moment I started these memoirs I have often thought how comforting it must be to have the assurance of a Rousseau, to be able to state, 'I am undertaking a work which has no example,' and then to say, 'Here is the only portrait of a man, justly painted according to nature and with complete truth . . . this man is myself.'

To describe oneself requires a generous ration of self-mockery and a keen awareness that we only confess our faults through vanity. In the ardent and arduous days of the Regency politicians often committed actual suicide instead of using the more cumbrous method of writing their memoirs. I have listened to and given myself so much advice, for a writer is always prey to self-doubt: it is the nature of the beast. And because the major part of my working life as a writer has been in the film industry, where advice from others is the force-fed staple diet, I am no stranger to my own reflection.

My career as a professional writer could well have been blunted at an early age, for the ghost of Palinurus, in the portly shape of Cyril Connolly, has walked my battlements since the first appearance of *The Unquiet Grave* in the, alas, now defunct *Horizon*. This book and the same author's *Enemies of Promise* are required reading for any aspiring young author, and at one time I almost knew them by heart. They describe in dauntingly concise prose where it is all likely to go wrong. *The Unquiet Grave* could, in many ways, be said to resemble Doctor Spock – listing, detailing and anticipating as it does every flatulence likely to attack or paralyse youthful literary bowels. I recommend it to anybody about to have a first novel.

Connolly, with his own arrogance, defines the true function of a writer as being the production of masterpieces: 'no other task is of any consequence'; and goes on to say that 'all excursions into journalism, broadcasting, propaganda and writing for films, however grandiose, are doomed to disappointment. It is in the nature of such work not to last, so it should never be undertaken.'

This story, then – this conceit – is not the journal of a disappointed man, nor a scrapbook of yellowing press cuttings, but an account of somebody who has spent the last thirty years making such excursions, undertaking a series of grandiose journeys, more often than not with no return ticket, and who now feels the need to come home and start afresh.

One

It was love beneath the table – dark, unrequited, innocent. I could only have been four years old at the time, possibly even younger, for although my earliest recollections go even farther back and I can recall the pain and panic of a serious, near fatal illness before the age of two, the remembered shadows on the nursery wall are thrown by brief candles and the early flame is not steady or reliable.

To say I fell in love is to exaggerate an unformed emotion with the hindsight of forty years. But it was a passion, and I can remember turning to it time and time again like a drug.

The object of my love was a photograph of an unknown little girl of my own age running naked along the edge of the sea. There is no point in concealing that my attraction to her was entirely physical, for she was a very *naked* naked little girl, and I have never ceased to be thankful to her. She was one of the illustrations in *The Glaxo Baby Book*, a publication given away to regular purchasers of that admirable product. I believe I can claim to have been a 'Glaxo Baby' as they were glowingly termed in the adverts. Certainly I wasn't breast-fed, and my mother later confessed that I was not a welcome pregnancy. She conceived me somewhat late in life. I was born in 1926 in the sullen aftermath of the General Strike in my mother's 41st year and some six years after the birth of my only sister, Betty. Even now, although memory has been strongly diluted by pride, my mother still frequently returns to a much-polished monologue – chronicling a long and painful labour in Queen Mary's Hospital, Stratford-atte-Bow, which is literally within sound of the fabled Cockney bells. It was there during a night thunderstorm that I claimed identity on the 22nd July 1926, which places me, in horoscopic terms, leaving Cancer and at the cusp of Leo.

The love-affair started in that back room at 43 Cranmer Road, Forest Gate, where I spent the first thirteen years of my childhood. I remember crawling under the dark, tasselled tablecloth, careful not to disturb my maternal grandmother who always sat to the left of the black coal range and who remained dozingly unaware of my illicit practices. Once concealed beneath the table I would turn to that page, and that page only, and gaze upon my beloved. In retrospect I can conjure guilt across the years – but was it really guilt, I wonder? Are we born with such prudery, or is it only the smear that forty years of living has thumbed on to the subconscious?

Beyond the safety of the tablecloth Grandma Seaton, deaf and devoted to me, remained convinced of my innocence in all matters. I must have had a certain basic cunning, for I committed all my acts of love and rebellion while she was asleep, sometimes turning out the entire contents of my father's desk, a crime which he treated as on a level with the Nazi reoccupation of the Rhineland. When awake she would roll dusters into a ball for me and throw them, her chuckling face in shadow, tears of laughter glistening on her old cheeks – a phenomenon which more than anything else about her always fascinated me, I remember. I would stand very close to her chair peering up into her lined face while the tears coursed silently down, for all the world like the end of a drought travelling across parched earth. And then, suddenly, in the midst of laughter, she would lapse back into sleep, her head falling forward with an abruptness that, to a child, seemed like death: as though invisible hands had snapped her neck. She was in her nineties, a farmer's daughter and a farmer's wife from Gedney Hill, Lincolnshire, the mother of nine boys and four girls.

I would back away from her when this happened, unsure but not afraid, and stand motionless at the other end of the room, seeking to solve the many mysteries of somebody so old, so unknown. Then, when convinced that the game was postponed, I would stealthily remove *The Glaxo Baby Book* from the cupboard on the other side of the hearth and take it to my lair. Safe beneath the table again, I would turn once more to the favourite page, amazed every time that the object of my passion was still excitingly the same. I kissed that page, kissed the naked image until the imprint of my lips stained the sepia-tinted shiny paper. The little naked girl had fair, curly hair, I remember, and was running from left to right along the edge of an unknown sea. I loved her beyond recall and included her in my prayers. I loved her until the book disintegrated, and then I forgot her.

Two

I was christened John Theobald Clarke, for Bryan Forbes is a stage fiction, chosen at random by the late Lionel Gamlin, the man who gave me my first professional job.

Over the years Bryan Forbes has become legal fact, although my mother increasingly and understandably reverts and will call me John again. Sometimes now, in the twilight of her years, the confusion tangles even further and she will address me as Ralph or Knowles, the names of two favourite nephews, one of whom is dead.

Theobald was the maiden name of my paternal grandmother and I have since discovered it is compounded from the old German of *theuda* 'folk' and *bald* 'bold'. Apparently names beginning with *theuda* were early changed to *theo* under the influence of such Greek names as *Theodore*, and my father has always been called Theo by the family. The usual Latin form is *Teobaldus*, the vernacular being *Tebald* or *Tibald*, which leads to *Tybalt* in *Romeo and Juliet*. A strange and somewhat heady heritage for a small Cockney boy to live with, who in any case was inevitably referred to as Nobby.

Clarkes are called Nobby because clerks used to wear top-hats in the City. Again, not the most sought-after nickname when, without comprehension, you find yourself so labelled aged five.

Miss Ivy Richardson, who called herself my Nanny but who was in fact the spinster who owned the house we lived in in Cranmer Road, used to try and cheer me up with the 'sticks-and-stones-will-break-your-bones-but-names-will-never -hurt-you' school of sympathy, but I remained unconvinced.

Ivy was a kindly soul who occupied the two front rooms on the upstairs floor. She was the neglected child of a large family and had gifts that the very young were quick to discern. I spent long hours with her, indulged and understood, inventing complicated games with wicker chairs which she allowed me to upturn and transform into railway engines, dark caves and chariots. Her only other companion was an enormous Persian cat who dined more regularly and substantially than its mistress. Ivy convinced me that when the cat purred he was really singing 'Jesus wants me for a sunbeam', a fact which I immediately imparted to the local Curate. 'Cats do not sing hymns,' he said without humour. I dismissed him as an idiot and a liar. What Ivy said was the Gospel.

Ivy was allowed to take me for walks in my push-chair and her route invariably took us to Wanstead Cemetery, a place I associated not with the dead but with 'conkers'. There, in the dank avenues leading to the pigeon-fouled mausoleums of Victorian tradesmen, the ground was thick with them. The wheels of my push-chair crushed the wet, spiky shells like so many helpless baby turtles, and I could lean down and select only the shiniest and fattest of the fruit. On the return journey home we would stop at a sweet shop to buy sherbert dabs and liquorice wheels, chocolate buttons and hundreds and thousands, all expressly forbidden by my mother and which, gloriously, I therefore had to consume before we turned the last corner.

Our shared guilt was exposed within seconds of arriving home, for apparently I had a compulsive need to confess the truth and would cheerfully betray Ivy and enjoy the consequent scolding she received from my mother. But if Ivy shielded me at home, providing sanctuary on those dog days when my over-worked mother's patience finally snapped, she could not protect me when I entered Godwin Road Elementary School.

That establishment was approached through a long corrugated iron covered way which held more dread than all the tombstones in Wanstead Cemetery. There, immediately plotted on that built-in radar screen that all young children seem to possess, I was quickly identified as a Nobby *and* a Theobald: doubly humiliated, isolated and mocked. I think part of the agony stemmed from the fact that Theobald belonged to my grandmother and the explanation that it was a maiden name only served to confirm in my mind that it was a deliberate attempt to saddle me with a female personality.

Naturally, since I embarked upon this remembrance of things past, I have tried to trace my origins. The search led me eventually to a small village called Walsham-le-Willows about ten miles north-east of Bury St Edmunds in Suffolk, which is clearly shown in Blaeu's Atlas of 1645. The church register in Walsham has an embarrassment of Clarkes, and there is a direct line from 1659 to the present day.

I do not intend this to be a long recital of dates, births and deaths, for there is nothing more boring or pretentious in narratives of this kind, and I will therefore limit my family tree to the barest branches necessary to support the story.

My grandparents lived in Odessa Road, Forest Gate, when I was born. This was a dismal thoroughfare, bordering at one end on the London and North Eastern Railway which ran, below street level, behind a blackened wall topped with jagged bottle glass. There was little, I fear, of the romance of steam about that particular stretch of line which terminated in the sooted vault of Liverpool Street Station. Pollution being then undiscovered, the belching tank engines were merely an accepted fact of life, menacing every washline and delighting only small boys – for to remain fearless on the wooden pedestrian bridge while a train shuddered beneath it was considered a supreme test. One of the punishments meted out to the bullied was for the victim's face to be pushed between the wooden floor slats of the bridge while a slow goods train passed jerking and clanging below. Apart from the terror produced by the noise, the sufferer was choked by the thick yellow smoke which took minutes to disperse.

My grandfather had some nameless job connected with the railway in his later years, and I dimly remember him wearing a nondescript uniform – always falsely impressive to a child. But perhaps my memory is at fault in this instance, perhaps I am confusing him with another branch of the Clarke family, all of whom served in the Salvation Army, that Sandhurst of the poor.

I think it is true to say that my grandmother Clarke was a unique and remarkable little woman. Totally unlike the stage idea of a Cockney (she would have been revolted by this generation's ready acceptance of Alf Garnett), she lived to be

98, having survived being made homeless twice during the Blitz, once from a land-mine and once from a doodle-bug.

She was frail in appearance and ate, almost literally, like a mouse, taking tiny pieces of dried bread and nibbles of orange-coloured cheese, cutting both cheese and bread with the sharpest of kitchen knives into minute triangular portions. Small of frame and delicate of feature, she was nevertheless blessed with enormous energy and scorned any form of self-pity. Proud and unenvious, she accepted her many and various burdens with a fortitude that, in the later Blitz years, welded with that of her neighbours into a calm defiance. She had pure white hair like the gossamer tresses immortalized in fairy-tales, and when she loosened it it fell to below her waist. She kept it to her death. Her skin, I remember, was truly transparent and seemed to a child to resemble tissue paper carefully pasted over an etching of wrinkles and veins.

Once a week I was taken to family tea in Odessa Road and it is only in retrospect, sitting here at this desk, that I begin to perceive the boundaries of her simple and ever-shrinking life. Conditions must always have been hard for her. My grand-father, although to a child an amiable figure most of the time, always good for an extra penny pocket-money, could not have been the easiest of men to live with, for he had a violent temper, carefully but not completely concealed in front of the grand-children but which my sister and I sometimes glimpsed when we were stroppy. He claimed to be an authority on horses and I gather that at one period he had been a groom to a titled family in London. Certainly the only time he became really animated was when he recounted some apocryphal story about his equestrian exploits. His eyes would sparkle and his smile – always faintly sinister – would reveal a row of broken stumps, jagged and forbidding like the glass embedded in the railway wall. The stories always ended the same way. He would repeat the tag line several times, making as it were his own echo, and then with much hissing of tobacco breath would lean forward and roll up one trouser leg – revealing first an expanse of grey combs and then the mottled pale flesh of his calf. He would point to some scar and repeat yet again how he had tamed the horse that inflicted it. I vividly remember the performance filling Betty and me with horror, for his legs, which never saw sunlight, were like grotesque and bleached pieces of driftwood.

When my recollections start, my grandparents occupied the whole house. Everywhere was spotlessly clean and kept that way until the bombs fell. Perhaps the years immediately before the Second World War were the swan-song of that particular type of working-class pride, when even in the most squalid districts the ritual of whitening the front door step was observed every morning by the majority, and the lino in the front 'best' room polished to shaving-mirror brightness, was guarded more closely than a daughter's virginity. There was no bathroom, of course, and no inside toilet in my grandparents' house. The house came down before electricity was installed, and heating was virtually non-existent, the only warmth originating from a minute grate burning the cheapest variety of coal and upon which was perched from morning to night a heavy blackened kettle simmering just off the boil for the endless cups of thick tea.

It was a doll's house, grimed and sandwiched between two other identical dolls' houses, with 'front' gardens just big enough to take a baby's pram lengthways, separated from the pavement by a thin barrier of privet hedges, their exposed roots cankered by vintage dog pee and their foliage crisped by soot to the texture of dried holly.

Inside, the tiny rooms were cluttered with a multitude of prized possessions. I remember bamboo shelves overloaded with what, today, would be considered bric-à-brac camp enough to make Islington antique dealers lisp all the way to the bank. There were pale blue china hands festooned with simple gold rings; gaping, pink-mouthed sea-shells; dainty silver frames housing sepia photographs behind fly-blown glass; pairs of infant shoes fossilized by some process, from which coloured pipe cleaners protruded. Dried and painted poppy heads gathered immortal dust in one corner, and on the mantelpiece were tiny translucent vases, picture postcards commemorating holidays other people had taken (my grandmother never travelled: she suffered from 'bilious attacks'). I remember a collection of hat pins piercing a crumbling heart-shaped cushion, a wooden doll's tea service and, of course, occupying the place of honour, in the 'best' room, a framed photograph of a Tommy – the absurdly young face anticipating death above the newly issued khaki tunic – Alfie, my father's only brother, killed before the age of nineteen on the Somme, his grave unlisted. The first time I saw adult tears was at tea in Odessa Road following an Armistice Service. My grandmother sat with her back to a window, sipped hot tea and cried.

The possessions, large and small, gradually disappeared. It was a slow process, for poverty is seldom instantaneous, and to a child almost imperceptible. It was the gold rings on the pale blue hands I noticed first, for the hands themselves had always held a sinister fascination for me and they were the first things I looked for when entering the house.

As the years advanced, so my grandparents withdrew further and further into the house, finally inhabiting only two rooms. The front bedroom was kept locked, but occasionally, as a treat, I was permitted to peer inside and I recall mysterious packages wrapped in old newspapers, a smell of damp and decay, and old clothes thrown across a large double bed, the brass frame of which was dulled with mildew, and the coiled springs of the mattress curiously naked, reminding me of entrails in the cheap butcher's shop in Forest Road.

It was as if, with the decline of their already meagre fortunes, my grandparents themselves became smaller, needing less and less room in which to exist. Just as the flesh fell away from my grandfather's collarless and plucked-turkey-like neck, so, it appeared, their physical demands withered. My grandmother took even smaller morsels of bread and cheese, my grandfather gave up shaving himself and his stubble grew whiter in a skin pocked with a lifetime's exposure to soot. This more than anything else dismayed my grandmother and she would bring a bowl of hot water into their living-room, place it on his lap and wash his face with a soft piece of flannel and Pears transparent soap. I have often observed that when a man and a woman live together over a very long period (and my grandparents celebrated their Golden Wedding together) even without illness one of the partners appears to give up the struggle before the other and gradually assumes all the attributes of a long forgotten child. Such was the case here. My grandmother never lost her keenness to participate in life, but her husband became morose, closing his eyes to the passing scene, muttering over the slights, imagined and real, that fate had dealt him, and only in some short-lived spurt of anger did he, from time to time, convey an impression of the original man.

There was a smell of age which met me as I climbed the stairs to the darkness at the top: sheets not aired, bundles of newspapers hoarded against a rainy day, the enamel slop pail beneath the sink in the kitchen, the door frame which did not fit, the tabby cat huddled, moulting, against the window pane, staring into the gaslit room with malevolent eyes.

While time and the river of poverty eroded the very fabric of the house, my grandmother remained triumphantly serene. If she had a difficult life with my grandfather she did not share it with the family or outsiders. As children we were never aware of what lay beyond the evidence. There was always cake for tea, and the best china brought out, a piece of butter muslin weighted with coloured beads over the milk jug, fish paste on thin bread and butter slices cut from a crusty cottage loaf, and the same welcoming face framed by the unreal white hair.

Three

The woman was mad and one morning she started to move all her furniture and belongings into the garden. I watched from my upstairs bedroom window, in that room in Cranmer Road that for the first thirteen years of my life I shared with my parents. She did it very methodically, and to a child there seemed little that was odd about her behaviour: she might have been embarked upon some definitive bout of spring cleaning. It wasn't until she began to hang pictures on the garden fence that I dimly perceived and was attracted by her growing madness. I remained at the window, fascinated, while below me she covered her pathetic patch of lawn with old and faded carpets, and then placed her dining table and chairs in a neat pattern in one corner. It seemed like a forbidden adult game. Next came the bed which she positioned tight against a garden shed, and brought out a standard lamp which leaned crazily on the uneven lawn.

When everything was arranged to her satisfaction the woman stripped off all her clothes, throwing them into beds of lupins and London Pride, Ophelia with a creped belly, and then began to dance very slowly. Her body, I remember, stood out white against the green of the lawn and seemed to belong to a younger person than her face suggested. While she danced she held her full breasts in her hands, crooning to them as she sang verse after verse of 'Ain't it Grand to be Blooming Well Dead'.

It was at this point that I was discovered watching and dragged inside, for while madness was acceptable, nudity was forbidden. But with a child's natural cunning, I managed to follow the working out of this strange drama. I remember other neighbours shouting out, some with words of encouragement, some crudely abusive, and my mother going around the house with a worried expression, genuinely distressed. I can also recall strangers in uniform walking through our house and climbing over the fence at the bottom of our garden – disturbing my swing which was hung between two poplars. Then the poor naked woman was trapped in the debris of her home. Her nudity inhibited her would-be captors – she seemed free and sane while they were stiff and sweating beneath peaked caps.

Years later, permitted with the passing of time to question my parents on vaguely suspect topics, I learnt that she had smothered a Mongoloid child. That morning she was finally overpowered, put into a strait-jacket screaming in sudden fear and carted away to the asylum. To be mad in 1930 was something very shameful indeed. My mother, who always had a good word to say for everybody, excused her. 'She had a lot on her mind, poor soul. I shan't speak ill of her,' she said. 'She was a good neighbour to me.'

That single bizarre episode remains fixed because the gentle flow of life in Cranmer Road was seldom disturbed. It was a peaceful neighbourhood with pretensions towards what used to be called the 'genteel': neat, undistinguished but solidly built rows of terraced houses, carefully painted every year on the outside, and the women used to hang striped canvas sunblinds during the summer months to protect the front doors. Forest Gate was a pleasant place to live in in those days. Originally a hamlet lying to the north of Upton at the edge of Wanstead Flats, it was, as its name denotes, the southern entrance to Epping Forest. Cranmer Road bordered on the Flats, the savannah of my formative years which I was forbidden to explore beyond a certain limit and which, in consequence, appeared to me to be as mysterious and boundless as an entire continent.

In reality it was a large area of sparse grassland dotted with irregular plantations of thin trees and some sandhills humped around what I assume must have been a derelict gravel pit. It had a pathetic boating pond like something out of Toy Town, with half a dozen rotting little paddle boats for hire, and a small bandstand where, some Sunday evenings, we were taken to hear the music, sitting on hard slatted seats and surrounded by discarded peanut shells. I thought it one of the most romantic places on earth.

Running parallel to Cranmer Road were four other roads named after the martyred bishops – Latimer, Lorne, Tilney and Ridley. They were considered slightly posher than my own, and Lorne the poshest of the lot. When I progressed to secondary school I suffered my first crush for a girl named Violet, and it was with a feeling of mingled awe and amazement that, walking her home, I discovered that she lived in Lorne Road. It was as if I had foolishly selected a future wife from the aristocracy, and when, in a matter of days, she threw me on the scrapheap for a close friend called Arthur Smith who was the son of a prosperous grocer, I tearfully justified my fate on social grounds.

But that is anticipating a whole series of unrequited loves, for I have always been self-destructively romantic. My dandelion days on Wanstead Flats were for the most part totally uncomplicated: it was football in the mud during winter and cricket until the light faded in summer.

However, it was there in the 'Giant's Basin' on the Flats that I was first initiated into the mysteries of the sexual urge. On Sunday mornings the French letters waved accusing fingers from every hawthorn bush, and another friend of the period, Cyril Cocksedge, explained their exact function in bewildering detail. Cyril, I now realize, was gifted beyond his years and had what my mother would undoubtedly have called 'a dirty mind'. I don't wish to blacken his remembered character, for I think that his vast sexual experience was mostly imagined and then vividly embroidered. Certainly everything he told me was anatomically possible, though at the time it seemed that each additional piece of information he imparted was more improbable than the last. He had all his basic facts right but gave them in the wrong order.

He again was a layer above me in the social strata, for his Uncle Len owned a car, a Vauxhall, which placed him well and truly above the mob. In fact I am sure it was the only car in the road, and bachelor Uncle Len was a truly glamorous figure in our eyes. The wildest treat imaginable was to be allowed to help polish the car on Sunday mornings.

Curiously, I didn't receive my sexual baptism in Cyril's

company. It happened while I was playing with another friend, Albert Herbert, and his dog Trixie. We had ventured as far as the Giant's Basin. I was in hiding and Albert was searching for me. It was Trixie who gave the first warning: at her bark I looked up through the tall burnt grass to see a stranger regarding me. He was dressed quite normally, if somewhat shabbily, in a fawn raincoat and trilby hat. He had a soft and calming voice and he offered me sixpence – a vast sum – if I would 'do him a treat.'

Some instinct warned me to refuse the offer (perhaps the bribe was too high? A penny would have been more comprehensible and thus less suspicious). He repeated the request and then, in classic style, whipped open the raincoat to reveal himself totally naked and to my eyes amazingly deformed. Nothing in Cyril's careful schooling had prepared me for this variation on an old theme. I ran, as we used to say, like the clappers, with Trixie barking defiance at my heels, stumbled and fell, gashing my left palm on a broken bottle. The man didn't give chase and I made my way home bleeding copiously. For some reason I concealed the true nature of the incident from my mother, who in any event was sufficiently worried about my cut hand, but I brooded over the experience until my father returned home and then blurted out the salient facts. My father said nothing to me, but left the house immediately and went to the police station.

The gentleman in the raincoat proved to be an escaped lunatic (it would appear that Forest Gate had more than its fair quota in those days!) and was apparently swiftly apprehended.

According to the popular sex journals this early encounter with the hidden realities of human nature should have marked me for life, but the episode was completely erased from my mind until 1969 when I went back to Cranmer Road with a BBC camera team who were shooting a biographical 'Man Alive' programme around me and revisiting my childhood haunts to capture celluloid nostalgia. I stood again on Wanstead Flats, the limitless vista now reduced to its true scale, shivering in the winter dusk while hordes of turbaned immigrants played hockey in the Giant's Basin – not the canyon I had remembered but just a slight dip in the arid terrain. It was only then that the memory of the naked man returned, though the physical scar has always whitened the skin beneath my left thumb.

Four

Mosley came to Wanstead Flats some Sunday evenings. He came in a sealed truck with a wire cage let into the roof. Surrounded by a black garland of close-cropped, scrubbed and waxlike bodyguards, he stood within his cage and screeched his British upper-class impersonation of Streicher to an audience that mostly consisted of children, derelicts and police.

Violence was something glimpsed from the top of a double-decker bus: the skirmish in a side-turning, old bearded Jews running across the tram lines in Whitechapel, a policeman's helmet in the gutter: unrelated clues to a struggle that was never openly mentioned. Anti-Semitism was a boy called Cohen who wore bi-focals and wet his trousers and nobody wanted to share a desk with him because he smelt of piss and fear. Politics was a closed book, for unlike so many of my contemporaries I will not pretend to an early political consciousness that did not exist. I did not grow up in a political household and the immediate circle of my parents' friends exhibited little or no awareness of the larger events waiting round the corner. For the most part they were torpid, seemingly prepared to wait and see, and grateful for any stay of execution.

Mosley spoke on Wanstead Flats. I can remember listening without comprehension: it was merely a strange but not unwelcome diversion from the sameness of everyday life. I can remember seeing bottles breaking on the wire cage close to the thin drawn face of Mosley and hearing his lunatic-amplified voice bouncing back from the houses behind him. Mounted police waited in the shadows beside the empty bandstand, edging their restless horses forward as the bullyboys started on the really important business of the evening. Mosley looked like Mighty Mouse in his mobile cage and departed the scene as battle commenced to spread his gospel on another corner of a foreign field.

Such was my introduction to the politics of the thirties, the age of Baldwin and Chamberlain, Edward VIII and Mrs Simpson, figures remoter to me than Henry Hall and Jack Payne, for we children seldom saw a newspaper – the only one that came into the house, the *Daily Express*, disappearing with my father when he left for work after his statutory breakfast of boiled egg, toast and three cups of tea. I saw newsreels, of course, for I was an inveterate cinemagoer, and in those days you got value for money. Most of my contemporaries patronized the 'Tuppenny Rush' at the Splendide alongside Forest Gate railway station. There, on a Saturday afternoon, we would rush the doors to tread the threadbare carpets inside that dark and welcoming cave. For threepence you could join the ranks of the elite and sit upstairs in the balcony, a privilege which carried with it the bonus of being able to hurl your ice-cream carton on the unruly audience below. The programme was lavish. There was always two feature films, an episode of a serial, a cartoon, and a newsreel. Our favourite was Buster Crabbe in *The Vanishing Shadow*, but we cried with Rin Tin Tin, booed lustily if any of the cowboy heroes so much as held a girl's hand, and were constantly in a state of readiness to pelt the unfortunate manager when the equipment broke down. To this day I can recall the agonizing delight of those afternoons, the bliss of coming out from the darkness into sunlight and crossing the road to Paterson's Dolls' Hospital on the bridge to spend what remained of our pocket-money on a penny bomb. This was a small but effective device, made of some cheap alloy and shaped like a hand-grenade. It had two sections which came apart and you put a cap between the two, clicked it together and then hurled it high in the air. There was a satisfying explosion when it fell to earth.

And beyond that the return home to tea, the favourite meal of the day; crusty cottage loaves cut lengthways into soft warm plates and spread thickly with butter and bright strawberry jam.

But if the Splendide was my village church, the Queens at the top of Woodgrange Road was my Westminster Abbey. This superior palace, glorifying the Cunard-liner-style of British cinema architecture, demanded greater respect and the collection started at sixpence. It was there, on Friday nights, that blissful childhood day of the week when school can be pushed to the back of the mind, that I first became addicted. I saw Laurel and Hardy there, and Will Hay, Graham Moffat, Ernie Lottinga, Moore Marriot, Sonnie Hale and Jessie Matthews. Miss Matthews was my first screen crush and I included her in my prayers, asking God to keep her for me until I was of age. When I discovered that she was married to Sonnie Hale my sense of deprivation was acute. Claude Dampier was another favourite, and of course Cecily Courtneidge and Jack Hulbert; I was moved to tears by *Soldiers of the Queen*. With the exception of Laurel and Hardy, who in any event were exports to Hollywood, my affections were mostly confined to British stars. I recall that in the company of another friend, David Usher, I once went at opening time to see *Oh, Mr Porter*. We sat through three complete performances to emerge after dark into the irate arms of two distraught mothers and a policeman. We resorted to all manner of subterfuge, not to say dishonest practices, to gain our ends when the fever ran highest and the kitty was empty. The simplest and most effective ploy at the poor old broken-down Splendide was to raise the money to buy one ticket. Once inside, the owner of the ticket would then work his way to the remotest exit, carefully open the door where his partners in crime would be waiting outside. They would dart in like rats and occupy the nearest vacant seats. The aged usherettes were too bored and poorly paid to give chase, but from time to time a new manager (pathetically attired in some second-hand dress suit) would brush the dandruff off his collar and attempt a purge. He didn't stand a chance, of course. Selected stooges would allow themselves to be captured and evicted whilst greater hordes, taking advantage of the planned diversion, would swarm through every orifice and occupy the house. Now, as a film producer, I cannot possibly condone such foul practices, but in those days it seemed a natural way of life.

Nazi Germany and the war in Abyssinia as seen in jerky clips on British Movietone News had little or no meaning for us. The Spanish Civil War and the tribal warriors of Ethiopia aiming spears at the Italian Air Force seemed like an episode from *Sanders of the River*. People didn't really die on films, they only fell down. Chamberlain dressed and looked like any of the other comics, and the goose step was better than Charlie Chaplin.

In fact, the only times the fear of a future war became vaguely real was when we rushed outside to watch the R111 float across the evening sky. I had many times been regaled with exaggerated horror stories of the zeppelin raids by Grandfather Clarke, for like many survivors of past carnage he had forgotten the waste of lives and remembered only the spurious excitement that war brings.

My father, I am sure, did have an awareness and more than most he was ready for the war when it came, but he never confided in me. He was a somewhat remote character, except during holidays, for he worked long hours; but occasionally I was permitted to accompany him to his office, The London Letter File Company in Farringdon Road where he was employed for the best part of forty years. The trains from Forest Gate were appallingly dirty, the third class being little better than upholstered cattle trucks, and it was quite normal to have eight people standing in bleak proximity in each crammed compartment.

My father belonged to a select group of dedicated card players, and the newspapers they carried were never bought to be read seriously but used to spread across their knees and form a card table. Since the trains were always late and always slow on that particular stretch of line, the games helped retain sanity.

I was proud of my father's appearance for he was and is a handsome man and wore the accepted dress of the City gentleman: black jacket, waistcoat, striped trousers, trilby hat, and always a clean shirt every day, religiously washed and ironed by my mother and laid out on his bed in summer, warmed across a chair in front of the fire in winter. He also wore heavy boots which my mother polished for him, for he pounded the streets in all weathers selling office files and equipment on commission. He lunched cheaply at Joe Lyons. The waitresses were called Nippies and wore shiny black uniforms. They were much admired by their regular male customers and considered somewhat too sexy and forward by the wives.

My father has always had an overdeveloped sense of social justice, and any increase in the price of a Lyons cup of tea would provoke an argument extending over several weeks. I once witnessed a scene which both impressed and embarrassed me. He had taken me into one of the famed Corner Houses for a mid-morning currant bun and lemonade. It was vast to my eyes, music was playing and the whole thing smacked of luxury and decadence. We were served by a dazzling Nippy who knew my father by name: her smile, her bosom beneath the black satin, hinted at darker secrets. Seduced by both atmosphere and the straw-sucked lemonade, I was totally unprepared for my father's violent demonstration. He suddenly struck and smashed his tea-cup with the handle of his umbrella. He then explained that it was against the law to serve beverages to the public in cracked cups because they were responsible for the spread of horrifying diseases (unspecified) and it was therefore every citizen's solemn duty to take the law into their own hands if not faithfully observed by the authorities. His cup had been chipped. He had therefore smashed it and prevented a recurrence of what I took to be the Black Death. This piece of eccentricity won him admiration from his colleagues and was apparently tolerated by Messrs Lyons for we were not thrown out into the street. The Nippy returned with an even broader smile, a fresh and unblemished cup of tea, and indulged in some ribaldry while she cleaned up the debris. I saw my father in a new light from that moment onwards. He has continued to tilt at windmills in equally dramatic fashion to the present day.

Since lung cancer was then an untabulated consideration in the quality of life, he smoked non-stop, going from cigarette to pipe and back to a cigarette, with the occasional cheap cigar on festive days. I must have inherited this propensity for I singed my eyebrows with a packet of Woodbines before the age of eleven, and save for a few short-lived and agonized breaks have been puffing away ever since.

It wasn't until he was in his late sixties that my father kicked the habit, so there is hope for me yet. But at the time in question his dedication to the weed provided me with a cigarette-card collection that was the envy of my circle. At one point I was the casual possessor of a collection which would nowadays command respect at Sotheby's, but I remember that we treated the cards with scant regard for the future. After school hours we rushed to gamble with them. The game was played by flicking cards from the gutter towards the nearest wall, and as each player took his turn the object was to land your own cards on top of your opponents. This entitled you to claim whatever number of cards were already on the pavement; a lucky aim could sometimes win a hundred or more cards if the game had been in progress for some time without a strike. Contestants were allowed to glue several cards together if they chose because this gave a better trajectory.

The Rembrandts of any collection were those cards issued in Kensitas packets. They were superior illustrations printed on silk and I longed without success for my father to switch brands, but he remained resolutely faithful to Gold Flake.

I can't remember any actual poverty, but then a child has little or no comprehension of adult finances. I know that we always ate well, if simply, for my mother was a superb housekeeper, somehow able to eke out her modest allowance of three pounds a week, and could turn her hand to most things when money was short. I now know that she went out to work herself, mostly charring, though the fact was concealed from me at the time.

Fortunately my father had a good governor, a Mr Robinson, who kept him on during the Depression, but his basic wages were never more than eight pounds a week and he has since told me that he did not get a raise for over twenty years. He relied upon his daily quota of orders to qualify for the all-important annual bonus. Every Friday night he would sit at his desk (another status symbol in my eyes) and carefully divide his wages, placing a number of small sums into separate bank envelopes and covering quantities of scrap paper with calculations in minuscule handwriting that only Betty could decipher with accuracy.

My father was also impressive to a child by virtue of the fact that he was then treasurer of the No. 88 (West Ham) Division of the St John Ambulance Brigade. This admirable organization has no real counterpart anywhere else in the world, and its voluntary members, although sometimes derided by more exalted sections of the medical fraternity, render valiant and unselfish service to their fellows. He joined in 1923 and worked his way through the ranks until he became the superintendent of his division and was given the Order of St John. During the Blitz he commanded a Flying Squad of ambulances throughout the worst nights in dockland.

During those early days in Cranmer Road his activities, like anything vaguely medical, had a certain aura of mystery about them, and once a week our living-room was used as the meeting-place for the committee. Every cupboard in the house was crammed with quantities of a product called *Iglodine*, which came in liquid and ointment form and could, according to my father, be used to good effect on every ailment known to medical science, and a few more that the doctors in their pedantic ignorance hadn't heard of! As children we drank it, gargled with it, put it on our cut knees, bathed our eyes in it, and even on occasions sniffed it up our cold-ridden noses. I have never seen *Iglodine* publicly advertised, but I am a living witness to its recuperative powers and to this day my father still dispenses it with undiminished fervour.

I joined the St John Ambulance Cadet Force, since the uniform had more attraction for me than the Boy Scouts. Albert Herbert accompanied me to a series of lectures at Barclay Hall in Green Street and eventually, armed with very little and I am sure dangerous knowledge, we passed our examinations and were allowed to buy and wear the grey flannel uniform and assist senior members at public functions. At one period in my life I was prepared to give artificial respiration to anybody who gave the slightest indication that they were feeling seedy, and I lived in the expectation of being witness to a national disaster at which, totally unaided, I would astound the entire medical world with the brilliance of my instant diagnosis and the skill of my bandaging. I nursed my secret, superior knowledge ('When in doubt, put them in a sling') and went about my ordinary business at school with a certain smug disdain. For months after my graduation, until the total absence of broken and mutilated limbs cooled my enthusiasm into boredom, I always carried a rolled triangular bandage in my pocket and haunted the ponds on Wanstead Flats in the fond hope of being on the spot for multiple drownings. The fact that I was unable to swim I dismissed as being of no consequence. I knew that the real test was my undoubted ability to dislodge 'foreign bodies' in the throats of those fortunate enough to be brought under my care.

My greatest triumph came when I was permitted to accompany my father and help man a First Aid post in front of Selfridges during the Jubilee celebrations of George V. A number of crushed spectators were misguided enough to faint in my presence. One, I was convinced, showed all the text-book symptoms of a convulsion. I knew that the correct treatment was to plunge the victim into alternate hot and cold baths – a somewhat difficult manœuvre to bring off successfully on the pavements of Oxford Street. It was one of our busy periods and there was nobody else to consult for a second opinion. I therefore acted unilaterally. I put two very grubby fingers inside the slack mouth of my elderly patient, but that was as far as I got. The old gentleman, with a sharp instinct for survival, closed his mouth and my probing fingers were trapped. In the struggle that followed I did succeed in dislodging my first foreign body – in this case a complete set of very nasty dentures. My patient, who was suffering from nothing worse than acute alcoholism, recovered consciousness and proved ungrateful in the extreme. It took two policemen to restrain him and as he was frog-marched away uttering foul oaths, I realized that my medical career was at an end.

On other occasions I did duty with my father at Upton Park. Football crowds seemed just as violent then and I always considered myself lucky to be on the touchline with the police. I remember my father added a chapter to his own medical glory when an extremely fat lady was passed over the heads of the crowd and deposited on the damp grass at our feet. The resident doctor being otherwise occupied with the walking wounded, my father as senior ambulance man on the spot took the law into his own hands. His efforts to loosen our patient's constricting clothing by all normal methods proved impossible, and by now she was turning an interesting shade of purple. My father didn't hesitate. He called for scissors in the best tradition. There, on the touchline, he proceeded to make the first incision. He cut the lady's corsets right up the back from the base of her spine. She came apart like a sack of condemned veal and seemed to spread over the polished boots of the watching policemen. The effect was electrifying to observers and patient alike. The lady recovered consciousness and her voice, gathered her shattered pink armour plate around her, and chased my father along the edge of the pitch screaming abuse. The game was halted until three or four policemen succeeded in heading her off and she was carried, to suitable applause, down the players' tunnel.

My father still recalls this event with some pride. 'I saved her life,' he says, 'but the public are never grateful.'

Five

I opened the tin containing the dead German soldier's finger and my mother promptly fainted. It was then my turn to feel scared, for the deception had succeeded beyond my wildest expectations.

The dead finger was one of my simplest tricks. In the company of Albert I conducted a series of increasingly complicated experiments into the bizarre, since we both had highly developed and somewhat gruesome imaginations and were never happier than when we found the occasional dead mouse or bird, for the phenomena of death fascinated us. Left alone in the house while his complacent parents were out for the afternoon, we would retire to the kitchen and melt down quantities of household candles. We sought to pierce the mystery of Egyptian mummification and would patiently spend long hours binding the tiny stiff corpses with layer upon layer of bandages impregnated with hot wax, finally encasing the messy whole with red sealing wax.

Alas, we never achieved success, for we looted our own tombs within a matter of days after burial. I don't think it ever occurred to us that mummies, like cheese, need time to mature. Having solemnly closed the entrance to the tomb (which was always beautifully constructed at the bottom of Albert's garden, with the entrance shaft lined with silver paper and supported by firewood baulks, and the coffin itself an intricate series of boxes within boxes, each one separately secured with wire and more wax), we couldn't wait to take it apart again.

Ignoring the stench of ripe putrefaction, we would hopefully peer into the final coffin only to find an oozing maggot-ridden and discoloured object which was neither mouse nor mummy.

We were never discouraged by each succeeding failure, nor did we ever question our methods. It was back to the old drawing-board, look for another dead mouse, and ruin for another of Mrs Herbert's saucepans.

Although I cannot claim credit for inventing the trick of the dead German soldier's finger, I can ask posterity to record that I perfected the technique. It was disarmingly simple. You merely took a flat tobacco tin and bored a hole in the bottom large enough to allow the insertion of a middle finger. This finger was lovingly dirtied with a secret mixture of burnt cork, Heinz tomato ketchup and small pieces of raw sausage. The tobacco tin was then lined with cotton wool stained with more ketchup or Stephens red ink, the finger pushed through the hole and carefully positioned. Then the lid was closed, only to be opened in the presence of a suitable victim.

My mother proved to be our most spectacular audience. We presented ourselves at the front door after school one summer afternoon. Albert – a past master of the hesitant delivery – rang the doorbell while I stood concealed to one side. When my mother answered he told her I had something fantastic to show her. I then stepped forward, holding the tin with care. My unsuspecting mother, curious as any woman towards door-to-door salesmen, came out to inspect. I then made my own speech. I explained that a boy at school whose father was a World War I collector had been persuaded to part with his prize exhibit in exchange for a quantity of my choicest cigarette cards. There was no doubt, I said, that I had got the better of the bargain. Albert suppressed his mounting hysteria. My mother neatly on the hook by now, I opened the tin lid to reveal a nauseatingly authentic-looking dead finger. My mother screamed and swooned and I remember helping to lift her with the tin still attached to one hand. Despite an equally dramatic aftermath with both sets of parents consulting on a suitable punishment, Albert and I continued to regard this episode as our greatest achievement.

He was the most perfect of friends, and in those days out-distanced us all. A gifted and original cartoonist from an early age, he later went on to become a gifted but spasmodic painter. Shy with everybody except me, he walked with an almost Groucho Marx-like stoop, giving the impression that he wanted to avoid people seeing his face. His sense of humour was far in advance of his years and in some ways anticipated Monty Python. The best of his oils that I possess is an echo of the days I am trying to recapture here. It shows two children fighting in the street and a third child stealing away from the scene. Albert later admitted that he had painted it to expunge a feeling of guilt. Apparently he had once failed to come to my rescue when I was being attacked by a school bully and the shame of the memory persisted. I had no recollection of the event.

In the immediate pre-war period of 1933–9 we were inseparable, and his extraordinary imagination spurred me and did, I know, sharpen my perceptions. I was very much the junior partner and it was Albert who set the pattern for our varied exploits together. One Christmas, I recall, we both made sure that we were given make-up kits in our stockings. We embarked on our Sherlock Holmes period and spent long, blissful hours applying quantities of crepe hair, fashioning elaborate moustaches and beards. Then, when mutually satisfied as to the effect, we walked the streets utterly convinced that we were middle-aged detectives with impenetrable disguises.

Obviously I was also preparing myself for a future professional debut, for it was always I who insisted that any public performance we forced upon our long-suffering families should command entrance fees. We wrote and performed endless sketches in which I was always the customer in a restaurant and Albert was always the waiter.

We became ever more ambitious and launched our own theatrical company, using the cellar of another friend's house as our rehearsal room. I can remember lying awake at night trying to think of the plot for a great play which would immediately put my name in lights. Lacking any original talent at that time, I turned to plagiarism, blatant and unashamed.

I cycled to West Ham Public Library and selected a volume of One Act Plays by A. E. W. Mason. I laboriously copied out one of the plays into a school exercise book, put my own name on the title page and duly turned up at the next rehearsal to announce our next production. Naturally I gave myself the best role and we not only rehearsed it night and day during the ensuing weeks, but also persuaded our English teacher to enter us into a local drama festival.

According to popular legend such infamous conduct should end with the culprit being exposed and caned in front of the whole school. I regret to say that we carried all before us, won the first prize, and I was highly commended for the brilliance of the writing. Again, in the best tradition of theatrical biographies, I should then have gone on to become a child star. But either there was a shortage of talent scouts during that period, or else the adjudicator was as suspect in his knowledge of acting as he was of the works of A. E. W. Mason.

Shortly afterwards our theatrical company broke up in a welter of recrimination and boredom and our enthusiasm withered like burnt string. Albert and I walked away from the theatre and my promising career as a plagiarist came to an abrupt end.

There was no feeling of time passing in those days, nor do I remember the seasons in any detail. We lived in a strange world of fantasy, reading and exchanging our copies of the *Magnet* and *Hotspur* and occasionally launching out for the more superior paperback editions of Sexton Blake. We concocted new languages, carried out hideously foul-smelling experiments with chemistry sets, and in short were never bored. We believed the impossible with consummate ease, and until the war tore us apart our friendship never faltered.

Six

One of my more spectacular efforts during childhood was to plunge a garden fork through my left foot on the eve of our departure for the annual summer holiday. My mother, rushing to my aid on hearing the screams, pulled the fork free and carried me on her back to the doctor's surgery. Although there was very little blood and scarcely any pain at the actual time, I remember her anguish for the possibly doomed holiday.

'Your father works hard all the year to give us a holiday,' she said, 'and now you do this. It'll serve you right if they take your foot off.'

If it takes a sort of genius to stick a garden fork through one's own foot, it also takes genius to avoid severing a main artery. The wound was surprisingly clean. I was injected against tetanus and pronounced fit to travel. The double relief gave me a spurious defiance and I returned home affecting a limp and already thinking of ways and means to colour the story to my country cousins upon arrival the next day.

Most years we went to Lincolnshire, either to one of my mother's family in the Wisbech area, or else to some distant cousins on my father's side who lived in a small hamlet named Martindale just outside Woodhall Spa. This was always my favourite holiday.

We would arrive at the small railway station which year after year took first prize for its flower displays and be met by a pony and trap. The River Witham ran parallel to the railway and once we were over the bridge we could see our destination in the distance across fields of waving corn. We drove for a mile down a straight fen road, past the minute church built of corrugated iron and painted rust red, and then we turned off on to a cart track which led to Simbooth Grange.

The excitement of those arrivals has never left me. The sterility of Wanstead Flats was behind me, not to be thought of again until the very end of the holiday. Instead one had the fresh bitter scent of nettles growing in profusion on the banks of the dykes and ditches, that heady smell of dung as the pony and trap came alongside the first outbuildings, and then the odour of the house itself – a mixture of so many things, carbolic soap and rainwater in the damp stone-flagged kitchen, the inevitable pan of freshly dug potatoes frying in animal fat on the ever-present fire, plates of flaky jam tarts cooked especially for our arrival standing on slate in the twin larders, fly papers hanging alongside whole home-cured hams, the jar of dead wasps drowning in sugar-water, patched jackets stiffened with sweat, the pail of foamy milk, the great slabs of new-churned butter.

Simbooth Grange was a large house, but not as large as a child's eyes remember. Two years ago I took my own children on a nostalgic pilgrimage and we revisited Simbooth. It is derelict now, the empty rooms damply rotting, the floors dusty with dried rodent and pigeon droppings. The vast dining-room I remembered was reduced to ordinary proportions, the bedroom where I slept with my cousin Clarence on deep feather beds nothing more than a squalid closet, the beamed kitchen piled high with potato boxes. Age and neglect have bent and twisted the very fabric of the house; the doors are crushed and distorted and the staircase I once climbed in candle-lit expectation of another enchanted day crumbled at the weight of my smallest daughter.

It was a romantic house. I shall never surrender that belief. Local legend had it that in Cromwellian times it had been used as a hideaway for priests, and there was supposed to be an underground passage leading from Simbooth to Crowthorne Abbey. I believed every word.

'Uncle' George Leggatt who owned it and farmed the land around was straight out of Thomas Hardy. He had a kindly, florid face, a straggly damp moustache, and smelt quite different from my father. Whenever I kissed his grizzled face I caught the pungent scent, strange but not unpleasant, of what used to be called honest sweat. His favourite place was in front of the kitchen fire which burnt even on the hottest summer day, and he would carve himself slices of dried pork with an ancient pocket-knife, hot bootless feet stuck out and into the hearth, his full belly fecund above a heavy leather belt. I could hardly understand a word he said to me, for his accent was pronounced and his voice surprisingly soft. I remember that I wanted him to like me, I wanted him to single me out from his many grandchildren, to grant me special favours. To be asked to accompany him around the farm in the early mornings would transform the entire day.

He kept a few cows to give milk for the house, and these grazed in a paddock behind the house where there was a cricket pitch with concrete wickets let into the uneven grass. Once a year, at the end of the harvest, the Leggatt brothers, who could more or less field a team from within the family, challenged the village to a match. The teams wore unaccustomed white shirts for the occasion and clouted the ball over the house. Tables were set up in the grass, laden with home-baked tarts and pies and stone jugs full of dark beer.

I must have felt an affinity with the land at a very early age, for my first attempt at a full-length novel, commenced at age sixteen under the splendidly pretentious title of *Nourished is the Grass*, was a prematurely ambitious exercise in trying to do for Lincolnshire what *How Green Was My Valley* did for Wales. Although not devoid of precocious merit, it was a pretty turgid piece and betrayed not only my vast ignorance of the novel form, but also my equally vast ignorance of the carnal side of human nature. A few chapters still remain, for I have always had a writer's instinct for preservation, which extended to the preservation of failure.

That part of Lincolnshire had its own legends. The Devil, for instance, was reputed to ride through the stables on a black pig on St Bartholomew's Eve and I was persuaded to keep vigil with my cousins. We made the classic mistake of taking up our stations far too early. The first hour was exciting enough for we had taken provisions, chocolate and baked potatoes and apples, and there was warmth and companionship in the hay-loft overlooking the placid horses. But later the bats flew circles in the gloom, unseen rodents rustled amongst the piles of rotting sacks, and our conversation grew more desultory. Soon the darkness was absolute. The bile of fear mixed with our revoltingly varied supper. Clarence, being the oldest, held out the longest, but when one of the mares below voided her bowels noisily it was the signal for even Clarence to retreat. We scrambled down the ladder, skidded across the dung-spattered stable floor, each firmly convinced that the Devil was at our heels, and by the time we reached the lighted warmth of Simbooth the legend had become fact.

I was a city child. I thought animals lived for ever. I had no idea they died in terror. I can remember to this day the sight and smell of the first ritual killing I was witness to. It was all performed with affable efficiency by the knacker man. He arrived rather in the same way that the master painter used to arrive at Cranmer Road, to be greeted with a cup of tea – I had no idea as to his true function and when my cousins told me of the real purpose of his visit I was inclined to disbelief and followed them to the place of execution with shared enjoyment.

The pig screamed every inch of its last ten yards. A rope was put through its nose ring and then thrown over a stout branch on the nearest tree. My cousins fought for the honour of hoisting the pig off the ground. The knacker man's knife flashed once and suddenly all was blood. My cousins danced as blood flew from the pig's slashed neck, just as children in Harlem dance round an open fire hydrant. The pig's last scream became a slobbering moan. The horror was too quick, I could not believe in the immediacy of death in the strong sunlight. I watched, diminished, isolated by new fear as the knacker man exposed the steaming entrails. He extracted the full bladder, I remember, scattering my excited cousins as he emptied it, bagpipe fashion, in their direction. Then he sealed one end, blew it up like a football, knotted the other end and threw it in my path. I ran from the scene and until I entered the army during the war and the need to survive surmounted scruples, I never ate meat again.

The holiday days seemed so long. I wonder, is memory at fault, or did the sun shine more often during those pre-war summers? I recall nothing but endless hours of heat, with no wind disturbing ripening fields of corn. The greengage and apple trees of Simbooth *were* glutted with fruit and we ate them until distended and suffered the resulting colic with fortitude. I have tried for fifteen years to establish an orchard here at Seven Pines, but such sparse and miserable offerings as survive the chaffinches bear no resemblance to the stolen fruit of Simbooth's golden days. 'Uncle' George used no sprays other than a bucket of soapy water, he didn't read books on the subject, or leave small fortunes behind at the garden centres like me, he just planted trees that bore fruit.

Lunch was always taken in the fields, and it was our happy chore to carry the enamel cans of strong black tea and the baskets of fresh bread and cheese to the men working at the harvest. There, beside the freshly arranged stooks, regular as stacked rifles on a parade ground, the taste of simple food was something rare and special. The men cut great slices of cheese with fearsome pocket-knives, revealing white flesh above the elbows when they rolled their sleeves, for whatever the heat they never removed their shirts. 'Uncle' George rode the harvester wearing a waistcoat and a spotted red and white kerchief at his neck. He and his sons tossed the sheafs at the end of pitchforks as though they were weightless, hour after hour, until it was too dark to see. Then, Constable-like, we would ride home through the gloaming, picking the wheat darts from our clothing, with the horses anxiously pulling against the shafts, scenting their supper as we scented ours.

The oil lamps would be lit for our return and we would wash in bowls of brownish rainwater, soft to the skin, and share the same damp towels before ducking the beams to enter the kitchen. Then the feast. The family around the laden table, the men talking of the next day's work, the children wilting from sun and a surfeit of treacle tart. We would mount the creaking stairs with candles in hand and pass into a drugged sleep on the soft feather beds, while below the men played whist for small stakes until the early hours.

Seven

I was destined to return to Martindale as an evacuee during the period of the phoney war from September 1939 to the fall of France the following year.

At the beginning of the war evacuation was a somewhat haphazard affair. There was no compulsion about it, the choice being left to the parents. Roughly half of West Ham Secondary School departed in official regimented fashion to Colchester, but the remainder stayed on in Tennyson Road and a few of us were tearfully dispatched to friends and relatives.

It's odd how one can recall isolated incidents whilst forgetting whole years. I was very conscious that war was coming. My father was greatly concerned with the preparations for Civil Defence that were accelerated after Munich, and my remembrance of those uneasy days is concentrated on a single evening.

We were having a party, I remember, given for the St Saviour's Tennis Club. Betty was one of the leading lights in the club and collected many admirers. They were all gathered together in the front room in Cranmer Road one pre-war summer evening, still in their white tennis clothes. It was thundery, and the air was heavy and ominous. In the middle of the supper my mother had prepared a stranger came to the door and shortly afterwards my father announced that he would have to leave. I was aware that following his departure a blight descended on the party.

Songs were sung around the piano and the storm clouds finally burst into torrential rain. It was during this storm that my father returned. He announced that a decision had been made to issue gas-masks. The piano lid was closed. As in any domestic crisis my mother went to make tea and the girls left the room to help her. The young men who remained clustered around my father and questioned him for further details. The scene bore no resemblance to those photographs of the 1914 hysteria I had studied in histories of the First World War. Voices were subdued. One of the young men announced that he intended to join the fire service which had been scheduled as a reserved occupation. I suspect he little imagined the part he would have to play in the Blitz on London. Outside the rain beat steadily down, and after cups of tea had been drunk the guests made a run for it, scattering into the darkness in their tennis clothes.

When it became obvious that war would not be averted a second time, my parents decided that I should be sent to Lincolnshire, not back to Simbooth Grange, but to another house – Wheat Farm, Walcott Dales, the home of Tom Curtis. Tom had married one of the Leggatt girls, Kath, and although once again I called them uncle and aunt, the family ties were even more slender. The choice of sending me to Wheat Farm rather than elsewhere was made because Tom and Kath had three children of their own, the eldest daughter, Mary, being roughly of my own age. Next came another daughter, Joan, and a son called Dick. I had, of course, played with them on many occasions at Simbooth Grange, but holiday relationships are different from everyday life and I departed in some dread, my mother's tearfully brave face doing nothing to allay my fears. I was convinced, like many others, that the bombs would fall within hours and that I would never see my parents, or Betty, or Albert, or my ginger cat, ever again.

Wheat Farm stands right on the banks of the River Witham within sight of Tattershall Castle. In those days it was an unprepossessing place with no electric light, inside lavatory or bathroom. The only accommodation available for me was a room shared with the waggoner, Jack Warrender. We slept together in a small double bed, while my three cousins occupied the second bedroom together and Tom and Kath had the third room.

The strangeness and excitement of the first 24 hours blotted out home-sickness. I had the transient added glamour of coming from the great city and could regale the innocents with lurid stories of air-raid shelters being dug in all the public parks and our own Anderson shelter being installed.

Largely, I think, as a result of my exaggerated horror stories, Tom Curtis decided to turn the best downstairs room into an air-raid shelter. He boarded up the only window in the room with stout planks and every available hand was commandeered to fill potato sacks with earth. These were piled pyramid fashion outside the window. The resulting airless chamber was, I now realize, a potential death-trap, but at the time the sense of floundering urgency gave much comfort.

We stood outside on the lawn, putting the finishing touches to the sandbags on the very day war broke out, and waved to the solitary RAF bomber as it staggered across the night sky on what must have been an early, if not the first, leaflet raid over Germany.

Then we retreated into the house, fixed the newly made blackout shutters into position and surrendered ourselves to the unknown. It was more than unknown to me, for my cousins, although scared, were at least in familiar surroundings. Although luckier than many, I was a thirteen-year-old evacuee possessed even then of a particularly vivid imagination and morbidly convinced that I would never see Cranmer Road again.

I hated the first few months at Wheat Farm. Although both Tom and Kath went out of their way to make me feel one of the family, I was always conscious of being the outsider. My cousin Dick and I managed to work out some uneasy boyhood truce, but the two girls proved more difficult to accommodate within my limited experience of their sex. Mary was slightly older than me and very conscious of her budding sexuality, while Joan felt compelled to challenge my male superiority at every opportunity and we spat like wild kittens. I had no roots, few toys of my own, I found it difficult to converse on their local level, and I could no longer claim indulgence for my own faults from my own mother. I wrote home every day but was often prevented from posting the letters for lack of funds. My mother sent me sixpence pocket-money by postal order every week: this was considered an extravagant sum by my aunt and caused friction.

Whenever I received a letter from home I would hurry away to the wooden outside toilet and perch on the worn seat, choosing to ignore the stale stench of newspaper-layered human excreta rotting six feet below, braving the flies that always clustered there in return for the chance to cry in solitude.

I suppose it was the most desperate period of my life to date, but something of Grandpa Clarke's cunning must have rubbed off on me, because I began to plot ways and means of escaping. I considered stealing, lacked the courage and then discovered that the fishermen who came to spin for pike on Sundays were prepared to pay for somebody to boil some water for their brew of tea.

With a bit of the Mile End Road street trader in me, I quickly organized myself. I cleaned up an old disused boiler in one of the farm buildings and laid in a store of firewood. The next Sunday I was up before anybody else, even ahead of Jack, creeping out into the first light to get a good fire going. The fishermen arrived about an hour later and I went along the river's edge collecting their bags of mash – tea and sugar mixed. I'm ashamed to say that I indulged in some early war-time profiteering and charged threepence for a can of boiling water. Once I had a few shillings' capital, I used part of it to buy some milk from a neighbouring farm and then increased my price to sixpence for the full service. On the very first day I made just over a pound which in those days was a rare fortune.

My parents had sent my bicycle from London and that night I retired early, packed my small fibre suitcase and went to bed wearing my pyjamas over my day clothes. I had no alarm clock to rely upon, but Jack Warrender seemed to possess a farmer's instinct for dawn – for it was his job to bed and feed the cattle before breakfast.

I woke when he left our shared bed next morning, waited until he had left the house, then crept downstairs myself. I stole a few slices of bread from the larder, then wheeled my bike from the wash-house, through the orchard and gained the riverbank road a hundred yards from the house.

It was about four miles along the winding bank road to the railway station at Martindale, and I suppose it took me the best part of an hour, for I didn't have a full-size bike. I had no clear escape plan worked out and merely assumed that my pound would buy me a ticket to London. But the wartime trains were few and far between and a strange Cockney child sufficiently unusual to attract immediate attention. There was nobody in the booking office when I arrived and I sat on a crate of live chickens on the platform and ate a slice of the stolen bread.

A three-wagon goods train was slowly shunted into the station and the driver got out to load the chicken crates. I stared at the driver and blurted out the first of many self-incriminating replies to his questions.

'You're out early then,' he said.

'Yes.'

'Who're you waiting for?'

'Nobody. I'm waiting for the London train.'

'Not here, you're not.'

'Why not?' I said.

'No London train today. Today's Monday. What d'you want to go to London for, any road? You don't want to go down there.'

'I live there,' I said.

'Aye. I could tell that.'

I was conscious that the conversation was not going my way. The station-master joined us at this point.

'Got a customer here for London,' the driver said.

I fumbled in my trouser pocket for my money.

'London, is it?' the station-master said.

'Yes, please,' I said, and offered him the money. He regarded me gravely.

'I know you, don't I?'

'We have met, yes,' I said, George Washington going to his doom.

'You're staying down at Walcott Dales, aren't you?' He turned to the driver. 'He's Curtis's evacuee.'

'Oh, yes. I heard they'd got one.'

'Does Tom Curtis know you're out?'

'Oh, yes,' I lied.

'Know you're going to London, does he?'

'Yes,' I said.

'Well, you ain't going to London today. Not today, you're not. Not unless you bike to Lincoln.'

'How far's Lincoln?' I asked.

'It's a fair way on a bike. Take you best part of the day. Don't you like it here?'

'I do like it, but I prefer London.'

'Well, it's a rum old do, if you ask me. See, I don't want to doubt your word, but it wouldn't surprise me if Tom Curtis there came looking for you. What d'you say to that?'

I stared past him.

'Course on the other hand, he might not have missed you yet. I reckon if you pushed the pedals a bit you could be back in Walcott Dales before breakfast. I hear they set a fair table down there. Don't go short of nothing. You'd be better off for cycling to Lincoln with a bit of fatty bacon inside you.'

I refused to look him in the face. I hated him. 'Well, if there's no trains,' I said, 'I shall probably go to London later in the week.'

'Aye, that's right.'

'That's what I shall do.'

I walked away, recovered my bicycle and started the journey back to Wheat Farm. He was quite right: nobody had missed me.

Eight

There were no more escape attempts, only endless days of captivity in kindness. Tom Curtis was an honest, bluff man who worked himself hard. I think he was proud of me in an inarticulate way and whenever visitors came to the house he would push me forward and praise me. About this time I developed a talent for mimicry – a talent to play the fool is an instrument for survival and I have used it to good effect at various periods in my life.

Urged on by my cousins and to Tom's keen delight, I once dressed myself in old clothes and walked along the bank to the next farm which was owned by a family called Pick. I stood on the bank shouting gibberish in a vaguely foreign language and gesticulating wildly, and before long the noise had attracted the entire Pick household. Mr Pick himself finally put in an appearance armed with his shotgun, and with an actor's instinct for a quick exit, I retreated back to Wheat Farm. A few hours later Walcott Dales were alive with rumours of German spies, for at that period in the war people in outlying districts were prepared to believe anything. Tom Curtis was delighted and basked in the reflected glory. He still recalls this minor episode with pleasure.

I also thrust myself into the limelight at the local chapel. Although still no churchlover, I was more taken with the free-wheeling, bible-thumping atmosphere of the chapel and its Wesleyan hymns than with the remembered boredom of St Saviour's. I was invited to take part in the Chapel Anniversary and recited the whole of Alfred Noyes's 'The Highwayman' – a feat of dramatic memory that astounded the entire congregation, so much so that I was invited to repeat the performance in several private houses. It was my first real test of public success and I dare say my conceit irritated my three cousins.

Against these triumphs I had to set the humiliation of having to attend the infant school in the village for a period, but eventually the bureaucratic muddles were sorted out and I was granted a place at Horncastle Grammar School. This necessitated the purchase of a new uniform and brought with it a fresh crop of worries. I was no longer the prize exhibit in a village school, merely a new boy with a strange accent who had to fight for any sort of recognition.

Again I resorted to my talents, such as they were, for making people laugh. I rapidly became the class jester and within weeks could turn in passable impersonations of all the staff, and in particular a devastatingly accurate parody of the easiest target – a Margaret Rutherford-type English mistress with a pronounced lisp. Undoubtedly I added to her existing torments and on several occasions reduced her to tears with that easy cruelty that children take to the classroom. But even though I was the protagonist in her daily humiliation, I learnt to respect her, for she was a fine teacher and the first to pull out of me an appreciation of the written word. I owe her a debt of gratitude as well as many apologies, for she brushed aside my slings and arrows and marked my essays with intelligence and compassion, encouraging me to extend myself so that in the end I was seeking secret ways to please her.

I made the First Cricket Eleven at Horncastle, wearing borrowed white trousers with pride and taking two wickets against all odds. I also managed totally to destroy the school piano by riding it down an incline straight into the door of the headmaster's study, and for this I received six of the best and became, for a time, the school hero.

It was now that I became more and more conscious of my own sexuality. We lived well, went to bed early and got up early. We were healthy and animal sex was an everyday event, for we all watched the stallion brought to the mare and saw the bull mount the cow. We knew all the theory but lacked practical knowledge. Dick and I spent hours studying a purloined copy of *Lilliput* which happened to contain a few nude photographs: they were the first we had ever possessed and they obsessed us. I was at the cusp of puberty, armed with a little knowledge, and the insistent demands of my body confused me. Added to this I was far from home, I had to cast my own raft out on the waters and there was nobody in whom

I could confide. I wanted, desperately, some assurance from without that the world contained tenderness as well as carnality. I lived in close proximity to my cousin Mary and I found her pleasing, but it would never have occurred to me to attempt to force our relationship into a deeper intimacy.

The war scarcely touched us. We had the black-out, it was true, and the air-raid siren went once or twice, but there was no feeling of menace and the shuttered room was never entered, the sandbags began to crumble. I had begun to lose my previous city identity and my Cockney accent began to blur. The bouts of home-sickness were now controllable. I missed my parents but I could now receive the regular letters from home without bursting into tears.

The war went on somewhere. We were playing tennis, I remember, on the small grass court by the side of the orchard at Wheat Farm, when the news of the fall of France reached us. I think it is true to say that my first reaction to the news, conditioned by the attitude of Tom and Jack and the other men around the farm, was one of anger towards France: she was a dead loss, we should never have trusted her in the first place, the French were too fond of wine, women and song, etcetera . . . The adult arguments were on a predictably mundane level and I can well remember that there was a great deal of admiration for the German Blitzkrieg that ran parallel with the contempt for French deviousness.

It was now, when the war seemed suddenly much closer, that my parents decided I should return to London. I thus went back to Cranmer Road just as the Battle of Britain was beginning, a piece of timing which perhaps perfectly illustrates the most baffling aspect of our national character.

The air-raids began almost at once and every night my mother, Betty, Ivy Richardson and I took our blankets and Thermos flasks and found comfort in the corrugated womb of the family Anderson shelter. It had a thick concrete base and reinforced concrete sides and a further concrete wall to act as a baffle outside the entrance. My mother put matting on the floor and we sat in deck-chairs, dozing or reading by candle-light.

The early days and nights of the Blitz were not all that

frightening. I felt curiously, irrationally secure in the fetid darkness of the small shelter and developed a method of determining the distance from our own house of the bomb blasts. I would put my cheek against the sweating concrete walls and calculate by the intensity of vibration carried in the earth. I suppose it was an extension of the old folk lore that makes children start to count after a lightning flash.

Immediately the All Clear sounded I would rush out into Cranmer Road to try to retrieve pieces of shrapnel, before walking to the top of the road to await my father's return from his ambulance duties in the Dock area. He was totally reticent about the part he and his companions were playing, and the only time I remember him showing any emotion was when he came home after the tragic stampede in the Mile End Road tube shelter. He was grimed and weary, having done 48 hours' continuous duty in the rubble and he ate his breakfast egg, with bowed head.

We listened to Lord Haw Haw in the Anderson, searching the dial of the wireless until that arrogant rasping voice filled the small enclosure. 'We shan't be dropping bombs on Earlham Grove tonight,' he said once, in a reference to the Jewish quarter of Forest Gate, 'we shall be dropping Keating's Powder.' Keating's was a brand of dustbin disinfectant. In repeating the remark here I am not trying to perpetuate that distant, vicious smear, I merely wish to record the absolute amazement and fear I felt at hearing my own locality mentioned by the remote voice of the enemy. For the first time I had a premonition of my own death, and I was very afraid.

On the Saturday afternoon when the second phase of the Blitz began in earnest I was inside the Odeon, Forest Gate, watching a matinee of *Gaslight*, starring Anton Walbrook and Diana Wynyard. Halfway through the performance the audience became conscious of what seemed to be a hail storm beating on the roof. The projector lamp died and the house lights came up. The limp manager, in black tie, came on to the stage and announced that the audience should disperse in the interests of safety. We trooped without undue haste into the bright sunshine outside and stood in groups on the pavement watching pattern after pattern of sun-silvered Dorniers winging high overhead. Urged on by police and wardens I ran the length of Woodgrange Road and along Godwin Road straight into the arms of my distraught mother.

We went immediately to the Anderson and except for hurried forays into the house for food and the use of the toilet during the rare lulls in the bombardment, we stayed in the garden shelter for the best part of two whole days and nights. During the night hours the sky was swollen red enough by the monstrous Dockland fires to make the regulation blackout meaningless. Sticks of bombs fell across Wanstead Flats, cutting a path through Cranmer Road at the top end, but the Anderson never shifted. I was terrified, convinced now that every fresh screaming descent was aimed directly at us. You have very little sense of direction if you are in the middle of a concentrated bombardment, the noise seems to press down and squash you. We could hear wardens shouting in the streets, and at intervals the mobile ack-ack units would stop and loose off a few random rounds very close at hand. Their transient comfort was lost in the general bedlam and nightmare. Barrage balloons, severed from their moorings, floated Disney-like across the slaughterhouse sky.

Our experience was nothing out of the ordinary and we were far luckier than most, for when at last the bomb with our number on it found its target the Anderson shelter still held, but our life at Cranmer Road was over for ever.

Nine

To be evacuated once is unfortunate, but to be evacuated twice has a Lady Bracknell quality of carelessness.

My second exodus from London took place in September 1940. This time I travelled with the bulk of West Ham Secondary School to Helston in Cornwall. I left London with a sense of selfish relief; relief tinged with the fear of never seeing my parents or Betty again, but nevertheless relief.

The crowded train zig-zagged across country, halted and detoured many times because of bomb repairs to the tracks, and it was nearly nightfall when we eventually reached Helston, home of the fabled Floral Dance, a small and in those days bigoted town that had scarcely altered since the turn of the century.

On the journey I had decided to join forces with a hitherto vague friend called Raymond Matthews who was in the same form. He lived in Lorne Road at Forest Gate with his widowed mother and another brother, John. Labelled, clutching the permitted single suitcase and gas-mask, we stood outside the strange station like the dispossessed anywhere, waiting for officialdom to give us some identity. Eventually the equally weary school staff compared lists with the local billeting officers and singly and in pairs we were checked off various forms, signed for and taken away by foster-parents.

'You're lucky,' the billeting officer told Raymond and me. 'You're going to a big house. You're going to live with Mrs Ratcliffe.' From the tone of voice he used we were aware that he drew a line of social distinction between the as yet unknown Mrs Ratcliffe and the other claimants.

It was a large house, standing in its own grounds in the affluent section of Helston. I can remember feeling dwarfed as we entered it for the first time and were conducted by an anonymous member of Mrs Ratcliffe's staff into her presence.

I can recall nothing of her features, only an impression –

Martita Hunt at her most forbidding – powdered and scented and icily disdainful. She condescended to show us to our 'quarters' personally, ushering us through the furnished body of the house until we reached a room at the rear. It was vast and clean and totally unlike any room I had ever seen before. In all probability it had previously been used as a utility room for the gardeners, for it had a long, scrubbed wooden work-bench which ran the length of one windowed wall, and there was a deep white sink beside this bench. Two camp-beds had been put for our use. They were unmade. The sheets and blankets were folded on top of the beds, together with a towel and a thin slice of what we used to call Cheese soap.

Two large and fearsome Alsatian dogs joined Mrs Ratcliffe and regarded us with suspicious eyes.

'Don't worry about the dogs,' Mrs Ratcliffe said. 'If you leave them alone, they'll leave you alone.'

She directed us towards another small table set up in the middle of the room. It was sparsely laid for two. A pot of jam, a loaf, a minute portion of butter and two slices of ham.

'What do boys like you drink?' she said.

'Tea,' we said.

'It's too late for tea,' she said. 'And tea is in short supply, you know.'

The dogs took a step nearer and she called them to heel.

'You won't be staying here very long,' she said. 'There is nothing personal in this, you understand, but I was not anxious to have evacuees. You were forced upon me by the authorities, but you may take it that your stay under this roof will only be temporary. While you are here I shall do what is expected of me, no more and no less. In return I shall expect you to treat me and this room with every respect. You will make your own beds and tidy up after you. You will take all your meals here and you are not free to wander elsewhere in the house. Is that understood?'

We nodded.

'There is nothing personal, you understand. I am as sorry for you as I am for myself, and I am sure we shall both be relieved when the mistake has been rectified.'

And with that she left us alone. We didn't dare to move or

breathe until the door had closed on her and the two dogs. Then, in the manner of all new prisoners, we examined the cell from wall to wall. We selected a bed each and helped each other with the sheets and blankets. We found a small selection of the works of Rider Haggard in tattered red covers, and after eating our meal to the last crumb we climbed into bed. She hadn't said anything about lights out, so I read myself to sleep with *She*.

The whole of the next day we were confined to the room. Occasionally we would hear the two Alsatians sniffing at the closed door, which was only opened by the same anonymous and silent member of the staff who brought us our breakfast and lunch. We felt like the Princes in the Tower.

Just before tea we were rescued by one of our own masters. He strode into the room and told us to pack our bags immediately. Mrs Ratcliffe had obviously pulled her strings. We left without ever seeing her again and were taken to the hostel at the bottom of Helston's steep main street. There we joined a strange band of outcasts, rejects from our new society, the doubly unwanted.

The hostel was a warm and comforting place, for we slept three or four to a room and ate in a communal dining area. The food was simple but ample, and the voluntary matron in charge of us all tried her best to give each of us some individual attention.

One of my room-mates was a lumpy, untidy boy called Cohen. He wore thick pebble glasses and without them he was as good as blind. His parents gave him a weekly allowance of Getty-like proportions compared to the rest of us, which he generously shared and we accepted without embarrassment. I suspect that he had always had to buy his friendships, for he was a shambling and somewhat gross character, but he had a keen and well-developed brain and used part of his funds to purchase the political bestsellers of that time. He was a member of the Left Book Club, a unique and daring thing in our circle, and under his patient tuition I read and had explained to me *Guilty Men*, that anonymous broadsheet that first pointed the finger at the causes of Munich. Cohen opened my eyes to many things. He actually bought two newspapers a day, the *Daily*

Mirror and *The Times*, both hitherto unknown quantities. We carefully cut all the savage Zec cartoons from the *Mirror* and pasted them round the walls. Cohen also supplied a large-scale map of the war-fronts and every day we moved the flags and plotted the shifting fortunes of enemies and allies.

We were by now back at school, housed in temporary premises in the basement rooms of a large Methodist chapel. My form master was Mr Smith, a wild and nicotine-stained character, a great breaker of chalk and strict disciplinarian, but a born teacher. His special subjects were Economics, Shorthand, Accountancy and Bookkeeping, and we started every day with whirlwind dictation practice – Mr Smith striding backwards and forwards amongst the disused prayer books whilst attempting to drum into sleepy heads the intricacies of Mr Pitman's system.

The hostel was only meant to be a temporary resting-place and before very long I had been allocated another billet. I was on my own this time and deposited some distance out of town in a pleasant terraced house. There, for the first time in my life, I had my own bedroom and slept in unaccustomed luxury on a foam-rubber mattress. I had scarcely finished congratulating myself on my good fortune when I was sent for by the billeting officer and cross-examined in the presence of one of the West Ham teaching staff. Apparently I stood accused of a sexual assault upon the person of my foster-mother, the charge having been laid by the husband. Since husband and wife were both in their sixties and the evidence, in cross-examination, non-existent, I left the room with my character intact, but was once again returned to the hostel.

I made a third move a few weeks later, this time being deposited with another elderly couple in a semi-detached house again on the outskirts of town. The husband here was a pathetic character, completely hag-ridden by his odious wife. The house was spotless and cheerless, and the husband was not permitted his own front door key. If he returned home and his wife was not inside he had to wait in the bicycle shed, as did I. He had some menial job on the railway and seldom if ever opened his mouth.

His wife's chief pleasure in life was to purchase quantities of black-market butter which she then proceeded to eat in front of me. My own meagre butter ration was put out every Monday at breakfast-time with seven paper flags stuck in it, each bearing the days of the week.

I loathed her. I plotted murder every meal. I equally loathed her thin, sexless daughter who lived next door, but I saved my real hatred for her spotty grandson. Granny searched far and wide for extra sweet rations which she then crammed into his acne-ridden face. He was always served the best piece of the joint on Sundays and allowed to sit next to the fire while her husband and I were pushed to the coldest extremities of the room.

She delighted in counting and rationing everything. Her husband was allowed to roll one cigarette per evening. She counted out the toilet paper, three sheets a day, come what may. No man was allowed to step over the doorstep wearing his outside shoes. Candles were limited to one per person per week. If you had a hot water bottle at night you were not allowed hot water to wash in the following morning.

I took a large paper round for which I was paid five shillings a week, and I used the extra money to buy such unrationed food as I could lay my hands on, but I was always hungry and would lie awake at night in the bedroom at the top of the stairs, made sleepless by longings for food.

I endured it for as long as I could and then one day I revolted. It was tea-time, and the loathsome grandson was being treated to cream cakes whilst I eked out my remaining butter ration on the allowance of two slices of bread. I suddenly leaned across the table and snatched the cream cake from his thin, chapped lips. I consumed it in one mouthful, then upended the table, sending plates, cutlery and her beloved slab of black-market butter flying across the mirror-surfaced lino.

I then went upstairs to my room, packed my possessions and waited for the billeting officer to arrive and take me into custody. As I left the house for the last time the husband gave a tentative thumbs-up sign, his solitary act of defiance for which, I am sure, he paid dearly.

Ten

My various declines and falls amongst the billets and foster-parents of Helston were no doubt duplicated all over the country, though I doubt whether many other fourteen-year-olds were accused of gross sexual assaults on elderly matrons with Lloyd George moustaches.

I was much wiser and tougher than I had been in Lincoln-shire and concealed most of the seamier side of my adventures from my mother. I was therefore quite prepared to face a further succession of experiments, and when one day I was told I had been placed in yet another home I accepted my fate with resignation.

'If you don't stay put in this one,' I was told, 'we shall begin to think there's something wrong with you. You're going to stay in a vicarage with the Canon of Truro. So you'll have to be on your best behaviour.'

I said goodbye to the hostel once again and climbed into the billeting officer's ancient Morris. We drove out of Helston, taking the winding coast road that eventually leads to Pen-zance. We came down the hills, past rugged Daphne du Maurier countryside where all the trees are distorted by the Atlantic winds, into the small fishing village of Porthleven.

The vicarage at Porthleven is built of local stone, a neo-Jacobean building standing at the head of a small valley, fronted by tall Scotch firs and with all its main rooms facing the sea. By my standards then it was a large house, certainly the largest in the village, and given a special significance in my eyes by virtue of the fact that it was the official residence of what I took to be a high dignitary of the church – for I had no idea what a canon was. The billeting officer had given me certain details on the journey, but they were mostly confined to descriptions of the extraordinary new life that awaited me.

Nothing he told me gave any cause for celebration. The canon's name was Gotto, the Reverend Canon Gotto. It conjured up some forbidding figure swathed in ceremonial vestments, and the billeting officer had further confused me by enquiring whether I was 'High Church?'

'Some of the locals don't care for it, you know.'

I was too alarmed to enquire what it was they didn't care for and I had visions of the church and the vicarage perched on some mountain. He also told me that the Canon and his wife already had three other evacuees, one of them a senior boy from my own school and the other two, much younger than me, from another East End school that had been dumped in the district.

We passed through the entrance gates and I remember that my overriding first impression was one of terror. High or Low church, I didn't care – I only knew that anybody concerned with religion struck a combined note of fear and boredom. I suddenly felt dwarfed by my own helplessness.

How wrong I was. The Reverend Canon 'Teddy' Gotto and his dear wife Innes proved to be the dominating influences in my life. They were both in their sixties when first I entered their house. Childless themselves, possessed of no great wealth, they took in four strange children of varying ages and gave us all a home we could, in every sense, call our own.

Mrs Gotto was a slight, wispy little woman who always wore a hat inside and out. I can only describe her inadequately. She was the sort of person who could have stepped straight out of a Dodie Smith play, frequently vague, often unconsciously funny and yet always in command of any situation. Never having had children of her own, she was still capable of becoming a mother to four boys, two of whom were incoherent, tiny East End urchins who had never before eaten with a knife and fork or slept between sheets; myself and a slightly older boy who was studiously withdrawn and given to whistling whole Bach Preludes without appearing to draw breath.

The Reverend Canon Gotto – known in the village as 'What-Ho-Gotto' – was a rugged individualist, given to driving his car with a reckless and unswerving faith in the benevolent generosity of his Maker. A great and violent preacher in the pulpit, an inveterate pipe smoker, avid reader of detective stories, hearty swearer when the occasion demanded, lifelong hater of cant and pomposity, he whirled about the countryside in a way that horrified his detractors and mesmerized his admirers.

He had been a Blue at Cambridge, as had Mrs Gotto's brother Dick who had also come to rest under the same roof. Perhaps his most endearing quality was his method of dressing. He cared little for his own appearance and sported flannel trousers worn so short that they revealed most of his bony calves. I used to love it when he was fully decked for the church service; then he took on a totally different glamour in my eyes, and I could never quite get over the fact, listening to his perpetually hoarse voice from my choir stall, that unlike the majority of the congregation, I was privy to his private life. He confided in all of us and we would have spirited conversations round every meal table, for he liked his grub and liked others to share his own enjoyment in his wife's excellent cooking. His own contribution was to provide the porridge for breakfast, and he made it with a flourish after he had returned from Early Communion.

We ate at an elegant table, where the silver glistened under a central lamp which was poised low on a long overhead flex. All the lights in the house were so positioned and, thinking back now, I can see the dining-room and the library and the Canon's study with their walls always half-shadowed. I can hear the Cornish wind howling outside, the vicarage like some solid lighthouse, the fires inside reflecting on the brasses, the chairs deep, battered and comfortable – a feeling of security and love. Two Pekes, wet and snotty, snuffled at the world from their baskets by the side of the wide staircase. Regiments of vintage copies of *Punch* in the library stood alongside well-thumbed editions of Dorothy L. Sayers and Agatha Christie and John Dickson Carr. My own bedroom, its windows looking towards the sea – a private world that nobody in the house ever entered without first knocking (something which totally amazed me). The warm kitchen with the Aga cooker that never went out upon which Mrs Gotto performed succulent wonders with the rations. She did not scorn my attempts to be a vegetarian, but instead encouraged me and cooked special dishes. Without benefit of black-market supplements, she also managed to vary every meal and we never went short.

If her husband could be described as an inspirational driver, Mrs Gotto was in a class of her own. Apart from the two Pekes, she reserved uncritical affection for a vintage Austin 7 which she more or less willed to perform. I can well remember the feeling of doom whenever any of us were asked to accompany her on a shopping trip. She was the only person in the household who could actually start the car by normal means. The minute engine would shake the rusting frame violently until the gears were somehow engaged. Then, with the driver hunched forward over the wheel, we would take off down the drive, gravel-scattering the Pekes and chickens, and hazard the narrow winding Cornish lanes. Dick, who had an amiable contempt, used to roar with laughter and shout, 'Ah, Sister's filled it up with kangaroo petrol again.'

Her attitude towards religion and her husband's parishioners was refreshingly unconventional. More than anything else I think she resented the fact that he had to drag himself out at first light in all weathers, every day of the week, in order to give early communion to one particularly cantankerous old biddy. Village churches are always hot-beds of intrigue and gossip, the flame of faith kept alive by the latest piece of scandal, and they invariably come to be regarded as the exclusive property of a small group of holier-than-thou regulars who border on the lunatic fringe and who insist that whatever else occupies God he must somehow find time to give them His undivided attention.

Canon Gotto rode it all with pleasurable cynicism. He would stride into the kitchen, his nose dripping from the cold, hurl the oats into the porringer and denounce the hypocrisy of his flock. 'If I used the milk of human kindness available to me this morning, we should all go short for breakfast,' was one of his favourite expressions. 'They all hate each other, of course. They almost fight to get to the altar first, blasted people. Old Mrs Whatsit buttonholed me when I left the church and complained that the communion wine was not up to scratch. I told her there was a war on. If I didn't grab the cup back she'd swig the lot.'

63

I was encouraged to join the choir, but not forced to. I rather enjoyed it, I enjoyed assuming a whiter personality for a few hours, especially when I was promoted to swinging the boat, for this was something of a star part in the service and I relished the theatricality of my role and dispensed the heavily scented incense with reckless disregard for the other altar boys.

The Canon was also the commanding officer of the local Home Guard with the rank of major. He recruited me, quite illegally, and I was decked out with a shapeless uniform and eventually, when supplies allowed, issued with an ancient .303 rifle which I kept oiled and ready by my bedside. I gave lectures on the disposal of incendiary bombs, illustrating my vivid talks with a near-perfect specimen I had picked up on the streets of Forest Gate. I even did all-night guard duties on the Cornish cliffs, peering towards France and aiming my unloaded rifle (we had not yet been permitted the luxury of ammunition) at anything that moved. The Canon took his own duties seriously and drove with even greater abandon from blockhouse to blockhouse throughout the night, rousing the inevitably sleeping occupants and cursing them in his cracked voice. Needless to say my army activities were not known to the school, for I was under the regulation age.

The war was closely followed in the vicarage and we had many spirited discussions around the dinner table. In common with most of my contemporaries, I was fanatically pro-Russian and Left Wing, but the Gottos never tried to impose their own opinions and we were encouraged to speak as we found it. I came across an old copy of *The West Ham Secondary School Magazine* the other day, dated summer 1941. In the section dealing with the activities of the Debating Society the motions we discussed throw much light on the prevailing mood. '*This House Deplores the Growing Americanization of this Country*', '*Future World Peace depends upon the Formation of a United States of Europe*', '*A War for Democracy cannot be Won by Undemocratic Means*', '*That Democracy as practised in Great Britain is Obsolete*'. I apparently spoke in a debate on '*Flats v. Houses in Post-War Britain*', flats having it by 31 votes to 13.

After dinner in the vicarage we would all retire to the library

Left John Theobald Clarke with gaps in his teeth
Below My mother as a girl

yrs sincerely
Kitty.

Above Giving my all as Bob Acres in *The Rivals* at Helston.
Unfortunately, no photographs exist of my performance as
Shylock, described in the school magazine as the 'finest
fourteen year old Shylock of his generation.' *Below* Lionel
Gamlin and BBC's Junior Brains Trust, 1942

to listen to the nine o'clock news. I remember that Mrs Gotto always preferred Bruce Belfrage as the newsreader. 'He makes the bad news tolerable,' she used to say. I dare say many of my fumbling, half-formed opinions must have offended her when they did not amuse, but she dispensed tolerance in the same way that she poured her rationed tea, a little at a time and always gracefully.

Mrs Gotto had a profound influence on me, but in paying her tribute I do not wish to denigrate my own mother. By an accident of war I was transported to that vicarage at a period in my life when I desperately needed to be given a sense of direction and purpose. Doubtless my own parents would have provided that guidance had the war not separated us. But, inevitably, it would have been a narrower view of life simply because their experience was necessarily limited. Canon and Mrs Gotto had travelled, they had seen the world. From Dick I learnt to appreciate the lore of birds, for he was consumed with an early passion for conservation and his room was decorated with watercolours of seabirds found on that coast. He also introduced me to the magic of Gilbert and Sullivan, playing his prized collection of 78 records on an ancient gramophone. From Mrs Gotto I learnt such manners as I now possess, and from the Canon the beginnings of tolerance towards others.

In later years the Canon retired from Porthleven. For a time he was the private chaplain to the family on St Michael's Mount, making the journey across the sands at low tide. I kept in touch over the years and visited them whenever I could. Mrs Gotto became increasingly infirm, for the Cornish climate is not kind to old bones, and in her last years her eyesight failed her. Towards the end of 1973 I had a premonition that she was ill. I caught the night train to Penzance. Arriving at their modest bungalow before breakfast I found the Canon distraught. Mrs Gotto had fallen and fractured an arm. Very much against her wishes and those of the Canon she had been committed to a hospital in Redruth. 'She doesn't mind dying,' the Canon said, 'but she wants to die at home. I've tried all I can, but they refuse to let her come out of hospital. Do you think you can do anything?'

I went to the hospital and found her, blind and frightened, in a ward full of geriatrics, many of whom were mentally disturbed. I talked to her in that Marat-Sade atmosphere and promised her that she would return home. She could not see me, but she trusted me. I bulldozed my way through the doubtless necessary but distressing red tape, located and hired a full-time nurse, and organized an ambulance, all within the space of a few hours. She was taken home the following day and died five days after that. It was not the end I would have wished for her.

Eleven

I was to stay at the vicarage until the summer of 1942 when, after sitting for my Cambridge School Certificate, I left for good to embark upon an acting career.

There was no theatrical precedence in my family, and the blossoming of such talents as I possess took place during the years spent in Helston. I suppose my English teacher, Miss Bray, was the first person who gave me the courage to chance my arm. I first tasted the heady fragrance of a live audience in the Godolphin Hall, Helston, on 28 March 1941 when the school Dramatic Society presented a production of Barrie's *Quality Street*. The school heart-throb, Bernard Hopkins, claimed the leading role of Valentine Brown and I appeared as Ensign Blades, complete with rosy cheeks and a haircut more befitting a borstal boy than an officer of the period.

I went on to greater things, attempting the father in W. W. Jacobs's *The Monkey's Paw*, stunning the school with a piece of vintage ham acting that was later surpassed by my Shylock. My Jew of Venice must have been a total horror, for I wore crêpe hair down to my knees and strained my unbroken voice into a parody of Tod Slaughter. The school magazine, with remarkable charity, described me 'as probably the finest fourteen-year-old Shylock of his generation.' And you can't ask for better than that! Armed with this notice and a further rave for my Bob Acres in *The Rivals*, I became convinced that Shaftesbury Avenue was beckoning.

I had no idea how anybody went on the stage, but I consulted the *Radio Times* and wrote a series of identical letters to anybody who caught my fancy. I wrote to Tommy Handley (who courteously replied), Sir Malcolm Sargent, Alvar Lidell, Ben Lyon and the entire cast of *Happidrome*. I enclosed copies of my notices, a press photograph of a pile of crêpe hair labelled 'John Clarke as Shylock', and gave each of the recipients to understand that the offer I was making would not be kept open indefinitely. The initial response, apart from Tommy Handley, was disappointing. Undismayed, I wrote a further batch, casting the net a little wider, and this time I had the luck to select Lionel Gamlin. He replied in all seriousness on BBC notepaper, suggesting that if I came back to London during the vacations I was to ring him and he would arrange an interview.

The Blitz was over by now, of course, and we were allowed to return home during the holidays. My parents had found another house in Newbury Park near Ilford in Essex. It was less substantial than the old one in Cranmer Road – anonymous almost, in a row of terraced, identical boxes. The war had interrupted the developer's progress, so that the road in which the house was situated petered out into scrub land, territory without any of the romance of Wanstead Flats.

I can remember nothing of that first holiday, I can only recall the return to Cornwall. I caught the train back at Paddington, not labelled and dragooned as on the first occasion, not in fear of the falling bombs, but as somebody going back to familiarity after a break.

I occupied the same carriage as a ravishing young schoolgirl, like me a returning evacuee, who wore the brown mortar board of a convent school and who proved to be just as vulnerable as myself. She was journeying to Newquay and destined to leave the train before me to catch another connection. Her name was Marguerite and I fell immediately and helplessly in love with her.

Love in one's youth is an endless purple passage and to attempt to disguise that fact is to deny the beauty and agony of a perfection that comes but once, for, to turn again to Connolly, 'once only are we perfectly equipped for loving: we may appear to ourselves to be as much in love at other times – so does a day in early September, though it is six hours shorter, seem as hot as one in June.'

Was I 'perfectly equipped' for loving? I thought I was. The first and most urgent fear that possessed me, the fear that the homing journey would come to an end before I had managed to make the force of my emotion felt, was soon dispelled. We were told at Exeter that the train had to be diverted – there had been a bad crash on the main line between there and Plymouth, with the consequent delay of some hours.

I am compelled to warn those who are now expecting to read a variation of Frank Harris or *Walter's Secret Life* that, unlike those two sexual athletes, I did not fall upon the delectable Marguerite the moment the train pulled out of Exeter. I wish I had, for one of the keenest pangs of advancing middle age is the remembrance of chances lost. My thoughts were totally impure, my motives towards her unashamedly carnal, but I lacked that first requisite of the would-be seducer – opportunity. We did not have the carriage to ourselves. Being wartime it was crammed to overflowing.

I should perhaps anticipate my reader's curiosity and reveal that the attraction was mutual. Although I can understand my own feelings, since I want this to be an honest account of my life and tribulations, I cannot comprehend why the enchanting Marguerite gave me a second glance. Studying the Box Brownie snapshots of the period, I appear to have been something less than God's gift to convent girls. I had an absurd haircut and a perky little face devoid of character. I looked rather like one of the dust-jacket illustrations to Richmal Crompton's *Just William* series.

But apparently I helped to pass the journey for her, and oblivious to the other occupants of the carriage, we embarked on the first tentative voyage of exploration which only erotic liars pretend to recall in detail. I have no such details, alas; I cannot remember a single word we exchanged, all I retain is the picture, blurred around the edges, of a young girl trapped within that budding grove of Proust's imagination, who indulged me, made me captive, enchanted and destroyed me and who now, some thirty-three years after the event, still has the power to rekindle the ashes of a lost personality.

She was, unlike any girl I had encountered before, soft in outline, with that pampered loveliness that comes but once. I began to make feverish plans, carrying on incoherent conversations which never began or ended, while my mind evolved the most fantastic schemes. With every passing minute I became more and more conscious of the need to declare myself before it proved too late. But at fourteen the words don't come. I was merely Ensign Blades again, the inky scrubby little boy, an immature Merchant of Venice stripped of his crêpe hair. First love can only be expressed in retrospect, and even then the middle-aged poet distorts the past with experience. At the time it is a race towards a winning post that never gets nearer, a waking nightmare.

Somehow I must have found the courage to ask for her address. I have no doubt that she was more in command of the situation than I was, for girls of that age are infinitely more aware. Even then I must have had some inner conviction that my pen would prove mightier than my spoken word.

We eventually arrived at Exeter. She left the train there and I journeyed on alone to Helston. I imagined her arrival at Newquay, tried, like any other young lover before me, to put myself in her place. I went over every inch of my own battlefield, cross-examined and reviled myself for the stupidity of my manœuvres, cursed my timid nature. I became convinced that all was lost, that she would never think of me again.

The moment I was back in the vicarage I made the long journey an excuse to retire early. Secure in my own room, the door locked, I put pen to paper and wrote my first love letter. I recall that for her part she had given me a *poste restante* address, for her incoming mail was intercepted and censored by the nuns. I think I wrote to her care of a local newsagent.

The new term began the following day, but all was dross. I had posted my letter and for the next week I experienced those pangs so achingly familiar to anybody who has ever been in love. One makes allowances. The letter has to get there. Probably one just missed a post and therefore it didn't arrive the following day. So no need to panic. She would have got the letter on the second day . . . No, probably she couldn't get out of school to collect it. So allow another day. Now she has it, she has read it, probably two or three times, and is wondering how to reply in kind. My letter must have been a revelation to her, for what young girl could resist such extravagant expressions of adoration? Even if she *replied* that same night she couldn't post it that night. She would have to wait for a suitable opportunity. So don't expect anything yet. No news is good news.

But after six days, no news started to become the unthinkable.

Even so . . . there could be other reasons. She could be ill. I wrote again in even more florid prose. I cribbed from Rupert Brooke, because all is fair. I made the excuses for her, I said that she wasn't to worry that I hadn't received a letter in return, because it made no difference to my feelings.

I waited again for a further week. My work suffered. I thought of nothing else. By the end of the second week I had convinced myself that she was dying, or worse still that my letters had been discovered and that her martyrdom at the hands of the nuns was in progress. My ideas of convent life were inexorably bound up in fragmented misconceptions gleaned from the turgid volumes of the lives of saints in Canon Gotto's library. I conjured up a startling vision of my beloved held captive, forced to deny me, doing penance.

Straightaway I began to make plans. I obtained a one-inch Ordnance Survey map of the district and planned the route I would take. Porthleven to Newquay proved to be some forty miles. Bright with my one desire, I obtained permission to absent myself on Saturday, carefully checked and oiled my bicycle, and retired early on the Friday evening.

I live as a jaded traveller now. A journey of seven thousand miles is a jumbo-sized chore, a boring race against the clock. The daily fight along the M4 to London, even in the smoothest of limousines, adds another crease to my belly – a mere seventeen miles in an insulated box, and we grow old in the traffic jams, breathing nothing but our own polluted air. The soul is no traveller any more.

That day, that Saturday when I folded and packed my best suit into the holdall on my bike, my spiky hair watered into submission, setting out on such a journey of promise, my legs anxiously spinning the miles away . . . that feeling will never come again. Yes, of course the temptation is there – how satisfying to colour yesterday's sketch-book with purple splashes – and yet sitting here at my desk, burning more of my midnight oil, I can without remembered guile pinpoint every turn of the wheel, older but no wiser, setting out once again as a fool, and certain to return so.

I left Porthleven at first light and was through Redruth before ten, pushing the pedals relentlessly, sustained by anticipation of certain joys to come. By a quarter to twelve I stood on the high land overlooking the bay at Newquay. There I went behind a hedge to change my clothes. That accomplished, I cycled slowly into town.

The map fades. I retain nothing of the geography of the streets or houses. I remember that I enquired the location of the convent school. Presumably I dismounted near by. Did I eat lunch? I have no recollection. I know I waited, but how long I waited ... Was the sun shining? Were there other people in the streets? Faded images. Negatives of snapshots that were never printed. But no suggestion of defeat, that much I do remember. It never occurred to me that I wouldn't glimpse her, that was inconceivable.

There was a sort of happy ending. She did appear, I did see her. At some point during that afternoon a group of school-girls snaked out of the courtyard, marshalled by nuns, and Marguerite was amongst them. The projector flickers, the action is jerky, a few frames are missing, but I can discern from this distance in time the progress of that giggling column as it crossed the street to the cliff-top and walked down the steps to the beach. I followed at a distance.

From the top of the cliffs I saw the group arrange themselves on the sand, the nuns black against the virgin beach, sinister blobs in the midst of all that innocence. I had never taken my eyes off Marguerite, watching her as a sniper watches his selected victim.

The rest is banal. Pulp magazine fiction. I went in search of some gift for her. I was blinded with love. I spent all my sweet coupons on a box of chocolates. I returned to the cliffs. They were still there below me, but now I saw that Marguerite was sitting apart from the rest, almost as if she sensed my presence.

I walked slowly down to the beach, watching the guardian nuns carefully every inch of the way. Taking a long detour once my shoes felt sand beneath them, I casually worked my way nearer to Marguerite. I dared not give any signal, I could only hope that she would look up and see me approaching.

I was almost alongside her before this happened. Then everything went very swiftly. All I could remember afterwards was that I no longer had the box of chocolates in my hand. I was filled with shame. It could only be that I had dropped it in the sand beside her, a panicky gesture, completely out of character with the suave lover of my preparations, but I could not bring myself to retrace my steps. Useless, drained, I walked on to the harbour and thence up another set of steps to the promenade. When I got back to her beach and looked down she was nowhere to be seen.

It was Tuesday before I received a letter from her. By then I had dispatched three, each one more passionate than the last.

Her letter was brief. She thanked me for the chocolates, which she said were scrumptious; she thanked me for taking the trouble to come all that long way, and she signed herself with love.

I was, of course, transported. Alone in my room I went from the writing-desk to the mirror over the basin, finishing a page of humbleness and then examining my face in reflection. It seemed scarcely possible that I had not changed. I started to wash with extra care. I felt the need to be perfect for her.

The following Saturday I received my second letter from her. It was a long letter and it returned my love in full. In it she outlined a plan for our next meeting. She was to receive a visit from an elderly cousin who, she assured me, would be sympathetic to our cause. Chaperoned by this adult, she would be allowed to go her own way for the entire day. It was to be perfection.

I was up at an unearthly hour that second Saturday. I completed my toilet with infinite care, arranged and rearranged my best shirt and trousers, saw that my shoes were polished, then washed again.

We had arranged to meet a short distance out of the town and when I arrived on the high ground overlooking the long sweep of the bay, everywhere was calm and a warm and lazy breeze flew in from the sea to dry the morning grass.

She came punctually and her 'elderly' cousin – who proved

to be a girl in her late twenties – wandered off after some desultory exchange of pleasantries, doubtless confident that her young charge was in no danger.

We were alone, and the summer day stretched limitless before us.

I have no faded snapshots of her, no mementoes, no trace whatsoever, and although my memory is as livid as a badly stitched appendix scar, I have no recollections of the actual operation. All I can recall is that she was not wearing her school uniform when she greeted me and that she was the protagonist throughout the hot blur of that day.

We walked to a deserted beach and there, presumably, took some picnic lunch. I can't be sure. I don't remember going into any cafe. I found it difficult to look at her – does that seem possible? We must have talked, we must have held long and involved conversations, so much is certain, and yet nothing remains. You would have thought that everything about that day would have stamped itself indelibly on my mind, but such is not the case. All that love I could so easily confide on paper vanished without trace. All I can evoke again is that sickening feeling of inadequacy that burnt into me more fiercely than the sun, the rising panic I felt at the realization that I was allowing the precious minutes and hours to slip away without progressing my cause.

She was, I now realize, bored with me, irritated by my passive adoration. I suppose I was totally unprepared at such close proximity for the revelation her superb young body offered. She too had made her plans and she came wearing a flowered bathing costume under her thin summer dress. There, beside me on the beach, she stood and removed the dress, artlessly, casually, then sank again to the sand, turning inwards towards me so that the full lushness of her breasts brushed against my arm. Nothing in my far from timid imagination had conditioned me for the real thing. That revealed and sunburnt flesh so close to my seaward-turning head, that mass of tumbled hair falling to touch the first swell of unkissed breasts had too much reality and I was powerless. With infinite regret I record here that we never exchanged one fumbled kiss – she was chaperoned by my turgid purity that day and perhaps that is why I remember her more vividly than those in whose arms I later lay with fonder delights.

How did I take my farewells? Did I see the cousin again? Were any promises given? Was hope completely extinguished before the afternoon ended?

I don't know. I suspect I was even more stupid than these recollections suggest. I began the long journey home, dissecting every incident with each push of the pedals. On one of the steep hills before Redruth I overtook an old woman bent with the weight of her shopping bag. I dismounted and went back to her and offered to carry her parcels. It was a deliberate action, not my good deed for the day. I was challenging God, I dared Him, in the face of my conduct, to shatter my happiness.

He gave me a completely Old Testament answer. A few agonizing days after that Saturday afternoon I got a brief note from Marguerite. In it she said that she did not wish to see me again, that she considered it a waste of time to continue our association, and she signed herself, With All Good Wishes, or some such cruelty.

There is a postscript. Two years after the events I have described I achieved a certain local fame by becoming the Question Master of the BBC's Junior Brains Trust. My photograph appeared in the now defunct *Illustrated* and I entertained certain conceits. Armed with these, I went in search of Marguerite. I remembered the town she lived in and went there. I enquired at the local post office and was given an address. It proved to be out of date, but the present tenants furnished me with the new one.

Boldness being my friend, I presented myself at her door. Her welcome, when she had recovered from her surprise, was quite genuine. My fame, such as it was, had apparently preceded me. We walked out together. I met her parents and she was taken back to Newbury Park to meet mine. For a few days we were inseparable, but as her enthusiasms blossomed, so mine withered. Despite her beauty (for the early promise had been fulfilled) she no longer had the power to destroy me. I kissed her goodbye one evening and I never saw her again. Her letters to me went unanswered, so that all we shared in the end was a common cruelty.

Twelve

That last summer in Porthleven I spent most of my time swotting up the subjects I was to take in the Cambridge School Certificate examination. The war was dragging on and it seemed depressingly certain that I would soon be old enough to be called to it. Because of this and because of the romance of the Battle of Britain pilots I had set my mind on the RAF. We had a school Air Training Corps squadron and were taught drill, Morse and navigation. Perhaps the main attraction was the chance of visiting the operational RAF station on the Lizard. There was a Beaufighter squadron in residence at the time, and against all standing orders the pilots smuggled cadets on board and took us for wave-top flips across the Channel to Occupied France. We had to stand behind the pilot's seat, there being little spare room in the cockpit, right over the escape hatch. Looking back, I am amazed that there were no reports of 'one of our cadets is missing', for quite apart from the illegality of the jaunts, the chances of being shot down must have been considerable. But we were all mad keen to fly, aped RAF slang and regarded the pilots as gods. The original idea of the ATC was to form a hard nucleus of semi-trained air crews who, upon receiving their call-up papers, would skip the basic training required of all raw recruits and go straight to the Initial Training Wings, but with the arrival of the US Air Force in Europe the need for a large number of spare pilots for the RAF proved a myth. Our squadron, along with many others, received a visit from a high-ranking RAF officer who gave us a speech of profound banality, explaining that, although the Chief of Air Staff was very grateful for all the hard work we had put in, our services were no longer a material consideration in the conduct of the war. Wasn't it splendid, chaps, he said, that although they had thought they would lose 50 per cent of our pilots, most of the pilots being shot down belonged to that other, Yank, air force. It was jolly good of us to have given up our spare time and he felt sure that when our call came we'd find much of interest and a job of work worth doing in the Army. Our somewhat misguided commanding officer called for three cheers, but we stood in total silence, and immediately after the top brass departed the majority of us turned in our uniforms in disgust.

I took my School Certificate during a series of long hot summer days. By now the idea was forming in my mind to follow a stage career, a decision which was greeted by my Form master Mr Smith with profound misgivings. 'You'd make a brilliant accountant,' he said. 'It's a great waste.'

I was conscious that my school days were coming to an end. It was not a time when one thought much about the real future that might lie ahead. At best the majority of us had less than two years before being conscripted, thus there was no incentive to plan any major academic career, although a few of my contemporaries did gain some deferment by winning scholarships to the universities. Perhaps that is my keenest regret, for to this day I envy those who went to pre-war Oxford and Cambridge. Life in the vicarage at Porthleven had given me a glimpse of another world (echoes of Grantchester) where there was always honey for tea.

None of that was destined to come my way. Instead, I embarked upon a stage career, a decision so arrogantly un-expected that it stifled all protest I might otherwise have encountered.

I was received back by my own family as the prodigal son – a son strangely withdrawn, introspective and in many ways alien. I had not the heart to draw comparisons between the vicarage and the small terraced house in Newbury Park, but the split had been made and I was restless to escape again.

Lionel Gamlin, as good as his word, immediately gave material help. He selected me to be the Question Master of the BBC's Junior Brains Trust on the North American Service, and then announced that it would be necessary for me to change my name. Another young actor, ahead of me in the game, was also named John Clarke and had recently made a success playing the leading role in the *Just William* series on radio.

Nobby and Theobald were laid to rest in the Aldwych Brasserie across the road from BBC Bush House where Lionel had his headquarters. To the scarcely believable strains of gipsy music, surrounded by genteel matrons up for the day from Pinner, munching a wartime meringue that looked and tasted like the substance one pushes between the bars of a birdcage, I listened respectfully while Lionel suggested a few alternatives.

He elaborated on the surname first. 'Forbes has a good theatrical ring to it,' he said. 'Forbes-Robertson, you know.' I nodded. I hadn't the vaguest idea what he was talking about. Had he suggested I call myself Joseph Stalin I would have agreed without a murmur. I had just given my first audition for him in a subterranean studio, reading, as I recall, Lincoln's Gettysburg address in a cracked soprano voice, and then surpassing that with a carefully rehearsed piece of Shylock and finishing with my celebrated impersonation of the entire cast of Tommy Handley's ITMA. I think Lionel had been stunned, in his turn, by the sheer untalented audacity of the performance. Unfortunately the recording has been lost to posterity, otherwise it would now be a collector's item.

Forbes it was, and then Lionel began to juggle with Christian names to go with it. 'You want a good sounding name,' he said, 'and one that *looks* right on the bills. These things are important – not now, perhaps, but later when you've made your name.' I savoured the flattery behind this remark. The gipsy king, sweating profusely and showing war-economy braces underneath his satin jacket, played 'I'm in Love with Vienna' with a fervour I took to be homage. I dimly comprehended that Lionel was asking if I would accept Brian.

'Bryan with a Y, I think.' He wrote it down on the menu and I studied my new self between the Brown Windsor stains. 'How does that strike you?'

The concrete in the meringue was setting fast, but I managed to blurt out my grateful acceptance of the miracle.

'Fine, that's it, then,' Lionel said. 'From now onwards you're Bryan Forbes.' He went on, somewhat obliquely, to give me an invaluable discursion on the dangers that lay ahead for any would-be young actor. 'You will starve,' he said. 'You will exist for weeks on end on nothing more than a currant bun and a glass of milk at the Express Dairy, you won't find any justice and you will be chased round a great number of desks.' My eyes, I am sure, widened at this point. He elaborated. The perils of Pauline, it seemed, were chicken-feed compared to those that surrounded juveniles in the West End theatre. 'Queers,' he said. The matron at the next table gathered her fox tippet and asked for the bill. 'Do you know what I mean by queers?' I didn't. Lionel warmed to his task. 'The theatre is controlled by queers,' he said. 'Most of them escaped being called up by shaving their armpits and you're going to have to make up your mind very early on.' I was too amazed to confess to further ignorance, although shaving one's armpits seemed a small price to pay for fame.

'I'll give you a word of advice,' he said. 'I take it you're not queer?'

'Well, I'm not sure,' I said.

'You prefer girls to boys?'

'What for?'

'Sex.'

It seemed a far cry from the *The Glaxo Baby Book*, but I hope I was equal to the occasion. 'Oh, that,' I said. 'I thought you meant something else. No, I prefer girls for that.'

'Well, that's fine,' he said. 'The important thing is never to be a tease. Don't tread both sides of the line, in other words. And always say No gracefully whenever you're asked by either sex.'

'Oh, I will.' I had a quick mental picture of a queue of people waiting to pop the question.

'I mean, you're going to be asked,' he said. 'And I would say you're going to have a lot of trouble. But as long as you remember what you are and stick to it, you should get by. It's all too easy to be camp.'

It was a foreign language. He meant it kindly enough and in later years when I knew him better and could talk on equal terms, I realized that not only was it well-intentioned advice, but also a cry from his own heart. He was for the most part a lonely and underrated man, brilliant at his job, destined to make enemies in a profession that does not forgive or forget easily. I little knew over tea that first day that the demons he described to me were demons he had fought himself. Looking back, I can see how comparatively simple it would have been for him to have influenced me in other directions. But from the very beginning he treated me as an adult and as a friend, and our friendship remained firm and intact until the day I buried him. Lionel was a homosexual himself, and when I first met him he occupied a position of prestige and influence with the European service of the BBC. Obviously he had more than one reason for introducing the subject to me, and doubtless his motives were not of the purest, but having put the question and received my answer he asked nothing else of me but gave willingly of his time and experience. He believed in me for some reason, chose not only my name but also the direction I should take. I shall always remember him with affection and I shall always be grateful to him.

Following my first professional engagement for the BBC, I secured a scholarship to the Royal Academy of Dramatic Art in Gower Street. Competition amongst the men was minimal and in the term I commenced the ladies out-numbered us by twenty to one. Of the dozen or so new male entrants at least five were noticeably odd (one wore chalk-white make-up night and day, always carried a copy of Stanislavsky and flung his coat around his shoulders like a cloak). Thus it was not so much a dramatic academy as a sexual finishing school, a subtle point which mercifully escaped the attention of the Principal, the late Sir Kenneth Barnes.

Sir Kenneth was the brother of Dame Irene Vanbrugh and gave us the impression that he had only wandered into the theatre under the mistaken impression that it was a church, for he placed greater reliance on morning prayers than the need to train for the cold winds of the second oldest profession. He didn't take any classes himself which was, perhaps, just as well, for most of the male students perfected quite stunning and unflattering impersonations of him. He had favourite pupils who got all the best roles in the end of term public performances, and it was a student joke that if you washed up in the staff dining-room you got to play Hamlet.

The first person to take me down a peg as I entered RADA

As can be seen my performance as Charley's Aunt
was not lacking in subtlety

Jean Simmons in the act of collecting my fallen hair during her 21st birthday party

on the first day was Pete Murray. He stood, I remember, looking down from the first-floor balcony. He carried a fencing foil and his hair was Byronically styled. He regarded me with utter disdain for some moments. 'So *you* are Bryan Forbes,' he said in the tones of an old Shakespearean laddie. 'So be it.' Then he turned and started to fence his way farther up the stairs, taking on two opponents in the swashbuckling manner of Douglas Fairbanks. His opponents were Charles Mander and Norman Bird. I watched it all with profound admiration. I was not even disconcerted at Pete's attempted humiliation of me, for to be noticed at all was a kind of triumph.

I entered the first class with some trepidation, conscious that, although we were all total innocents, it would be necessarily a survival of the fittest. Here, I thought, is the cream of future acting talent. This conviction was short-lived. With very few exceptions the entire intake of my year vanished almost without trace, and I suspect that the majority of the girls were only admitted to bolster RADA's sagging financial fortunes of those war years.

At the time the academy was housed in the inadequate Gower Street building, for the large theatre at the rear had been demolished during the Blitz: the gallery hung shredded over the ruined auditorium and the stage was open to the skies. There was a much smaller theatre in the basement at Gower Street and it was on these boards that I first trod.

The lean and hungry Neil Porter was my first teacher. He was a Shakespearean actor of some note with many seasons at the Vic behind him, but was definitely of the old school. The first play we studied and rehearsed was *Hamlet*, and during the opening sessions we were all required to read a variety of roles so that Mr Porter could judge our capabilities before making his final decisions.

I was very green, but not so green that I didn't know that if you're going to be in *Hamlet* you don't want to end up playing Polonius. Mr Porter, however, had other ideas.

'All good actors spit,' he said, tearing the text from my hands and striding about the rehearsal room with a beady eye for the girls.

'When you read that piece you must *see* the forked lightning

in the skies and say, "And like an oak, *blas-ted* with ecstasy." '
I was showered with spit from a reasonable distance and much
impressed. He handed me the book again and I did my best to
emulate him. He stroked his beard. The girls sighed.

'Now read To Be or Not To Be,' he commanded.

I found the page and commenced acting. A pale and interesting fellow student named David March mouthed the words
without benefit of book directly in my eyeline. Minus spit,
with a mouth dried by fear, I did my best.

Then doubtless borrowing a much quoted saying of the
formidable Lillian Bayliss, Mr Porter snatched the book away
from me with the words: 'You've had your chance and missed
it, Forbes. Polonius, I think.'

And Polonius it boringly was. I have no doubt that aged
charactor actors are thrilled to earn a weekly stipend by por-
traying that dreary, pedantic figure, but for a sixteen-year-old
first-term student it was like being condemned to the galleys.
I hated every minute of those rehearsals and yet I learnt much
from them, for Neil Porter cut the ham he served us in thin
slices and had the dedicated actor's honed knowledge of his
text. For the first time in my life I began to understand
Shakespeare. Porter made the words come alive. It was no
longer a set book for the exams, it was a way of life.

David March played Hamlet and played it well with a
technique way beyond his years. I finally understood Polonius
but gave a flat and unprofitable performance that I was happy
to forget. At end of term Sir Kenneth doled out the honours
like any other headmaster and I recall that when he came to
me he shuffled his papers and said, 'Accent, Forbes. Get rid
of your Cockney accent or you'll never amount to much.'

To have a Cockney or provincial accent in those days was a
grave disadvantage to anybody's career. It meant in practical
terms that you would never play leading roles, for the simple
reason that the majority of fashionable dramatists and screen-
writers seldom created true star parts for working-class actors
or those with provincial accents. Theatre managements often
seemed to cast on a snob basis.

As Lionel had said, the West End theatre was virtually
controlled by a homosexual clique. By that I do not mean that

every young actor had to lie face downwards on the casting couch before obtaining his big chance, but it was certainly true to say that you offended that clique at your professional peril. Even if you did not join them you were expected to applaud them. Charm was their armour, charm that concealed a biting scorn for those outside the inner circle. They were talented, ruthless and extremely vindictive to those who questioned their way of life. Far from being exploited, they were the exploiters. If they went, as is commonly supposed, in fear of blackmail and exposure, then they concealed their fears with amazing skill. I stress this because the general public has always been invited to believe that young girls who go on the stage run the immediate risk of being seduced or sold into white slavery. This runs contrary to my own experience. Actresses are no easier to seduce than secretaries. The call-boy was in much greater danger at all times.

Another prerequisite was height. Leading men were always tall. I went for audition after audition only to be told that I wasn't tall enough. I bought lifts which I put into my shoes when knocking on agents' doors, and falsified my entry in *The Spotlight* (the actors' casting directory) by adding a couple of inches – but all to no avail. Platform soles had not yet come into fashion and the rubber aids that I slipped beneath my heels merely gave me a somewhat alarming forward slant and failed to advance my ambitions.

At the RADA the outnumbered men were the only ones who got a chance to play a variety of roles from beginning to end. The aspiring actresses were not so fortunate, and it must have been bewildering to friends and talent spotters alike to visit the RADA theatre during a public performance, for in an effort to be just, Sir Kenneth insisted that the leading female roles be shared. Audiences were therefore treated to the numbing spectacle of one young actress playing the beginning of a scene, exiting to fetch the tea tray, and never being seen again. Instead she was replaced in the wings by the next relay runner, who would come on and say the next few lines and then hand the baton over to *her* successor. It was democratic, but it was hardly art.

The experiences I had at RADA bore no relationship whatsoever to conditions existing in the professional theatre, and a group of us decided before the middle of the first term that, if we were to progress at all before the war snatched us away, we had to get into a professional company. We were allowed to take jobs during the vacations, and various producers from provincial repertory theatres, desperate for talent of any quality, raided the cheap larders of Gower Street.

My first encounter was with a lady called Yvonne le Dain, who ran a theatre in Rugby. She accosted me one afternoon on the stairs at RADA and asked if I was familiar with a play by Eugene O'Neill called *Ah! Wilderness*. With an actor's instinctive regard for self-advancement, I lied without twinge or blink and told her it was one of my favourite plays.

Did I know the role of Richard? she asked.

Know it? I replied. I was reared on it.

Miss le Dain was impressed. Well, in that case, would I consider reading the part for her the following morning, with a view to joining her company in Rugby later in the year? I would indeed.

The moment she departed, having fixed an appointment for the next day, I caught a bus to Foyles in Charing Cross Road, bought a copy of *Ah! Wilderness*, and stayed up all night learning the lines. The next morning, thanks to the stamina of youth, I was word perfect, gave a passable audition and landed a contract for the season as 'juvenile lead plus assistant stage manager' for three pounds ten shillings a week.

On my return to RADA I found that Miss le Dain had also signed Norman Bird, Charles Mander and Wolf Morris, my principal partners in crime. She had also taken an actress from our class called Hilary Bamford. We were practically the touring Good Companions.

When the term ended we all journeyed to Rugby to find that our debuts were to be made in the Temple Speech Room, a vast cavern of a place that had been converted into a theatre for the repertory company.

Norman, Charles, Wolf and I shared digs. The other three also shared a bed to the best of my recollection, but for some reason I had a room to myself. We existed in a state of perpetual chaos, since weekly repertory demands endless stamina and fortitude. The days were carefully allocated. We rehearsed the first act on Tuesdays, the second act on Wednesday and the third act on Thursday. Thursday afternoon there was a matinee, Friday you went through the entire play, Saturday morning was laughingly 'free', another matinee Saturday afternoon, and following the evening performance every member of the company was expected to strike the old set and put up the new. This labour of love usually finished in the small hours. Then it was back to the digs for cold Spam and a beer, a few hours' sleep, then a return to the theatre for the first dress-rehearsal. This was invariably such a shambles that by midnight on Sunday you were usually only halfway through Act One. You were then granted a few hours' rest and expected to be back in the theatre by nine o'clock the next morning. It was quite commonplace to be struggling through the dress-rehearsal of the Third Act as the Monday night audience was coming into the house. And of course, on Tuesday, the whole process began again – you were acting one play and learning the next one, a process that frequently led to unexpected dramatic twists. It was not uncommon to come on stage and be greeted by a fellow actor quoting next week's dialogue at you.

My scrapbook reveals that we opened the season with a piece called *The Crime at Blossoms* in which I played a character described in the programme as 'A very Late Visitor'. I remember that I wore a trilby hat and a thick layer of Leichner make-up in an effort to convince the good patrons of Rugby that I was a middle-aged gentleman with a past. The local critic described my performance as 'masterly' and I doff my cap to him across the years.

The following week I had my big chance, and duly appeared as Richard in *Ah! Wilderness*. It was originally performed on Broadway as a vehicle for George M. Cohan and is a charming look at small-town American life. It traces the faltering sexual experiments of the younger son of the house in somewhat sentimental terms, but like most of O'Neill's work it retains the power, even in its more overblown moments, to capture and hold an audience's attention. Certainly it offers a great opportunity for a young actor and in the week allotted to me I made a passable stab at it. That performance more than any other determined my destiny, for it gave me my first taste of centre stage and I can remember still that curious, bowel-twisting feeling of power that comes to any actor when he is made aware of his influence over an audience. To make people laugh or cry is both humbling and exhilarating, an experience difficult to describe to anybody outside the profession. The whole craft of acting is a mixture of arrogance and humility.

Ah! Wilderness also had a more personal significance for me, because during the course of the action the character I played had to visit a brothel where he there encountered that well-thumbed old tart so beloved of American theatrical fiction and had his first sexual experience. The part of the prostitute 'Belle' was played by Hilary Bamford.

During the Christmas vacation from RADA it had been decided at government level that the only actors pure enough to present a Nativity Play to the troops were RADA students. As a result a party of us were recruited into ENSA, rehearsed at Drury Lane itself, and then thrust upon the long-suffering licentious soldiery. We travelled around Southern Command in a rickety army coach doing one-night stands. Whatever innocence we portrayed on stage was not emulated in our off-stage performances. Everybody slept with everybody. The Virgin Mary paired off with one of the Arch Angels before the coach had left the Greater London area, and by the time we reached our first base in Salisbury it is no exaggeration to say that Mary Magdalene had probably conceived.

It was on this tour that my friendship with Norman Bird set firm in the cement that binds us to this day. Like me, he was destined to be burdened with an accent that blunted his progress for many years. On the face of it, we were the most unlikely of friends, for I am extrovert where Norman is introvert, I am brash where he is modest. But we complemented each other and we shared a common sense of the ridiculous.

It was in the Sun Hotel, Chatham, that I kept watch and guard outside our shared room while Norman deflowered a nubile member of the cast. I was vastly impressed at his nerve and desperate to join the club, but my basic romanticism delayed the great day. I had entertained the hope that a particularly stunning young waitress in the hotel would somehow fall into my bed, but my major passion of that nativity tour was the delectable Hilary Bamford. For a few brief days she allowed me to neck with her during our long, cold journeys in the army coach. It was bliss beneath the shared blanket as the coach shuddered across Salisbury Plain, sad and tortured walks through the bracken during the daylight hours, exchanges of undying love, desperately earnest conversations about our joint careers, stolen kisses. But with that inexplicable fickleness that is not peculiar to actresses, Miss Bamford transferred her affections to another member of the cast and the remainder of the tour convinced me that I was destined to love in vain. First Marguerite and now Hilary.

So when, some months later, I found myself on the stage of the Temple Speech Room in Rugby being paid three pounds ten shillings a week to publicly kiss and fondle Miss Bamford, my sorrow was tempered with revenge. Being by then a dedicated actor, I did not take advantage of the situation, but it was my first experience of art imitating reality.

The season ended in disaster for Norman and me. We exhausted ourselves in a series of unsuitable roles, gave, as they say, our all and somehow eked out and survived on our meagre salaries. Then came the moment when we were rehearsing yet another new play, never before performed, called *Charlotte Corday*. This was a dramatic episode of the French Revolution written by Helen Jerome and Yvonne cast herself in the name part. I was given the minor role of an aged jailer which I played as Charles Laughton in *Mutiny on the Bounty* down to the last lisping intonation. Norman got the flamboyant part of Marat, and of course the action included his murder in the hip bath at the hands of Charlotte Corday.

We took our work very seriously and it was tacitly understood that we would keep a watching brief on each other's major performances and feel free to proffer advice without fear or favour.

Since I only appeared briefly in the closing moments of the play I was able to sit out front during the dress-rehearsal and evaluate Norman's big scene. I thought he played it well enough but I was critical of the staging.

'The real problem is,' I said when we were once again in

our shared dressing-room, 'that Marat took endless baths in order to relieve himself from a foul skin disease. Now, from the front, you look completely healthy, and when Yvonne stabs you with the knife nothing happens, there's no blood. I mean, it stands to reason that if anybody stuck a bread-knife into you with that force there'd be a great gush of blood, a fountain.'

Norman was only too anxious to agree with me and in the short time available to us between the dress-rehearsal and the first performance we devised ways and means of correcting the glaring faults.

I first concocted and then applied to Norman's body a mixture of cornflakes and glue to simulate Marat's foul scabs. Warming to my task, I then coloured them with sticks of carmine and brown until he resembled a leper in the last stages of deterioration.

Next I gave all my attention to the problem of the missing gush of blood. I unearthed an old motor car horn bulb in the prop room, filled this with liquid paraffin and tomato ketchup and then taped it under Norman's upstage arm with a roll of sticky plaster. I then carefully rehearsed him and was fairly confident by the time that Overture and Beginners was called that dramatic justice would be seen to be done. So engrossed were we that it never occurred to us that we should inform our leading lady and employer of these added pieces of finesse.

When the curtain went up on the second act Norman was revealed in his hip bath covered in suppurating scabs. With the added incentive of an audience to play to, he picked at them with ghoulish pleasure, causing a wave of horror to sweep through the Temple Speech Room. Then Yvonne made her appearance as Charlotte Corday and the scene progressed to the point where she plunged with the assassin's knife. I watched with a scientist's detachment from the wings. As Yvonne struck with the knife Norman timed his movement to perfection, bringing pressure to bear upon the bulb with his upstage arm, just as I had instructed. Yvonne was saturated with a great gush of imitation blood: it burst from Norman's imaginary wound with a force and authenticity that startled even me. Two people in the front row of the stalls leapt scream-ing to their feet and poor Yvonne must have thought she was going mad. She was drenched in our viscous mixture and quite unable to continue with her dialogue. Other members of the cast, rushing on stage, were equally dumbfounded. Norman, meantime, had died. He slumped half out of the hip-bath, a naked, blotchy corpse, diseased and bloodied. Yvonne, being a trouper, eventually recovered, and the play staggered to the curtain fall.

During the interval she committed verbal assassination on us both and we were given our notices on the spot. I don't think we were too dismayed, because we still had the rest of the week to go and were delighted with the startling success of our innovations. We took comfort in despising Miss le Dain for failing to recognize true dramatic genius.

The war caught up with Norman while we were at Rugby. He received his call-up papers and departed for the RAF. We walked the midnight streets of Rugby in embarrassed silence on the eve of his going, searching for the right words that would give some meaning to our friendship. We made a pact that for as long as we survived we would keep in touch, and I gave him some token gift. We kept the pact, exchanging frequent letters throughout the war years and on into the period when I served in the army of occupation. Every one of those letters survive, and although the great majority of them have no literary merit whatsoever, they do chart in great detail our many declines and falls.

My brief taste of the real theatre had made me openly scorn-ful of the insulated and for the most part phoney world of RADA. I was impatient to make my name in some small way before I too disappeared in the Forces. I therefore took the initiative and applied for an understudy job at the Saville Theatre in Firth Shepherd's production of the Broadway success *Junior Miss*. For this I received eight pounds a week, but the venture had to be kept totally secret: scholarship students were not allowed to supplement their grants by taking outside jobs during term time. I got away with it for about three weeks and then the Registrar sent for me. I was given no choice. She informed me that my contract at the Saville had been terminated by Sir Kenneth and that I would have to appear before a disciplinary committee. I explained that I couldn't make ends meet on the grant alone.

'It has been carefully calculated,' she said, 'as being sufficient for all normal needs.'

I asked for a personal interview with Sir Kenneth. Despite my pleadings, he remained adamant. There and then, in his office, I decided to burn my boats. 'In that case,' I said, 'I shall throw up the scholarship.'

'If you leave here, Mr Forbes, under a cloud, I shall see to it that your name is mud. Furthermore, I shall make the matter known to your own educational authorities who will doubtless demand that you return in full such monies as you have already received.'

Roughly a week before this dramatic confrontation I had won the Forbes Robertson prize and this carried with it a bonus of five pounds. Before leaving Sir Kenneth's office I asked if I could have the cash.

'It will be sent to you, Mr Forbes,' he said. 'Do not bother to try and collect it in person, because you will not be admitted to the ceremony.'

So I packed my make-up box and quit Gower Street during the middle of term. I was sorry to lose the comradeship and the easy access to a bevy of very attractive young ladies, but I never had any second thoughts about the wisdom of my decision. I knew that I had outgrown the insular atmosphere of RADA, that I had taken from it all it had to offer, and that time was not on my side.

Envy My Simplicity, a new play we had previewed during the season at Rugby, had been put together again under a different management and was to have a further try-out week at the Theatre Royal, Brighton. It was a somewhat melo-dramatic piece and concerned with two brothers living on a remote farm with their aged grandmother. The younger brother was a simpleton who could only converse with his dog, whilst the elder brother plotted the murder of granny, finally accomplished the foul deed and cunningly switched the blame on poor Sammy. It was an effective piece of theatre, despite the improbabilities of the plot, and provided me with a showy role.

There was one major snag, however. During the original production at Rugby we had been fortunate to secure the services of an aged local dog who performed admirably and without mishap. Its owner, understandably, declined to let him tour and we were therefore faced with the problem of recasting. It was finally decided that I should pay a visit to the Battersea Dogs' Home and select a replacement at random – the argument being that any animal condemned to that place would repay its rescuer with slavish devotion.

It wasn't my place to argue. I went to Battersea, spent fifteen agonized minutes and then picked an appealing mongrel who was given the name Micky, since that was his name in the play.

Micky came home to Newbury Park and during the period of rehearsal was a model pupil. He never left my side and obviously regarded me as God. The producer was delighted.

We duly departed for Brighton on the Sunday morning and I booked into some well-known theatrical digs called Ross Mansions. These consisted of bedsitting-rooms equipped with small basins and stoves concealed in a cupboard. Micky, of course, shared my room and this immediately presented considerable problems. Either the prospect of my first starring role in a real theatre unbalanced me, or else I was genuinely stupid, because I went out and bought a dog-fish. I then attempted to cook this object, complete with head and innards, in my kitchen cupboard. Naturally Ross Mansions didn't provide a pot big enough, so I put the head in first and was quite astounded to see it blow up like a balloon with an accompanying stink that passed description. It was too late to turn back and I stood and watched while the scaly monstrosity inflated, overflowing on the minute stove until it filled the whole cupboard. The play was aptly named where I was concerned, because I was too stunned, even then, to avert the inevitable disaster. The dog-fish exploded, splodging the walls with a sickening mixture, and filling the entire neighbourhood with a foul smell.

I scraped most of the evidence off the walls and put a saucer-full of the remains down for Micky. He quite understandably refused to entertain it. By then it was time to go to the theatre for the dress-rehearsal.

Micky behaved impeccably during the chaos that always precedes an opening night, and performed his role to perfection for the actual first public performance. He even collected a notice from the local critic and I can only assume that this went to his head. In the middle of the second performance he went berserk, bit the stage fireman, made his entrance through the fireplace instead of down the stairs, and totally destroyed the play during the all-important love scene between Mary Mackenzie and Robert Griffith. The rake on the stage of the Theatre Royal, Brighton, is a violent one. Micky made an unrehearsed and unscripted appearance, ran to the sofa where Mary and Robert were in a clinch, cocked his leg and proceeded to void himself of one of the longest pees in the history of the theatre. Gradually made aware of the flood that was gathering around their ankles, Mary and Robert carried on valiantly in the best traditions of the profession, but the trickle became a torrent, gained momentum and rushed down the steep incline to the footlights. When eventually it hit against the footlights it started to explode them in a chain reaction that sounded like machine-gun fire. The Brighton audience collapsed, as did the rest of the play.

Having emptied his bladder, Micky responded to the applause and laughter and embarked upon a solo comedy routine, jumping over the furniture, racing round the set and evading all attempts at capture. He eventually ran out of the stage-door and was never seen again.

The management and producer called an emergency meeting after the curtain came down and it was finally decided that the play would have to be rewritten. My character was made even more of a simpleton. I still conversed with a dog, but extra dialogue was introduced to explain that my dog had been killed and that I refused to acknowledge the fact. The mechanics of the change worked, but it was something less than a perfect solution and the play folded on the Saturday night for the second time.

Thirteen

So it was then in 1943 that I turned towards the parallel career of a writer. Possibly there was an instinct for self-preservation, for I had already tasted the precariousness of an actor's life. I also knew that any progress I might make as an actor would be cut short by the war.

I invested in an ancient typewriter, bought a ream of paper and started writing. My first stories and my many unpublished novels were stumbling creations borrowed from a new world I had just discovered. Starting from the time I entered RADA I had been made aware that I was sadly deficient in my knowledge of literature. Other students would mention authors I had never heard of and I began to question my own past tastes. I was introduced to Joyce, Aldous Huxley, Richard Aldington, Charles Morgan, Saroyan, Hemingway, Thomas Wolfe, Faulkner, Proust, Flaubert and Sitwell – there weren't gaps so much as voids in my education.

I spent every penny I could spare haunting the second-hand bookshops, my blood fevered with the virus I carry with me still – consumed with the need to collect books. I have been very poor at various stages in my life, compelled sometimes to sell possessions in order to survive, and although on such occasions I have divested myself of furniture, clothes, cars, records and other material junk, I have always resisted selling my books. When I was out of work as an actor I frequently served in bookshops and took payment in kind. I cannot bear to part with a book and I would rather make a duplicate gift than part with a favourite volume. People who borrow my books and never return them are people I avoid thereafter.

Naturally I was influenced by what I read. In attempting to emulate those authors I admired I merely succeeded in paraphrasing them, yet I remained undismayed. I think I always had the self-honesty to admit my shortcomings, and gradually a glimmer of originality illuminated the darkness. It was not

unusual for me to write a new short story at one sitting, perhaps four thousand words or more in length, and I can remember working hour after hour, day after day, in the front room
at Newbury Park on a novel called *Awake and Wander* which
was such a slavish imitation of Aldous Huxley that even now I
can still blush at my temerity.

My literary efforts were sandwiched between odd theatrical
engagements. I played in other repertory theatres in Salisbury,
Palmers Green, Swindon and Worthing. I was forever answering advertisements in *The Stage*, and with a true actor's panache
I invariably exaggerated my experience. The manner in which
I got to Worthing is worth recording. I had seen a famous wartime film directed by Leslie Howard called *The Gentle Sex*. I
was greatly taken by one of the leading ladies, Joan Greenwood, and immediately upon my return from the cinema I sat
down and wrote her a fan letter. She sent me a charming reply
almost by return of post, and after some persistence from me
was persuaded to meet me in the flesh. I was totally enamoured,
decidedly in awe of her film-star status, but sufficiently brash
to intrigue her. We used to go for trips in Epping Forest and
she gave me copies of Kafka and Stendhal. We had long serious
discussions about life, held hands, exchanged a few chaste
kisses and vowed to act together. Joan had considerably more
influence than me and was as good as her word. Having been
invited to appear in a season at the Connaught Theatre,
Worthing, she persuaded the producer, Anthony Hawtrey, to
include me in the company and we played in *The Corn is Green*
together. Journeying to the barbed-wired seafront of wartime
Worthing, I readily entertained fantasies of a grand affair and
squandered most of my modest salary on a room in the same
hotel, only to discover upon arrival that she was heavily
involved with a rather rich young man. It was early Françoise
Sagan, for the rich young man and I both failed to capture
Miss Greenwood's heart: she departed back to the West End
and I moved in as a guest in the young man's enormous house.
He was exceedingly generous in every respect and we sat up
night after night smoking his cigarettes trying to outdo each
other in our praise of the delectable, if departed, Miss Greenwood. The pain of my own loss was apparently short-lived,

because I fell in love with a photograph of his cousin and was persuaded to write to her. It was a romantic gesture, but got me nowhere. I returned to the Connaught Theatre to play Mercurio in crumpled tights and a very inefficient jock-strap which offended the management but delighted certain prurient tastes in the audience.

After Worthing I did a short tour in a play called *Fighters Calling* by Ronald Adams which, as the title suggests, was about the RAF in the Battle of Britain. It starred that fine and underestimated actor Francis Lister, and the posters proclaimed that we were touring 'immediately prior to London production,' but it died a natural death on the road and the cast dispersed.

During the week we played at the Theatre Royal, Brighton, I had a visitor after the show who came unannounced to my dressing-room. It was Terence Rattigan, and after complimenting me on my performance he told me he was writing a new play and would I call on him at his Albany chambers when I returned to London.

I duly went to see him and he said that he would like me to appear in the new play which he was writing especially for Gertie Lawrence and Ronald Squire. I almost blotted my copybook there and then by enquiring who was Gertrude Lawrence? I was overawed by the occasion and acutely conscious that time was running out. The title of the play was *Less Than Kind*. I was the first person to read the finished manuscript.

Terry gave the play to the Lunts for their opinion during a weekend in the country, and they came down to breakfast the following morning saying that, with a few minor adjustments, they would be willing to appear in it. This presented Terry with a dilemma. The Lunts were then at the height of their fame and to have them select a new play, even if you were Rattigan, was the accolade. In the first shock of the announcement Terry was unable to bring himself to mention the existence of Gertrude Lawrence, and the Lunts sailed on.

Their 'minor adjustments' proved to be another Munich. When Terry showed me the original version, the balance of the play was hinged between the mother – to be Gertrude Lawrence

– and the son – to be played by me. The third role of the father, designed for Ronnie Squire, was in the minor key. But a vehicle for the Lunts was a vehicle for the Lunts and they set to work on Terry to persuade him that he would have a much better play if the role of the husband was considerably enlarged. It could only be enlarged at the expense of the son, and thus it was.

I read for the Lunts, perhaps the most harrowing experience of any young actor's life, for they had the appearance and manners of royalty. After a sleepless week I was informed that my impending call-up presented a hazard, and the much reduced role of the son eventually went to another young actor, Brian Nissen. The play by then bore little or no resemblance to the original. Even the title was changed, and the Lunts duly appeared in a vehicle called *Love in Idleness*. I happen to think that it was not such a good play as the version I read with such mounting expectations. By the time it reached the West End I was in the Army and I remember that I went to see it during a weekend leave, an act of masochism that left me emptied and suicidal.

By way of a consolation prize, Terry arranged for me to take over a part in his long-running success *Flare Path*. It was during my stay in that production that I received, at long last, the official envelope that requested my appearance at Warley Barracks, Brentwood, Essex, where I was duly given the number that to this day I can repeat without thought and became 14942447 Pte Clarke, J., a very humble member of No. 5 Platoon 'A' Company of the Initial Training Corps in an infantry regiment.

Fourteen

'You men will attend in your best battledress and boots for the ABCA lecture in the canteen at 1400 hours. The subject of the lecture this week is Keats and I want to see everybody paying attention, because I don't suppose any of you know what a keat is.'

I was the only one in 'A' Company who laughed and I was immediately put on a fizzer and given two days' jankers in the latrines. I welcomed the physical nausea as a change from the mental stagnation.

The life of a raw recruit has been chronicled many times before. It is a subject that is beyond parody. My own experiences at Warley Barracks were as degrading, as funny and as tragic as most, but they were not original and most of them don't merit repeating. We were admitted, jabbed, shorn, issued with kit, greasy eating irons, straw biscuits to sleep on, and a First World War rifle to clean.

We slept, in fetid confusion, forty to a room, watched over by a malevolent corporal who viewed life from groin level. He saw himself as one of Nature's humorists and greeted every new day with the immortal joke, 'Hands off cocks, pull on socks.' This was delivered between the rickety bunks at the top of his phlegmy voice, and the early morning sight of his soiled, grey form at the foot of the bed filled me with a deep loathing.

The army machine had to spew out its end products every six weeks and it relied upon the tried and tested method of a chain of fear. Our loutish corporal became craven in front of the sergeants, who in turn licked dry lips when face to face with the C.S.M. Only the R.S.M. seemed totally removed from officers and men alike, moving god-like between the ranks, like one of Kapek's robots with a red neck.

Once again I consciously opted for the role of jester. I solemnly changed into pyjamas every night and smoked

Turkish cigarettes in a long Jazz Age holder, told endless theatrical jokes, blatantly exaggerated every back-stage anecdote I could recall. I was once again a Nobby, of course, and I swallowed this, for nicknames are also a protection in a mob.

The officers were totally remote and the only one I can recall was a fat, preening little major who delighted in addressing us on the horrors that lay ahead. 'Remember, you chaps,' he would say, 'the Boche is no man's fool.' He delivered his orations in a squeaky impersonation of Montgomery, mixing catch-phrases from both world wars. It was 'we are going to knock the Hun for six' or 'never forget that although we shall fight him on the beaches, we shall kill him in his guts with good old British cold steel.'

During one parade he asked for a volunteer to perform a job of national importance. Nobody stirred, for if we hadn't learnt much we had at least learnt not to fall for the oldest gag in the army book.

The question was asked again, and the R.S.M. let his eyes travel slowly across the front rank.

'Now, look here,' the major said, 'I'm not just talking to hear my own voice. This is a job of national importance. Is there anybody amongst you who has any experience of this broadcasting thing?'

I stared straight ahead. I could vaguely sense that the R.S.M. was moving in my direction. He stopped in front of me.

'Speak up, lad,' he said. 'Answer the major.'

'Who is it, R.S.M.?'

'Name, lad!'

'Clarke, J., sir. 14942447.'

'One pace forward . . . *march*!'

I stepped out from the ranks.

'Have you ever done this sort of thing?' the major said.

'Yes, sir.'

'Then why didn't you speak up?'

'Don't know, sir.'

'The War Office has asked us to provide a young soldier who is willing to broadcast his experiences.'

I said nothing, still suspecting the trick ending.

'What is he, R.S.M.?'

'Actor, sir. One of those actor johnnies.'

'Actor, eh? In the chorus, were you?'

'No, sir.'

'Think you can handle it?'

'Yes, sir.'

'Don't want any slip-ups, you know. Got to be the real thing.'

He eyed me up and down.

'Have him report to me after parade, R.S.M.'

I was duly marched to the Company office at the end of the parade and there told that I would be granted an immediate one-day pass to London. Half an hour later I was on my way back to freedom.

I did the broadcast and found that I still had a few hours before I need report back. I went straight to Charing Cross Road, parched for the sight and smell of books. My favourite shop in those days was Better Books on the corner of Old Compton Street. It was presided over by a young man called Ken Fyfe. A true bookman, prematurely stooped, giving an impression of vagueness to strangers, he nevertheless had an encyclopaedic knowledge of everything published this century. When answering some obscure enquiry from a customer he never hesitated, but immediately quoted back the publisher, year of publication, even the colour of the original jacket. 'Yes,' he would say, peering past the customer as though looking straight at the book on some distant shelf, 'yes, I think I could put my hands on that, given a week.' I owe a lot to Ken, for although I was addicted to books before I became friends with him, he shaped and guided my taste, leading me to many twentieth-century authors I had never previously heard of – John dos Passos, John O'Hara, Horace McCoy and Gide. Better Books was an unprepossessing place in those days, but its dingy basement, crammed with dusty books, provided a haven of sanity during many dark days.

It was in Better Books that particular afternoon that I encountered a young woman in her late twenties. I will call her Edith, though that was not her name. She had an over-ripe figure and her face, surrounded by luxuriant auburn hair, was sensual and appealing. We got into conversation and I invited her to take a cup of tea with me in the nearby Express Dairy. There I learnt that she was married but that she hadn't seen her husband for over two years. He was apparently in the Merchant Navy. She had recently come out of hospital after an appendicitis operation. I listened politely, glad of her company, but I can honestly say that, although attracted to her, I had no designs upon her. Married women, especially married women with husbands serving in the war, formed no part of my sexual expectations.

During the course of our indifferent tea she suddenly stretched a hand across the table and grasped mine. 'I'm very lonely,' she said. 'Will you come to bed with me?'

It was the most amazing offer I had ever received. Up until that moment I had wandered through life in the old-fashioned belief that gentlemen always made the running, and I carried with me a rosy picture of love pure and undefiled. I was, of course, still a virgin in the technical sense and the events of recent weeks had, if anything, heightened my romantic conception of life rather than diminished it. In an effort to survive the crudities of Warley Barracks I had steered myself towards a Charles Morganesque view of women. I convinced myself like Morgan's hero in *The Voyage* that 'when we are ready we shall know what to do.' Alas, when Edith propositioned me, I had no idea what to do.

'I can't,' I said. 'I have to get back to barracks, I don't have an all-night pass.'

'I want to make love to you.'

She gripped my hand very tightly. Apart from Edith and me the Express Dairy was full of derelicts dunking pieces of toast into slopped cups of tea.

'When will you get another pass?'

'I don't know. It depends.'

She took my hand and placed it on her breasts. I felt like Maugham's Philip in *Of Human Bondage*: this was my Mildred, in the tea-room, and I was the cripple, my mind club-footed with inexperience. She held my hand there and I could feel her nipples.

'I'm not a whore,' she said. 'I'm just lonely.'

I wondered when I could decently withdraw my hand.

'D'you think I'm a whore?'

'No, of course not.'

'Do you like me?'

'Yes.'

'I watched you in the shop for a long time before you noticed me. I haven't done this before, you know. How old are you?'

'Nearly nineteen,' I lied.

'I'm twenty-eight. This is the first time I've ever said what I'm saying to you. I didn't even say it to my husband.'

Then in that dim tea-room she proceeded to amaze me further. She described in some detail exactly how we would make love, what she wished to do with and to me. Around us the disgruntled elderly waitresses started to stack the chairs. I listened, quite content to let her do the talking, strangely and erotically disturbed by her confession. I wanted to accept there and then, to risk going absent without leave, but I lacked the ultimate courage. She came with me to Liverpool Street station and waved me goodbye on the train. I had agreed to meet her again when I next obtained leave.

That night I felt more isolated than before. I was of course closely questioned about the broadcast by my companions who regarded me in some awe. Even the ghastly corporal felt unsure of himself and declined to bait me. I lay in my lower bunk and pondered the strange events of that afternoon. Part of me was afraid of what the future might hold. I had never before entertained the idea of possessing a woman I did not love.

The following morning the physical efforts required pounded all carnal thoughts from my head. The brutal relentlessness of army training accelerated by the needs of war ensured that the mind was kept numbed. As far as I can judge we were still taught by methods out of date in 1914. We were encouraged to charge with the bayonet – 'In, Clarke! Twist, feel his guts – poke it around a bit you useless clot! Don't stick it like you would a woman. You're trying to kill the bleeder, not fuck 'im.' We were marched to the rifle ranges and allowed to fire one magazine at a distant target. Grotesquely shaven of head, we resembled zombies staggering around a deserted landscape, isolated from all normal contacts and feelings. I drifted into the same patterns as the rest of my companions, for I no longer had the energy or will to stand outside. And when one of our intake hanged himself in the wash-house I confess to no sorrow or shock. He had escaped.

The body was brought into our barrack room and laid out on the trestle table. The face seemed strangely peaceful despite its mottled appearance.

The R.S.M. was hastily summoned. He strode into the room, took one look at the body then turned on us.

'What you are looking at is a coward. A man who took the coward's way out. There is no room for cowards in the British Army. Right, I want two volunteers – you and you! Double over to the M.O. and fetch a stretcher.'

He rounded on the corporal. 'Got his A.B.64?' The corporal handed it over. The R.S.M. thumbed through it. 'No distinguishing features, I see. None in life and none in death.'

At the end of our initial training we were given our first weekend pass. By now we had each been granted a ten-minute interview designed to uncover all hidden talents and upon the outcome of which depended our army future. I have never shone at interviews or auditions. I can recall that the officer who conducted my session was openly sarcastic when I enquired as to the possibilities of a commission. 'What makes you think you could be a leader of men, Clarke?' he said. 'According to the reports of your N.C.O.s you're a very average soldier. But convince me. That's what I'm here for, to be convinced.'

On the spot, I could think of no plausible reasons. I could hardly hope to convince him by comparisons with his own appearance, and my statutory ten minutes ticked away without any discernible progress on my part. My examiner listened expressionless, made a brief notation on my papers, and then said, 'Field Security, I think. Intelligence Corps. That seems about your mark.' He made it sound like a life sentence in the latrines.

A few days later I received notification that I had been posted to the Intelligence Corps. I was the only one in my intake destined to take that route. We took our farewells, exchanging soldiers' lies about keeping in touch, and we were even craven enough to club together and buy the ghastly corporal fifty cigarettes as a parting gift. He matched our insincerity with the pronouncement that we were the best bunch of recruits that had ever passed through his hands.

During those weeks my thoughts had revolved around Edith's amazing offer. She had given me a number to ring, and the night before I left Warley Barracks for good I queued to use the one telephone kiosk. Mercifully she answered the phone herself. I explained that I had forty-eight hours before journeying to my new camp and that, apart from visiting my parents, I would be free to see her. Her ardour appeared constant and she said that she would arrange everything. I couldn't visit her where she lived because of the neighbours, but she thought she could borrow a flat. At her suggestion we agreed to meet in Better Books. I was committed.

My last act before leaving Warley was to indent for a free ration of contraceptives. I viewed them with a certain amount of suspicion because according to the old lags they were left over from the Boer War. The elderly lance-corporal in charge of the stores must have taken pity on me because he gave me four dozen. At that stage in my sexual career they seemed likely to last me to my grave. I filled one with water to test its efficiency and packed the rest.

My mother cried at my changed appearance, stuffed me with her week's meat ration and insisted that I take away some long underpants. I lied about the duration of my pass and took a hasty and tearful farewell. Lust allows of no conscience.

Edith was waiting for me as arranged. She seemed older than I had remembered. After a meal we went to the Unity Theatre to see a stage adaptation of *Citizen Kane*. I remember little of the performance, for I was mostly concerned with mentally rehearsing my own first appearance as an adulterer. I kept wondering what her husband was like and where he was at that particular moment. I had visions of him drowning in icy black waters, his white, cuckolded face floating away in a sea of tears. By the time the play ended my appetite for Edith had been drastically reduced.

The flat she had borrowed for the night was in a mews somewhere behind Victoria Station. Striking a proper balance between fantasy and reality I had brought a round dozen contraceptives with me. After a cup of watery coffee, Edith suggested that perhaps we ought to go to bed. She undressed quickly. Nothing in the pages of *Lilliput* had prepared me for the revelation of the real thing. Her breasts, freed from the constrictions of clothing, were enormous and topped with proportionately large nipples. I was desperately trying to be casual and man-about-town, but I found myself staring open-mouthed at the sheer naked bulk of her. For one thing, she had no pubic hair and I dimly worked out that she must have been shaved in hospital for her operation. The scar shone like a stroke of smeared lipstick. It had been crudely stitched and looked very insecure. I wondered whether it would stand up to the strain of coming events. This and other morbid thoughts all combined to extinguish what remained of my ardour and I embarked upon a stammered apology for leading her astray.

'I've thought about it every carefully,' I said, 'and I don't think we should go through with it. After all, your husband is out there fighting for us, and it would be very wrong for me to take advantage of you in his absence.'

That sort of speech is difficult to deliver in a strange, cold flat at midnight when you are standing in the nude in a state of patent unreadiness for the fray.

Edith behaved very well. She appeared to agree with me and complimented me on my concern. Lulled into a false sense of security, I immediately fell into the trap.

'Of course I'll spend the night with you, but I don't think we should do anything.'

She agreed again. It was all too easy.

'You have the bed,' I said, 'and I'll sleep in a chair. I'll be fine, don't worry about me.'

'All right,' Edith said. 'I won't pretend I'm not disappointed, but perhaps you're right. Just kiss me good night.'

That seemed to me a reasonable request in the circumstances and I approached the bed. I was immediately engulfed between her strong white breasts. Her naked body in the cold sheets seemed inflamed and her idea of a good night kiss became a full-scale assault. I ended up on the lino and scrambled to retreat.

At this her personality underwent a profound change.

'If you don't come back to bed,' she said, 'I shall scream the place down. I shall switch on all the lights and tear down the blackout. When the wardens or the police arrive I shall say that you were trying to rape me. You know what they do with soldiers on a charge of rape?'

She delivered this message with chilling conviction. I had never felt less like rape in my life. My dozen contraceptives, army issue, troops for the use of, might just as well have been finger-stalls.

I changed my own tactics and pleaded with her. I explained that it was nothing to do with her, it was merely that, stupidly or otherwise, I could not bring myself to deceive another man.

'I haven't heard from him for two years,' she said. 'For all I know he's dead.'

She lay on the crumpled bed, a supine study by Renoir, the offered naked receptacle of all my dreams. We talked and argued for what must have been half an hour, and by now I was blue with cold and desperately in need of some comfort. It was then that I suspect she began to realize the truth of my situation. Her attitude changed yet again.

'Haven't you ever done it before?' she said. 'Is that what it's all about?'

'I have done it,' I said, 'but not very successfully.'

'Well, why didn't you say?' She held out a hand and the movement raised her breasts and for the first time they had a terrible beauty about them. I walked back to the bed and climbed in beside her. She folded me into her arms and treated me with great tenderness.

'I'll make it all very nice for you, you'll see.'

It was a very long night. She scorned the use of my french letters and by some triumph of her mind over my inert matter I was finally initiated into the second oldest mystery. Not content with one triumph, Edith then flattered me into a repeat. I was amazed, not so much at having done it well, but having done it at all. The conceits of converts are well known and before I took my leave the following morning I managed the hat-trick.

It wasn't until I reached the railway station that the full implication of those jumbled events hit me. My movement order was examined by the Military Police and pronounced invalid. I was dumped into a waiting-room while various official telephone calls were made to determine my immediate future. I asked permission to relieve myself. This was grudgingly granted, for I was technically under arrest. I went downstairs to the public conveniences and found myself facing a poster which graphically described the consequences of VD.

I stared at it in horror. We had been given a short lecture on the subject at Warley Barracks, but since I had not then matched performance with desire the gruesome warnings had little or no effect.

Now all was changed. The projector went into reverse and the jumbled images of the previous night suddenly took on a sinister appearance. Standing there in the station loo I looked down at my genitals. Was it merely the wartime lighting or did I detect the first signs of decay? I raised hurt eyes to the poster yet again. VD, it said, can kill. I was immediately given a preview of my own military funeral. The flag-draped coffin containing my diseased remains was lowered into the grave. A firing squad raised, not rifles, but syringes, and my bereaved parents lowered their heads in shame.

I couldn't linger too long because the Military Police were awaiting my return, but as I mounted the steps to the platform I went over the events of the previous night. How did I know Edith had been in hospital for an appendicitis operation? I only had her word for it. She had picked me up in a bookshop. Very odd. She had said that I was the first, but that was obviously just a bit of sales talk. What an idiot I had been. Green. Stupid. Betrayed by lust. The wages of sin.

I came face to face with the Military Police. They had sorted out the mistake. I was to return home and report to Wellington Barracks in the morning where I would be issued with a new and correct Movement Order. I thanked them. For a moment I considered asking their medical advice, but just in time remembered that VD was a serious offence in a serving soldier.

Only one step removed from desertion. I walked out into the night.

I was up early the next morning and went to a library. There I unearthed a tattered copy of a Family Medical Dictionary and thumbed my way to the pages that dealt with social diseases. I studied the entries for Gonorrhoea and Syphilis as though about to audition for them. I decided, with some further sinking of the heart, that I had not contracted Gonorrhoea, the lesser of two evils, but in my first excursion between the sheets I had hit the jackpot with Syphilis. I based this diagnosis on the known medical evidence: loss of hair (hadn't my comb contained a mass of fallen locks that morning?), headache (I hadn't slept all night), and a rash around what the dictionary defined as the 'private parts'. I read the page once again and then rushed to find the toilets. Safely behind locked doors, I examined every inch of my bare flesh. There was no doubt. I had a blinding headache, my hair was falling, and to cap it all my penis was definitely inflamed.

An hour later I was in the queue outside the M.O.'s office in Wellington Barracks. I was finally admitted into the presence and found myself confronting a middle-aged army major, chain-smoking Woodbines.

'Yes, soldier?' he said without looking up.

'I think,' I said, 'I think, sir, that I may have contracted a venereal disease.'

'Name, rank and number.'

I gave them.

'Drop your trousers.'

Up until now he hadn't actually looked at my face. He dragged himself out of his chair, balanced the burning cigarette on the rim of his tea-cup and peered at my genitals.

'Was she a pro?'

'Sir?'

'Tart. Was she a tart or your girl-friend?'

'Girl-friend, sir.'

He flicked my penis with a nicotine-stained finger badly in need of a manicure.

'That hurt you?'

'Not badly, sir.'

'You're lucky it didn't drop off. It has happened, you know.'
He went back to his chair.

'When did you do it?'

'Last night, sir.'

'*Last night?*'

He looked at me for the first time.

'What's your bloody game, soldier?'

'Sir?'

'Get out of here!'

'But, sir, have I got it, sir?'

'I'll tell you what you've got, soldier. You've got a bloody nerve, that's what you've got. Now get out or I'll have you on a charge.'

I stumbled to the door, one hand trying to pull my trousers up, the other hand saluting.

On my way to the Orderly Room I decided that I could place no confidence in his medical opinion. I waited around for two hours while the indifferent staff made a desultory attempt to find my file. The beauty of red tape is that it very often works for rather than against you. My file hadn't come through and therefore I officially didn't exist. They gave me another piece of paper and told me to get lost for twenty-four hours.

I checked into the YMCA after having purchased a bottle of strong disinfectant and some carbolic soap. I locked myself in the first vacant bathroom and proceeded to anoint all so-called erotic zones with undiluted disinfectant, then scrubbed myself with carbolic soap. In the process of making myself free from infection I managed to remove a layer of skin from my most sensitive parts. I walked out concealing a portion of lobster Newburg in my crutch. Then it was back to the library to swot up the medical dictionary again. By now I had all the symptoms in abundance and it was obviously time for more drastic action.

I wandered out into the streets and descended into the public conveniences at the junction of Tottenham Court Road and Oxford Street. There I found the address of the nearest VD clinic. It was in Endell Street – ironically enough the home of

Angus McBean, the well-known theatrical photographer who had captured my image for front of house stills. I walked past his studio thinking: *he has got the last negatives.* I also paused in front of the Winter Garden Theatre, which was featuring a play called *Fly Away Peter* starring a young contemporary named Peter Hammond. I thought: you lucky sod. There you are, in the best of health, starring in the West End, and here I am, diseased, in the army, my life and career almost at an end.

I somehow found the courage to continue and descended the steps into the subterranean clinic. It was a squalid place and consisted of a long corridor, badly illuminated, with wooden benches down the length of one side. There was a glass cubby hole in the other wall. I tried not to look at the other occupants of the benches and presented myself at the cubby hole. A young man in a white overall gave me a card with a number on it.

'Sit down,' he said. 'You'll be called when it's your turn.'

I went and sat on the bench. A middle-aged workman was next to me. He straightened up as I joined him and gave me an unshaven smile.

'First time?' he enquired.

I nodded.

'That's nothing. I've been coming 'ere for bleeding seven years, mate. My arse is like a pin cushion.'

I nearly fainted. 'What do they do?' I finally managed to ask.

'Depends, don't it? What you got?'

'I don't know yet.'

'Same bleeding treatment anyway. They take a bloody great syringe, stick it in your arse and Bob's yer uncle.'

I staggered in search of a toilet and was violently sick. When I returned my companion was nowhere to be seen and a few moments later my number was called.

Beyond the cubby hole there were a dozen cubicles. I was directed into one of them. A young doctor entered, sat down and began filling in a form. He paid no attention to me other than to tell me to take off my jacket and roll up my sleeve.

He finished writing. 'Right,' he said. He reached for a syringe. 'Ever had a Wassermann before?'

I didn't even know what a Wassermann was.

'I don't think so,' I said.

'Clench your fist.'

I did as directed. He jabbed the needle into the vein and to my horror the syringe filled with black blood. It confirmed my worst suspicions: I was rotten, decaying.

He pulled the needle out and dabbed a small piece of cotton wool over the wound. Then he emptied the contents of the syringe into a test tube and labelled it with my number.

'Come back tomorrow,' he said.

'But don't you want to examine me?'

'Do what?'

'I thought you'd examine me?'

He stared at me. 'Well, I presume you're here because you've sat on a dirty lavatory seat. That being the case, I don't need to examine you. I've got your sample. It'll be tested in the labs. If it's positive you get the treatment. If it's negative you can live to shit again.'

During the course of an endless night I made a pact. I swore that if the test proved negative I would never touch another woman until marriage. It seemed a small price to pay.

The next morning I reported back to Wellington Barracks. A different and equally unconcerned Orderly Room staff kept me hanging about all day before informing me that nothing had come through and I was therefore entitled to another 24-hour pass. I remember that I paid frequent trips to the latrines to stare at my face in the cracked mirror, looking for signs of accelerating baldness.

That evening I went back to the clinic, sat on the bench until my number was called, and was finally informed that my test was negative. Life began again. I danced, literally danced in the streets, and treated myself in the St Giles High Street Tea-Rooms to a blow-out of horse steak, fried Spam, chips and onions. I had come back from the dead.

Fifteen

The remainder of my orthodox army service was devoid of interest, blank spacing in the continuity of my life. I was eventually posted to a Holding Battalion for sixteen weeks' Corps training where I learnt to be more cunning and somehow endured such refinements as crawling through sewage pipes strewn with offal – an exercise designed to give infantrymen the smell and taste of the real thing.

I spent most of my spare time writing incredibly pompous letters to Norman who, by now, had completed his training and was a fully operational rear gunner surviving his first tour of Germany. He was hopelessly enmeshed in a *menage à trois*, the unwilling member of the trio, and I wrote him page after page of quite useless advice, which sensibly he never acted upon.

The only thread connecting us to the outside world was a weekly session in the padre's hut. He played ancient classical records to a few of us and served Empire sherry, but we quickly discovered that his sexual tastes were also classical. That and his halitosis, both mental and physical, dwindled the flock and it was back to the NAAFI for the watery beer and Vera Lynn.

Although we were allegedly being prepared for the Intelligence Corps we still had to endure our share of infantry drill, and this was deeply resented by all the inhabitants of my hut. We were a fairly stroppy lot and numbered amongst us were two lawyers who came equipped with a well-thumbed copy of King's Rules and Regulations which they quoted to great effect whenever the N.C.O.s became too tiresome.

This period in my life was notable for one thing only: I began to form, hesitantly and with much soul-searching, a political consciousness. (I am always suspicious of people who contend that their political attitudes appeared in liquid form one night and had hardened by the morning.) We had many political discussions round the central stove in that wooden army hut. They were confused, irrational and emotive, but curiously they had one distinguishing feature. At the end of the debate or slanging match we did not divide and depart, we went to our beds under the same roof and slept in the same smoke-filled atmosphere. I realize now that this had a significance, in the same way that married couples, if the marriage remains a valid, living entity, find it difficult to sustain transient differences whilst sharing the common bed. This is neither profound, nor original, but it seems to have escaped the notice of many of our political pundits, for the Commons has ceased to be the equivalent of an army hut and most of the decisions are taken beyond its walls.

Granted that it had to happen, then the 1939–45 war was a just one – there was at least a known cause, and the later revelations at Dachau and Belsen made that cause manifest. We could therefore talk far into the smoky night without cant of the possibility of a better world once the war was over. At that point in my life, apart from a glimpse of the caged Mosley, I had never seen a politician in the flesh, I had no idea of the differences between the two main parties, and apart from Churchill's orations during the Battle of Britain I had never listened to a political speech. I was sufficiently naïve and ill-educated as to half-believe that our Royal family played an active political role. During my time in the ATC our squadron had been inspected by the then Duke of Kent. I remember that as he came along the ranks I was stunned by his appearance. His face had a glow to it that I was prepared to accept as supernatural. I now realize that in all probability he was wearing some form of make-up for the benefit of the newsreel cameras, but at the time it served to confirm my ready belief that the ruling classes were beings apart.

Many of my previous misconceptions were turned inside-out in those barrack-room debates. I had no idea, for instance, that there were people who actually questioned Churchill's competence and who furthermore held nothing but contempt for his political convictions. For the first time in my life I began to understand the significance of the events which had led to Munich and many a night I crept between the blankets with a sense of utter futility. I think I had the intelligence to keep my political ignorance reasonably hidden from my companions, but I kept track of the various arguments and took the first steps along that endless road that is reputed to lead to political salvation.

I was eventually posted to a Field Security Unit. I freely admit that I was ill equipped for the job in hand, but like the majority of my fellow soldiers content to muddle through and trust in providence. By some process I found myself in Normandy where my inadequacies as a soldier were swiftly exposed. I contracted pneumonia and was sent back to an army hospital in Rhosneigr on the Isle of Anglesey.

It was in this hospital that my orthodox army career came to an end and the rest of my service until demobilization belongs more properly to Monty Python's Flying Circus than the official history of the war.

Sixteen

The Medical Officer of the day waved the telegram at me accusingly.

'What's all this about, Clarke?'

'No idea, sir.'

'Says here you're to report immediately to War Office Section 6 Upper Grosvenor Street, and you say you don't know anything about it?'

'No, sir.'

'Well, it's bloody rum. How sick are you?'

'I don't know, sir.'

'Well, I mean, do you feel well enough to travel? What're you supposed to have had?'

'Pneumonia, sir.'

The M.O. took my chart from the foot of the bed and stared at it. Then read the telegram again. 'Report immediately,' he muttered to himself. 'God, I don't know. Is it something hush hush? You're Intelligence, aren't you?'

'Yes, sir.'

'Well, you'd better go, hadn't you? Can't ignore this. No telling what it is.' He put a hand on my forehead. 'Coughing, are you?'

'Not much, sir.'

'Feel fit enough to travel then?'

'Yes, sir.'

'Yes, well, I'll arrange a railway warrant. Only for Christ-sake don't pass out before you get to wherever you're going. You'll have to sign a form saying you're A1, then, you know, it's somebody else's pigeon.'

He wandered off down the ward as confused as I was. The other inmates immediately started to question and congratulate me. I got out of bed and started to get my kit together. It was an army rule that one travelled in best battledress and boots, fully Blancoed-up, and it was two hours before I was passed presentable and had been issued with the necessary papers. I got a lift in the back of a five hundredweight truck to the station and caught the next London train.

As I recall it was about six o'clock in the evening when I finally staggered out of the train, having been forced to sit on my kitbag in the corridor the entire journey. By now I was feeling distinctly under the weather and sweating profusely, since traces of the disease still lingered. I made my way across London to Oxford Street and then humped my kit to Upper Grosvenor Street. The house had obviously been a private residence of some quality before the war, but now it bore all the signs of commandeered army property. The impressive entrance hall and staircase was deserted and bare of furniture except for a trestle table and the inevitable notice-board for standing orders.

I stood there for a few minutes and eventually a captain came down the stairs, looked at me and then disappeared into a side room. I had naturally come to attention as he approached and I found it a little odd that he failed to return my salute, but merely gave a somewhat enigmatic smile. I remained there at attention.

The captain returned, started up the stairs again and then retraced his steps.

'What can I do for you, young man?' he said.

'Sir!'

I threw him up another salute and handed him the telegram. He read it.

'You're not what it says here, are you?'

'Sir?'

'I mean, this isn't your stage name, is it? You're Bryan Forbes, aren't you? Do stand easy.'

I relaxed slightly.

'Are you Bryan Forbes?'

'Yes, sir.'

'We've been so looking forward to you getting here. My name's Brandon-Thomas, by the way.'

He held out his hand. I shook it, then dropped my hands to my sides again. I realized I was being put to some sinister test. I calculated that I had been posted to some strange Intelligence

Unit and that my future would be determined by my reactions to a series of trick questions. I tried to take a grip of myself. I was exhausted and hungry and somewhat obviously running a temperature.

'Have a good journey?'

'Not bad, sir.'

'Where've you come from?'

'Anglesey, sir.'

'No, I mean, what unit were you in?'

'I was in hospital, sir.'

'When?'

'This morning, sir.'

He took a step back and looked genuinely shocked.

'*This morning!* But that's dreadful. What were you in hospital with?'

'Pneumonia, sir.'

'And they let you travel like this, all that way. Well, it's perfectly disgraceful. You don't look well.'

'No, I don't feel too good, sir, as a matter of fact.'

'Jevan. My name's Jevan. You don't have to call me sir. Here, let me help you off with your pack.'

I was now convinced there was a catch in it. Full captains did not help privates remove their heavy packs, but I was a little light-headed and allowed him to loosen my shoulder-straps and remove the pack.

'You've got a ghastly rifle too, haven't you. You had to carry that, I expect. They've no right to send people out of hospital like that. Have you had anything to eat?'

'They gave me some rations for the train, sir.'

'Jevan. Please call me Jevan, we don't have much formality here. Look, we must fix you up with something to eat. Come and meet the C.O. We knew you were coming, of course, but we'd no idea you were in hospital. You should have let us know and travelled when you felt really well.'

He carried my pack and rifle upstairs and I followed him, by now utterly convinced that I was on a lunatic collision course. We went up to the first floor, which was ornate, with a lot of marble and gilt scuffed by army boots and army disregard, and he led me towards large double doors. Pinned to one side of the door was a notice which said: Commanding Officer. Instinctively I braced myself.

'Noel,' the captain said as he entered the room, 'you'll never guess what they've done to Bryan Forbes. He's had pneumonia in some hospital and they let him travel!'

I found myself face to face with a dapper major who got up from behind his desk as we came in and advanced to meet us.

'This is Major McGregor,' the captain said.

'Noel McGregor,' the Commanding Officer said. I had never known a more matey set of officers. 'Get him a chair, Jevan.'

'He hasn't had anything to eat, of course.'

A chair was produced. I sat down on it, but managed to sit down at attention. Whatever game they were playing they weren't going to catch me out on discipline. The Commanding Officer offered me a cigarette from a rather elegant case. I was just about to take it when he withdrew the case.

'D'you think you ought to smoke?'

'Well, I wouldn't mind one, sir. Thank you.'

'Would you like a cup of tea? We can't offer much in the way of a meal, I'm afraid.'

'Well, if it wouldn't be too much trouble, sir, yes, I'd like a cup of tea.'

'No trouble.' He turned and shouted towards an open door. 'Sergeant-Major! Would you get Bryan Forbes a cup of tea.'

I stiffened in my seat. This was the crunch. However eccentric officers might be, there was no question of senior N.C.O.s making cups of tea for private soldiers. I tensed myself for the rabbit punch on the back of my neck. Sweat dripped down into my eyes. My steel helmet sat like a ton of lead on my throbbing head.

The blow never came. Instead a slim and youthful sergeant-major, sporting non-regulation length hair and carefully tailored battledress, put his head round the door and said: 'How many sugars?'

I was on my feet standing to attention by reflex action. 'Two, sir.'

'That's Sergeant-Major Hall,' the Commanding Officer said with pride. 'And do take your helmet off.'

I sat down again and removed it. Sweat poured down my face. The Commanding Officer showed great concern.

'You look as though you've got a temperature, you know. Where're you going to spend the night?'

'Sir?'

'Have you got somewhere to go to?'

'How d'you mean, sir?'

'Somewhere to sleep?'

'I've got room in my place if you're stuck,' the captain said.

'You mean I shan't be staying here, sir?'

'Oh, good lord, no. Nobody sleeps here. You get a London pass, you see. You merely have to report here.'

'Well, I could go home, sir. Newbury Park.'

'I think you ought to take leave,' the Commanding Officer said.

'Not entitled to leave, sir.'

The elegant Sergeant-Major Hall returned with a cup of tea and a biscuit in the saucer. 'Hope you like it weak,' he said.

'I was saying, Sergeant-Major, he ought to take leave. He's just come out of hospital.'

'Disgraceful,' the sergeant-major said. 'They just don't care, do they?'

'Can we fix him up?'

'Course. Just on medical grounds alone.'

'Now look here,' the Commanding Officer said. 'When you've had your tea we'll get you a taxi . . .'

'I can get him a taxi,' the captain said.

'Take you to the station, you go home, get a good night's rest, and in the meantime the sergeant-major'll fix you up with some leave papers and a railway warrant. Where would you like to go?'

I said the first thing that came into my stunned mind. 'Helston, Cornwall, sir.'

'Right, well, we'll arrange that. You take a fortnight's leave, and if you don't feel well enough at the end of that, just ring in and we'll extend it. We've got nothing for you at the moment, so you won't be missing anything.'

I thought: this is how the Gestapo work. They give you a cup of tea and a cigarette and tell you you're going home, and then they slam you in the kidneys. Either that or they were all three mad. The rest of the building appeared to be deserted. I was alone with three uniformed lunatics. I sipped my hot tea and kept my head down.

'Going to be great fun working with you,' the captain said. 'I'll nip downstairs and see if I can bribe a taxi.' He disappeared.

'There are one or two interesting things coming up,' the Commanding Officer said. 'But you just take your time, get yourself fit, and then we'll talk about them.'

'Yes. Thank you, sir.'

A voice shouted from down below. 'Got a taxi.'

Sergeant-Major Hall came back and thrust some papers at me. 'They're all in order,' he said. 'And I've put this phone number on the back of your warrant. Don't lose it.' He picked up my pack and rifle and helmet and started for the staircase. The Commanding Officer gave me a paternal smile.

'Have a nice leave.'

'Thank you, sir.' I couldn't salute without a helmet or cap, but I brought my heels together, did a smart about turn and followed the sergeant-major.

The captain was waiting at the kerbside with the taxi. My kit was deposited inside and the door held open for me.

'I'll wait for you to phone,' the sergeant-major said.

I hesitated. 'Sir. Could you tell me what unit it is I've joined?'

'Oh, didn't you know? Army Theatre Unit. Stars in Battle-dress.'

He closed the taxi door and I travelled into the night feeling better every second of the way.

Seventeen

Once I had recovered from the initial amazement at being posted to No. 10 Upper Grosvenor Street, I quickly became bored and querulous. I was in uniform, denied some freedoms, but not a captive and not quite a soldier. The basic lunacy belonged to the War Office, for only officialdom could have brought into being an outfit run on army rules but with all the reasons for those rules removed. It was joke stuff, of course, and we quickly ensured that nothing went according to plan. The War Office instructions were that serving actors, properly administered, could and would provide entertainment of a suitable nature for the troops. The result was an absurdity.

In the first place it had been decided at top level that acting was not a suitable occupation for officers. Commissioned ranks could produce plays but not appear in them. Further, it was laid down that there should never be more than twelve personnel in any one production, such complement to include the stage management staff as well. This naturally limited the choice of material. All female roles had to be played by serving members of the ATS, and since there was only a handful of professional actresses in khaki, a recruiting drive was launched. The War Office held auditions. I am only sorry that I didn't get an opportunity to witness any of these sessions, for the idea of a group of desk-bound brass-hats solemnly sifting through possible female candidates for an army theatre unit is in the best traditions of British farce.

We were allowed enormous freedom, which we cheerfully abused. Additional premises were commandeered for our rehearsals and before long there were a number of flourishing rackets in progress. We had the run of an enormous house on the corner of Grosvenor Square and another in Lower Sloane Street. Once the ball had been set in motion it rapidly got out of control. Recruits flooded in. There was a variety section which included Sergeant Harry Secombe, Terry Thomas,

Charlie Chester and many other soon-to-be-famous names. It was an open secret that most of them were appearing, quite illegally, in West End Cabaret in the evenings. The legitimate actors, myself included, spent abortive weeks rehearsing unsuitable plays. At a given moment these were deemed to be in a state of readiness, and we would then give a dress-rehearsal in front of 'referees' from the War Office. In the majority of cases official approval was withheld, the cast read the verdict in standing orders the following morning and started rehearsing a different play.

Since there were so many different regiments represented in our ranks, it was the custom to identify them on pay parades. A truly amazing assortment, we would form up in the street and be called to the pay table on the sidewalk. Poor Sergeant-Major Hall had the unhappy public task of reading out the names. The whole operation was something of a charade and passing spectators would be greeted with the unmilitary spectacle of Sergeant Harry Secombe blowing kisses as he received his money, tripping on his way back to the ranks, where he was given applause and then, when the next man stepped up, letting rip with one of his famed Goon Show raspberries. Most of us sported long hair, every battledress had been tailor-made (those in the wardrobe department supplemented their pay with bespoke service) and several were collector's items.

Some hint of what was going on must have percolated through to the War Office because a new Adjutant arrived, stiff-necked and glaring, who immediately announced sweeping changes and a general tightening up of discipline. Terry Thomas had to cancel a few cabarets and actually show his teeth at headquarters, there was a rush to unearth ordinary issue battledresses and a supply of Blanco was doled out by the scenic section. For a few days the entire unit tried to give their impressions of the regular army. The Adjutant established his desk in the front hall so that he could personally check everybody entering and leaving the building, and this ultimately proved his undoing.

By this time, of course, certain productions had been passed fit for human consumption and we had units departing to various theatres of war. These were given special passing out parades by the Adjutant and sternly lectured on codes of behaviour. He was determined, he said, to stamp out any criminal activities and there was to be no black-marketeering. It was common knowledge that a tin of coffee could command a small fortune in the recently liberated parts of France and Germany, and the Adjutant had somehow deduced that the property baskets were leaving Upper Grosvenor Street laden with high quality beans. 'This evil practice will cease forthwith!' he shouted, 'as will the various sexual perversions peculiar to your profession. It is an offence under the Army Code for any male serving soldier to cohabit with a female member on active service. It is an even greater offence for two members of the same sex to dirty the King's uniform in the act of buggery. Do I make myself clear?'

By some mischance a certain Sergeant Eric Whittle was absent from parade when these edicts were given out. He was shortly to leave for Germany in charge of a unit and had made his plans accordingly. So one day the Adjutant was sitting behind his desk in the lobby when a lorry drew up outside and two very obvious spivs in civilian clothes sauntered into the building.

'Yes? What can I do for you?' the Adjutant said.

'You got a Sergeant Whittle 'ere, 'ave you?' one of the spivs said.

'We have such a man on the establishment, yes.'

'Right. Sign 'ere then.'

A grubby delivery note was put on the desk. 'Against number seven. Two hundredweight of coffee. Where d'you want it?'

The Adjutant never recovered from this and shortly afterwards vanished as mysteriously as he had appeared. Life quickly went back to normal.

My own day-to-day existence was equally bizarre. Following an unexpected leave back at the vicarage in Porthleven, I had returned home to Newbury Park. I journeyed to London every day, signed myself in and then, if there were no rehearsals, went in search of paid employment. I adapted some stories for the BBC and even got myself a solo programme broadcasting news and events to students in India. In the course of this series I chalked up what must surely rank as a BBC first, for during a live broadcast I was groped under the table by a very excitable Indian homosexual. We were alone in a small studio, facing each other on either side of a narrow table. The moment the green light went on and I announced myself with the immortal words 'Hello, India,' the Indian gentleman made a grab for my parts. The announcement came across the air waves as 'Hel-LO! India' and the rest of the fifteen-minute programme made even less sense than usual.

I spent V.E. night in Newbury Park and remember going to the end of the road to see the celebration bonfire being lit. I find that I wrote a long letter to Norman on the actual day, but the only reference to it is contained in a postscript which says with some lack of modesty: 'This letter is likely to become famous as the one Forbes wrote on V.E. Day.' For the rest it was merely another of my advice notes, this time concerned with helping Norman make a start as a novelist. I was writing furiously myself and many of my letters to him during this period were padded out with long quotations from 'work in progress' – my straight pastiche of Aldous Huxley called *Awake and Wander*. It is amazing that our friendship survived.

By the time V.J. Day came around I was writing from another address: 19 St Giles High Street, which now lies demolished and buried beneath Centre Point. This was the home of Valerie White and Albert Lieven. It was a cheerful household and Valerie, a generous and talented person, gave shelter to a passing population. When I arrived the house was also occupied by Wendy Toye and the ballet mistress of the Tauber show at the Palace Theatre, Eileen Baker. Valerie was playing a leading role in Esther McCracken's hit *No Medals* at the Vaudeville. I can well understand why I was attracted to her, but to this day I can't think why she took pity on me. I had a splendid room to myself, and there was a distinct air of La Vie Boheme. The bathroom led off the warm kitchen and we invariably shared our rations round the communal table whilst one of us took a bath. Albert Lieven was much in demand in films and often away, and I would collect Valerie at the stage door after the show and escort her home, for it was a tough neighbourhood in those days and most of the houses around us were brothels. I think my parents imagined that I was living in a semi-brothel and doubtless they were hurt at my wanting to leave home yet again.

The victory celebrations soon faded for those with high demob numbers, and it was back to the Central Pool of Artists as we were now known. George Doonan, Jnr, the son of the famous comedian, had recently joined us and we both found ourselves rehearsing a depressing little drama called *The Day is Gone*. I was cast as a drab, middle-aged man who murdered his shrew of a wife because of his passion for 'a younger woman'. ('Ideal choice for the troops, you know.') We were told that we would eventually be taking the production to India, but rightly placed little reliance in the rumour. George was an amiable companion, hedonistic and totally relaxed. He was living in his parents' flat just off Queensway, a vast warren of a place that always seemed full of people and life whenever I visited. We shared the same sense of humour and cheerfully despised most of our amateur companions in the cast. George went from affair to affair with a succession of girl-friends like the daring young man on the flying trapeze and I was much impressed, for my own romanticism denied me the pleasures of emulating him and despite opportunities and an understanding landlady I remained resolutely celibate.

Eighteen

The colonel who came from the War Office to vet our dress-rehearsal of *The Day is Gone* was the tangerine-coloured works: monocle, riding boots and British Army warm slung over his shoulders. We performed in an unheated room in November, and when we had finished he stomped out without a word. We waited around for an hour or so feeling like lepers, and then word was got to us that we had been passed as suitable for exhibition to adult audiences.

By now I was back in Newbury Park. Albert Lieven had finished his filming and not unreasonably wanted his own room back. I found it even more difficult to live at home, though I hope I concealed this from my parents who must have found my comings and goings very baffling.

Betty had fallen in love with a young man, William Meldrum, serving in the Scots Armoured Division. Their happiness was short-lived, for he contracted TB and died shortly after their marriage, leaving her to bring up a daughter, Judith, born after his death. Poor Betty had been demobilized from the WAAF by now, of course, and returned to her old job in order to support her child. She deserved a kinder fate. Thus my mother, by now in her sixties, had the day-to-day responsibility of a babe in arms. With an energy that is still undiminished she took this in her stride and also cared for Grandma Clarke who had been bombed out again in the closing months of the war by a V.1. Indeed, both my parents surprised me by their cheerful acceptance of all adversities.

I was still writing furiously. *Awake and Wander*, the size of the London telephone directory and slightly less interesting, had been rightly rejected. Undismayed, I started another, this time taking my inspiration from H. E. Bates's *Fair Stood the Wind for France*. I sent it to Terry Rattigan, which must have been a severe test of friendship. He wrote back a gentle letter of great pith and moment which started with the words, 'My dear Bryan, Even Tolstoy at the age of eighty . . .' but he was also kind enough to introduce me to the greatest of all English literary agents, A. D. Peters. 'Peter', as he was known to all his many friends, took me on as a client and remained my literary agent and mentor until his death in 1973. Devoid of ambition to be a writer himself, he had a true eye for spotting and then nourishing talent in others, and his criticism, expressed with an economy that many a reviewer could emulate with advantage, was unfailingly dead centre of target. Publishers respected him, and he drove the hardest of bargains with an old-world courtesy that completely disarmed. He always treated me like a son, and although there was a twenty-year gap between my first and second books his patience with me and his belief in me never wavered. Perhaps the real secret of his long success with many authors immensely more distinguished than me was his ability to be a good listener. To take lunch with him in his rooms at 10 Buckingham Street off the Strand was to enter another world that is fast disappearing if it has not already gone for ever. He loved books and painting and the cut and thrust of Grub Street and his Gioconda smile was praise more welcome than a lead review in the *Sunday Times*.

Peter's first advice to me was to forget the novel form and to concentrate on my short stories for the time being. 'It won't be easy, but I'll place those for you,' he said. 'We'll take it in easy stages. Get a collection together, ones that you're pleased with, and then we'll have a try.'

Merely to be accepted by Peter as a client was an accolade in itself, and I returned to my typewriter with renewed hope. He was as good as his word and shortly afterwards succeeded in placing my first story in Reginald Moore's *Selected Writing* 4. I think I received the sum of three guineas.

I eventually left England on the first stage of my flight to Egypt on 18 January from Lyneham, in a converted Stirling bomber. Air travel was decidedly primitive in those days, especially if you were a private soldier. George and I were the last to be allocated seats since we were designated Priority 4. The rest of the cast had gone ahead. There was no heating in the plane and we waddled across the tarmac festooned with sweaters and greatcoats and carrying equipment (for the army still insisted that we were soldiers on active service) and boxed rations for the journey.

The other passengers consisted of high-ranking officers, who viewed us with undisguised disdain, and also Roger Livesey and Ursula Jeans who were en route to India for some star-studded ENSA production. They took pity on us and made the trip bearable.

Instead of the scheduled eighteen hours the flight took five days. Our first touch-down was in Rabat in French Morocco. I had never been out of England before and so much of the unpleasantness was discounted by an excited, if short-lived, curiosity.

The moment we landed all the officers and V.I.P.s were whisked away to the mess. George and I were left on the tarmac surrounded by Arab ground staff. Nobody came near us and we hadn't the slightest clue how we were expected to behave or indeed what was happening. It was Roger Livesey who came back to rescue us and who insisted that we join him for a meal in the officers' mess. We tried to point out that such a move would hardly be greeted with applause, but he disregarded all protocol and took us to the bar rather in the manner of Lawrence introducing his Arab boy-friends and ordered massive drinks in his inimitable plummy voice. The red tabs choked over their double gin and tonics, but amazingly lacked the courage to challenge him, and he treated us to a slap-up feast.

We finally arrived in Tunis after six and a half hours' flying time, and my journal records that I had tangerines for the first time in six years. Roger gave us a night on the town and we visited a cabaret where the principal attraction was a ballet dancer very visibly pregnant.

The next day, 21 January, we landed in Cairo. Naturally it was a total bog-up. George and I were eventually taken to No. 152 Transit Camp in Abassia – 'city of the dead' – and told to fend for ourselves. We spent that first night sleeping on concrete with a couple of scrounged blankets thrown over us, and huddled together for shared warmth. George woke me some time before dawn. 'Don't move,' he whispered. 'Don't do anything.'

Standing over us was an emaciated and extremely unpleasant-looking Alsatian guard dog. We lay like petrified babes in the wood, while the dog sniffed at the edge of the blankets. It apparently found something familiar because it proceeded to first pee and then defecate all over us. We were prepared to be grateful for such small mercies and the dog, having completed its ablutions, wandered off into the fetid darkness. It was a memorable introduction to the land of the Pharaohs.

We eventually made contact with the rest of our party. They were somewhat smug, having got settled in before us. The rest of their news was not good. One of the cast had been struck down and was in hospital. The local Welfare Officer had never heard of us, had not been expecting us and was not prepared to receive us. As far as officialdom was concerned we did not exist. It was enough to daunt even Montgomery. But actors are curiously resilient. We laid siege to the Welfare Officer, quoting non-existent War Office authorities and hinting at court-martial and dismissal with ignominy if he failed to pull his finger out. We were sufficiently convincing to make him telegram London for further instructions, but in the meantime it was back to the dog latrine at Abassia and the prospect of having to live on our wits for another two weeks.

George took his own escape route and immediately set about finding himself a girl-friend affluent enough to support him in the manner to which. He broke his previous best time for the event and by nightfall on the second day was installed in a comfortable apartment with a half-caste of disturbing beauty but distinctly unwashed. Being a generous friend he invited me to move in with him and share what was going, but even in my misery I found it possible to decline.

It wasn't until the tenth day that the red tape finally got sorted. We were given a replacement actor for the one in hospital and somehow galvanized ourselves into the necessary rehearsals. It was all totally unreal.

So began our Middle East tour, the play inflicted upon various audiences so starved of entertainment that even our pathetic efforts were well received. My journal records that on occasions I was so ashamed that I was tempted to leave the stage in disgust. A handful of army actors and actresses, living in tents, journeying long distances in swaying three-ton Bedford trucks, the men compelled to unload the scenery, set it up, fix the lighting (such as it was), then dress and make up and perform the play. Afterwards our females were whisked away to the mess while we loaded the scenery again and then joined them for the remainder of a drunken party. At such times we were accepted in the mess, despite the fact that we were all in the ranks. But it was only a temporary dispensation. For the rest of our days we were constantly reminded of our true station in life: those same officers who had entertained us the night before would cut us dead the following morning or else put us on a charge for being incorrectly dressed.

Sometimes we were the guests of the sergeants' mess, and just in case I am accused of unfair bias against the officers let me record that I found the non-commissioned hospitality just as condescending. I remember one particularly drunken evening where we were exposed to several alarming rituals. One must admit that these were desert veterans, most of them over the hill with boredom, awaiting their turn to catch the Blighty boat. The sergeants seemed very elderly to me, pot-bellied, swaying men consuming endless pints of the local beer and anxious to recount their war experiences. They invariably became maudlin as the night wore on and sang repeated choruses of sentimental songs like 'It's a Sin to Tell a Lie' before finally passing out. On this particular night there was a cabaret of sorts. I have noticed that in nearly every mess I have visited, be it sergeants' or officers', there is always one character who, given sufficient drink and encouragement, will perform a drag act, eat gramophone records, or else strip. There are few sights sadder than false breasts above hairy legs. That night the cabaret progressed from female impersonation to various degrading sex acts. Topping the bill, as it were, was a performance by a middle-aged staff-sergeant who smeared his parts with sardine oil and allowed the mess kitten to fellate him. Of such was the Kingdom of Heaven in Middle East Command in 1946.

I had an acute sense of time lost and my premonitions as to the eventual outcome of the tour became curiously urgent. On the 15th February I noted in my journal: *I feel, though I cannot articulate my feelings to the others, that something traumatic is going to happen to us. The sense of being isolated before an impending disaster fills my whole body.*

Later that same day, after the evening performance and following the customary leery skirmishes in the officers' mess, we set out in our three-ton Bedford truck for the journey back to Lake Timsah. I remember that I had taken extra care not to drink more than the minimum socially required of me. When finally we gathered together in the cold night air I was icily sober in contrast to the majority of the party. The girls were merry, some of the men maudlin, others fairly stewed to the gills. We sat huddled together for warmth and comfort while the truck gathered speed along the road that ran parallel to the Sweet Water Canal. I was conscious that we were going much too fast, but I lacked the courage to voice my fears. And then it happened.

Some years later I sat down and wrote a short story based on the events of that night. It was called *The Morning it All Came True*. My fictionalized account included a death, though the real story stopped just short of that final ingredient. The actor sergeant in charge of our party was the central character in the real-life drama, and the only reason he didn't die was that George saved his life. My journal records in great detail what took place and I used much of this detail to colour my short story.

The sergeant was a Scot. When he was sober he was an endearing character with a keen, if sardonic, sense of humour, but after a hospitality session his personality changed completely – the humour changed to biting sarcasm first of all and then he became totally vicious. That night he was really tanked-up, and earlier in the evening he had been looking for a fight.

Using his rank, he travelled in the cabin with the young driver. Nobody argued, because the rest of us were glad of physical separation from him. He must have ordered the young driver to put his foot down and then, on a sudden drunken whim, told him to make a violent stop. The truck lurched off the road until the front wheels were halfway down the slope to the canal. Those of us in the back were thrown together in dark confusion. We heard a cry from the driver – 'He's on the rocks.'

We tumbled out and saw the sergeant as a black object thrashing lazily in the water. George, drunk, bemused, merely let his body relax and then he, too, was in the water striking out for the drowning man. He rescued him, somehow, in the darkness and they were both dragged on to dry land. The sergeant was badly injured, bleeding profusely from a head wound. We got him and George back into the truck and did what we could for both of them. The sergeant vomited and then lapsed into a coma.

Those of us sober enough to give coherent instructions bullied and dragooned the young driver into getting the truck back on to the road. Then began a nightmare journey without maps. We lost our way many times for in the original confusion we had taken the wrong direction. The sergeant lay in his own vomit and would obviously bleed to death unless we got him to hospital. George, dressed in an assortment of borrowed dry clothes – an ATS shirt, my greatcoat, somebody else's spare trousers – was too chilled to take any further part in the proceedings.

We drove aimlessly for at least two hours with a mounting sense of panic before chancing upon any directional signs. We found that we were heading back for Cairo. By then we were committed.

Unbeknown to us serious rioting had broken out in Cairo. Totally isolated and concerned with our own personal problems, travelling on secondary roads, we somehow slipped through the network of army roadblocks which had been hastily set up during the night to divert all traffic away from Cairo.

When eventually, just after dawn, we entered the outskirts of Cairo with an apparently dying man on board, we drove into the middle of the rioting. Naturally we were unarmed, unprotected and worst of all unprepared. As luck would have it I was now sitting beside the driver up front. I can remember suddenly seeing a mass of people converging on us, but I still didn't take in what was happening. It wasn't until the first piece of broken paving stone shattered the windscreen that the often-imagined nightmare fused into reality. But by then we had travelled another hundred yards and were in the thick of it. I urged the driver to keep his foot down and we surged forward, blind, into the angry crowd. Rocks and bottles bounced off the truck as we zig-zagged crazily from one side of the street to the other, relentlessly mowing down anything in our path. It was simply a matter of them or us and what little luck we had left. The luck held. We got through the main body of the crowd and then accelerated down a comparatively empty stretch of road, a body of the rioters still in pursuit. We still had no idea where to go and though we doubled back several times on each occasion we found the road ahead blocked with marauding gangs. We turned off again and this time we were spotted by a British armoured car. This provided an escort and led us to the nearest military barracks.

It wasn't until we were safely in the courtyard and the gates had been closed behind us that the full impact of what we had gone through came to me. The rear of the Bedford truck was in tatters, the canvas rent by a score of missiles. Smoke was rising over various parts of the city for the rioters had set fire to many buildings. Our ATS girls were understandably in a state of shock and were swiftly taken into care. The sergeant, who had somehow survived the night, was removed to hospital and the rest of us, after a meal and interrogation, joined several other hundred refugees in the packed courtyard.

The riots lasted three days and during that time many of the British buildings were destroyed and looted. It was a week or more before the curfew was lifted and the authorities considered it safe for us to walk the streets again. There were stringent rules that no British soldier was to walk out alone, and all female personnel travelled under escort.

The incident itself was of no great pith and moment, merely a transient, squalid little escapade. I hated the Cairo of 1946. I hated the surface gloss and the seething maggot-ridden interior. I felt as I had once felt on the farm in Lincolnshire when I had chanced upon a dead and bloated rat lying in a field of poppies. I lifted the corpse with the toe of my boot and exposed the soft, decayed underbelly – it glistened white in the sunshine and then disintegrated, the corruption bursting through the paper-thin skin. That was how the Cairo of 1946 appeared to me.

My life changed because of the incident. On the army level it changed because I was promoted on the spot and given my sergeant's stripes. On a personal level I had been tested and found wanting, and I despised myself for that.

The whole episode lasted thirty-nine days, for by the 1st March 1946 we were entrained for Port Said and the boat home.

Nineteen

I dare say the good ship H.M.T. *Empire Ken* had seen better days. Since my previous seafaring experience had been confined to a day-trip from Weymouth to Lulworth Cove and back, I embarked with mixed feelings. We were lucky to have secured our passage for there was a rush to get the veterans home for demobilization and every ship leaving Egypt was packed to suffocation.

Our quarters were below the water-line and we slept in close proximity in three-tiered metal bunks. There were no such refinements as air-conditioning, and for the greater part of each day we were confined down below in a rarefied atmosphere of sweat, sick and slopped urine. The food dished out to us was indescribable. Much of it looked as though it had been regurgitated by the previous sitting then hurriedly reheated in the same filthy utensils. We queued in long dispirited lines for hours on end, our patience being finally rewarded with a tray of ladled swill, for it was by no means uncommon to be served three nauseating courses on the same metal dish – yellow-fatted meats, greens, rock-hard potatoes and semi-congealed gravy all mixed together with a dollop of chocolate pudding and a portion of tinned fruit-salad.

This was just bearable while we steamed sedately through the Mediterranean, but became the food of revolution when our overloaded vessel lurched into the Bay of Biscay.

Two-thirds of the men on my deck, myself included, were immediately prostrated. I can remember lying on my bunk, which was at floor level, praying for a quick death. Vomit from the two upper bunks, filtered through ancient army blankets, dripped continuously. The latrines had long since become blocked and with every roll of the ship a dark tidal wave of liquid human excreta rushed over the metal floor of the deck and slopped high against the bulwarks.

The storm abated after forty-eight hours, and a few of us

managed to stagger up on deck. Gulping in the first lungfuls of fresh sea air, I resolved there and then that I would somehow beat the system. I volunteered to serve in the second-class dining-hall. There I waited upon a motley collection of WAAFS, ATS, WRNS and pregnant Egyptian wives. Like all the others the married couples were segregated from each other; in many cases I suspected that this was welcomed by the returning husbands who were mostly veterans of the desert campaigns. Doubtless they had been attracted to their wives a few years previously, for Egyptian girls have a sleek nubility when they are in their teens, but removed from their natural surroundings the gloss soon goes off their coats. Perhaps prolonged exposure to British Army cooking hastened their decline. Certainly they were a sorry lot when I chanced upon them, for the majority were already going fat. They sat on deck, huddled together, looking up with sad, suspicious eyes at the watery sun, for all the world like stranded seals.

There was method in my menial madness. My stints as a waiter entitled me to remain above deck most of the day, and with a little discretion and guile I was able to widen my scope of activities. I discovered the whereabouts of the ship's entertainment officer and made that harassed individual aware of our professional presence. I planted the seed that perhaps it would relieve him of some anxieties if we gave two or three performances of *The Day is Gone*. We were both desperate men, and I correctly judged that with conditions of near-mutiny prevailing below decks even our inadequacies would be gratefully received. 'Perhaps,' he said, 'you could also get up a ship's concert. Bit of a sing-song and a conjurer, you know. Is that up your street?'

It was before the days of the Chanel advertisements but I promised him anything. He thanked me with half-mad eyes and departed to get sanction from the captain. I returned to my second-class dining-room scenting victory.

I had previously glimpsed a lithe and attractive Wren at one of the sittings. There had been something about her that set her apart from the others. She wore, I remember, the regulation navy-blue jersey and her skin was the perfection of pink and white, as though it had never been exposed to the coarsening heat of the Egyptian sun. I looked for her again and made a point of serving her at the next meal. I longed to find out her name.

At that moment the entertainments officer returned. Permission had been granted for the performances of the play. 'I hope it's a comedy,' he said. 'Plenty of laughs, are there?'

It didn't seem the moment to disillusion him about *The Day is Gone*. My own performance as the middle-aged murderer was about as funny as an open grave.

'It's okay for the concert too,' he said. 'So try and drum up something for that. There must be heaps of talent just lying about the ship.'

'We'll need somewhere to rehearse,' I said, thinking quickly. 'Can you fix anywhere?'

'Yes, I'll get on to that.'

'And I'll need permission to get the rest of the cast together. They're all over the place, and of course we're not allowed up here.'

He looked dubious.

'I mean if we don't all rehearse together the thing'll be a shambles.'

'Well, we don't want that. Look, you go ahead and round them up and I'll fix it somehow. But don't make yourselves too conspicuous.'

'When do they want the first show?'

'Soon as possible. Tonight.'

He departed again. I looked around for my Wren but she had finished her meal and was nowhere to be seen. I went below decks and broke the good news to George and the rest of the male cast. I got a message to the girls and about an hour later we all assembled in one of the state rooms and went through a rapid word rehearsal. Rumour was already on the grapevine and some of the senior officers came to gawp: actors have the same fascination as the zoo for many of the general public.

The remaining hours before the first performance were spent in locating our props and costumes. The main dining-hall was cleared for us, but there was no stage as such, and no

One of those carefully posed publicity stills that fool
nobody. Yvonne de Carlo behind the camera. Rock
Hudson and Raoul Walsh discussing my socks

This is an authentic example of British 'B' picture acting

Above Night shooting in the streets of London on *Seance on a Wet Afternoon*. Bunter (Richard Attenborough) is wearing a false nose. We were both contemplating suicide at the time. *Below* Hayley Mills listening to a bearded and apparently desperate director on *Whistle Down the Wind*. The gentleman with the loud-hailer was my First Assistant Basil Rayburn

curtains. We got together some furniture and a programme was hastily roneoed by the ship's purser.

We played to a packed and amazingly appreciative audience, and by some curious piece of alchemy the thing worked better than it had ever done before. It was very early theatre-in-the-round, possibly the first theatre-of-cruelty, but the proximity of the audience somehow worked for rather than against us and we were listened to in rapt silence and wildly applauded at the end. As we took our bows I saw my Wren in the audience.

The rest of the voyage we were given the freedom of the ship. We attended dances in the afternoon on the so-called 'sun-deck'. I danced with my Wren. Her name was Alice and she came from Glasgow. She was engaged to a Canadian Wing-Commander. The fact that he was not on board gave little comfort.

By now we had started to assemble a programme for the ship's concert. I held auditions and sifted through some stunningly untalented baritones, bird impersonators, would-be Max Millers, Jew's-harp experts, conjurers and drag acts. It became all too obvious that we would have to pad out the bill with some improvisations of our own. I put myself down to recreate the immortal Sid Fields, being fortunately able to remember his famous golfing sketch verbatim. I must ask you to believe that this monstrous piece of conceit was born of desperation.

I had skilfully recruited my delectable Wren into the cast for totally ulterior motives. By now I had fallen in love with her, performing my oft-repeated routine of the daring young man on the emotional trapeze with a growing desperation. Alice remained enigmatic and although our relationship deepened as we came in sight of the shores of Scotland, my lack of real progress depressed me.

For once Service red tape worked for me. Although Glasgow was her home town, Alice was not allowed an immediate return to her family. Instead she had to catch the night train to London with the rest of us because officialdom decreed that she must travel south to report to her base depot before being granted disembarkation leave.

Segregation of the sexes extended to troop trains, but I was in no mood to embrace that form of idiocy, and the moment the journey began I walked the length of the train to her compartment, determined to press my case one last time. It was not a successful reunion. She felt guilty about her absent Canadian, and although we stood in the corridor until 1 a.m. we talked like strangers. We parted again and I went back to my own carriage numbed with anguish.

The train had a long wait at Carlisle and most of us got out to stretch our legs and smell the smoky night air of England. I could not resist parading in front of her carriage in a masochistic urge to take one last look. Her face was circled in the steamed window as I drew level, and to my amazement she mouthed an invitation for me to join her. I managed to buy a bar of chocolate from the WVS trolley on the platform and gave it to her as a peace offering. Long before we reached London she was asleep on my cramped arm.

The story did not end on that railway station. Within twenty-four hours I was travelling on another train, back to Glasgow for a journey's end in lovers meeting. She had phoned me on my return home and I had immediately set forth again, puzzling once more my doting, indulgent parents. It was a time for madness. My romantic conception of life was being proved and I could not resist the challenge. I know now that it was a selfish act on my part, for it brought little happiness to Alice. Because of me she broke off her engagement to the Canadian Wing-Commander, because of my insistence she became for a time what I imagined her to be and it was an alien role she could not play without deception. I cherished her too well and unwisely for a few months and we had many good times together, but divorced from the counterfeit setting of a sea voyage our relationship had no chance of lasting success. She was more perceptive, more honest than me, a dear, sweet and beautiful girl who found the courage to tell me that what I really wanted was not a wife but a fictional mistress. I denied it, of course, many times, but with diminishing conviction, and in the end we drifted apart. I lost touch with her for many years and then discovered that she had married happily. I was glad for her and I always thought of her with tenderness and affection.

A few weeks ago I had a letter from her husband, whom I have never met. He told me that she died of cancer after a mercifully short illness. He said that she had often talked of me and that they had both followed my subsequent career with interest. Reading his sad and generous letter, I was reminded once again of those brief days on the *Empire Ken*, days the locusts have not quite eaten.

Twenty

By the time my twentieth birthday came around I was in Germany, the sergeant in charge of a 'Stars in Battledress' production of James Bridie's *It Depends What You Mean*. This engaging play, one of Bridie's minor works, was built around the Brains Trust. It was an uneasy mixture of near-slapstick and Bridie's own brand of philosophy and it confused many of the army audiences we played to, the majority of whom were seeing a play for the first time. Perhaps part of the confusion stemmed from the fact that it was indifferently performed: the cast was two-thirds amateur and without exception we were all playing beyond our range. Absurd though it undoubtedly was, I was recreating Alistair Sim's original role of the Padre, and since I still had a featureless pudding of a face without a line on it, the effect was patently not what Bridie had intended.

There were side benefits, however. I discovered the power of the dog-collar by chance one afternoon when I was holding a dress-rehearsal to try to bring the cast up to scratch. Still wearing my stage uniform I wandered out into the streets for a breath of fresh air. Before I had gone a hundred yards I was approached by two privates, who saluted and then asked if I would give them some help and advice on personal problems. Too surprised to stammer an immediate explanation, I found myself listening to lurid accounts of adultery in distant Newcastle. Discretion, I decided, was necessary, for I had the conviction that the sentence for impersonating a man of God was likely to be a prolonged stay in the glasshouse. I heard them out, told them to apply for legal aid and, for good measure, to go and commit some therapeutic adultery themselves with the nearest German girl. I also gave them my blessing, and they departed strongly converted. One of them actually said, 'If I'd met you sooner, Padre, I'd have been a better man.'

This sobering encounter gave me other ideas. I tested the deception elsewhere and found that nobody questioned my youthful appearance above the dog-collar. I had an officer's battledress with three pips on each shoulder and I could therefore be said to be a gentleman. The clerical collar was an added, and all-powerful, fetish. I brushed up my hail-fellow-well-met dialogue and embarked upon a brilliantly successful career in the Church.

It is clearly laid down that the senior rank in any group of soldiers in the field has a duty to make sure that those under his command are kept well fed and watered and free from infection. Although we lived fairly comfortably, decent liquor was hard to come by. Only sergeants and above were allowed to draw a ration of spirits from the bulk issue stores, since it was a fact of life that Scotch and gin fetched astronomical prices on the black-market. Being a sergeant I was entitled to indent for two bottles of Steinhager gin every month, a fluid with many of the characteristics of U-Boat fuel. I was concerned for the welfare of my troops who, in desperation, were turning from the watery German beer available in the canteens and acquiring illicit bottles of wood alcohol. We all knew that the good stuff was to be had in abundance in the officers' mess and hotels frequented by the layabouts in the Control Commission. Having given the problem much thought, and having perfected my holy technique, I borrowed a jeep (without permission or driving licence) and sallied dangerously forth complete with dog-collar on the first of many crusades.

It all went alarmingly well. I drove boldly – without being able to shift out of second gear – into the nearest officer-restricted compound, parked the jeep in a reserved space and breezed into the mess. Nobody gave me a second look. I had the sense not to go into the bar, but instead located the quartermaster in charge of stores. He was such an obvious old villain that I knew I was home and dry.

'Look, Quarter,' I said, 'I'm prepared to give you a clean ticket for all your notorious sins if you'll help me out.'

'Beg your pardon, sir?'

'You can do that too,' I said in my best strangulated voice. 'Don't want to pull the old rank on you, but you've been tumbled. And since it's coming up to harvest festival, I wondered if you'd be prepared to make a reasonable offering for the Church?'

His eyes glazed.

'Well, as you know, sir, I've got a difficult job here . . . What exactly did you have in mind?'

'A little liquid offering, perhaps? See, I'm not on the establishment here, mostly swanning around, and I get a little parched after evensong.'

'Say no more, sir. It so happens that I have a little tucked away for just such emergencies.'

'I knew you were C. of E.'

'In me A.B. 64, sir. Shall we say half a dozen of each?'

'Well, shall we?'

'May as well make it dozen, then. You don't want to run short, do you, sir?'

Minutes later I had a crate of Scotch and a crate of gin under the tarpaulin of the jeep. Both were then eight shillings a bottle, payable in the equivalent in marks. The mark was thirteen to the pound and a packet of Players fetched 100 marks minimum. I returned home a hero and threw my own birthday party.

Twenty-one

I was in a bookshop (even then in war-shattered Germany my first haunt when we arrived in a new town). The shopkeeper was quite young and had a deformed hand, a relic of the Russian front. He was polite and quite helpful, neither too much one way or the other. I don't think I was aware of anybody else in the shop. Then the small man spoke to me.

'Are you interested in German literature?'

He had a dark, enquiring face and very expressive hands, beautiful hands. I thought at first he was just another black-market operator, perhaps more cultured than the average and obviously working with some subtlety. I took it for granted that his smile, his interest, his gesticulating hands, his apparent ease and command of English were merely means to an over-familiar end. But no, cigarettes were not mentioned. We made conversation – it was all a little frigid.

'Do you speak or read German?' he said.

I told him that I spoke schoolboy German but found great difficulty in reading German script.

He offered to lend me some books from his own library. Still no mention of any barter. It was all curiously British, reserved. We made a date for the same hour two days later at the bookshop. When he had gone I enquired his name from the young bookseller and was told it was Dr Lehmann. Years later, watching *The Third Man*, I was reminded of this encounter, for there had been something of Holly Martins about me and Dr Lehmann resembled most of the minor cast in that remarkably accurate film.

I kept the appointment and Dr Lehmann duly arrived. He brought with him a small briefcase filled with books and we went into a back room. I was still convinced that the episode would end in barter. I wondered what the black-market rate was for second-hand books. But no cigarettes were asked for and it became apparent that he had no intention of selling any of his books, they were too precious. He merely wanted to lend them.

I discovered to my concealed shame that he was a Doctor of Philosophy at Kiel University. Sir William Beveridge had recently spoken there to 2000 Kiel students. Dr Lehmann had heard the lecture but was non-committal when I questioned him, and we went on to discuss the political situation in England. He was profoundly impressed by the fact that Churchill had been removed from office before the end of the war. 'Inconceivable,' he kept saying. 'Such a thing is inconceivable to the German mind.' He seemed to take it very personally.

I liked him. He had none of the mock-humility of the defeated. At that time it was almost impossible to find a German who would admit to having ever supported the Nazis. The majority were unctuously willing to volunteer the information that Hitler had been a transient evil influence on an otherwise blameless nation. Equally unconvincing was the much-repeated excuse that England had never been the real enemy. The real enemy had been and remained Russia, as we would soon discover to our cost. But the dismissal of Churchill remained the main topic of discussion and future historians could well determine that this single democratic illustration did more to convince the average German of the practical possibilities of our imperfect system than any other piece of laboured post-war propaganda. They found it fascinating, alarming, inexplicable.

Doctor Lehmann and I then broached the subject of Belsen which I had visited a few days before. His reaction – the first I had received from a German face to face – was startling. He struck his head with his white hand. 'There is no hope for most of my people,' he said. 'They don't believe. They cover their faces and say they don't want to hear. Jewish propaganda. English Jewish propaganda. I should not say this of my own people, but for fifty years they will be a menace.'

It was the voice of a man who for twelve years had been forbidden to think. A schoolteacher who had not been allowed to teach the truth, who had continually to pretend that Russian and English literature did not exist, that there was no culture outside the sterile confines of the Nazi doctrines.

I looked at this man, this small man, with his narrow bespectacled face, his shabby clothes and neatly laced boots, and I began to comprehend what life had been like for some Germans since 1933. He was unreal in many ways, and much of what he said sounded curiously stilted and insincere – his emotion embarrassed me because experience had taught that there was no real truth in the Germany of 1946. I wanted to believe him, but part of me held back. He questioned me closely about Belsen. Had I actually seen it, were the ovens still there, did I think the actual numbers had been exaggerated? With every answer I gave he became visibly more distressed until he was openly crying, and removed his ancient, repaired spectacles to wipe weak eyes.

He invited me back to his home. He and his family no longer occupied the whole building, for Military Government had moved in several other families. He had somehow come through the war with his library intact, and this was now crammed into a single small room. Many of his books were in English and he showed them to me with unconcealed pride.

I took a tin of corned beef and he handled it with the respect that a stamp collector would give to a Cape of Good Hope triangular. Only then did I offer him a single cigarette, which he accepted gravely – turning it over and over between his fingers, examining it like some clinical specimen, and politely asked me not to be offended if he did not smoke it straight away in my presence but saved it for later. I told him of my first impressions, how I had been convinced that he was just another, slightly more subtle, black-market operator.

'Yes, I can see,' he said. 'Why should I be different? I understand perfectly.'

He then went on to tell me that, in his turn, he had thought my attitude towards him had been very correct – not unkind, but merely frigid and correct – almost Germanic!

'I had to summon up courage,' he said. 'Should I speak? Yes, I decided that I would. You see, forgive me, but one does not often see your British soldiers in a bookshop. They have other interests.'

He insisted that I accept a book from his library and we finally agreed that I would take a volume of Leonardo de Vinci drawings. I have it still.

I returned to Dr Lehmann's home the following day and this time I was greeted by his daughter – a dark-skinned girl of nineteen with unlimited charm and a plausible English accent. From her I discovered, to my further embarrassment, that her father was a well-known minor German poet and that in his youth he had been regarded as an innovator, his early work having taken the form of rather advanced novels. She showed me some of his work. We went on to discuss Kafka, Rilke, Edith Sitwell, and most surprisingly – Edward Young, that all-but-forgotten poet whom Johnson described as a genius. Dr Lehmann said he felt his own poetry had much in common with Young, though he was modest enough not to quote Johnson.

We let the flood of enthusiasm carry us forward, he drawing his chair closer so that he might listen more intently. The room grew dark, for electricity was rationed and only came on at certain hours. From time to time he would jump up from his chair, hair disordered, and fetch me fresh volumes. He asked me to read some Shakespeare aloud to him, then a favourite poem of Keats, 'Ode to Autumn'. I read it very badly, but he sat silent, nodding his head in approval.

He insisted that I shared their tea, a weak ertsatz brew which they took with dry bread. I gave them what cigarettes and sundries I had with me – soap, a bar of chocolate, a packet of razor blades – the currency of victory rather than friendship. I also gave him half a dozen Penguin paperbacks and he treated these with reverence: they were the first new English books he had seen for over eight years.

Before we parted for the last time, he talked of responsibility and authority. 'The trick will be if we comprehend the difference between the two,' he said. 'I shan't live long enough to see the outcome.'

I wrote to him once or twice and received his replies. Then after an interval I wrote again, but this time my letter was returned with the German equivalent of *Return to Sender,* *Address Unknown* stamped across the envelope. I often wonder what became of him and his family. Presumably by now he is dead. I hope he died amongst his beloved books, those books he could now read in freedom of a kind.

Twenty-two

Most of my letters to Norman during this period were concerned with our joint future after we had been demobilized. During my stay at 19 St Giles High Street I had formulated the idea that we ought to enter into a financial partnership, each agreeing to put aside the same sum of money each week and deposit it in a joint account. Valerie helped make the necessary arrangements, for neither Norman nor I had ever possessed a bank account. With her usual kindness she introduced me to the manager of Lloyds, 16 St James's Street, and after due ceremony in that imposing building an account was opened in our joint names.

In September 1946 I was writing to Norman: 'I haven't drawn any pay since I arrived out here, so I should have accrued about £30 and by next January we should have £100 in the joint account. Not a bad effort for just over a year since we broached the idea.'

To Norman and Norman alone I was ruthlessly honest about my attempts to become a writer. 'Self – perhaps that is the key to it all: self-discipline, self-knowledge, complete honesty regarding ability, the conscious knowledge of my failings. I can reveal to you that, taking the bulk of my work to date, I have borrowed flagrantly. Seldom have I begun from scratch. Yet, contained within the schoolboy's attempt at a crib has been a tiny spark of my own life. If only I could work my own bellows I might ignite the spark and produce the complete hidden work that I feel lies somewhere beneath my skin.'

My first German tour ended the following month and towards the end of November I was 'lingering on the brink of existence on Salisbury Plain' in a great corrugated-iron plantation.

We lived like the dispossessed, stateless and seemingly without identity. It was a scrounging, day-to-day existence quite unlike any other period in my life, confined within the corrugated-iron boundaries of partially rotted army huts, and I sometimes had the feeling that we were the sole survivors of some disaster. In some adjacent huts was a group of ATS girls, equally adrift, who shared our food and misery. Some of them also shared our beds. Numbered amongst them was a girl destined for public tragedy. She was anonymous then, just a fellow sufferer, but I can claim to have had a passing premonition about her. My own midnight companion, who shared an innocent cup of gritty cocoa, was an ebullient and intelligent girl called Ros Chatto who later went on to a distinguished career in theatrical management. She hated the squalor of our surroundings as much as I did. I was glad of her feminine company and sense of humour. We discussed earnestly, as young people will, a more intimate relationship but decided, equally earnestly, that companionship without the burden of sex was more immediately valuable. In any event I think we were both too particular to venture into an affair in such depressing surroundings: the idea of making love in those sordid huts between soiled army blankets was very off-putting, and we settled for an undemanding friendship which happily has survived to this day. Having taken the decision we became somewhat smug and holy about the less scrupulous in our midst whilst discussing them with a tinge of envy.

In particular, we were fascinated by the behaviour of this other girl. I am no student of criminology, but I have noticed a certain morbid truth. Time and time again one reads of a sex murder and the accompanying blurred snapshot alongside the inflamed text shows the familiar bovine features of a girl who looks older than her stated years. I don't know whether I am alone in thinking this, but I am convinced that certain people are attracted to the idea of violence and actively contribute towards their own sad destiny.

Years later I was to recall our existence on Salisbury Plain when I read the first reports of a murder on board a pleasure cruise. The accused was a steward and his defence was that he had been invited to the victim's cabin in the expectation of enjoying certain familiar favours. As the moment of truth approached, the girl had suddenly denied him. He was then the victim of his own lust, panicked and strangled her, later pushing the dead body through the porthole. Despite the fact that the body was never found, he was convicted of murder. Studying the reports of the case I was confronted with a photograph of the victim. I recognized her as that same ATS girl. Her name was Gay Gibson.

Our gipsy-like existence on Salisbury Plain ended as suddenly and inexplicably as it began. By now many of the old members of Stars in Battledress had been demobilized. Major Noel McGregor and the inestimable Sergeant-Major Stanley Hall had secured their release. They were to go on to greater things, for they banded together to form Wig Creations, a very successful business enterprise which flourishes to this day.

By January 1947 I was back in the Intelligence Corps barracks in Aldershot, attending drunken sergeants' mess parties where 'the R.Q.M.S. was deprived of his pants and tied to a radiogram so that he could more easily assimilate the message of 'One Meat Ball.'

There is evidence to show that I forged my pay book and put in for some more leave. Apparently I was successful and got away with seventeen days. It turned out to be another embarkation leave, for shortly afterwards I went back to Germany, this time to Hamburg to join a quasi-military outfit called Combined Services Entertainment Unit. Our headquarters were the partially ruined Hotel zum Crownprinzen in the Haupt-Bahnof Platz. The cold that winter was intense. I occupied a fifth-floor room, sharing it with another young soldier-actor called Basil Hoskins. It was a room devoid of comfort, situated at the rear of the hotel, and half the glass was missing from the single window. There were power-cuts every day, sometimes lasting twenty-four hours, which in turn meant that the indifferent food was served uncooked. We stayed in bed most of the day in semi-gloom, washing and shaving in cans of water carried up five flights of darkened stairs from the kitchens. There were daily food riots in the streets, for if our existence was miserable the plight of the citizens of Hamburg was grim indeed. People were murdered every day for nothing more than crusts of bread and their threadbare clothes. It was not uncommon to see people drop dead in the snow from the cold and starvation – the only Germans who survived in comfort were those working for the Occupation Forces or prominent in the black-market. I have never known such cold, nor have I ever lived in an atmosphere of such grimed despair. The degradation and misery of Hamburg that winter is something I would like to erase from memory.

My own life staggered along, restricted as always by a net of incompetence and red tape. Officially we were rehearsing a production of Edgar Wallace's *The Case of the Frightened Lady*, a pathetic production which would have reduced any actor's body temperature below freezing point without the help of the elements.

I somehow managed to scrounge the use of an ancient type-writer. I bought a ream of yellowing paper and worked every available hour of daylight in that fifth-floor room on yet another novel. With the help of endless duty-free cigarettes and whisky, I managed to commit 40,000 words to paper. I sent these to Norman for his opinion and criticism, and with much perception and not a little friendship he eventually found the courage to tell me that he thought them less than excellent. Our letters to each other trace the progress of the novel and my gradual acceptance of another failure. I was slowly learning that my literary talents did not match my literary ambitions. I felt that I was gradually being stripped of all hope; the rehearsals for the play filled me with despair and I began to drink heavily and my health suffered. I was never drunk – the cold saw to that: my body could burn a whole bottle of whisky just keeping warm, but the daily intake of alcohol dulled what remained of my imagination. Apart from Basil I had few friends, and although my letters to Norman reveal that I occasionally wandered forth in aimless fashion to find some temporary solace in female arms, it was all worm-wood.

The dreary tour ran its course and I mercifully remember little of the actual performances. Then it was back to Hamburg again, a return to the fifth-floor room where I somehow found the necessary energy to start writing again. This time I wisely turned my back on the novel and embarked on some new short stories. These efforts met with some success and I was able to post three new stories to A. D. Peters. They showed a marked improvement on all previous attempts. The long winter was finally over and I was rehearsing for *The Hasty Heart* under the direction of a professional called Mac Picton.

Once again we took to the road for a tour of *The Hasty Heart*. There was only one female role and this was played by a civilian actress, Eileen Murphy. She became the unpaid psycho-analyst for a group of very neurotic actors, a function she dis-charged with down-to-earth, no-nonsense efficiency. It was, by the standards of those days, a happy tour, and I learnt much from it.

I spent my twenty-first birthday in Iserlohn without any remembered or recorded jubilation. Certainly my coming of age was not notable.

It so happened that due to the usual army bog-up I was still officially listed as Field Security with a knowledge of German and therefore my demobilization was exasperatingly delayed. After *The Hasty Heart* tour finished I somehow wangled another home leave.

During this leave Mac came back to London and informed me that I had been cast in the name role in *Charley's Aunt* for his next C.S.E.U. production. He had returned to audition three young ladies for the unspeakably boring juvenile roles and I was asked to attend these auditions with him. I little suspected that this would turn out to be my Judgement of Paris, for included amongst the final selections was a young lady who was destined to be the cause and the measure of my future discontent.

To say that I fell in love at first sight with my usual regularity would be to compound the previous mistakes of the heart, but I cannot conceal the fact that Elizabeth and I were immediately and dangerously attracted to each other. After the audition I made it my urgent business to find out where she lived and before I returned to Germany at the end of my leave and in advance of her journey we had become lovers.

For once I did not betray myself in advance; for once I did not share the experience with Norman, and this in itself was an admission of sincerity. On my return to Hamburg I found there had been few changes made at the Hotel zum Crown-prinzen. The derelict foyer was as crowded as ever with vaguely resentful faces. I was directed to my old fifth-floor room: it occurred to me that it was a long way to come to embrace a familiar despair.

Climbing the dimly lit stairs I found myself face to face with an alarmingly good-looking young officer and was just about to salute him when a Jewish sergeant jumped on to the landing, flung his arms round the Adonis with one pip on his shoulder, and screamed, 'Roger, darling! When did you get in?'

Roger darling took it all in good part and I was kept waiting on the stairs while he and the sergeant exchanged show-business reminiscences. I had time to study the young first-lieutenant, who I decided was either on his way, in costume, for a dress-rehearsal of *Journey's End* or else was a travelling salesman for Alkit, for he appeared to have stepped straight out of their window. I don't think I have ever seen such a handsome creature, and in my travel-stained battledress I was prepared to hate him on sight. But with that considerable and totally genuine charm which distinguishes his public and private behaviour, First-Lieutenant Roger Moore dealt with the ebullient sergeant, then turned to me and introduced himself. Thus began a long friendship which survives to this day and is unusual in that we have never worked together despite the fact that our professional paths criss-cross.

My ancient namesake John Clarke wrote in his *Paroemiologia*, '*A man hath many enemies when his back is to the wall*,' and such is my character that I have often found myself rubbing shoulders against brick. I am not by nature Machiavellian, and I have a habit of saying what I think at the time I think it. This, I have found, does not endear me to all and sundry, and I have several times been my own executioner, hacking at my own vines before the grapes were ready. It is a fine art, the art of making silver bridges, and I have never mastered it. But I will admit to being very good at defending my friends.

I have known Roger when he was down on his luck and at the height of his success, and although it may infuriate his detractors I will record that he never changes. Perhaps the most amazing thing about him is that he has survived his good looks and his basic niceness in a profession which hates even as it admires. Easy-going and enormously tolerant of bores and rogues alike, he possesses in abundance that rare quality in leading men, the ability to send himself up. Because of his looks he has always been underestimated as an actor and he has learnt to live with grudging praise. I know him to have remarkable qualities.

We broke a few rules together that autumn in Hamburg, sharing not only high demob numbers but also a common cynicism towards the behaviour and attitudes of the army social set, who lost no time in re-establishing their *Tatler*-view of life in that shattered and occupied country. Officers who consorted with other ranks were not considered worthy of their peace-time commissions. The army then was the ideal stage for the best and worst human comedies.

Although we met socially we both went our separate ways within the Combined Services Entertainment Unit. I was rehearsing *Charley's Aunt* under Mac's direction and becoming more and more depressed, for without an audience that perennial comedy is heavy going. There was a moment when I asked to be released from the principal role, so agonised was I with my progress. My performance seemed to be devoid of inspiration and refused to come to life. I was in despair.

The play opened in Celle during September, and much to my surprise I scored a resounding, if local, success. *Charley's Aunt* in front of an audience is watertight, and granted that the leading actor has a modicum of talent he cannot fail utterly. It was my first experience of that heady power – the ability of an actor playing a superbly constructed comedy role to convulse an audience. I am sure it was a disgraceful perform-ance, for I remember adding bits of business each succeeding night, some of it original and improvised on the spot as the mood infected me. I enjoyed myself enormously and in the process became somewhat conceited with the rest of the cast. Since I was also in charge of them, off-stage relationships were often strained and unpleasant.

By now Elizabeth and I had resumed our affair. It was the first constant liaison I had ever entered into, and with a mixture of arrogance and immaturity I made many mistakes. We were circumspect and discreet in front of the rest of the cast for reasons which, at this remove, I cannot fully comprehend. It was easy enough for us to spend the nights in one bed for it was my responsibility to allocate the rooms. We drained each other emotionally and physically, wandering through the days, now living in tenderness and lust, now in doubt and recrimination. In love and loving we yet managed to destroy each other on many occasions, and although the subsequent reconciliations added another ingredient to our love-making in various hotel rooms, there was always a feeling of unease, of something about to end.

I was to be touched by real tragedy at long range during this period, for Betty's husband died on 24 October. The letter from my mother giving the news pursued me for nearly a month and by a curious irony arrived in the same post as another letter from A. D. Peters informing me that Methuen had offered to put me under contract for a volume of short stories and two further novels.

What do I really remember of that time with Elizabeth in Austria? The long, quick quarrels, the afternoons of love-making, the evening rides – all is trite when set down on paper. I was to write it subsequently, making my act of atonement for the misery we caused each other, in a short story called *Love is a Debt*, and perhaps my fiction, so thinly disguised, gives a more truthful description than I could ever reconjure here.

On the fine days we could eat outside on the terrace and three ponies would wander up through the orchard and stand quietly below us until we fed them crusts. There was an old dog, quite blind and flea-ridden, who used to lie on the stone steps of the terrace and remember his bark whenever the ponies came near. The main road lay parallel to the house below our window. There was a lot of traffic on that road, but for all that it was quiet in our room behind the double thickness of glass. We did not stay up very late. The lights and water went off every evening at eight. Usually I remembered about the water and filled the wash-basin, but there were times when we brushed our teeth in flat cold white wine. This didn't bother us. Very little bothered us. The darkness certainly didn't. We went to bed in the dark and smoked endless cigarettes. We slept when we were tired and then we slept very well. I loved her very much. But the war seemed to have done something to me and I did not love her enough.

It does not need a very discerning critic to detect the influence of Mr Hemingway in my prose of that period, and there were conscious echoes of *A Farewell to Arms* in my relationship with Elizabeth. The setting helped. Austria seemed like an exaggerated picture postcard come to life, a gigantic stage backcloth with all the hills cut out in stiff cardboard and mounted against skies of impossible blue. It was the country of the novel – the Hemingway pine trees, the Vicki Baum freshness in the air, the Charles Morgan stillness. Purples and blues and still black rivers below the roads. The greens were too green, the scent of the fields and the trees too poignant. Everywhere was clean and bright, I could not imagine that there had ever been a war.

We lived like feudal kings in that Gasthof by the lake at Krumpendorf, taking our meals in the open, grapes and wine being set before us, and the shuttered room to return to when replete, deadening the sounds of the outside world and conscience alike.

She still went riding, leaving the room before I was awake and then coming back to me, cold and flushed, to surprise me from sleep, undressing with beautiful haste. Our love was a long sickness by now, it weakened both of us. I remember that she once said to me, 'It wouldn't be so bad if one never got anywhere near the bullseye – but just to nick the outer edges, to get that close but no closer, that's the really tragic thing.'

We performed the play at infrequent intervals, and for a period of a week or more the authorities appeared to have forgotten our existence and we were left entirely to our own devices, tourists by chance rather than design.

Then we were routed to Vienna and our days at Krumpendorf were over. I was destined to remain behind, the first and only time I have ever missed any performance in the theatre. I suddenly developed a very high temperature and was taken to a military hospital babbling deliriously. My illness was diagnosed as pneumonia once again, but I have a sneaking suspicion that it was partially self-induced, for my emotional bank balance was heavily overdrawn. I had a ward to myself and lay in great comfort, attended by a succession of pretty nurses (shades of Mr Hemingway yet again!), exhausted but strangely at peace, removed from the cause and the measure, free of the responsibility of living up to my own conception of love. It was one of those rare periods in my life when I was able to give up smoking. I read everything the nurses brought me from the sparse library – the poems of John Pudney, some Evelyn Waugh, Nigel Balchin's *Darkness Falls From the Air*, and, once again, *The Good Soldier*. The curtains were kept drawn in the ward and I had the feeling of being totally isolated, my batteries on slow charge, savouring the singing time of the blood.

I was discharged from hospital when the company returned from Vienna and we returned to Hamburg via Dusseldorf. My relationship with Elizabeth was never again to achieve the happiness we shared at Krumpendorf, for the enforced separation had proved to both of us that life was possible apart – the unthinkable decision had been taken for us.

A few weeks later she returned home to England, the tour having finished. We made love for the last time in the very early hours of the morning. I bought her a present of *The Fountain* – surely a pedant's farewell? – and saw her on to the train.

Afterwards I went back to her room and touched the still-warm bed. It was all strange, I remember, strange and lonely and yet not overpoweringly so: it seemed in that moment the best thing that could have happened to us. I stayed in the room for the best part of an hour, and then went down to the bar and drank my way through a whole bottle of Benedictine.

The story I wrote, the story for Elizabeth, which A. D. Peters thought the best one in the collection, began with the words:

Roughly four years ago I promised a girl named Julie that I would one day sit down at this machine and write for her my first happy story. She has had to wait a long time. But the promise you make when you are in love is a promise that returns.

Dear Elizabeth, I repeat the promise twenty-eight years later, and if by chance you ever read this, thank you for being nicer than I deserved.

Twenty-three

I selected a pin-stripe suit that looked and felt as though it had been cut from sheet metal, shoes, shirt and, for good measure, an absurd trilby hat, and came out of the demobilization centre resembling a bit-player in an early Warner Brothers' gangster movie. Then I caught the train back to the Criterion Theatre.

It was 28 January 1948. I was home, out of the army at last, and fortunate to have landed an immediate part. *Envy My Simplicity*, extensively rewritten and retitled *Gathering Storm*, was being produced for the third time under a West End management. Stephen Mitchell and Sam Goldwyn, Jnr had joined forces to present the play at the St Martin's following one week's try-out at the Theatre Royal, Brighton. Sad to relate, the role of the dog no longer existed.

The new cast was headed by Nancy Price, a lady of formidable appearance and reputation. She was known irreverently as Nancy Half-Price, and sometimes as Nancy Not-At-Any-Price, a brace of nicknames acquired from her days as a manager. I was terrified of her from the first meeting. She was not a generous actress and using the weapon of her advanced years she succeeded in getting her own way in most things. Miles Malleson was directing the play this time round and he offered only token resistance to her calculated whims. I bore the brunt of her selfishness for most of my major scenes, until she was killed off at the end of the second act, were with her.

Throughout rehearsals she tried every trick she knew to get the play rewritten, for she was all too aware that characters who die at the end of the second act in a three-act play are unlikely to receive the final applause. She conducted vehement public arguments with the author Gordon Glennon, who was studiously polite but unmoved. Finally, when she had run the gamut of her repertoire of persuasion, she retired with ill grace in a fit of the sulks and announced that she wasn't well enough to rehearse in a cold theatre and that henceforth the actors would have to come to her. She was all too obviously made of solid teak and impervious to everything except death-watch beetle, but the management were craven and gave in to her. From that moment onwards Emrys Jones and myself had the dubious privilege of rehearsing our scenes with her in her flat off the Brompton Road.

Her major success had, of course, been in the long-running *Whiteoaks*, she and her parrot Bony having passed into theatrical legend. She still had a parrot and for all I know it could well have been the original. Certainly long familiarity with its mistress had ensured that it reproduced several of her least endearing qualities, and in the half-light and from certain angles they could be mistaken for mother and child.

The first morning I presented myself at the flat, dubious but still keen, I was astounded to find her lying on a couch swathed in shawls and rugs and with the beady-eyed parrot perched on her shoulder.

'Good morning, Miss Price,' I said. 'I hope you're feeling better?'

'I don't want your sympathy,' she said. 'Just get on with the dialogue.'

The parrot shifted its weight to another leg and seemed to be sizing me up for the kill. Since most of my scenes with Nancy involved throwing my arms round her neck in an excess of affection, I began the rehearsal with considerable misgiving. But as luck would have it my alien presence spurred the parrot to commit a social indiscretion. I was on my knees, careful to keep at a respectful distance, and stumbling through my dialogue when the parrot did his Long John Silver impersonation, lifted one leg and relieved itself of a quantity of green slime. This shot with alarming velocity across Nancy's face.

Miss Price was as if carved from granite. Waving me to continue with the scene, she merely shouted, 'Cloth!' Immediately an elderly crone appeared from behind a grandfather clock, armed with a piece of rag.

'Mop it up,' Nancy ordered, 'and then take it out.'

I watched in fascinated horror while the crone with practised dexterity removed both perpetrator and perpetrated.

'Go on!' Nancy said. 'Go on, boy, what're you waiting for?'

The rehearsal continued. I gave a sterling performance of devotion which was a triumph of matter over mind. Many of the subsequent reviews remarked on the tenderness of the scenes between the boy and his grandmother. The public end result is the only thing that matters but, O God, how I loathed every minute of it.

We duly opened in Brighton to polite noises, and at the end of every performance Nancy made a speech which began 'When we dead awaken . . .' and made the rest of us cringe. Rationing was still in progress and at the matinees, when local farmers traditionally formed part of the audience, she would add to our embarrassment by openly soliciting butter and eggs 'to help me get through', ending her speech with an invitation for members of the audience to come back-stage and purchase her latest book. One had to admire the sheer arrogance of it all, but the charity she demanded of others was notably absent from her own behaviour.

We opened at the St Martin's in a blizzard, and the following day it was patently obvious that we had a copper-bottomed flop on our hands. The notice went up at the end of the first week. I was grateful for the many chances that the play had given me over the years, for it was a showy part, and I accordingly received my fair share of what praise was going. During the short run we were visited by Queen Mary and that is the only performance I remember in any detail, for in an effort to impress our Royal patron Miss Price totally changed her reading of the role, altered all the moves and in general behaved like the ageing prima donna she was. Between shows several members of the cast complained to the stage manager, who happened to be a woman, and she relayed the complaints to Miss Price. Flushed with her afternoon triumphs, Miss Price was not in a mood to receive criticism and during the evening performance took it out on me. Instead of patting my cheeks in mild grandmotherly reproach during one of the scenes, she gave me a crack across the jaw, with the result that my masterly portrayal of a village idiot became a masterly portrayal of a mute village idiot for the rest of the act. I shed few tears when the final curtain came down, although I was sorry for the author.

Accepting my out-of-work status with an actor's obligatory resignation, I went back to Newbury Park and started to write with frenzied energy. My commissioned collection of short stories for Methuen was somewhat thin on the ground. When I re-read what was available I was forced to the unhappy conclusion that I needed to do a great deal better and I therefore set to work and finished what was eventually the title story, *Truth Lies Sleeping*, and wrote the first version of *Story for Elizabeth*. I now had some nineteen stories that I judged possible for inclusion, and had outline plots and titles for a further ten.

Fortunately my performance in the ill-fated *Gathering Storm* had not gone totally unnoticed and one day I received a call from Dennis van Thal who was then a casting director at Pinewood Studios. I took the tube to Uxbridge and caught the bus to Iver Heath. Dennis had been non-committal on the phone and merely said that he wished to discuss future prospects. He interviewed me with great courtesy and then said that since I was in the studio he would like me to meet Mr Ian Dalrymple who was the head of Wessex Films. I was ushered into a much larger office and there met Mr Dalrymple who proved to be the very antithesis of what is commonly thought to be a typical film producer. Throughout the entire interview, which lasted perhaps ten minutes, he never spoke to me, but remained at the window with his back to me, only turning briefly to wish me goodbye. Dennis seemed to find nothing odd in this behaviour.

Outside the door again I said, 'Well, that was obviously a waste of time, but thank you very much for trying.'

'Oh, no,' Dennis said, 'don't be put off by that. He liked you. I know him very well. He's a very shy man and if he hadn't liked you he'd have left the room.'

I departed unconvinced, but a few days later Dennis rang me again and said that, although he had no news from Mr Dalrymple, he had cast me for a small role in Michael Powell's new film *The Small Back Room*, based on Nigel Balchin's wartime best-seller. It was only one day's work as The Dying Soldier, and I was to receive £25. I accepted gratefully. I asked when I would receive the script.

'Ah,' Dennis said. 'I don't think that you actually say any lines. But it's a very important part nevertheless.'

Actors have such faith that I believed him and duly presented myself at Worton Hall Studios. I was put into uniform once again and led on to the set. Michael Powell was then a director of great eminence and had a reputation for giving short shift to actors who didn't know their job. I certainly didn't know mine, because nobody had told me what it was beyond the fact that I was required to die. I walked on to the sound stage and found that the setting was a sea of imitation grass. David Farrer, the star, was conversing with a man I took to be Mr Powell but who subsequently turned out to be the third assistant. He was dressed rather more elegantly than Mr Powell. I did my best to look inconspicuous, but nobody came near me for the entire morning and during that time I saw little activity of any kind. Filming in those days was an unhurried affair.

After lunch in the works canteen I returned to the set and finally got to meet the legendary Mr Powell.

'Who's this?' he enquired in his high-pitched voice.

I was brought forward and introduced.

'I hear you're a very good young actor,' Micky said. 'I hope they're right. Lie down there.'

I did as directed. Micky and two other men peered at me from all angles for at least twenty minutes.

'He looks too clean,' Micky said. 'Dirty him up.'

Two men moved in with sponges and cakes of black pan-stick. Micky watched with a critical eye.

'What do men look like who've been blown up by plastic bombs? Does anybody know?'

'Their faces are pitted,' somebody volunteered.

'What?'

'Pitted, sir.'

'Well, his face isn't pitted,' Micky said. 'It's merely covered in make-up. Very unconvincing. How do you pit a face?'

The make-up men shifted uneasily.

'I'm asking you a question. How do you make a face look pitted?'

Nobody had the answer, but a passing painter made a suggestion.

'Crumble a gramophone record and press it into his face.'

Much to my horror this idea was immediately taken seriously. Micky called for the prop man and told him to get a gramophone record. Nobody paid the slightest attention to me. The prop man duly returned, knelt beside me and, taking a handful of powdered gramophone record, started to press the fragments into my cheeks. Micky watched.

'Useless. You know what looks like that? Powdered gramophone record. We're making films, you know, not play acting.'

He walked away from the scene and the set went very quiet. 'He's probably going to turn very ugly now,' the prop man whispered to me. 'Famous for it, he is.'

Micky returned and stared down at me. 'Bandage him,' he said. 'I want him bandaged, just the eyes and mouth visible. Got that?'

The prop man went in search of bandages. Ten minutes later I was the poor man's version of Claude Rains in *The Invisible Man*. Micky and the cameraman took turns to peer at me through the viewfinder, and this time I apparently passed the test. The camera was pushed into position and the process known as lighting commenced. From time to time Micky would sit behind the camera and stare down at me. He was obviously still possessed of doubts.

'Messy,' he said. 'It all looks messy. Get all those leaves and stuff away from him.'

The first assistant shouted for the man whose job it was to sweep the set of any debris.

'Sweep the leaves up, Bert.'

Bert took his time sizing up the situation. 'I don't sweep up leaves,' he pronounced finally. 'I only sweep up woodshavings.'

'What's he say?' Micky shouted.

'Not his job, governor,' the first assistant answered.

'Well, whose job is it?'

'Gardener,' Bert said. 'That's a gardener's job, that is, sweeping up leaves.'

I listened amazed while half a dozen grown men discussed the situation seriously. The shop steward was sent for and added his authority to the argument. He confirmed that the job could only be tackled by a fully qualified gardener.

'Well, get a bloody gardener, then,' Micky shouted.

'I have to inform you, there is no gardener in the studio.'

'What does that mean?'

'It means there is no gardener in the studio.'

'We'll have to send out for one,' the first assistant said.

'How long will that take?'

'How long, Bert?'

'No telling, is there?'

During all this I was still lying on the dead leaves trussed about the head like a mummy. By now it was late afternoon. Following another involved discussion about the subtleties of the situation, it was decided to ring another studio to see whether they had a gardener available. The rest of the unit sat around and waited for the result of the phone call. Nobody seemed very concerned.

'Interesting problem,' the prop man said to me. 'I haven't come across this one before. Lines of demarcation, you see. Have to be observed, otherwise we'd all be out of a job.'

He suddenly looked at me. 'You all right in there?'

I mumbled that I was feeling somewhat hot.

'Mr Powell, governor. What about the artist?'

'What about him?'

'He says he's feeling hot.'

Micky came over to me. 'Why doesn't anybody think about these things?' he said. 'Leave an artist lying on the floor, like that. Get him up and take his bandages off.'

I was lifted to my feet and three people from wardrobe, make-up and props unwound the bandages.

'Doubtful whether we'll get this tonight, sir,' the first assistant said when he returned to the floor. 'We've located a gardener, but can't promise he'll get here before time.'

'Right, we'll make it first shot in the morning then,' Micky said.

'That's it, chaps. It's a wrap for tonight, but don't strike anything. This is first shot in the morning.'

I was put on the call sheet for the following day and the next morning I was duly encased in bandages again. The imported gardener had made a splendid job of sweeping up the leaves and some time around the mornng tea-break I made my debut before the cameras for a first feature film. I died, slowly and inarticulate, from many angles, face-acting furiously behind my bandages. I was amazed at the trouble that they all took about what appeared to be a very minor episode in the film. Micky Powell was kindness itself to me, and my fellow actors David Farrar, Michael Gough, Roddie Hughes and Walter Fitzgerald, experienced players all, were flatteringly considerate. I went to see the rushes on the third day and was kissed passionately by Hein Heckroth, the large and excitable German art director. The spectacle of myself enlarged twenty times on the screen was a disturbing experience, and unless one had been gifted with X-ray sight it was difficult to discern any signs of acting. I looked, I thought, like a gigantic boil, but Micky Powell, a gentleman not given to praising actors lightly, pronounced the scene acceptable and sent me home in his Rolls-Royce. I departed in style, thinking, My God, if this is the way they treat you when you are playing a one-day part, what happens when you land a lead? I had been paid £50, thanks to the dead leaves, and came away totally amazed with it all.

The story about the dead leaves is, alas, not even faintly apocryphal: it was vintage *Nobody Ordered Wolves*, and by no means an isolated incident. The boom war years were over, and from 1948 onwards the British cinema began its glacier progress towards the melting waters of insolvency: great masses, like Korda, broke off and floated out to sea to sink their City Titanics: Lord Rank made repeated and valiant attempts to plant the British flag amongst the crevices of Wardour Street, going out into the cold time and time again with Methodist zeal and Captain Oates-like courage only to find, on every occasion, that the base camp had been obliterated by marauding Sherpas. The British cinema faithfully aped all the excesses of Hollywood without any of its ruthless discipline. There were major talents around, a wealth of actors and directors, cameramen and technicians. They were given artistic freedom and generous budgets, and some of them squandered both the money and the opportunity. There were very simple rules: to make a great film you took a long time and spent too much money, to make an average film you took less time and spent too much money, and to make a bad film you shot it in three weeks on a shoe-string. Looking back I see nothing but a crowd-call of collective villains and it is un-rewarding to single out individual culprits: every section of the industry made its contribution to the decline and fall. There were some monsters, for the film industry breeds monsters quicker than most. But in the end even the con men were conned, just as a single prostitute can infect an army. Lord Rank was a saint, Lord Rank was a sinner; Korda was a genius, Korda was the architect of ruin; Sir Michael Balcon was the road to salvation, Sir Michael Balcon was a cul-de-sac. Various lesser gods entered the temples and the oracles spoke to us in foreign tongues, but each in turn came to the Ides of March and either fell upon their own swords or else were dispatched with the assassin's dagger. There was only one thing we all had in common: we lived on borrowed time with borrowed money in a borrowed country. We attempted a transplant on an imported corpse. We tried to impose an industrial pattern on to what was and will always be a shared creative process: the experiment, brave, often imaginative, always undertaken with optimism, was doomed to failure. It failed then, it has failed since, and it will continue to fail for as long as the industry continues in its present form.

Twenty-four

I don't think I ever succeeded in gaining a role through an audition or test. There is an old theatrical chestnut which tells of a character actress who was a familiar figure at every audition. On one occasion, after years of total failure, she was miraculously short-listed and asked to come back the following day. She duly reappeared and gave another reading. The short-list was narrowed yet again and she found herself amongst the last three. She gave a third audition and was asked to stay behind. The producer handed her the script. 'At last,' he said. 'The part is yours.' The lady looked shocked. 'Truly,' the producer said, 'we've made our final choice, you've got it.' He tried to force the script into her hands but she refused to take it. 'You don't understand,' she said. 'I don't actually accept parts. I only give auditions.'

It's a very theatrical story and any similarity between that anecdote and my life is not even coincidental. I tried desperately to find success by auditioning, and I was never short-listed. Shortly after my baptism in films, I read for Peter Glenville who was about to produce Sartre's *Red Gloves* at the Lyric, Hammersmith. I later learnt that the role had always been earmarked for Michael Gough, but some producers feel compelled to go through the motions of interviewing a score of actors. It is a depressing process for everybody concerned, and when eventually I directed my own films I made it a matter of principle never to test an actor. In the first place all you record on film are varying degrees of fear, and secondly it is an admission of defeat before the event. I loathe interviewing actors because I know what they are suffering. There are never enough jobs to go round and casting sessions inevitably mean that one has to disappoint the majority. The director's bible is a massive publication called *The Spotlight*, the brain-child of a one-time actor named Rodney Millington. It consists of page after page of photographs of actors and actresses.

Since the majority of actors are vain, the photographs often bear but fleeting resemblance to what comes through your office door. I often think it is like a book of remembrance for those slain on the Somme – a printed graveyard of hope. It is published twice a year and every edition it grows fatter. If you read it from cover to cover you are left with the inescapable conclusion that all actors are divine, but mad.

Having been rejected by Peter Glenville, I quickly renewed acquaintance with an old mentor, Ronnie Kerr, who had been the guiding force at the Intimate Theatre, Palmers Green, and who was now running the theatre at Bromley in Kent. Ronnie was an erratic, paradoxical character with many endearing qualities and considerable talent who was always his own worst enemy. He was later to commit suicide rather than face a court appearance for a minor and inoffensive aberration.

At Bromley I played the leading juvenile role in *The Guinea Pig*. It now seems impossible to believe that this play created a minor furore because the schoolboy hero used the word 'arse' during the course of the action. I remember feeling sickly daring when I uttered the word for the first time on the Monday night, and afterwards Ronnie told me that several regular patrons had complained at the lowering of standards.

I stayed on to repeat my Worthing performance in *The Corn is Green*, and used my transient influence to try and get Norman a job in the company, but without success. Our letters of the period are full of unrealized plans to get a flat together, for our joint and several financial resources were at a very low ebb and we argued that two could live as cheaply as one. In one letter I made an arrogantly prophetic statement: '*I bought a book on the Art of the Cinema today and I intend to specialize in this field for some time to come. I have made up my mind that one day I shall direct a film – preferably a film of one of my own scripts.*' There it was, the bald statement with no qualifications and no elaboration, for in the next sentence I related an anecdote about Randolph Churchill who was reputed, when asked by the great Reinhart why he didn't like the theatre, to have replied, 'You can't smoke there.'

Being at that time only too anxious to earn my living by any means open to me, I accepted a part in a BBC television

Play of the Week. It was Somerset Maugham's *The Breadwinner* and produced by John Glyn Jones. Nicholas Hannen played the lead and I noted in my diary, 'I get the feeling that I am working in a bank – Hannen dresses like a Branch Manager.' In those two days there were two performances, given live but without an audience – the first on the Sunday evening and the repeat the following Thursday.

Conditions at Alexandra Palace were primitive, and although the television audience was minuscule by today's standards, the demands upon actors and technicians alike in transmitting a 'live' performance of a full-length play were considerable. The equipment broke down during transmission with a regularity that did nothing to bolster confidence or quell the normal first-night nerves. The early television cameras were ponderous things, requiring cables as thick as a navvy's wrist, and since the studio was of modest proportions it was always an obstacle race to get where required on the set.

Television in those days combined the worst of filming with the worst of the straight theatre. There were no short takes, just the normal theatre intervals between the acts. Once the show was on the air, it was every man for himself. I once had the lead in a play concerned with a young gambler who spent most of his time having involved telephone conversations. There were normally three cameras operating during the Sunday night television play and the actor could always tell which one was transmitting at any given time because, like some portable brothel, they had bare red bulbs mounted on top of them and the one actually transmitting was illuminated. I was engaged in a long and, I suspect, boring soliloquy and turned, as rehearsed, to face Camera 1. To my horror this was surrounded by sweating technicians armed with screwdrivers who were taking it to pieces. The floor manager waved at me frantically and looked around for Camera 2. Even as I turned to it, the red light went out and smoke poured out from all sides. The by-now demented floor manager tripped over cables to get into my eyeline and pointed at the only remaining camera which was desperately trying to manœuvre into a shooting position. The rest of the play was visually as boring as my necessarily ragged performance. And all this for a fee of forty guineas, spread over three weeks' rehearsal.

During the course of rehearsing and performing *The Bread-winner* I received a call from Dennis van Thal to say that my interview with Ian Dalrymple had not been the wash-out I suspected and that I had been cast for a very important role in their forthcoming *All Over the Town*.

All Over the Town started on location in Lyme Regis. It starred Sarah Churchill and Norman Woolland and I was included amongst such featured players as Cyril Cusack, Sandra Dorne, Eleanor Summerfield, and my old Cairo bed-mate Pat Doonan. The script had been taken from a novel of the same name by R. F. Delderfield who was then the most successful playwright in London. It was a gentle comedy about a small-town newspaper office and I played a character with the improbable name of Trumble. The director this time was Derek Twist and I suspect that he allowed me to overdo the charm – certainly studying the still photographs in my scrap-album I appear to have cultivated a very coy hair style and I undoubtedly wore too much make-up. Being engaged for the entire run of the picture, I came into what was then untold wealth, earning no less than £700.

When the unit returned to Pinewood Studios to complete the interior scenes I decided that the time had come to change my life style and took a room of my own in a flat occupied by the assistant art director on the film, Geoffrey Drake. This was at No. 11 Strathern Place, just off Hyde Park Square. I occupied a somewhat damp basement room at first, sharing the kitchen, living-room and bathroom with Geoff. The bedroom had a stone floor and heavy bars on the window, and I was frequently disconcerted by the edifying spectacle of the local dogs using the basement as a toilet. To wake and find that the world consists of an Alsatian's arse pushed through the bars of your window was not quite in keeping with the public image I was trying to foster. The sophisticated young actor, star of stage, screen and television, would invariably be transformed into a screaming lunatic, banging on the window with a shoe in an attempt to avert the inevitable. I tried my bed in a dozen different positions, but the room was not big enough to achieve success and I was forced to live behind the scenes at

Crufts for the first six months until a larger room became available on the ground floor.

Some mornings Sarah Churchill would call for me in her car and we would journey through the deserted streets to Pinewood. It was difficult, if not impossible, to divorce the actress from the daughter of the great man, and when I got to know her better I naturally steered her towards the legend. She told me many fascinating things about Churchill's home life during the years when he was in the political wilderness, minor and unimportant details of domestic happenings which have no significance in history but which, more than anything else I had ever read or heard about her father, made him believable.

Twenty-five

I slept long and late in those days, snug and cocooned and, sad to relate, mostly alone in my bachelor basement, and I woke resentful and irritated by the shapelessness of my existence and my inability to discover what it was I wanted from life.

I had ambition, of course, but the edges were blurred: I was torn between the need to advance myself as an actor and the need to see myself as an author between stiff covers. I was making modest progress as an actor, but *All Over the Town* failed to make any real impact and went the way of most British films of the period.

The writing on the wall, so easy to distinguish at this distance in time, was carelessly ignored in 1948, for few people linger to study their own graffiti. The publicity departments, content to pee on their own doorsteps, painstakingly recorded some of the great non-events of our time. Two decades later, when I took over the old ABPC Studios at Boreham Wood, I was shown tomb after tomb of this material: humble details of the daily life of the citizens of Pinewood and Denham, Elstree and Gainsborough, philosophical enquiries of scribes and whores and the wise men who came from the City, discourses on the wealth of dynasties, kings, queens and colossi long since tumbled from their pedestals. There were a thousand boxes of curling, glossy stills – yesterday's heroes and heroines staring out from waxlike Max Factor masks, replicas of gods and goddesses no longer worshipped, some dead, most of them forgotten, all buried face upwards alongside the trappings of their reigns: it was like chancing upon some new Valley of the Kings and finding that all the gold was dross. Perhaps saddest of all was the awareness that none of the tombs had ever been pillaged: they were all intact, dusty, dumb witnesses to a now incomprehensible way of life.

But in 1948 nobody was prepared to believe that the great

days would ever end. Beyond the city gates the accountants were gathering, led by the then inconspicuous figure of John Davis. From time to time scaremongers would relay horror stories of films being cancelled, scripts rejected, actors taken off the payroll, but these were shrugged off. The film industry is no stranger to political assassination, and indeed the majority of the inhabitants enjoy nothing more than the swift demise of a rival and will then perform endless verbal mutilations upon the corpse. I was very small fry in those days and the dagger that ended my contract with the Rank Organization was the size of a penknife, others were retired from the scene in more spectacular fashion, but whatever the method employed, the end result was the same, and as the tables in the studio restaurants emptied it didn't need a publicity department to spell out the message: the good old bad old indifferent old luxurious old magnificent days were over.

I had been cast in Irene Henschel's production of Daphne du Maurier's new play *September Tide*, the vehicle selected by Gertrude Lawrence for her long-awaited return to the London stage. By now, of course, I was well aware of Miss Lawrence's rightfully exalted status and conscious that I was privileged to join the small cast – Michael Gough, Anne Leon, Cyril Raymond and the then comparatively unknown Dandy Nichols.

My role, that of Miss Lawrence's son, didn't appear until the third act. By today's standards *September Tide* might seem ludicrously tame, but as an undisguised romantic vehicle for one of the most unique talents ever to grace the English stage it was most expertly tailor-made. From the moment Gertie stepped on the stage she had every capacity audience eating out of her elegant hand, giving not reality – for she was never real – but an aura of total glamour. Prior to the start of rehearsals I had never seen her in the flesh nor witnessed any of her previous stage performances, but from day one there was no mistaking that she belonged to that select band of actors who are rightly legends in their own time. I think she liked me from the start because I was a fellow Cockney and she was always urging me to remember Cockney stories, the dirtier the better. During rehearsals she took me to lunch at The

Caprice and ordered fresh asparagus. I had never eaten it before. Not wishing to appear gauche or rude, I solemnly started at the wrong end and attempted to chew my way to the green tips. Half an hour later I was still trying to dispose of a wodge of cellulose and wondering why everybody made such a fuss about so inedible a vegetable.

Rehearsals proceeded smoothly, with little of the expected temperament. Irene Henschel was another extraordinary lady. The wife of the distinguished author and critic Ivor Brown, she dressed and behaved like some amiable eccentric from an Agatha Christie novel. Chalking up success after success with a charm and ease that her detractors found frustratingly baffling, she achieved her ends by using a velvet fist in a velvet glove.

We opened out of town at the New Theatre, Oxford, on 8 November. I was very nervous in a detached sort of way, and somewhat put out because my name had been spelt incorrectly on the bills. The theatre was sold out for the entire week in advance.

The train calls every Sunday, which somehow seemed to epitomize the essence of a theatrical tour and now conjure up a lost world, were usually hilarious events. Ossie Morris, our diminutive, snuff-taking manager, would have reserved two first-class compartments and it was normal for the station-masters to turn out in frock coats to escort a star of Gertie's magnitude to her seat. Gertie loved train calls, she liked having the cast closely confined and all to herself, and I remember the miles and hours slipping by while she reminisced about her early days.

She told us many things about her early home life. Her father drank heavily, but was well liked for all that, and always came home in a hansom cab after a blind, then beat his wife – 'beat hell out of mother.' Gertie confessed that she was terrified of her mother and often wet herself on the doorstep before entering one of their many homes. Apparently her mother had also had twins and these had died at an early age. Gertie amazed us by saying that she held herself responsible for their death. 'I think I finished off the twins. I used to have to mind them, rock them in the pram, and I was only four myself and I often gave them a shake-up. I'm sure they died of concussion from my rocking.' I listened fascinated, for it was difficult to reconcile the Cockney urchin wetting her knickers in fear with the ultra-sophisticated spellbinder who sat opposite me in scented splendour in the first-class compartment. Although she demanded the homage due to her in the theatre, Gertie had surprisingly few affectations and her flashes of temperament were soon forgotten.

We travelled across the bleak November countryside, playing Blackpool out of season, Liverpool, Leeds and Manchester, and my journal notes that we endured endless fogs. It was in Liverpool that I faced a theatrical Waterloo. The final curtain came down on Gertie and me singing a duet. We had rehearsed and opened with a song from the current success *Annie Get Your Gun* – 'Anything You Can Do, I Can Do Better' – and from the very beginning this proved to be something of an over-statement. Gertie sang in her celebrated cracked voice, but she was Gertrude Lawrence. I for my part sang in a considerably weaker cracked voice and it is doubtful whether I would have made much impact on *Opportunity Knocks*. However, after a great deal of rehearsing and three weeks on the road I didn't make an absolute fool of myself, and since every member of the audience was looking at Gertie and not at me, I got by. That was until we reached Liverpool.

Irene Henschel and Daphne arrived in the middle of the week with the bowel-constricting news that the owners of *Annie Get Your Gun* had taken violent objection to our using the song out of context and had withdrawn permission. We therefore had to look for another song with which to replace it. The field was somewhat narrow, because the new choice had to be one we could legally use and at the same time convey the same feeling as the original. We spent a whole morning listening to records and eventually decided to use 'Miss Annabelle Lee'.

It was a matinée day and Irene rehearsed Gertie and me behind the iron curtain while the cleaners were collecting the discarded ice-cream cartons and tea-cups. Perhaps I should also mention that my singing contribution to the end of the play was but the climax to a great deal of complicated stage 'business' I had to accomplish without detracting from Gertie's tearful farewell at the upstage window. I was required to light a cigarette, put the record on the machine, ensure that the speed, tone and volume controls were correctly adjusted, get out the backgammon board and set up the pieces, throw some darts into a dartboard without hitting anybody on or off stage, do some clowning, then toss a few unfeeling words over my shoulder to mother and launch into 'Who's wonderful, who's marvellous? Miss Annabelle Lee.' I had to accomplish all this while lying full length on a settee close to the footlights since I was supposed to be immobilized with a broken leg.

I learnt the new lines in the interval between the afternoon and evening performance and then retired to wait in my dressing-room where, without benefit of audience, I foolishly gained a spurious confidence. The play ran its normal course until the time came for me to make my appearance. Then everything went wrong. I burnt myself with the cigarette, put the wrong side of the record on the machine, scored a bullseye on the assistant stage manager with one of the darts (thus collecting an unwanted laugh), and in general managed to perform like a bumbling amateur. Came the moment when Gertie joined me on the sofa and we launched into the new song. The Caruso-like qualities of my dressing-room voice vanished in the wide open spaces of the Royal Court Theatre. I seemed to shake my voice at the audience like a tiny fist, demolishing the mood of the play in seconds, and for the first time since we had opened the curtain came down to something less than tumultuous applause.

There was an immediate and alarming post-mortem conducted on the empty stage while the audience was still filing out. To say that I took part would be an exaggeration. I heard what was going on as though under water, but there was no mistaking Gertie's fury. 'I didn't stay out of the country eighteen years and then come three thousand miles to work my arse off for two hours to take part in a comic charade' would be a fair sample, heavily expurgated, of her dialogue. 'The boy,' she said, 'can't sing. He ruined the whole bloody play. So you'd better solve it and solve it quick, because otherwise I'm catching the next boat back.'

176

The rest of the cast dispersed, carefully avoiding my eyes, and I crept away like a leper to remove my make-up and return to the private hotel and the inevitable and very jugged hare. Long after everybody else had retired I remained in the deserted dining-room, chain-smoking and wondering who would replace me. My career, it seemed, was in ruins.

Some time after midnight the hotel phone went in the lobby. I answered it and a woman's voice at the other end asked to speak to Bryan Forbes.

'Speaking,' I said.

'This is Gee,' the voice said. 'Why are you still up?'

'Well, I wasn't feeling too happy, Miss Lawrence, not after the events of this evening.'

'Why the Miss Lawrence suddenly?' she said. 'You call me Gee. And forget about tonight. It was bloody awful and you ruined the end of the play, but that wasn't entirely your fault. I always sound off like that when I'm in a tizz, but you don't want to take any notice. I suppose you were sitting there crying into your beer, were you?'

'Not even beer,' I said. 'Some cold cocoa.'

'Well, don't be such an idiot. Go to bed and forget it. We'll get it right tomorrow. Call for me at the hotel at eleven and we'll go out to lunch together.'

I put the phone down in a haze, totally in love with her and unable to believe my good fortune. The following morning I presented myself at her hotel and she took me out, bought me an expensive silk scarf and treated me to a dozen oysters. After lunch she took me back to the theatre and rehearsed me herself, showing me how to use what little singing talent I had to the best effect. At the performance that evening everything went smoothly and the incident was never mentioned again.

The tour finished on 11 December in Manchester and I said goodbye without regret to the dubious charm of the open road and headed back to London. We opened at the Aldwych Theatre four days later to a packed and emotional house, and the action of the play was held up for fully five minutes by the applause which greeted Gertie's first appearance.

I was conscious of personal failure. I was dulled by nervousness and made little or no impression. I think I was objective enough to realize that I wasn't yet a good enough actor to surmount an indifferent role.

The first person to come round to my dressing-room that night was Jean Simmons. It was a case of the Queen coming to see the cat.

Twenty-six

I cannot pretend that I enjoyed the nine-month run of *September Tide* except spasmodically, for after the excitement of the opening night there was little or nothing to look forward to. I sat in my dressing-room listening to the play's progress over the relay system until my call came, then went down on stage and performed mechanically for my allotted fifteen minutes or so. Except for matinee days there was little or no contact with the other members of the cast and only the occasional 'bad' house gave cause for comment. An actor craves the security that only a long run can bring, but it is that very security that proves his undoing as an actor. We were not meant to be complacent, for the regular pay packet brings staleness and boredom in many cases.

I think what kept me sane during the run was a chance encounter with a young man called Derek Yorke. He came backstage to see me after a performance and outlined his plans to make a full-length film on a co-operative basis, inviting me to play the star role. He had an interesting Saroyanesque script he had written himself and explained that it was his intention to force the film through by fair means and foul, borrowing equipment, begging locations, using every spare penny he had and scrounging the rest.

The title of the film was *Saturday Night* and the stylistically simple story-line was concerned with a young man who finds himself bored and alone in London, wanders the streets, visits a cafe and there has a chance meeting with a girl his own age. The teenage brief encounter provides no solution and they part again.

I believe that the original budget was £100. Everybody in the unit, technicians and actors alike, worked for nothing. Naturally much of the shooting had to be done on Sundays and we embarked upon the experiment in the cramped back bedroom of the art director's house in the suburbs. Derek

179

proved to be an exacting taskmaster. His energy and determination could not be dented and he drove us on with relentless enthusiasm.

Somehow he had managed to assemble a talented group around him who were infected with the same maniac love for the medium. He chose well, for the five main characters in this very early piece of *cinema verité* were all to make their individual mark in later years. The young and extremely temperamental cameraman was Walter Lassally, who later gained recognition as the photographer of *Tom Jones* and went on to win the Academy Award for his brilliant work on *Zorba*. The camera operator was Gerry Turpin. His struggle to establish himself took longer than Walter's, but after many disappointments he joined me as my cameraman for *Seance on A Wet Afternoon* and never looked back.

The focus puller was Desmond Davies who later directed the much-acclaimed *Girl With Green Eyes* and then ran foul of the idiotic distribution system, for his subsequent film *The Uncle* failed to obtain a release and his promising career was blighted for a time.

Derek was not only a contemporary with whom I had an immediate affinity, he was also the first person I had ever worked for who gave me an insight into the limitless possibilities of film. We assembled Sunday after Sunday, week after week, month after month, spending many hours shooting in a small cafe in Shaftesbury Avenue. Derek had somehow persuaded the Italian owner of the cafe to loan him the premises free of charge. The difficulties were many, for the entire film was a night sequence and this meant that we had to black-out the windows of the cafe before we could commence shooting. Walter and Derek argued the merits of every set-up and the continuity problems mounted as the weeks went by. The equipment we were using left a great deal to be desired, and on at least two occasions we had to reshoot a whole sequence because an actor had gone absent without leave. But Derek remained ruthlessly optimistic, pushing us forward, placating here, bullying there, and although his ambitions sometimes bordered on insanity, I owe him a great deal, for he demonstrated that to be a good director you must print your signature on every frame.

I gave him some anxious moments, because after six months my enthusiasm for the project got a little ragged at the edges. I had been flattered by my 'star' status in the early days, but it is difficult to maintain the illusion that you are next year's Marlon Brando when forced to change and make up in a public urinal at three o'clock in the morning. Derek couldn't understand my disillusion. He listened politely to my complaints regarding the slow rate of progress, but it was obvious that he regarded me as an ungrateful idiot.

By now it was the beginning of summer. We were still playing to packed houses, though Gertie had announced that she would not continue indefinitely.

Gertie liked nothing better than to plan surprises for the rest of the cast. I arrived at the theatre one evening and knocked on her dressing-room door, as was my custom, to enquire how she had spent her day. 'I rang you several times this morning,' she said, 'but never got a reply.' I explained I had been out and about all day. 'I was going to ask you if you wanted to come to the pantomime at the Palladium with me. I had the Royal box this afternoon and there was a seat to spare. I thought it might have amused you.'

I made polite noises of regret, but didn't feel too badly because since childhood I have always considered pantomimes boring.

'Did you manage to get rid of the spare ticket?' I asked.

'No. I didn't bother in the end. There was just the two of us.'

'Who did you go with?'

'G.B.S.'

She turned with a smile from her dressing-table mirror and doubtless enjoyed the stunned disbelief on my face, for she had timed the revelation with her usual perfection. I thus missed my one and only opportunity of meeting Bernard Shaw face to face. I still remember the incident with keen regret. To have met Bernard Shaw in any circumstances would have been honour enough, but to have spent a whole afternoon with him in the Royal box at the Palladium in Gertie's company might have changed the course of my life. But I didn't.

I was out when she phoned.

I had an arrangement with Michael Gough whereby I partly shared the services of his dresser, an engaging and eccentric character named Herbert. Herbert's principal responsibility came during the second act when Micky had to dive from the balcony of the house into the harbour to rescue the drifting boat. He dived, of course, into a pile of mattresses strategically placed off-stage and out of sight of the audience. He then had to plunge into a bath of lukewarm water to simulate the real thing for his reappearance. Herbert had to be standing by to assist.

During one matinee when the Aldwych was packed with middle-aged matrons all balancing tea trays on their knees, one of the cleats securing Michael Relph's weighty set suddenly gave way. Ossie dashed in search of stage-hands to repair the damage before the set caved in. Now it so happened that this incident took place a few minutes before Micky was due to make his celebrated plunge into the harbour. Herbert was waiting in the wings and before he disappeared Ossie handed him a support rope and told him to hang on to it until help arrived.

Meanwhile on-stage Gertie and Micky continued with the scene, unaware of the drama being enacted in the wings. Micky leapt from the balcony and groped his way in the semi-darkness to the bath of water.

During his absence Gertie went to a cupboard in the supposedly totally deserted house and took some towels out in readiness for Micky's drenched return. It was a vital plot point and carefully established in the dialogue that she and her son-in-law were isolated and alone – the storm was raging and there was nobody for miles around.

Unbeknown to Gertie, Herbert was standing holding the rope on the other side of the cupboard door. It was a hot afternoon and he was curiously dressed in pin-stripe trousers, collarless shirt and white tennis shoes. I should also add that he had a small Hitler moustache. The total effect was startling.

Gertie opened the cupboard door as she had done for the last two hundred performances and revealed Herbert. She was too dumbfounded to close the door again, and for a few seconds she and Herbert stood transfixed like characters in a Disney cartoon. Herbert, being of the old school of theatrical dressers, was also a stickler for etiquette. He couldn't help himself. He gave a little bow and said, 'Good afternoon, Miss Lawrence.'

Up to this point the audience had been mystified but not unduly alarmed by this sudden plot twist. After all, since they hadn't seen the play before, it was conceivable that Miss du Maurier had intended that her central character be suddenly confronted with Hitler in tennis shoes inside a cupboard.

But when Herbert paid his respects to Miss Lawrence the game was up. Gertie managed to close the door and then started to collapse. She turned away up-stage in a futile attempt to conceal her mounting hysteria and, of course, minus towels, bumped straight into the wet and unsuspecting Micky. He clambered back over the balcony and was greeted with a howl of laughter from the audience and a leading lady staggering around as though inexplicably drunk.

In such circumstances an actor's first instinct is to check his flies, which Micky did. Finding that everything was intact, he began his dialogue as per cue, but received no answering cue for by now Gertie – one of the world's great gigglers – was on the floor. Micky assumed that she had gone temporarily insane and carried on, giving her dialogue as well as his own and attempting to retrieve the situation. Needing a towel, he went back to the cupboard. Renewed hysteria, this time in anticipation, from the audience. Micky opened the cupboard door. The cupboard was bare. And so the second act staggered to its conclusion, Micky having to wait until curtain-fall for an explanation.

I know many a star who would have reacted in anger to such a situation and had the polite and unfortunate Herbert fired on the spot, but Gertie loved a joke.

Years later I was reminded of the events of that afternoon, for the second act of *September Tide* seemed accident prone. I went to see a performance of the play by a touring company. Gertie's and Michael's original roles were being played by a couple who were perhaps a little long in the tooth. The gentleman wore a toupee in an effort to help credibility. The moment came in the second act when the famous omelet had to be cooked. The woman left the stage for a few moments to fetch the bottle of Nuits St George while the husband stirred the concoction in the omelet pan. To everybody's stunned horror, as he bent over his task the toupee came unstuck and dropped into the mess of eggs. He stirred it in. The wife returned, gay and expectant, prepared to play a tender scene with a young lover, and found herself confronted with a demented bald-headed old man cooking a pan of hairy eggs which eventually they would have to eat. It was almost too painful to watch.

Twenty-seven

At the beginning of 1949 my worldly wealth totalled £134, and there was a tax demand for £171. I wrote a polite letter to the Collector of Taxes, explaining that it would be difficult if not impossible for me to clear my debt in one go, but that I would make modest but regular contributions to the Exchequer. Surprisingly enough this offer was accepted and I breathed again. I had few prospects other than my weekly salary, though I did the occasional broadcast which brought in a few guineas. I lived simply, buying cheap cuts of meat which I simmered with a variety of vegetables, existing on the soup for days on end until the very sight of the saucepan revolted me. I saw few people outside the theatre and confined myself to my room to finish some more short stories.

The finished manuscript was delivered to Methuen at the beginning of April. I felt none of the expected elation: it no longer seemed part of me though the £50 advance was a welcome addition to the sinking fund. The only thread of continuity in my life was the letters that Norman and I continued to exchange at regular intervals. He was in love again, this time with an enchanting young actress called Nona Blair whom he was eventually to marry.

At one point I thought that I too had discovered the secret of true happiness, for I embarked on a pleasant affair with a very intelligent girl who had her own flat and proved to be an excellent cook. This was sufficiently unusual to intrigue me, since most of my previous girl-friends had been singularly lacking in any domestic virtues – one of them had actually succeeded in burning a boiled egg.

I savoured the novelty of three-course meals followed by other pleasures, but gradually became aware that she was looking at me with hurt eyes over the main course. She wanted, it seemed, to put the liaison on a more permanent basis. Although she continued to feed me she withheld equally basic favours, a subtle form of blackmail that drove me back to my lonely basement with a thoughtful expression. Several pots of my own revolting stew later I decided that I missed both her cooking and her comfortable double bed, so I returned with a suitably chastened expression on my face. Over the reconciliation dinner we discussed the life to come. There was no formal proposal on my part, for I was cunning too, but we agreed that, as a start, I should be taken home and inspected by her parents.

They were decidedly upper class, living in some splendour in a large house in the Eaton Square area. Mummy was very Joyce Grenfell and aloof, but I seemed to strike it off with Daddy, who was something in the Foreign Service. He plied me with sherry and asked the standard questions about my future prospects. 'I enjoy the theatre myself,' he said, implying that the rest of the human race were not as broadminded, 'but tell me, do you actually learn the words, or do you make them up?' When I explained the elementary aspects of my trade, he seemed slightly annoyed and baffled. 'How very novel,' he said, 'must be jolly difficult.' He spoke and acted like a parody of a parody, but I was grateful that he appeared indifferent to his daughter's fate.

When I left the house to share his daughter's bed in another part of London, she seemed very pleased with the result. 'They liked you,' she said.

'How can you tell?'

'Oh, I know they liked you. Especially Daddy. I think it intrigued him, you being an actor. Normally he doesn't talk to anybody outside the Service.'

A few days later she told me that I had been invited to accompany the family to a Sunday night show at one of the theatre clubs, with dinner afterwards.

During the first interval Daddy asked me if I'd like to have a drink at the bar. He didn't ask his wife or daughter to join us (something they apparently took for granted), and I followed him up the aisle with some foreboding. He wants me on my own, I thought, to ask when I'm going to name the day. By now some of the novelty of marriage to his undoubtedly attractive and talented daughter was beginning to wear thin. I rehearsed a few desperate answers in the short time it took us to reach the crowded bar.

Daddy looked around in some distaste. 'All these people can't be wanting a drink, surely?' I shrugged. 'Extraordinary collection for a Sunday night. I suppose they're all theatricals.'

We waited a few more moments, but the crush increased. 'Well, let's forget it, shall we? D'you want to have a wee wee?'

I didn't, but I was willing to make the social effort. We retired to the gents' cloakroom which was surprisingly deserted. He proved to be one of those men who carry out a thorough examination, double-checking as it were that everything is in the right place, before commencing. I stood alongside him and stared at some partially erased graffiti of a male torso afflicted with elephantiasis. He cleared his throat.

'I dare say my daughter has told you that you're a very attractive young man.'

I stood like Lot's wife, exposed but unfunctioning. A somewhat unconventional opening, I thought, but here it comes. But Daddy had quite another proposal in mind.

'I know that I find you very attractive,' he said.

I suddenly became conscious that Daddy wished to perform a certain foreign service.

'You dirty old bugger,' I said. 'I thought you wanted me to marry your daughter.'

'What's that got to do with it? I always understood you theatricals were double-gated.'

Mercifully this unrewarding dialogue was cut short by the entrance of another patron. I had a zip start on Daddy and made the most of it, walking out of the cloakroom and continuing on out of the theatre – out, in fact, of his and his daughter's life.

She wrote me a perplexed and despairing letter and I attempted a reply but gave up after several confused pages, and left my phone off the hook. My behaviour now seems callow beyond belief, but twenty-five years ago I was totally inadequate for the occasion and took refuge in silence. She was an only daughter and I am convinced that she was unaware of Daddy's double life. Without wishing to excuse my behaviour towards her, which was undoubtedly cruel, I can only record that the alternative seemed to me then to be unthinkable.

'The initial difficulty is in the sensitive writer's inability to live alone,' Connolly wrote in *Enemies of Promise*. '*The more he is alone the more he falls in love.*' (The italics are mine.) This seemed to me to be holy writ and I hastened to quote it back to Norman. Further on in the same passage I found, 'Children dissipate the longing for immortality which is the compensation of the childless writer's work. But it is not only a question of children or no children, there is a moment when the cult of home and happiness becomes harmful and domestic happiness one of those escapes from talent which we have deplored, for it replaces *that necessary unhappiness without which writers perish*.' (And again the emphasis is mine.) 'Most young writers are weak and know little about their weaknesses or their predicaments . . . In general it may be assumed that a writer who is not prepared to be lonely in his youth must, if he is to succeed, face loneliness in his middle age.'

I didn't question any part of Connolly's dictum and consciously willed it to apply to my own destiny in every particular. I was lonely in my fast-fading youth and therefore I must fall in love again – it was no use swallowing only half the medicine.

Thus, following a chance meeting at a rare party I attended, I launched myself upon another unknown sea. The young lady in question was June Sylvaine, the only daughter of that fine and grossly underestimated playwright Vernon Sylvaine. When I first met June she was appearing in the latest success of her father's, *One Wild Oat*, at the Garrick. Vernon was a handsome man, actorish in appearance and behaviour and generous to a fault. He and his wife Marie lived in a luxurious flat in Gloucester Square which by happy coincidence was but a stone's throw from my basement.

Once we had met we became inseparable. I would call for her every night after our separate performances, rushing from the Aldwych to the Garrick, while on matinee days we would meet between the shows and take tea in one of those sedate cafes that used to dot the Strand. Our days were spent in blissful excursions, and as Connolly had predicted I no longer had time to write. Slipping easily into the robe of self-deception, I persuaded myself that the stolen hours were not time lost but merely a period of adjustment. After all, I reasoned, I had a book awaiting publication, there was no need for undue panic.

Panic of another kind was no stranger to our relationship, however, for although we drifted through that summer in a haze of discovery, we were soon adept at the gentle art of self-destruction. There was a sweet tyranny in our relationship, quite unlike anything I had experienced before. I quickly discovered that I was not her only suitor, though I would hate to give the wrong impression. Her only fault was that she was young, and she was faithful in her innocent fashion and never attempted to conceal the existence of her other admirers. I don't believe she deliberately engineered my many jealousies, though she would have been less than human and certainly less than feminine had she not enjoyed the reaction such jealousy revealed in me. Equally, if goaded beyond endurance, I could provoke extremes of remorse in her, and our temporary final partings were many, anguished and dramatic.

We would agree to part for ever during the afternoon and then seek each other out for a tearful reconciliation a few hours later. I would assert my freedom of choice, studiously avoid phoning her for a few days, but spend most of the time writing anguished letters of justification, closely followed by roses I could ill afford. We were both ambitious to succeed in the theatre and to that extent we were rivals. I had the greater experience of life, she had a woman's instinct for survival. We both twisted the blade, we both bandaged the wounds until finally there was no novelty in the act or the compassion that invariably followed the act. We parted, not as enemies but as two people who happened to have taken the same boat for different destinations, but who had nevertheless enjoyed the voyage and took their farewells without remorse or regret.

Twenty-eight

September Tide finally came to an end after a nine-month run. Gertie went home and the cast dispersed. I landed a film job, a small and unimportant part in *The Wooden Horse*, taken from the famous epic story of escape by Eric Williams. This time I was working for Korda's London Films, and the director was Jack Lee.

Despite the fact that there were still hundreds of derelict DP camps available all over Europe, the film company started from scratch and built a brand new one on Luneberg Heath in Germany. This fake Stalag Luft III cost a relatively small fortune and immediately had to be aged to look like a derelict DP camp.

The leading English actors, headed by Leo Genn, David Tomlinson and the latest heart-throb Anthony Steel, flew out and were checked into a small German hotel close to the location. I went with a seven-week contract, for which I was more than grateful, not to say amazed, for my role consisted of a few heroic coughs and a spit.

We arrived to find the camp only half finished and the script being heavily rewritten. We sat around for three weeks listening to rumours of rows in the front office, acquiring sun tans and growing bored and irritable with each other. My seven-week contract only had a fortnight to run by the time the cameras eventually turned.

I shared a hotel room with Tony Steel, who had got married a few days before the plane took off. He confessed that he was incapable of writing a letter to his new wife. It was difficult to phone home, there being only one operative phone in the entire neighbourhood and this was in the private house rented for Leo Genn. Tony became ever more morose at his situation, but still couldn't pick up a pen, so I did it for him. The marriage was short-lived and I have often wondered whether my literary efforts on his behalf contributed to the failure.

The film finally got under way but without much enthusiasm, and there was a great deal of ill-feeling circulating amongst the crew and cast. Although a great deal of money had already been wasted in various directions, such are the contradictions and absurdities of the film industry that somebody had decided to make economies where the extras were concerned. The real Stalag Luft III had been occupied by RAF officers to a great extent, but these were impersonated by truck-loads of Polish DPs all hastily costumed to represent the flower of British youth. During the first week we shot most of the large crowd scenes – Leo, David, Tony and myself, together with half a dozen other English feature players, were placed alongside the cheap slave labour. We raised eyebrows at the time, but who were we to question the director's decision?

A week later we duly assembled to view the first results in a make-shift cinema. The first slate number came up on the screen and the camera tracked past a line of men. There was Leo, looking every inch the real thing, there was Tony, totally believable, there was David and me . . . and next to me was somebody who looked like Ghengis Khan wearing the uniform of an RAF Wing-Commander complete with DFC and bar. Next to him was the Mongolian Wee Georgie Wood with a drooping moustache, and next to him was Himmler disguised as a padre, and so on down the ranks. The effect was hilarious.

There was an immediate and acrimonious post-mortem amongst the higher echelon and a decision taken to scrap the first week's work and get rid of the DPs. In their place they recruited real army and RAF personnel from nearby camps who, since they were merely marking time until demobilization from the occupying forces, treated the whole thing as a welcome and trivial diversion. Jack Lee, who had a Scoutmasterish personality, grew daily more irritated, for by now the film was well behind schedule. The script was still being rewritten and one result of this was that my own role was enlarged. We vaulted over the actual wooden horse for days on end, from every conceivable angle, risking hernias every time the clapper board went in. Tempers wore thin, and on one occasion there was a punch-up in the local beer house and one of the actors was fired and sent home.

Leo Genn had brought his Rolls-Royce with him and somebody thoughtfully filled the petrol tank with sugar which rendered it something less than the best car in the world.

When the camp scenes were finally completed the majority of us were flown home to enjoy a holiday on full pay while Leo and Tony and the technical crew went to Flensburg to shoot the post-escape sequences. We still had weeks of studio interiors to complete, but these were further delayed because many of the vital continuity props were put on the wrong ship and ended up in Norway. Then Korda put in an appearance and saw the first assembly of the film, decided he didn't like parts of it and ordered extra shooting and retakes. This meant a change of cameraman, some added scenes for me, and the sum total of it all was that my original seven-week contract was elongated into seven months.

Most of this time I was stupefied by my obsession with Miss Sylvaine, which had been kept alive through correspondence during the time I was away on location, and resumed its old tortured routine on my return home. I decided that the time had come for a complete break. The flat in Strathern Place I found damp and irksome. I was now forced to share the bathroom and kitchen with two complete strangers, one of whom was a particularly truculent Irishman who boiled what looked like squirrels in the communal saucepans and, in the days before household sprays, made the bathroom uninhabitable for hours on end.

David Tomlinson came generously to the rescue and offered me bed and board in his luxurious flat in Upper Brook Street. He was an impressive character altogether, drove the last of the classic Jaguars, had a highly volatile French girl-friend, and a very distinct life style. He took one look at my wardrobe and pronounced judgement. 'Don't bother to give those suits away,' he said. 'Burn them.' Impressed, I allowed myself to be taken into Mr James's establishment in Sackville Street. Mr James was a Swede of conservative if impeccable taste whose only eccentricity was to bite the temporary stitches during the first fitting: he literally tore the shoulders to pieces with his teeth.

David had warned me that the real attraction of Messrs

James and James was the manager, Mr Ted Tremble. Given the right audience, David confided, Ted could be relied upon to surprise. He had perfected the art of saying the most outrageous statements with the blandest of expressions, looking his victims straight in the eye so that they were never certain that they had heard him correctly. If, on rare occasions, he was challenged, he would immediately give an innocent repeat variation. David liked nothing more than to urge him on to greater excesses and I was once present at an encounter between Ted and an extraordinary tweedy female client who patronized Mr James for all her riding clothes.

Ted was running a tape measure round me when the lady arrived. She was wearing a suit made of thick carpet felt and her face was as mottled and bristly as the material, so that it was difficult to decide where her features began and the jacket ended.

'Good morning, Mr Tremble. Are you ready for me?'

'Good morning, my lady. Shan't keep you a moment. Just park your old arse on that chair while I'm measuring Lord Forbes for his fur-lined jockstrap.'

He rattled off the entire sentence without a pause. The lady seemed unaware of anything out of the ordinary and sat down as invited. She took out a cigarette case.

'Mind if I have a gasper?'

'Of course not, my lady. You take your stays off and relax.'

'Stay what?'

'I said you stay as you are and relax. Be with you in a tick. Which side are you dressing today?'

She inhaled on the cigarette like a horse blowing into a nosebag of wet oats. 'I hope my breeches are ready,' she said.

'I hope they are,' Ted replied, kneeling to take my inside leg measurement. 'Once more into the breeches or we'll close the wall with our English dead.'

'English what?'

'No, I was talking to Lord Forbes.'

'Oh, sorry.'

'Have you met Lord Forbes?'

'No, I don't think we have. How d'you do?'

I was unable to reply.

'He's very shy,' Ted explained. 'Especially when we cut his trousers too tight in the crutch. Well, I think that's all we can do today, my lord. If you'd like to slip into your pyjamas, I'll attend to this lady.'

He advanced on the lady and slipped his tape-measure round her. As I made my exit just in time, I heard him say, 'Why, you're nothing but a bag of bones, are you?'

Under David's guidance I acquired three good suits, the first I had ever had made. They cost the then unheard of sum of twenty-eight guineas each.

Then out of the blue I was offered a leading role in a new play by Wynyard Browne, a gifted young writer who was to die tragically young before his Chekovian view of British life could find its true level. Frith Banbury, an ex-actor turned director, was to mount it for Tennants, and this time my salary was increased to £35 per week.

The play was called *The Holly and the Ivy*, and although I was greatly impressed by it at first reading, I had no idea that it would prove such a success. The distinguished cast was headed by that fine old actor Herbert Lomas. Minimising his height by stooping (he was nicknamed 'Tiny'), rasping out the words past ill-fitting dentures and with one side of his face drawn down by an old illness, he was hardly the drama school text-book ideal of a leading man, and yet he was one of the truest actors I have ever worked with. The star dressing-room he occupied by right was devoid of creature comforts. On the dressing-table he kept two small and well-used sticks of Leichner make-up, a spare clerical collar and a bottle of beer. That was all. He once asked me what I used for sticking on moustaches and beards. I told him I bought spirit gum. He shook his head in troubled concern. 'D'you know what I use?' he said. 'I bought a can, a gallon, of painter's varnish, just after the First World War and I've had it ever since. I'll give you some. You don't want to pay fancy prices for that other stuff.'

Although I did not enjoy the rehearsals – Frith Banbury depressed me by his constant references to my 'film technique', and at one time I again felt convinced that I would be given the sack before the play opened – I quickly made friends with the rest of the cast. Jane Baxter, who was usually cast in unrewarding roles which did scant justice to her beauty and talents, had the 'stick' part opposite Andrew Crawford. The word 'stick' is usually applied when you have all the words and few or none of the laughs. Jane had to carry much of the plot while the more showy part of her journalist sister went to the late Daphne Arthur. The small cast was completed by Cecil Ramage (later replaced by Patrick Waddington) and two widely different but splendidly eccentric old ladies – Maureen Delaney and Margaret Halston.

The theme of the man of God who can love and understand and when required forgive his flock but who fails to recognize the same frailties in his own family is one that has been used time and time again in the theatre. Wynyard Browne's triumph was that he fashioned his play with literate dialogue and most skilfully avoided any suggestion of preaching to his audience. Tiny Lomas's performance in the central role was craggy and uncompromising, rock-hard until the final revelation of his children's lives and then almost unbearably moving. I learnt more from him than any other actor I ever worked with, and although the play eventually ran for eighteen months, I never lost a sense of excitement before the big scene I had with him in the third act.

Years later I was driving home from London and heard his death announced on the car radio. I pulled into the next lay-by and wept at the passing of somebody I greatly revered. Such is the way of the theatre sometimes that we had never met again after the last night of the play. Perhaps my memories of him and my affection for him were intertwined with recollections of the years spent in Porthleven vicarage.

Truth Lies Sleeping was finally published during the run of *The Holly and the Ivy*. Despite a dust-jacket which suggested it had been written by an elderly spinster contemporary of Jane Austen, it achieved respectable sales and was eventually reprinted in paperback form. Short stories by unknown writers usually sink without trace, so I was bolstered by the fact that most of the serious papers and journals gave it review space. I got favourable reviews from Elizabeth Bowen, Angus Wilson, J. D. Scott and John Betjeman, and the general impression was that my forthcoming novel (announced on the dust-jacket as 'work in progress') would be worth waiting for. Little did they know how long the wait would be.

I purchased as many as I could afford at full retail price, going from bookshop to bookshop and asking for it in a curiously strangulated voice, half fearing and half hoping for recognition. Alas, I was never recognized, and half the shops hadn't bothered to stock it. Dreams of a Foyles Literary Luncheon soon faded, though my good friend Tony Godwin of Better Books in Charing Cross Road went to the expense of commissioning an amusing cartoon from Ronald Searle which he used in an advertisement for me.

Norman summed it all up when he wrote 'in years to come I dare say the *unsigned* first edition will be the rare one' – hitting the target fair and square and giving me a *bon mot* I have since claimed as my own and used to considerable self-deprecating effect.

Twenty-nine

Shortly after *The Holly and the Ivy* opened in London my life
style changed yet again. I was approached by other publishers,
notably one of Hamish Hamilton's senior partners, Roger
Machell. He came to see the play and later wrote that he would
like the opportunity to publish my 'next novel or two or
whichever marks the point where you can go to a publisher
who will give you a less poisonous dust-jacket and fewer
printer's errors per page.'

Roger obviously intended to provoke my interest and spur
me to a reply. He succeeded and before long we had embarked
upon one of the most treasured friendships of my life. In his
company, and at his lunch table in Albany, I met many of the
distinguished authors who graced the Hamish Hamilton list.
Roger sets a good table. His cook, the superb May Collins,
can translate her employer's enjoyment of food so that every
meal you have there is a new poem. An invitation from Roger
is something that you starve for in advance of the event. He
likes to see his friends rise from the table in tottery splendour.
When I remember those lunches at Albany, I conjure up the
unexpected peace that is in that part of Piccadilly, the noise of
traffic stilled beneath the Rope Walk roof, the finely propor-
tioned windows open, revealing flower-boxes filled with
seasonal plants, and most of all I remember laughter. Roger
likes nothing more than to provoke outrageous statements in
others, which he will then placidly top, adding as it were the
dressing to the salad that somebody else has tossed.

He chose his guests for their entertainment value, for he has
never suffered bores easily, and it was with a sense of real
excitement that I used to approach those distant lunches. There
I met René Macoll, Arthur Koestler, Sam Behrman, Judge
Learned Hand, Alan ('Jock') Dent, Raymond Chandler, John
Gunther, Cecil Woodham Smith, Marjorie Sharp, and Jamie
Hamilton himself. Crossing the courtyard of Albany House,

being greeted by Mercer or the astounding Farrell, two of the elegant porters, then entering the coolness of the hallway, the excitement mounted, for there was always a chance that one would meet one of one's gods. I would nod to, though I never had the courage to approach, Graham Greene. I often held open the door for Harold Nicolson to pass ahead of me into the Rope Walk. Sometimes I would glimpse Dame Edith Evans, soft of feature and seemingly always dressed for Ascot, emerging from the chambers opposite. She occupied a first-floor set in the same block as Captain 'Fanny' Adams, who for many years was Secretary of Albany and ruled it as though it was peopled with junior officers in the Indian Army. Sometimes my entrances would coincide with one of the rare exits of Mr Stone, the 'Squire' of Albany, and Roger's landlord, a man who had pioneered with Rhodes and who lived to be over a hundred and worth in excess of a million pounds, hoarding both his memories and wealth like Miss Havisham, a true English eccentric. He owned a great number of the Albany freeholds, including Roger's – in itself a strange story, for Albany is one of the few habitations in London where there are separate freeholds in the same building. Roger and I often speculated as to the legal niceties attendant to such an arrangement. Above us, on freehold rafters, paced Jack Priestley. Above J.B., Marjorie Sharp and her husband breathed more rarified free-hold air. 'Supposing,' Roger said, 'I was to remove one of my supporting walls. It's an interesting point. Marjorie would fall into Priestley's study, then they'd both continue on through until they reached here, and I could have them both for trespass.' He raised his glass to the ceiling, looking at the problem through a drink darkly, eyes crinkled with amusement behind Nunn-May spectacles. 'Of course they're neither of them on the Hamish Hamilton list, so I'd have to be careful they didn't sue for malice aforethought.'

One of his most frequent guests is Arthur Marshall. Seemingly a totally content man who has managed to combine an Establishment façade with a semi-showbusiness interior, he is one of the most gifted mimics I have ever encountered. The richness of his varied life embraces being a well-loved House-master at a prominent public school, book-reviewer to the

New Statesman, author and star of his own radio programme, and private secretary to a scion of one of the oldest banking families in Europe. I have always regretted that the price of a tape recorder was beyond my means in those days, for I could have preserved some classic episodes. The major hazard whenever Arthur came to lunch during the summer was the fear that he would provoke and contribute to too much merriment and thus cause Captain Adams to make one of his dapper protests to the occupants of B.1. Adams was impossibly snobbish and the well-established inhabitants treated him with the contempt he often merited. For years he frowned whenever I crossed his eyeline and was only persuaded to acknowledge my existence when he discovered that I was on Christian-name terms with Daphne du Maurier's husband, General 'Boy' Browning, who was then Comptroller of the Queen's Household. Captain Adams's form of relaxation was to play the organ, and Arthur had something to say about that. Following a complaint about our boisterous luncheon behaviour, Arthur said in ringing tones: 'That man should leave the country under a cloud no bigger than a choirboy's hand.'

I have fortunately preserved notes of one splendid luncheon when Sam Behrman and Jock Dent were present. Jock arrived clad in a hand-knitted overcoat and a felt hat that looked like a hot-cross bun out of season. Sam had recently come from staying with Maugham and much of the talk that day was concerned with comparisons between Maugham and Max Beerbohm. Speaking of Beerbohm's abject circumstances, Sam had told Maugham, 'He lives in the poorest hotel at the very top of a hill, he couldn't afford one even halfway up.' To which Maugham had replied: 'Why shouldn't he be poor? He hasn't done any work for forty years.' The fact that Maugham obviously resented Beerbohm's reputation fascinated Sam, who recounted that, when he confessed he did not think himself capable of undertaking a full-scale biography of Beerbohm, Maugham had said, 'How could you? Max had no life.' Sam also spoke of Maugham's anxiousness to accept a Nobel Prize and his obsessive meanness, made apparent by his relish in revealing the cost of a recent illness in a Swiss clinic. Sam said, 'He made one think that the only thing to do was to go there immediately and have a kidney carved out.'

During the same lunch, talking of the Shaw-Mrs Patrick Campbell correspondence, Sam speculated on whether they had ever been to bed together. Jock replied, 'I believe he did knock on her bedroom door on one occasion, in Sandwich, but he only had his quill in his hand.'

During that same year I gained another unexpected friend whose life and life style was totally different from Roger's. I have no record or recollection that accurately pinpoints the actual event, but by the end of March 1950 I was living at 43 Warwick Gardens, just off Kensington High Street. My new landlady was Daphne Rye, that legendary lady of the period who steered a faultless path through theatreland as H. M. Tennent's casting director. Students of the theatre will readily appreciate the niceties of the situation, for the offices of H. M. Tennent were hardly a bastion of feminine liberation, and yet Daphne – hedonistic, emotional Daphne – had somehow made herself a permanent feature of that establishment. She was a tireless champion of young and undiscovered talent and twice a year endured the rounds, visiting every major repertory theatre in her quest. She had enormous power which she seldom abused and was responsible for the majority of new-comers who appeared under the make-or-break Tennent banner.

In the days before I became an intimate, I was very conscious of her influence, for she was never remote and could frequently be seen taking lunch with a group of favoured actors and actresses in Taylor's Sandwich Bar in Rupert Street, then the 'in' place.

She was responsible for my being cast in *The Holly and the Ivy*, and shortly after the play opened I joined that select band of young men known with some malice as 'Daphne's Lodgers! The Roll of Honour included the young Richard Burton, Kenneth More, Terence Longdon and Richard Leech. We paid a modest stipend for our glamorous board and lodgings, for Daphne was generous to a fault, always lived beyond her means and shared everything she had. Although brilliant at dispensing advice to others, she was hopeless when it came to sorting out her own invariably complicated emotional life.

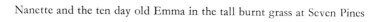
Nanette and the ten day old Emma in the tall burnt grass at Seven Pines

Opposite page above Peter Cook and Dudley Moore
on top of a hearse in the Royal Crescent, Bath,
during the making of *The Wrong Box*. *Below* Deciding
where to put the camera for the next shot on
The Wrong Box. Ray Simm's inspired train-wreck in
background

Above Typical study showing how simple it is to direct. The photographer, of course, was the ever-vigilant George Courtney Ward who has charted me through the years and – this specimen apart – is the best stills man I have ever worked with. *Below* Most of the cast and crew of *King Rat*

She had once been married to Roland Culver and had had two sons by him, but when I came on the scene she was divorced and in the death throes of a long and exhausting love-affair with another well-known actor. I had scarcely parked my suitcase in the allotted bedroom before Daphne burst into tears and poured out the latest tangled instalment. Halfway through the saga she announced she would have to take a bath, disappeared from view and mingled her sobs with the sound of running water. Being a newcomer to these domestic episodes, I started to unpack. Burton, an older and more cynical hand, shook his head. 'You have to follow her into the bathroom,' he said. 'It's your turn on duty. Beginner's privileges.' Sure enough, a few seconds later I was summoned into the steam. I sat on the edge of the bath rather than on the loo, since it seemed unfeeling to listen to a tale of such personal unhappiness while perched on the seat. Daphne, it must be said, was no hardship to behold in her bath.

I lacked Burton's superior attitude to the problem, nor was I bold enough to take advantage of the situation and give Daphne the solace that invariably dried her tears. I listened. During my first weeks at Warwick Gardens I listened long into the night, a sort of latter-day Isherwood confronted with a more elegant version of the fascinating Sally Bowles. I was a very tired camera by the end of it, but Daphne blossomed. She was one of those women who took refuge in food whenever emotionally upset, and since she prepared and cooked some of the best meals in London, her Camille periods differed widely from the original. She cried, she ate, she dried her tears, she ate, she never wanted to see her lover again, she ate, she couldn't live without him, she ate. It was only when the situation stabilized that she gave a thought to her figure. By then, of course, the gentleman, having been brought to heel, wanted to sample the noted delights of Daphne's kitchen as well as the tried and tested recipes she brought to her generous double bed. Perversely, it was at this precise moment that Daphne decided to go on a starvation diet and thus before long the whole cycle would begin again. The gentleman would take exception to the meagre fare he was forced to share, depart into the night yet again, leaving Daphne to rouse me from sleep with another lurid plea for help, and in her fresh despair attack the contents of the icebox.

Perhaps I was unique amongst the Lodgers in that I brought the faintest of literary flavours to Warwick Gardens. Shortly after *Truth Lies Sleeping* had been published I had the barefaced cheek to write the same letter on the same day to the Literary Editors of *The Spectator* and *The New Statesman* asking for work as a reviewer. Presumably Derek Hudson and T. C. Worsley never compared notes, for I had favourable replies from both and for a few months collected my humble two guineas from each in return for copy delivered to those distinguished periodicals. I reviewed mostly fiction for *The Spectator*, but T. C. Worsley, less of a flannelled fool than he eventually claimed, put me to stricter tests and sent along some weighty tomes that were beyond my limited experience. I quickly cottoned on to the trick of reviewing, which is to select more books than you can possibly find space for with a high quota of expensive volumes which are then swiftly flogged at half published price to certain booksellers who specialize in such transactions. I thus usually managed to increase my two guineas to ten or twelve, cheerfully embracing the time-honoured deceit without conscience, for the average reviewer's lot is a breadline activity.

Life at Warwick Gardens was never dull. It in some ways resembled a play by Dodie Smith rewritten by Henry Miller, with additional scenes and dialogue by Tennessee Williams. There was even a classic Cockney charlady who dusted around the debris, cigarette dangling from the corner of her mouth, cup of tea always to hand, turning a blind eye to every fresh arrival or eccentricity and totally loyal to Daphne and the Lodgers. Occasionally when the general pace dislodged a few of her hairpins she would permit herself some mild words of near-reproach. 'We're a bit busy this week, Mr Forbes, so if you do have a young lady to stay, don't bother to rumple the spare bed for appearances' sake. It's all the same to me and it saves extra work.'

She also possessed a daughter of such startling sexual attractiveness as to cause total havoc amongst the Lodgers. I recall with some affection and tenderness an evening when

Burton and I were alone in the house, Daphne having departed to find solace in some corner of a foreign bed. Food in generous quantities had been left for us and the nubile daughter recruited, with her mother's permission, to stay behind and serve. Burton and I invited her to join us at the table for dinner. She was a perfectly stunning creature and wore a blouse, I remember, with maps of all nations on it. Wales fell across one ample breast, and before we had finished the first course, Burton was insisting that his home town stood on the hill of her nipple. She was a sweet girl, not one of Nature's great conversationalists, but she took our cross-talk in good part, perhaps flattered by the attention being paid to her by two actors, one of whom was already laying claim to his eventual legendary existence.

I envied Burton. He had so many qualities that I lacked and was totally without inhibitions. He was then appearing in *The Lady's Not For Burning* and constantly in hot water with the management. His various escapades were eagerly awaited and exhaustively discussed in Taylor's and Warwick Gardens: they encompassed some beguiling sexual conquests from amongst the flower of Shaftesbury Avenue as well as some bizarre practical jokes. Esme Percy, that eccentric actor who had enjoyed a distinguished career despite the fact that he had lost an eye, was one of the cast in *The Lady's Not For Burning*. In some Celtic mood of boredom Burton purchased a collection of glass eyes which, aided and abetted by Richard Leech, he secreted all over the stage. At the following performance the rest of the cast, Mr Percy included, were horrified by the surfeit of glass eyes that confronted them at every turn. Somebody proposed a toast and found an eye staring at them in magnified liquid fashion at the bottom of the glass. People trod on glass eyes, slipped on glass eyes, opened purses and were confronted with an abundance of glass eyes. Whether or not Burton exaggerated the effect in the hilarious retelling, I cannot say; I only know that I hugely and callously enjoyed the joke at the time.

I was intent upon living beyond my fiscal and emotional means while *The Holly and the Ivy* continued to draw packed houses to the Duchess Theatre, and we entered 1951 with the 300 performance mark behind us. I was frequently bored and hungry for change. I had formed a relationship with a beautiful young actress who cut her hair like Ingrid Bergman and who cooked for me and washed my shirts, and was patient and loving. I bring no pleasure to the task of recording that I betrayed her in more ways than one. All my life I have had to fight against the dragon of self-destruction. I derive real as opposed to imagined pleasure from anticipating my own failures, surely a perverse and totally unrewarding aspect of any personality? The spore of pessimism grows overnight on any culture I possess. Perhaps I feel compelled to test my good fortune to the limits, perhaps there is some deep-set guilt I am fearful of uncovering. Literary detectives might some day find the vital clues in my written work, for most writers scatter but a thin layer of earth over their buried skeletons. So many of us work in the Rillington Places of the mind, strangling aspects of personality in the dead hours of the working night, betraying no trace the following morning to our families and friends, but instead going about our everyday business, Christie-like in our conceits with the midnight crimes erased, presenting the bland face of innocence for the world to judge.

I have to judge myself harshly in the section that follows, for if the act of writing an autobiography proves anything at all, it proves the absurdity of one's own life, recording as it should a series of self-seductions.

Thirty

To copy truth may be a good thing,
but to invent truth is much better.
Verdi

At the beginning of 1951 I had no premonitions of the events
that were to swiftly overtake me, and yet before the end of
February I was married to a girl I scarcely knew and by the
middle of the year I was living in another country with an
alien's passport, having abandoned home, family, possessions
and career.

In the circumstances it is hardly surprising that the marriage
was an immediate failure, and that the fault was all mine.

My first wife was the Irish actress Constance Smith. I met
her by chance in the home of two mutual friends, Mary and
Peter Noble. By a quirk of Fate that so often determines
human relationships, I had unwittingly been the instrument of
her own unhappiness. A few weeks before our first real meeting she had been engaged to director John Boulting. Taking
pity on his grass-widow status (for Connie was in Hollywood
under contract to Twentieth Century Fox), I invited John to
a dinner-party with a few other friends. During the course of
the evening he became totally infatuated with the mistress of
an eminent film critic (the Boultings have always been fearless). That very night the girl left the film critic and moved in
with John. To his credit the critic continued to give me
impartial notices, but in the course of one dinner-party I
somehow managed to complicate many lives.

Thus, when I met Connie a few weeks later she was quite
openly on the rebound; we had, as they say, something in
common which in retrospect was patently insufficient for any
lasting relationship, but intriguing enough to ensure that we
fell victims to circumstance.

Connie had just been cast in the star role opposite Tyrone Power in the remake of *Berkeley Square*. Confronted with the unwelcome *fait accompli* that their new discovery was intent upon marrying an unimportant British actor, the Twentieth Century Fox publicity machine moved into a well-oiled routine. It was a dull story, but the investment had to be protected, so they gave it the works. I don't want to give the impression that our whirlwind romance was in the Taylor–Burton category, but it was carefully exploited and became, for a time, front-page news.

We were married at Caxton Hall, where my parents met the bride for the first time during the course of a ceremony taken at the speed of a Keystone Kops chase. Even the flowers were rented.

Twentieth Century paid for the reception which was held in what is now the White Elephant Club. A good time was had by everybody except the groom. When the newsreel cameras had exposed their quota, family guests retired to Perrins Walk and there, in the two hours before I had to leave for the matinee at the Duchess Theatre, I was introduced to a host of Connie's relatives. They viewed me with the utmost suspicion. I was not only an English Protestant, but I had compounded that sin with a pagan civil ceremony. My brain dimmed by unaccustomed quantities of champagne, I listened with sinking heart to a series of maudlin monologues about the necessity of a second ceremony in a Catholic church.

Let this be an honest account. I knew then, at the wedding breakfast, within hours of the tenuous knot being tied, that the marriage was doomed. I remember whispering to Connie, 'Can't we get rid of these bores?' and hearing her nettled reply, 'They're my best friends.' The day ended in tearful recrimination, as unreal as the events that had led up to it. We had both been seized with a passing madness and whereas, in another profession, the results of that madness might have perished naturally in the desert of our basic incompatibility, we were swept up by the publicity machine, bewildered converts to the false religion of fame, merely used, as I now see, to provide some transient fillip for a commercial end-product.

There was no honeymoon in fact or feeling. Connie was

unhappy on the film for she had been elevated too fast to a position that she could not, professionally, sustain. We woke up one morning in Perrins Walk to read in our daily papers that she had been replaced in the role by Anne Blyth. Nobody had bothered to tell her. Her contract was suspended and the weekly pay cheque ended. The blow to our joint finances was critical, for in the general euphoria we had easily persuaded ourselves that we would walk the yellow brick road for ever. Our collective stupidity, so readily observed now at such far remove, plunged us into near despair.

It was difficult for outsiders to appreciate the extent of the blow to Connie. The role opposite Tyrone Power was considered to be the plum of the year and carried with it all the statutory prerequisites of a film star. It is easy in one's maturity and greater experience to dismiss such things as meaningless fabricated dross, but if you are just turned twenty-one and the glass slipper has been made to fit, you can be forgiven for believing that midnight will never strike.

When the blow fell she was totally unequipped to deal with the aftermath. The old-style Hollywood system allowed of no mercy. She was immediately reduced to the status of a Hindu road sweeper, all privileges were withdrawn overnight, and the army of sycophants and glad-handers avoided us like the plague. The publicity machine shifted into top gear for Miss Blyth, all Connie's scenes were quickly reshot at a cost of some £100,000, and the incident written off in the balance sheets.

It was at this moment that the West End run of *The Holly and the Ivy* came to an end. I was compelled by contract to undertake the post-West End provincial tour and faced the depressing prospect of once more returning to the landlady circuit. I managed to negotiate a few extra pounds per week, but we had no other source of income. Connie came with me to Bournemouth and was taken ill there. I was forced to leave her in hospital while I journeyed far north to Glasgow.

There, one night after the show, she told me that the studio had given her an ultimatum: either return to Hollywood immediately or have the contract terminated. She left the decision to me. I knew she wanted a second chance, for I had gained some insight into her character, and my fumbling immaturity as a husband embraced sufficient knowledge to persuade me that the distance between Glasgow and London was as great as the distance between London and Hollywood. All we really had in common was a book of press cuttings and our signatures on a marriage certificate. I told her that she must go and that I would somehow try and follow when I had raised the fare. She left the following day without fanfares.

As luck would have it, I had just been told that David Lean had selected me for a vital role in his forthcoming film of Terence Rattigan's *The Sound Barrier*. To work for David Lean has always been caviar for the actor, and the offer was potentially the turning-point in my career. I somehow endured the rest of the tour and we finally returned to London for the final two weeks at Streatham and Golders Green.

Connie was writing from Hollywood that things had started to go better for her. She had been cast in another film and was to journey to Montana for the location. She felt that if I took the plunge and joined her there I would soon obtain work, and she was sure that her salary could support us both until I got established. I allowed myself to be convinced for separation had dimmed the memory edges and everything in my upbringing persuaded me to the belief that marriage was something to be taken seriously whatever the cost.

I studied the balance sheet of my life. I had no money but I was poised for a leap forward in my career: in addition to the David Lean film I was also going to recreate my original role in the film version of *The Holly and the Ivy*. But an actor's conceits are many and complex, and the very name Hollywood beckoned like Shangri La. I set about obtaining an American resident's alien's visa and took stock of my meagre assets. If memory serves me the air fare to Hollywood in those days was around £175 one way. By selling my car and some of my possessions (the rest were distributed amongst friends, Norman becoming the guardian of my books), I scraped together the bare amount necessary.

I went to see David Lean, told him of my situation and asked if he would release me from *The Sound Barrier* contract. 'Of course you must go,' he said. 'This is just one role and you're talking about the rest of your life.' He was so gracious and understanding that I took fresh heart and the very real disappointment I felt at turning my back on such an opportunity was softened. I often wonder how different my life and career would have been had I played my cards in another order. The role I relinquished in *The Sound Barrier* was played by Denholm Elliot. He made such a success of it that his career was launched and he was given a long-term contract by Korda. The strangest irony of all was that he also played my role in *The Holly and the Ivy*.

My affairs in order, the holder of a valid visa and work permit, and with just enough money to get on the plane, I set out from the old trans-Atlantic departure buildings at London Airport on my twenty-fifth birthday. The journey took 32 hours, for I changed planes in New York, finally seeing the amazing expanse of Los Angeles on the evening of the second day. Due to the non-arrival of my telegram, Connie was not at the airport to meet me and I didn't have the price of a taxi. I must have presented a strange sight in my thick and unsuitable English clothes, half-dead from 8000 miles of propeller vibrations, struck senseless by the wall of humidity and heat, penniless in the land of plenty where oranges could still be bought for $1 a sack by the roadside but where nobody gave a sucker an even break. Something – perhaps my accent or my general air of despair – persuaded a taxi-driver to trust me until we reached our destination, an apartment on Olympic Boulevard in Beverly Hills conveniently close to the Fox Studios that Connie had rented as our home. Fortunately she was in when I eventually arrived and was able to pay the fare.

That was in July 1951. By Christmas of that year the marriage was over.

I see no merit in chronicling the private anguish of those months of the locust, for the day-to-day details can be of no possible interest to a third person. Re-reading my letters of the period to Norman, I am confronted with a mad stranger, and to quote by selection would be to quote by omission and nothing more. Like Henry James, I had to 'stagger out of my dust' as best I could.

The first few weeks were spent trying to make some tenuous contact with agents. I was just another actor in a town full of out-of-works and such slender reputation as I might have possessed had not crossed the Atlantic with me. My second letter to Norman, written on 14 August, records that I had given forty interviews without success. Despite daily humiliations I persisted in my quest for work, and by the middle of September my luck had changed with a chance introduction to Bob Goldstein who was then one of the top executive producers at the old Universal Studios. He took me to see Raoul Walsh and much to my amazement Raoul remembered me from London and cast me in a small role in *The World in His Arms* alongside Gregory Peck, Anthony Quinn and Anne Blyth. I was required to grow my side-burns and cultivate an American accent for a contract that guaranteed me $300 a week for six weeks. For the first time since my arrival I had money I could call my own, for up until then I had been totally dependent upon Connie's salary.

Jean Simmons and Jimmy Granger had proved generous friends and much of my enforced free time had been spent by the pool of their Bel Air home. Jimmy was never the one to do things by halves and had correctly judged that the only way to survive in Hollywood was to act bigger than life. Never noted for his reticence, he had quickly acquired a swashbuckling reputation that quite a few of the locals resented but none ignored. He lived in the grand manner dispensing hospitality like some latter-day Hearst, and his home was open house for any passing British chum.

Jean was ill at ease in Hollywood, for she didn't conform to any of the local patterns. When first I arrived in Hollywood she was in near despair waiting for the ultimately ill-fated *Androcles and the Lion* to commence shooting. She was bound hand and foot by some hideously complicated contract that had passed through many hands, and she could never discover who finally controlled her destiny. She was working at RKO, then the property of Howard Hughes, and alongside Jean and Jimmy I must be one of the few who frequently met Hughes face to face. He came regularly to their home in Bel Air, always accompanied by silent henchmen who performed such necessary tasks as opening toilet doors for him, legend having it that he was obsessed by the fear he might catch some nameless disease if he turned the handle for himself.

Apart from Hughes, the regular visitors to the Granger house were Mike Wilding and Elizabeth Taylor, who were just beginning their headline relationship. Mike, I suspect, didn't comprehend Hollywood and Hollywood didn't comprehend him, but he treated that period in his life as just another extended joke and, unlike Jimmy, couldn't be bothered to storm the sacred citadels. He has always had unlimited charm and a gift for gentle self-mockery. For as long as I have known him he has drifted through life, enjoying the moment and seemingly unconcerned about what the next day brings. He has always seemed to me a truly happy man, as indifferent to success as he is to failure. Conscious that his diction will never win elocution prizes, he enjoys telling stories against himself and his account of finding himself in a Russian hospital during the shooting of *Waterloo* is grotesquely funny. He tells how Jack Hawkins, hearing of his plight, went to the hospital and with no voice managed to effect his release. 'I was concussed, you see,' Michael relates, 'and dear old Jack said it was the only time in his life he could understand what I was saying. The moment I recovered, it was back to the old mumble.'

Mike and Elizabeth, together with Jean and Jimmy, supported me through some very black moments. In Jimmy's case the help was material as well as moral for he insisted that I be paid most generously for performing some vague secretarial work, which was merely a device to save my face.

I enjoyed making *The World in His Arms* and struck up a friendship with that quixotic renegade Tony Quinn. It was he who commissioned my first screenplay. I had given him a copy of my short stories on the set and he was sufficiently impressed to ask if I would write a script for his newly formed production company. His partners in the venture were Akim Tamiroff and the veteran cameraman Jimmy Wong How. A contract was drawn up for $150, and on the strength of it I rented a typewriter and got to work. The story was called *Vacant Lot* and was intended to be one of a trilogy built around three contemporary paintings. *Vacant Lot* opened with Ben Shahn's canvas of the same name and it was my task to invent what happened next. What did happen next was that I slaved over the script, delivered it on time, collected my money and never heard another word.

I was vastly impressed with the speed of shooting a film in Hollywood, for Raoul Walsh drove everybody at a fantastic pace compared to England. For no good reason that I could think of he took a liking to me and had my role built up. The few weeks I spent on the film were the only endurable part of that period in my life, and it is true to say that had I not been lucky enough to make the acquaintance of Raoul my story might have ended there in squalid tragedy. I had no further luck, for my option was never picked up, and apart from testing at Fox and the odd day's dubbing an English voice on a few reels of foreign film, I remained totally unemployed. Connie was away for various periods, for the studio rushed her from film to film, the majority of which had distant locations. I somehow eked out an existence on $5 a day, eating the cheapest meals I could find and occasionally, with all pride gone, inviting myself to Jimmy's table. He would have given me four square meals a day every day of the week, but with an actor's instinct for survival in a town where failure is like terminal cancer, I was desperate to conceal the real facts even from my friends.

Two other good people who took pity on me during this time were Betty Garrett and her husband Larry Parks. McCarthyism and the Blacklist still enveloped Hollywood like the smog of after years, and I can remember watching some of the public interrogations on television in total horror. Because of his testimony at the McCarthy hearings, Larry became unemployable – from being the top box-office star of *The Jolson Story* he was now a pariah, denied the basic right to earn his living in a profession he had previously dignified. It must have been a ghastly period for him and yet he and Betty went out of their way to try and help me. Word of my friendship with them reached my agents, and although they could not be bothered to try and find me a job, they found the time to warn me that my association with somebody like Larry was tantamount to professional suicide. I could hardly fall any farther from grace and I told them what they could do with their advice. My phone never rang again.

The end came over Christmas, the sad final chapter echoing the improbable plot of the worst B movie, for the news that my marriage was irreparably over was relayed to me in error by a Western Union operator who read over the phone a cable from Connie patently intended for my successor. In retrospect the episode is not without its own brand of bizarre humour, but at the time it lacked the traditional ingredients that make for a festive season.

Rescue came from a totally unexpected quarter. It was Raoul who somehow discovered the cause of my many disenchantments, took me out to his ranch home in the valley, plied me with Jack Daniels, gave me some good homespun advice, and then drove me to the TWA offices in Beverly Hills where he purchased a one-way ticket back to London in my name. 'Go now,' he said. 'Go tonight. I know this town very well. If you stay here you'll become a bum. Don't go back to the house, don't pack, don't do anything, just blow.' He drove me straight to the airport and we drank together until the plane took off.

'How will I ever repay you for the ticket?' I said.

'Oh, we'll meet up, maybe sooner than you expect. Don't worry about it. You'll pay me one day.'

It is an improbable scene. The tough old Hollywood director, dressed in riding breeches, rolling his own incombustible cigarettes from the sack of Bull Durham tobacco – the man who, as an actor, played John Wilkes Booth in *The Birth of a Nation*, who directed the first *What Price Glory* and most of the vintage Cagney movies that came out of Warner Brothers, the last person on earth one would cast to befriend a minor British actor in the midst of an emotional crack-up. All my life I have been lucky in my friends.

The weather was bad in New York and nothing was flying out. I had no money, but once again I was rescued at the eleventh hour. I phoned Gertie Lawrence from an airport call-box and she quickly invited me to stay with her until there was a flight out. While there I bumped into Roger. He was on his annual visit searching for new authors for his publishing house. I told him everything over a drink and he immediately offered me the use of his Albany chambers while he was away. There is irony in the fact that, totally penniless, I should return home to live in such splendour.

Once home, I kept low. It was a hard, cold winter and for the most part I seldom ventured far from the fireplace in Roger's library. I remember that I seemed to sleep for most of the day and would often wake in front of the dead grate in the later winter afternoons, shaking from head to foot like somebody in the grip of a tropical fever. I saw few people. If I went out at all it was merely to get the papers or take a hurried meal in Lyons Corner House in Piccadilly.

A few unsubstantiated rumours trickled through about Connie's situation in Hollywood, but it was like receiving news from another planet. My pride had been destroyed and most of my self-confidence had withered like burnt string. I was still in this sorry condition when Roger returned home. If he was put out at finding me still in residence, he betrayed no sign. There was only one bedroom which obviously I had to vacate, and I was steeling myself for the inevitable when he announced that he would buy a settee-bed to put in the dining-room, giving me the information in his usual tight-lipped fashion, for he was chary of betraying any emotion. Roger was the right person at the right time, devoid of false sentimentality and generous in the very best way, making no demands, asking no questions, offering no unwanted advice. His tolerance during that period is something I shall never cease to marvel at because I must have been a pain in the arse.

My absence from the London scene, short though it had been, had emasculated my career. Olive Harding used her best endeavours to obtain me work, but there were no takers. I made a determined effort to pull myself out of the mud. Taking stock of my meagre resources I decided that the only thing I had to sell was experience. I went to the old *Picturegoer* offices in Holborn and managed to bluff my way into the editor's office. *Picturegoer* was then the most influential film magazine. In what I now realize was one of my better performances, I talked Connery Chappell into commissioning a series of articles which eventually appeared under the nauseating title of 'A Husband in Hollywood'. I got a hundred and fifty pounds for them which enabled me to make some contribution to the housekeeping.

For obvious reasons I employed a variety of pseudonyms when writing about my fellow actors. 'Daniel Knowles' was one of my improbable pen-names, and he wrote a series called 'So You Want to Break into Films'. Looking back through my press cuttings I am amazed at the assignments I covered during this period. I interviewed Bill Holden, went very moral with a piece entitled 'Divorce is Disgracing Hollywood', demanded that people 'Let Liz Taylor Shine', issued an impertinent open letter to Mrs Joe DiMaggio, tried to do a friend a favour by asking 'Whatever Happened to Larry Parks?' and posed the question 'Are They Wasting Maggie Leighton?'.

Perhaps my greatest *coup* with *Picturegoer* was to persuade Connery to let 'John Seton' do a piece on Bryan Forbes. Under the challenging title 'Behind the Forbes Frown', Mr Seton wrote 1200 words with an insider's special knowledge which included:

When you meet Forbes for the first time, he seems, in the politest sort of way, preoccupied. Confined to a room for an interview, he gives the impression that his regiment is leaving at dawn and that he is anxious to rejoin it. As he listens to the questions, the worried look takes shape – one can see the reflection of the firing squad in his eyes.

To get paid for interviewing yourself is an achievement of sorts and the publication of this bogus piece of self-publicity marked the end of my run of bad luck.

Thirty-one

From time to time I made determined efforts to get back to some serious writing, hoping that the act of putting pen to paper would be the instrument of personal salvation. I commenced the novel that two decades later appeared in print as *The Distant Laughter*. For twenty years I carried the first hundred pages like some furtive atom spy who has only managed to steal half the formula. But the long hours I spent at Roger's elegant desk in Albany proved ultimately abortive. I could get so far and no farther, and in the end I resorted to premature editing of the initial chapters, polishing and repolishing like some old army sweat breaking in a new pair of boots with spit and bone, boots he has no intention of wearing but which he might have to produce for inspection. Each succeeding version became more sterile with perfection, there was no fire in my works, only the embers of a burnt-out imagination.

At Roger's prompting and with Roger's money I hired a car and took a casual pick-up to a hotel deep in the New Forest. The setting was a strange mixture of Agatha Christie and Graham Greene, for there was mystery in the fact that my companion and I were strangers, and an all-embracing sense of guilt. The hotel was seedy, every floorboard creaked at night, and our fellow guests seemed semi-mummified, wrapped in woollens and half-concealed with copies of *The Tatler*. We arrived late on the Friday evening, and as the grumbling porter humped our cases to two separate rooms rain slanted across the skylights. I tipped him generously, since I had once read that this was a necessary precaution in such situations, tested the springs of my damp bed and immediately lost all heart for the coming test. We retired early, our stomachs queasy from the set dinner and indifferent wine. After what I judged to be a proper interval I made my way to her room, armed to disarm an obligation masquerading as lust. She had cold limbs between cold sheets and my first conscious attempt at adultery failed.

Since we had nothing else in common the relationship ended there and we endured two rainy days in cold proximity, paying the penalty without having committed the crime.

I never repeated the experiment, yet so confused was I and so anxious to atone that I sought out the girl I had betrayed at the time of my marriage. I felt the need to confess to her the failure of my marriage. She was appearing in a successful West End play and agreed to meet me one evening after the performance. We went back to her small service flat and over coffee I told her that I had not bought happiness at the expense of her unhappiness. She did not pity me and she did not revile me. She listened to my story in a detached sort of way, as though no part of it had ever touched her life. Yes, it had been awful for her at the time, but she was over that now. She had made a new life for herself and the success of the play meant she moved in different circles. She had no particular emotional involvement with anybody, although there was no shortage of offers. She hoped things would work out for me. It was as clear-cut as the final paragraph of a Maugham short story, and when we had run out of shillings for the gas fire, I kissed her cheek and said goodbye.

Multa praeter spem scio multis bona evenisse. A remembered fragment of Plautus, sparse memento of a dusty classroom in Cornwall. *Many a stroke of luck has come to many a hopeless man.* Why should I recall this when I have forgotten all else? Because it is apposite or because, as Malcolm Muggeridge once said, a writer's mind remembers those things he can best write about?

The self-incarceration was not in vain. I had made many mistakes, but I had correctly judged the priorities of my interrupted career. By keeping my head below the level of the slit-trench I had escaped the sniper's attention. I might have passed out of circulation for a time, but I had not devalued my own currency – the private hurt had not overlapped into my professional life and as far as potential employers were concerned my credit was still good.

The offer of work, when it came, came out of the blue and with no strings attached. I was offered an important role in a new film called *Appointment in London* which was to star Dirk Bogarde and Dinah Sheridan. It was a well-constructed tearjerker about Bomber Command and I was to play a young pilot who ultimately failed to keep his 'appointment in London' at Buckingham Palace to receive the DFC. Little Anne Leon was cast to play my wife and widow. The money was good and I did not have to fight for co-star billing. I was suddenly back in the swim.

The location scenes were filmed on an operational RAF airfield outside Peterborough and I teamed up with Bill Kerr, the Australian comic who was then enjoying a considerable success on radio. He was a wildly extrovert character who could find something funny in any given situation. The last vestiges of my long depression vanished in his company. Bill literally laughed girls into bed. He would return to our shared hotel room every night, wake me up and recount the latest conquest in lurid detail. It is no secret to him that I made use of one such exploit when I came to adapt Kingsley Amis's novel *That Uncertain Feeling* for the screen. The film was retitled *Only Two Can Play*, and Peter Sellers played the randy librarian with notable finesse. Perhaps one of the funniest scenes in the film (which was directed by Sidney Gilliat) was the attempted seduction of Mai Zetterling by Peter in an American convertible parked in the middle of a herd of cows at night.

Although *Only Two Can Play* was considered very daring in its time, Bill's real-life adventure left it standing. His hilarious retelling of an episode that was both erotic and farcical could not be translated intact for the cinema. Censorship demanded that Peter and Mai be denied consummation, but in Bill's original he and his girl-friend had been surprised stark naked by an irate farmer. The farmer had fired both barrels of his shot-gun just as the moment of truth approached for the two lovers, and the blast stampeded the cattle. Bill described in great detail how he and the girl had coped with this dilemma. They were both in the back seat at the time in the missionary position. Bill insisted that the actual explosion had not thrown him off his stroke and that only when a terrified cow landed across the bonnet of the car did he become aware that all was not well. Still naked, he scrambled back into the driving seat, pressed the electric hood release instead of the starter in his understandable confusion, then drove round the perimeter of the field looking for the exit, narrowly avoiding the frenzied cattle, while behind him in the now open tourer his poor girlfriend attempted to put some clothes on. They finally made their escape, but wishing to put some distance between themselves and the farmer, Bill drove to the outskirts of Peterborough before he became conscious that he was the nude version of Eric von Stroheim in *Sunset Boulevard*.

Thirty-two

'What're you up to, kid? Anything happening?' The voice belonged to Raoul Walsh.

'Listen,' he said over the phone, 'I'm in town. Got myself involved with a piece of horseshit called *Toilers of the Sea* and I need a few friends around me. Now, I tell you what you do. They've got a part in this film they want Barry Fitzgerald for, but if we play the cards right I think I can swing it your way.'

He then proceeded to outline a barefaced deception. 'You'll get a call from the casting director in a few days to come and see me at the Dorchester. Play it straight. Don't shave, talk in an American accent, and you never saw me before in your life. Leave the rest to me.'

I stayed close to the phone for four days and left my razor on the shelf. Sure enough, I received the call to present myself at the Dorchester for an interview.

When I arrived there the queue of hopeful actors stretched halfway down the corridor, for a Raoul Walsh picture was an event, the more so in England since the success of his *Captain Hornblower*. Actors entered and exited the door of his suite with depressing speed, and by the time I reached the head of the queue my confidence was nil.

Raoul had his back to me when I finally entered, and I was greeted by the producer, David E. Rose, a kindly but ineffectual soul. He was flanked by the casting director and his associate producer.

'Who're we seeing now?' Raoul said.

'Bryan Forbes,' the casting director said.

We were introduced. Raoul shook my hand. He gave nothing.

'What've you done, kid?'

'Well, I played in quite a few films, both here and in Hollywood, Mr Walsh.' My accent was thick and unconvincing.

'The kid looks virile,' Raoul said. 'Look at that beard.

Certainly a change from some of those fags you've been show-ing me all the afternoon.'

'Yes, he's a good young actor,' the casting director said. 'We were thinking of perhaps the part of the young sailor in the first scene.'

'What about the part of Willie?' Raoul said. He was rolling one of his cowboy-style cigarettes, thin as a toothpick.

'Willie?'

David E. Rose spoke for the first time. 'You don't mean Willie, surely, Raoul? That's earmarked for Barry Fitzgerald.'

'Yeah, well, I've been thinking, we got to get some young blood in the picture. We're starring Rock Hudson, right? We don't want to put him against some vintage Irish ham. Give the kid the part.'

David E. Rose and the casting director looked as though they had both been struck by the same bolt of lightning. In the first place you never told an actor he'd got any part until you'd negotiated the price, and in the second place you certainly didn't substitute Bryan Forbes for Barry Fitzgerald without going into an intensive care unit for the weekend.

'Don't you think we ought to talk about it, Raoul?' David said when he finally managed to recover his voice.

'Listen, I'm tired. I've interviewed every out-of-work actor in England this afternoon and the kid here is the only one who impresses me. Let's sign him up.'

'Well, let's you and I talk about it, and ask Mr Forbes to come back later.'

'He doesn't want to come back later. Give him a contract now otherwise you'll lose him.'

'We don't have any actual contracts here, Mr Walsh,' the casting director said.

Raoul turned to me. His one eye twinkled briefly. 'Do you have a ten-per-center, Captain?'

'I have an agent, yes, Mr Walsh.'

'Well, get him on the phone.'

'It's a her.'

'Jesus, they got women agents over here? Fine, well talk to her and have her make the deal.'

David E. Rose had aged visibly during this exchange. His

associate producer looked like an exhibit in Madame Tussauds, and the poor casting director was already looking for another job. I duly phoned Olive Harding, gave her an expurgated version of what had taken place, and the deal was concluded. At one point in the proceedings Raoul passed close to me and whispered, 'You've got 'em over a barrel, kid.'

Less than half an hour after I entered the room my deal had been agreed. Then Raoul produced his masterstroke.

'Course the part as written is no good for the kid. I mean, it's written as an old man.'

Time has conveniently blotted out the identity of the author of the original screenplay, but when I entered the circus any resemblance to Hugo's *Toilers of the Sea* was insanely coincidental. Rock Hudson was a very raw newcomer, a Raoul Walsh discovery in fact, and although possessed of considerable charm and a personality which came over on the screen, lacked any real acting experience. His female co-star was the exotic Yvonne de Carlo and the villain of the piece was our own Maxwell Reed. Hugo's novel had become a vehicle for pirates and swooning heroines and the dialogue was unspeakable. The part of Willie had been written to accommodate an older man as a side-kick to Rock. Even without Raoul's chicanery on my behalf it is doubtful whether Mr Barry Fitzgerald would have entertained it for he was then at the height of his popularity and an appearance in this particular role would have guaranteed professional suicide.

'D'you know anybody over here who could rewrite it?' Raoul asked. 'We need a fast rewrite man.'

'Well, I write,' I said.

'You don't say?'

Out of the corner of my eye I saw David E. Rose clutch at the nearest piece of Dorchester furniture.

'You good on dialogue?'

'Yes, I think so.'

'Well, that's the answer then. Let the kid rewrite his own part.'

'But, Raoul, we need a screenwriter.'

'How d'you know the kid isn't a screenwriter? What have you written, Mr Forbes?'

'A novel, a collection of short stories, and one screenplay for Tony Quinn.'

'How about that! That's a pretty impressive list of credits, David.'

David E. Rose was too shell-shocked to put up any sort of resistance by now, and after some more insane conversation it was agreed that I should be engaged to do the rewrite. A second contract was quickly negotiated and I went back to Albany demented with happiness.

Half an hour later Raoul called me.

'You put on a pretty good show there, kid. You'd have fooled me. What're you doing for dinner?'

'Nothing.'

'Come round and have dinner and we'll crack a bottle or two to celebrate. Over dinner we can figure out how the script's got to go.'

In many ways it was a shameful episode, although hugely enjoyable at the time. But Raoul had come up the hard way. From long experience he knew there was no way he could overcome the basic absurdities of the whole operation and he had therefore decided to enjoy himself in the company of a few friends.

Raoul's own life-story reads like an improbable movie scenario. During the making of *Toilers of the Sea* in Brittany we had broken for lunch which was being taken in a small restaurant none of us had ever visited before. Halfway through the meal the proprietor came up to Raoul and told him he was wanted on the phone. Raoul took the call at the bar and returned to the table with a smile on his face. 'That was a jockey I know in Ireland,' he said. 'Just gave me the winner for the four-thirty at Newmarket.'

'How did he know you were here?' we all said.

'Oh, he always finds me. Terrible jockey, but a great man on the telephone.'

'Are you going to place a bet?'

'Sure. He knows better than to give me a phoney.'

The horse came in at incredible odds.

During the time when I was rewriting the script under his supervision he told me to insert a particular line of dialogue.

The line was, 'I'm going to get out of here faster than I left my first wife.' I queried it in the context of the story.

'That's my trademark,' Raoul said. 'I put that line in all my films. You see, my first wife took me to the cleaners and I still have to pay her alimony. Now I know she goes to see all my films, just to check up on me and make sure I'm working for her. So I think of her sitting there in the cinema hearing that line every goddamn time.'

It is difficult to convey the true flavour of his dialogue, for I would hate to give the impression that he is some loud-mouthed parody of the Hollywood tough-guy. While he would never pass unnoticed in a crowd, he dresses conservatively, most of his clothes being tailored for him in Savile Row, and his immaculately polished boots are handmade in Jermyn Street. When on the set he works without temperament. When you meet him for the first time he seems to be measuring the chances of beating you to the draw. He is now in his eighties, still erect, still handsome, holding himself like a prize-fighter of the bare-knuckle school, a man who is unfailingly polite when there are women present, graced with unaffected good manners.

Raoul never mentioned my Hollywood episode nor did he ask me to repay the air fare he had provided. Privately I had determined that I would one day refund it in full, in Holly- wood, and in local currency. He had to wait until 1964 when I returned on my own terms to direct *King Rat*. I took him out to dinner and together we drained a bottle of Jack Daniels. Then I handed him an envelope. He opened it and took out a wad of notes.

'What the hell's this?' he said.

'It's the price of an air ticket,' I said, 'with twelve years' interest.'

'What're you talking about? What air ticket?'

I reminded him. He looked at me in genuine astonishment. He had forgotten all about it.

Thirty-three

In the early spring of 1953 I was compelled to assume a double
identity. After giving the matter careful thought I became a girl
named Patricia Fenton. This Philby-like existence continued
for over two years until it was time for Miss Fenton and her
entire family to disappear: her brother suffered a fatal car
accident and she emigrated to Australia with her parents. In
many ways I was saddened to see them go, for I had grown
quite fond of them; Patricia in particular was a kindly soul with
a friendly and generous disposition.

The story really begins one cold February night. Given
freedom of choice I doubt whether any full-blooded English
male would opt for Marylebone shunting yards as the ideal
place for selecting a future wife, but God, British railways and
the film industry all move in mysterious ways, and by a fruitful
combination of these divers factors I chanced, in 1953, upon
the mother of my two daughters.

My own reasons for being in Marylebone shunting yards
that particularly cold night were transparently obvious. I was
starring in one of those Neolithic happenings known as
British Second Features. We made them on what was known
as a 'tight schedule'. In second feature language this was translated into a maximum of three weeks. Conditions were
primitive. Scripts, if they existed at all, were the Dead Sea
Scrolls of Wardour Street, mostly written in blood. Actresses,
if cast in them, needed to retain some of the old pioneering
spirit, and many a four-minute mile was run, pre-Bannister,
between Hammersmith and Merton Park. Make-up consisted
of being stained (if male) and disguised as a newly varnished
GPO pillar-box (if female). Costumes, unless period, were un-
mistakably one's own, and talent was measured by an actor's
ability to say the right lines on the first take without benefit
of rehearsal and above the noise of the carpenters building the
next set on the same stage.

Thus it was on the cold February night in question that I found myself lying on the railroad track, adding another chapter to my distinguished career. The script called for me to commit suicide under a train. This had been scheduled as the last shot on the last day of three forgettable weeks. The budget did not stretch to such luxuries as a stunt double, and the producer had sold the director on the conception of total reality. So it was to be me in my own second-best suit lying on a real railroad track, facing a real train.

Keyed up to a point beyond which few actors seldom venture in their right minds, I had agreed to perform in order that my agent should not starve. In a rare burst of temperament I had requested that some form of primitive cow-catcher be fixed to the front of the engine. At a given signal from one of the assistant directors, the engine driver was to provide a cloud of concealing steam. I was then to throw myself on to the cow-catcher and hope for the best. I was a Method actor in those days – my own particular method being to try and ensure that I stayed alive to star another day.

I noticed that for the first time during the entire three weeks the producer was smiling at me. He gave the thumbs-up sign from a distance and he even allowed me the rare luxury of a rehearsal, though I suspect that this humanitarian gesture was prompted more by a close study of his insurance policy than by a desire for artistic perfection.

The train started to move towards me. The signal was given. I rushed forward. Steam hissed to envelop me as, miraculously, I hit the edge of the cow-catcher and was propelled forward like some broiler chicken. I dimly heard confused shouts all around me and in the semi-gloom, from an upside-down position, I finally made out the figure of the director.

'Bryan,' he said with a generosity hitherto concealed, 'Bryan, that was *great*! I wish we'd shot it. But Harry thinks the train ought to go a little faster. How d'you feel about that on the day?'

I felt terrified but ambitious, and I needed the money, so I gave him my John Garfield smile and agreed that the train should be faster. At speed, death was more likely to be instantaneous.

While the details of my demise were being explained to the engine driver, I decided to ask for a blindfold and my last cigarette. I strolled across the track (John Wayne going to parley with the Indians) and it was then that I first saw Miss Newman standing under the lamp-post. Casually (Jimmy Stewart in *The Spirit of St Louis*) I walked past her. I sat in the only chair available, which had the word ACTOR written on the canvas back. I looked back at her and offered a cigarette (Paul Henreid in *Now Voyager*).

'No, thank you, Mr Forbes, I don't smoke,' she said.

I lit mine with a Swan Vesta (stars never used cheap matches).

'Have you come to watch the shooting?' I said, trying to sound like Cagney in *White Heat*.

She nodded. I sensed that it needed all her self-control to stop her throwing herself at my feet.

'Well, not exactly,' she said. 'Actually, Mr Forbes, I came down here to audition. There's just a chance I might get a small part in your film.'

I liked the possessive way she had said 'your film' but, like Leslie Banks in *Sanders of the River*, I heard those old jungle drums and was immediately on the alert for foul play.

'In *this* film?' I said. The cigarette stuck painfully to my upper lip. Miss Newman looked so very innocent.

'Yes, Mr Forbes. I read the part for the producer this morning and he said that if I came here tonight and met the director there might just be a chance.'

'You read it for him?'

'Yes.'

'Where?'

'In his office.'

'Which scene, which part did you read?'

'Your secretary.'

I inhaled like Bogart. I needed time to think. It isn't often that one has a chance to save a young girl's honour in Marylebone shunting yards, and time was at a premium.

'The secretary, huh?' I said, and it came out sounding like Peter Lorre in *The Maltese Falcon*.

I knew the role well. The girl who had played it on the first day of shooting was a well-known nude model.

'What's your name?' I asked.

'Nanette Newman.'

'Well, look, Miss Newman . . . Nanette, I'm afraid I've got bad news for you. The part in question has already been finished with. This happens to be the last shot in the film. When my mangled body is taken from under that train in a few moments' time, it's on with the bloody motley, I fear, for all of us. You have a simple choice before you. The future holds a trip home with me in comparative safety or else a long night's journey into a longer night with our distinguished and lecherous producer.'

'You mean . . . ?'

I nodded (Lewis Stone telling Andy Hardy the facts of life). 'The only role likely to be on offer to you tonight is the female lead in a two-handed tragedy known as Dodging the Producer's Bed.'

To do her credit, Miss Newman did not cry. She stared at me with wide open eyes and I fell in love with her on the spot. I could not wait to die in front of those eyes.

'What d'you think I ought to do? My father will kill me when he finds out.'

I carefully filed that last piece of information, for I suspected it had some future pertinence for me as well.

'Go and sit in my car,' I said. 'Wait for me there.' I gestured towards an ancient Austin Ten, Roger's property, which served as a star's limousine. Miss Newman looked worried in another way.

'Won't he think it odd?'

'Probably, but I'll sort it out.'

'What if he says something to me?'

'Tell him you're an old friend of mine.'

'But I never said that before. I said I didn't know you.'

'Listen,' I said desperately, for by now my own evil designs had become sanctified, 'please believe me, it's the only way. Just sit in the car and leave everything to me.'

At that moment I was called towards my other destiny. I gave her my Ronald Colman smile and crossed to the wrong side of the tracks so that I was facing the guard's van. Somebody shouted at me. 'I'm just getting into the mood,' I shouted back. An assistant in the last stages of Woodbine consumption hurried to guide me to the start mark. Arc lamps screamed into life: blinded by something approaching eternal love, I tried to focus on the spot where Miss Newman had stood. She was nowhere to be seen. There was also no sign of the producer.

'First take, eh?' the director shouted. I nodded. I was in no mood for his acid humour. I heard something which sounded like: 'Don't cut unless there's a real accident,' and then the train started to move. I ran forward like Scarlett O'Hara rushing to meet Ashley Wilkes and flung myself into the steam. I embraced the metal cow-catcher like a warm winter bed. I lay in bed and thought about Miss Newman until the scene went dark.

Somebody touched me on the shoulder. A voice said, 'Is he conscious?' and another voice said, 'Check the gate.' I sat up in bed and smiled. The crowd, cheated of blood, wandered away to commence packing the gear.

'Are we going again?' I asked.

'Just waiting for the word now.'

'Gate's clear, no hairs in the gate,' the focus-puller shouted from the camera.

'Right! That's it, boys,' the first assistant said. 'That's a wrap. See you, Bryan.'

I took out a crushed cigarette and lit it. The director was having a violent argument with the continuity girl. 'Who cares?' he was saying as I approached. 'With the light we're using even his mother won't recognize him.'

He broke off as he saw me.

'Great,' he said. 'Great end to a great picture. Going to take nothing but money.' Then he forgot about me. Nothing glowed in the darkness, not even a carbon.

I went over to my Austin like Paul Muni going to meet the mob. Miss Newman was waiting for me. There was a God after all.

'Have you seen him?'

She nodded.

'What did he say?'

'He said I was making a big mistake.'

'What d'you think?'

'Oh, I checked,' Miss Newman said. 'I asked one of the carpenters. Who was the safest, you know.'

This wasn't the dialogue I would have chosen for the scene. 'And what did the carpenter say?'

'He thought that by and large I'd be better off with you.' She said it very seriously, looking like Ingrid Bergman in *Going My Way*.

I put the car into gear, asked the directions and drove her home to Streatham.

Just before we said good night I told her two things. I told her I was married but living apart and that I wanted to see her again. Miss Newman agreed to meet me the following afternoon. Listening to a distant echo, I did not escort her to her front door.

There is, of course, a moral to this story and I wonder if I shall ever heed it when my own daughters bring home their own variations on the same theme, as bring home they undoubtedly will.

Nanette later told me that when she recounted the night's events to her father, that good man reacted with understandable dismay. 'You are never,' he said, 'to see Bryan Forbes again.'

She met me as arranged the following day, and I took her to tea at the Tate (culture first, lechery afterwards) then walked her past the Leicester Square theatre where, surprise, surprise, there was a photograph of me in *Appointment in London*.

'How fantastic,' I said. 'One of my films is showing. Would you like to see it?'

She would and she did. I had taken the precaution of ringing the manager in advance, and we were greeted like Royalty and shown to the best seats in the house. When I died one of my usual brave deaths during the course of the film, I reached for Miss Newman's hand just to reassure her.

When we left the cinema I took a taxi to Albany. As we entered the elegance of B.1, Nanette was suitably impressed.

'What a marvellous place to live,' she said.

'Yes, isn't it,' I said, Cary Grant at his most throwaway. I sat beside her on the sofa in front of the open fire.

'Did you tell your parents you were meeting me today?'

'No.'

'Oh, why was that?'

'My father doesn't like actors.'

'What does your father do?'

'He's in variety. He's an adagio dancer.'

I had a quick mental picture, subsequently confirmed by the true-life facts, of an immensely strong man who bent iron bars, did press-ups all day, and was capable of crushing me with a handshake.

'Why doesn't he like actors?'

'He says they only want one thing.'

There seemed no ready answer to that, so I stared in the fire and tried to look hurt.

'He said that if I went out with you the first thing you'd do would be to bring me back to your flat.'

'Well, it was the third thing, so he's wrong.'

I took some comfort from the fact that Miss Newman didn't look too disturbed as she explained all this. She was absurdly young, of course, and devastatingly pretty. I was not so young, absurdly married and with a healthy respect for fathers capable of reducing me to pulp. The situation called for extreme caution and not a little ingenuity. It was obvious that if I wanted to continue to enjoy Miss Newman's favours, and of that I had no doubt, I would have to exercise considerable imagination. One false move and the game would be up.

I can't claim to have invented Patricia Fenton that first night. She came later. I confined myself, on that first night, to a reasonably honest account of my marriage and future prospects. Divorce in those days was inevitably protracted and messy. Unless one was prepared to 'give grounds' by the time-honoured routine of the shared breakfast tray in the hotel bedroom with a professional stranger, it was a question of sweating out the statutory period of three years before petitioning on a plea of desertion. Since Connie was still in Los Angeles, collusion towards a mutually desired release seemed a remote and costly exercise. Since I had already determined that Miss Newman would one day be my wife, a decision that has never given me a single moment's regret, it was obvious that I would have to adopt long-term strategy, fighting, as it were, on two fronts at once. Her father had to be kept at bay until I was once again in a position openly to solicit his daughter's hand in marriage.

This earnest and one-sided discussion that first night was interrupted by Roger returning to his own fireside. Nanette now swears that I had conveniently forgotten to tell her that the flat was not mine, but women are pedantic on such details. Thus when the ever-understanding Roger made his appearance, she greeted him as a visitor who, like herself, was enjoying my hospitality in gracious surroundings. With a forbearance that will do him credit to his dying day, Roger did not reveal my guilty secret on the spot, but merely gave me an owlish look behind Nanette's back.

His arrival was the signal for our departure to darkest Streatham. I drove her home once more and we agreed that, despite my situation, we had to continue to meet. I promised to find a solution.

And that is how Patricia Fenton was born.

Thirty-four

I realize now that until I met Nanette I had been in love with love. I believed, as Pierre Drieu la Rochelle believed, that there had never been a single day in my life, however happy, however filled with people, or even with just one person, when I had not dreamt of solitude. Nanette was to change all that.

The two years that followed my invention of Patricia Fenton determined the course of my life ever since. They were two years of intense happiness, two years of torment. For the greater part of those two years we met in secret, concealing the substance and even disguising the shadow of our love for each other from all but Roger.

I was a married man and Nanette's parents were concerned to protect their only child. I felt no resentment towards them because of this, nor did Nanette or I derive any spurious pleasure from the deception we swiftly perfected. We acted not out of malice but from that selfish necessity that has ever decided the behaviour of lovers.

Naturally, being the older of the two by many years, and the guardian of that curious commodity we label experience, I was always the protagonist. Nanette looked and behaved like the innocent she was. Having chanced upon the device of Patricia Fenton, we proceeded to perfect her. In the early days she served a very simple purpose. When I telephoned Nanette at home she would answer me in one of two ways. If she said, 'Hallo, Pat,' I knew that her parents (and more critically, her father) were in the same room and that therefore conversation was impossible. She would do all the talking, inventing absurd but plausible gossip such as two girls of her age might enjoy, terminating the call as soon as convention allowed without arousing suspicion. Then, at the earliest opportunity, she would slip out of the house and call me back from a public call-box. If, on the other hand, she answered my call with some endearment then I knew that the coast was temporarily clear.

But even the most casual crime compounds like interest, and before long we were drawn into a more complicated deception. Patricia's parents would invite Nanette to spend an evening with them. Where did they live? What standard of living did they enjoy? What income bracket were they in? How old was Patricia, what did she do?

The dictates of my heart demanded that I showered Nanette with gifts – how could she accept them? Mr Fenton became a rich and generous man who insisted on treating Nanette as he did his own daughter when they were out together.

Mr Newman harboured the normal suspicions of any doting father, and before long he was enquiring why Nanette never brought Patricia home so that he could return her father's hospitality? It was a good question, and it stumped us. The Fentons went abroad for a time, taking Patricia with them. She could only ring long-distance. We breathed again.

Looking back, what astounds me is not the deception itself but the fact that it succeeded. I was a semi-public figure in that I frequently appeared on television and in films, and therefore the Fenton umbrella only afforded partial protection. We had to observe other precautions. The majority of our public meetings took place in the crowded basement restaurant of the Buxton Club, a favourite haunt of the period across the street from the stage door of the Theatre Royal, Haymarket. They served simple meals of generous proportions at reasonable prices, and the tables were so close together that even a Maigret would have been put to the test to decide who was eating with who.

Nanette's own background was vastly different from my own, for she comes from a theatrical family and has been schooled in the vagaries of our profession from the cradle. She had sung at Covent Garden as a child, starred in a children's film, studied ballet and tap dancing, spent most of her holidays in the back-stage atmosphere of summer shows, gone to the Italia Conti school which was then situated alongside the Windmill Theatre, been an unwilling recruit to her father's cabaret act, and then had obtained an exhibition scholarship to the Royal

Academy of Dramatic Art. She had just graduated from RADA when I met her. The amazing thing is that she had remained curiously untouched and uncorrupted by such a spectrum of experiences. Although steeped in theatrical traditions and folk-lore she had none of the more obvious and unattractive affectations that most young actresses feel compelled to adopt. She seemed totally unaware of her own beauty and could pass the acid test – the proximity of a mirror – with flying colours. She was not and has never been rabidly ambitious and perhaps, in theatrical as opposed to human terms, that has worked to her disadvantage. If her ambitions had equalled her talents her life would have been very different. Equally, I suppose, our marriage would have been very different. The chances are it would not have survived, for the really ambitious person always goes it alone – indeed, he or she has no real alternative and the roar of the crowd holds more attraction than the devotion of the individual. I have always been more ambitious for her than she has been for herself.

Thus while my career took several modest upward turns, my emotional life remained static, hemmed in by the prevailing divorce laws. Connie had petitioned in Los Angeles on the conventional grounds of mental cruelty. This had become public knowledge and I had been relieved of any further deception where my own family was concerned. But the petition failed and I was back where I started and faced the prospect of another two years before I would be free to marry Nanette.

Because she is not by nature a devious person, and because the burden of sustaining our secret proved too much, Nanette had confided in her mother. We were now able to see each other in her own home when Mr Newman was absent on tour. We had not expunged the guilt, we had merely extended it. Like the useful old soldier she had become, Patricia Fenton began to fade away.

Nanette was also working, having attracted considerable attention in a smallish film role. Principally because she wished to get away from the restrictions of home, she joined the Under Thirties repertory company in Hythe. By coincidence my old friend Tony Godwin from Better Books had recently moved to Hythe and thus I was able to visit her there. By now our relationship was total. We were impatient for the time when we could be married and we were oblivious to all else. We exchanged vows and I bought her an engagement ring which she could not wear in public and which I retained for safe keeping. She only wore it when we were together, giving it to me when we parted. It was a second-hand ring, chosen from the window of a jeweller's in Burlington Arcade, a turquoise in a Victorian setting, and I gave £42 for it when my bank account totalled £48.

We were together in Hythe when my life changed direction yet again. It was a Saturday, I remember, and we had gone into town to do some shopping before lunch. When we returned to Tony's house he said that somebody had telephoned me from London – a Mr Broccoli – and it was apparently very urgent.

I placed the return call. Mr Broccoli answered. He said he had once met me in Palm Springs with Jean and Jimmy Granger. He was a film producer in partnership with a man called Irving Allen and they were in trouble. They were half-way through making a film with Alan Ladd called *The Black Knight* and they needed a writer.

At this point I found myself talking to Mr Allen. He didn't waste words. 'Listen,' he said, 'I understand you're a very fast rewrite man.' I was too amazed to disillusion him. 'Well,' Mr Allen continued, 'we need a rewrite like yesterday. When can you begin?'

'Depends,' I said, playing for time. 'What's the film about?'

'What d'you care what the film's about? Can you start work today, this afternoon?'

'But I'm not in London.'

'So where are you?'

'Hythe,' I said.

'So get a train. They have trains down there, don't they?'

'Yes.'

'Okay, come straight to this office.' He gave me an address in Jermyn Street. 'What's your price?'

'Price?'

'Yeah, how much d'you want paying?'

236

'Well, I don't know what's involved.'

'I'll tell you what's involved, we've run out of words. Today's Saturday, right? We have to shoot on Alan Ladd first thing Monday morning and right now he ain't got any dialogue. So what do you want?'

I had no idea what I wanted. I wasn't even sure that I wanted the job.

'I'll give you six hundred,' Allen said. 'Is it a deal?'

Nanette and Tony were listening fascinated by my elbow. They urged me to accept.

'Yes,' I said.

'Fine, well get your ass up here. Catch the next train.'

Nanette went to her matinee and I caught the first available train. I went straight to the address in Jermyn Street where I met the redoubtable Mr Allen for the first time. His partner, Albert 'Cubby' Broccoli, whom I dimly remembered from that chance meeting in Palm Springs, sat on the opposite side of the vast, shared desk. Irving thrust a dog-eared script at me.

'You can read that if you like, but it won't mean anything. I'll give you the story-line.'

He then proceeded to detail one of the most unlikely plots in the history of motion pictures.

During some distant script conference Irving and Cubby had commissioned a story about King Arthur and his knights. The screenwriter, instructed to provide Alan Ladd with a suitable star role, had elected to make him the simple village smithy – not a happy choice, perhaps. In relating what follows I do not wish to be uncharitable about Mr Ladd's attributes. He was, in classic fashion, a film *star*, which is an entirely different animal from an actor who appears in films above the title. His public personality was meticulously invented and then grafted on by the old studio publicity machine. He was exceedingly handsome by the standards of those days and the roles he played were tailored to fit his talents. What he brought to the screen was a brooding, almost sullen quality which, I believe, he perfected over the years to conceal a basically shy personality. By the time I met and worked with him all reality had gone, he had discarded his true self and now sheltered behind the publicity mask.

As Irving related the plot that Saturday afternoon, England had been invaded by Saracens disguised as Vikings. Against these improbable forces King Arthur had given battle on a Spanish field. The said bogus Vikings had sacked Camelot and now convention demanded that Alan Ladd somehow became a Knight of the Round Table and single-handed achieved final victory. That much I could embrace, but there were darker forces to contend with. In addition to the normal fantasies, the exposed footage also took into account the evil revelries of the Druids at Stonehenge. These stone-age priests had somehow imported a bevy of Vestal Virgins – the Tiller Girls of Ancient Rome – and were intent upon sacrificing them as the sun came up over Pinewood Studios, thus posing yet another problem for King Arthur and Alan Ladd. And just in case the audience might feel it wasn't getting value for money, the Christian 'Bishop' of Stonehenge (one of the more inspired and endearing inventions of the script) was scheduled to consecrate a new abbey to replace the edifice destroyed by the aforementioned Saracens inadequately disguised as Vikings. Naturally there was also a Fair Maiden, played by Patricia Medina, horribly threatened in some ivory tower by a foul and lecherous knight and waiting for Alan Ladd's stunt double to leap a few parapets and rescue her. And it was at this cliffhanging point that the existing script came to a full stop.

The winter light was failing in Jermyn Street by the time Irving finished his digest of such notable events. He seemed reasonably calm for a man in the process of changing film and English constitutional history on such a heroic scale. There was no real problem in his view. My task, for which I was being suitably rewarded, was to resolve all the loose ends by Monday morning, give them sufficient pages to shoot during the critical period, and then to proceed on a day-to-day basis until completion.

'We have a slight situation with Ladd,' Irving said. 'See, under our deal he has script approval.'

'You mean he's approved it so far?'

'Well, yes and no. He doesn't concern himself too much with the details. Sue Ladd gives all the approvals. You go through her.'

'How does that work?' I said.

'You submit the pages to her. She okays them, we're back in the ball game.'

'And if she doesn't approve them?'

'You do another rewrite.'

'How about the director?'

'Listen, he'll be happy just to see pages. Don't complicate matters. Just put something down on paper and keep Ladd monosyllabic, don't give him any long fancy speeches. Got it?'

I nodded.

'You got paper?'

I nodded again.

'What're you waiting for then?'

I walked out into the night, treading a sombre route back to Albany. There I seized upon Roger's copy of *Morte d'Arthur*, put a blank sheet of paper in the typewriter, shook my blank head and wrote the first of many Forsooths. By a sustained act of desperation, working until late the following evening, I managed to produce half a dozen pages of inspired dross. I rang Irving to give him the good news. He seemed impressed and told me to take the pages round to Mrs Ladd at the Dorchester Hotel.

'I'll have a car to pick you up at seven tomorrow morning,' Irving said. 'You'd better work out at the studio from now on.'

I duly went to the Dorchester with my burnt offerings, and left them at the desk. In my innocence I did not wait to get word back from the oracle. That was the first of many mistakes.

Cubby's enormous Gestapo-like Mercedes was waiting for me in the Albany courtyard the following morning and I journeyed in some style to Pinewood Studios. There I was introduced to the director, Tay Garnett, and the rest of the crew who regarded me with mingled pity and contempt. I was given an office and ample supplies of paper and told to await the call. After an interval of some two hours I was summoned to Ladd's caravan on the set where I met him and his wife for the first time. Alan was polite, but distant, for which I don't blame him – he had, after all, problems above and beyond the normal call of duty; Mrs. Ladd, on the other hand, got straight down to business, dispensing with the social formalities.

'Alan Ladd,' she said, 'does not steal a horse, period.'

I looked round for an interpreter.

'I'm sorry, Mrs Ladd, I don't quite follow?'

'Get Irving Allen down here,' she said, firing her voice to some acolyte standing behind me. Irving duly put in an appearance together with Tay Garnett.

'What's the problem, Sue?'

'I'm telling you, Irving Allen, Alan Ladd does not steal a horse.'

'What horse, Sue? What're you talking about?'

'This Limey writer you got here, he's got Alan Ladd stealing a horse. He steals a horse, we lose the Boy Scouts Association of America. So unless you change it we're catching the next plane out of here.'

Irving was magnificent. He not only understood what she was talking about, he had the answer at his fingertips.

'He's not *stealing* a horse, Sue, he's *borrowing* a horse.'

'So show me the difference.'

Here I should perhaps let my readers in on the secret. My midnight oil, so painfully burnt, had illuminated the script with a scene of, I thought, great ingenuity. Alan, at the point where the previous pages ran out, had been trapped on the battlements of a flaming castle. My revisions required him to vault down into a conveniently placed wagon-load of hay, cut a Saracen *née* Viking in half with his double-bladed sword, seize the nearest horse and gallop across the rising drawbridge through a hail of arrows. Mrs Ladd obviously did not share my enthusiasm for the scene.

'Let me see the pages again,' Irving said, playing for time. He studied them with a reverence worthy of the First Folio.

'It's a good, ballsy scene, Sue, what more do you want?'

'I don't want him to steal a horse.'

'He's got to get out of the place, hasn't he?'

'Not on a stolen horse.'

'You want him to take a taxi?'

'That's your problem, Irving. I'm just telling you the way it's going to go. You keep the stolen horse in, you'd better look for another star because we're going to be on the plane.'

Irving, Tay Garnett and I retired to another corner of the stage to consider the ultimatum. To my growing amazement they discussed the situation rationally, but to be fair perhaps they had no alternative. Having listened to a series of insane counter-suggestions, I felt sufficiently light-headed to weigh in with one of my own. 'Why don't we,' I said, 'do it this way? The stunt double jumps from the parapet and lands behind the burning hay-wagon. Cut. Another angle, and Mr Ladd appears unscathed. He rushes up to the sentry and says: "Is this the horse I ordered?" The sentry is so taken aback – as indeed he might be – that he says yes. Mr Ladd jumps on to the horse and rides out, across the drawbridge and into the sunset. Dissolve.'

'I'll buy that,' Irving said.

Tay Garnett took his weary cue and nodded. We went back into the caravan.

'Bryan here has come up with the answer,' Irving said. He turned to me. 'Go ahead, tell them what you just told me.'

I launched into a repeat with even less conviction, fully expecting to be thrown out of the studio at the end of it, but to my total amazement the idiotic invention was listened to in respectful silence by the entire Ladd entourage.

'That solves everything, doesn't it?' Irving said when I finally got to the end.

'Tell me again, what's the line for Alan Ladd?'

The constant use of Alan's full name by his wife in his presence was strangely disconcerting, for it seemed to convey that he was both regal and non-existent.

'Is this the horse I ordered?' I said for the third time.

Mrs Ladd weighed it against the possible loss of the Boy Scouts of America. 'Yeah, I'll go along with that,' she said.

The entourage nodded at such wisdom.

'Okay,' Irving said, 'let's shoot it then, we've wasted enough time as it is.'

'It's never a waste of time to get things right,' Mrs Ladd said.

And in due course they shot it.

My tour of duty at the front lasted nearly seven weeks. Every day I was collected in the chauffeur-driven car and transported to my cell at Pinewood. I had no official status and indeed Mrs Ladd appeared never to know my name, mostly referring to me as 'the writer' or 'that Limey fixing the script.' I did manage to exchange a few words with Alan from time to time, and although I suspect that, like his wife, he was not quite sure who I was, he was always friendly in a distant sort of way.

The film contained several memorable moments, but the one I cherish most took place in the newly completed Abbey of Stonehenge. Irving was not the producer to do things by halves. For this sequence he had recruited the Westminster Choir and they followed the abbot singing a *Te Deum*. Alan, in his role as the simple village smithy, observed the proceedings at a discreet distance, and as the procession drew level he stepped forward and posed what I shall always consider an immortal question.

'My Lord Abbot,' he was required to say – though I will not claim authorship – 'this Christianity – can anybody join it?'

Ronald Adams, playing the abbot, paused, then handed Alan a copy of the St James's version of the New Testament and replied: 'Read this, my son, and have faith.'

I was bold enough to draw Irving's attention to the fact that within this hallowed scene he had brilliantly encompassed six hundred years of history and managed to get every single detail wrong.

'So who cares?' Irving said. 'They won't know the difference in Little Rock, and that's where it's going to take the money.'

My apprenticeship as a screenwriter on *The Black Knight* proved invaluable in later years. It was my bridge over subsequently very troubled waters. In the years that followed I encountered and worked through less arduous shambles, but nothing ever gave me the same feeling of doing a bad job really badly. The final postscript came when Alan Ladd took a full-page advertisement in the annual trade-bible, preaching expensively like many of his fellow actors to the already converted, announcing in the boldest type that he had just 'complated' *The Black Night*: whether the error was typographical or wholly Freudian we shall never know.

I found him a sad man. He seemed to get little or no enjoyment out of his work, living as he did in that twilight world between the hotel room and the studio stage. I recall that on one of my regular pilgrimages to his suite at the Dorchester to present my paltry wares, I was confronted by Mrs Ladd having a massage. She told me to read the script pages to her, but to read them quietly because Alan had just retired to bed. Perhaps taking pity on me, she then enquired whether I would like a cup of chocolate. I accepted gratefully and the waiter was instructed to serve it with the minimum of noise. What followed was like something out of a vintage Laurel and Hardy comedy. Reappearing with a loaded tray, the unfortunate man caught his heel in the carpet as he entered the room, did a variation of the 'Skater's Waltz' for a few yards, then completely lost his balance and shot the entire contents of the tray against the door of Alan's bedroom. Mrs Ladd's first concern was whether the incident had disturbed her husband. I was instructed to put my head round the bedroom door and find out. He was not in his bed. He was in the bathroom, shaving himself. The crash of crockery had triggered him like some Pavlovian dog. The sound of tea-cups meant only one thing: it was time to get up, shave and walk downstairs to the waiting car, the treadmill of the star living in isolation from most human comforts, condemned to the routine of luxury, to a life that began and ended with the pink pages of instructions written by strangers.

Thirty-five

As a reward for good behaviour Irving and Cubby kept me on the payroll and gave me another job. This was completely to rewrite the script of *Cockleshell Heroes*. I sat down at Roger's exquisite Carlton House desk and drew upon my own army experiences, since Irving had insisted that he wanted the true-life adventure spiced with humour. It was a good story, epitomizing as it did the dead-pan wartime heroics of our fighting forces. In this particular case the story centred around the exploits of Colonel 'Blondie' Hasler, R.M., who had conceived the idea of taking a team of canoeists up the Gironde to plant limpet mines on the German fleet at anchor. Within the framework I was licensed by Irving to take liberties.

I duly presented my first draft and was, I admit, fairly flushed with confidence, for it seemed to me to read very well. Irving liked the jokes but was less enthusiastic about the action sequences. He decided that he would send me and his associate producer, a kindly man called Phil Samuels, to Lisbon to look for suitable locations. So we caught the next plane and spent three weeks travelling up and down the Tagus which, as any student will tell you, has little in common with the Gironde. I went to my first bull-fight, loathed it and vowed never to go to another. Phil was a pleasant enough companion and became very excited about the possibility of using a Portuguese wind-mill as a hideout for the escaping Marines. On our return he sold Irving on this idea and I began again at page one and wrote an entirely different script set in an alien location. Irving seemed content to pay me my weekly stipend, and although I complained bitterly to Nanette about the mutilation of my first draft, I felt I had to weather these violent changes of direction.

About this time I felt that I could no longer take advantage of Roger's continued hospitality. Despite the fact that Nanette was a daily visitor, he had never complained and indeed the three of us – a somewhat unlikely trio in many respects – were constant companions. Since I had paid off all my debts and was once again solvent, I made a suitable contribution to the household budget, but it was hardly sufficient to repay Roger for his past generosity. So whilst he was away on a business trip Nanette and I completely remodelled his bathroom and brought it into the twentieth century. Albany is a distinguished address, but many of the chambers lacked creature comforts and Roger's previous bathroom was a somewhat austere room.

It seemed only right and proper that I should look around for more permanent quarters of my own, since I was confident that my divorce would be heard within the next six months or so and I had every intention of marrying Nanette the moment it was final. We eventually found an unfurnished flat in East Sheen, the upper half of a newly built detached house in a tree-lined street, with a shared garage and a modest rear garden. The rent was more or less within my means and we immediately set about collecting some decent furniture and carpets.

I remember that when we showed Roger around the bare flat for the first time he made a remark on a par with Marie Antoinette's much misquoted 'let them eat cake.' There was one spare guest bedroom in the flat and we were at some pains to assure Roger that he would be our first and most welcome guest. 'How odd,' Roger said, 'it'll be the first time I've ever slept in a room that faced on to a street.' It seemed then a perfect statement to come from the publisher of Nancy Mitford and we have never let him forget it.

Nanette and I still had to be circumspect about our relationship, for I had not yet come face to face with her father, but we were fortunate that, around this time, we were befriended by Mary and Johnny Mills. They lived quite close, in what I have always considered to be one of the most beautiful houses in England – The Wick on Richmond Hill.

Although I had known Johnny for some years I could not have claimed him as an intimate friend, but during this period we worked together on *The Colditz Story* at Shepperton and our relationship blossomed. It was on this same film that I got to know another dear and close friend, Lionel Jeffries. He shared my dressing-room at the studio and on the first day amazed me by calling me sir. He and his wife Eileen also lived on Richmond Hill – but in a basement, for they had just had their first child and money was short. Nanette and I spent many evenings in their basement living-room, cramped but consumed with the warmth of new-found friendship. Like Mary Mills, Eileen has always had the gift of making people feel welcome and both she and Lionel are instinctively generous people. They were heady days, days of promise and expectations fulfilled. There were parties at The Wick – Nanette, Eileen, Lionel and I very much the newcomers in the midst of such luminaries as the Oliviers, the Nivens, Deborah Kerr, Noel Coward, Emlyn and Mollie Williams, and Dickie and Sheila Attenborough (who were also Richmondites).

The house was always filled with the most exotic flowers and the sound of children – the three totally different, extraordinary Mills children, Juliet, Hayley and Jonathan. We would come away convinced that the Mills led the perfect life, for their halcyon existence at The Wick was repeated on the farm Johnny owned in Cowden. By some miracle of deceit and organization we would somehow manage to spend weekends there without Nanette's father being aware. It was an old Elizabethan house, totally different in character from the formal elegance of The Wick, but still possessed of the same warmth and family atmosphere. Whenever I think of those days we spent at Cowden I think of laughter: life was one long joke.

And then the spell was broken. Within the space of a few months, separation and death scattered the dandelion head of our happiness.

Jose Ferrer had been signed to direct *Cockleshell Heroes* and Cubby Broccoli phoned me on Christmas Day to say he wanted me to fly to Hollywood. A reservation had been made for me on the first flight out on Boxing Day. I packed that evening and managed to meet Nanette for a brief farewell.

It was a strange flight, with only seven fellow passengers on the plane, four of those being nuns who refused all food and sat, with heads bowed, counting their beads.

There were plastic Father Christmases on the manicured lawns of Beverly Hills when I arrived, and the sun was shining on the newly gifted Cadillacs. The studio had booked accom-

modation for me in the Sunset Tower, a tall block of apart-
ments which stands on the Sunset Strip close to the original
location of the *Garden of Allah*. It is a totally impersonal
building, half lodging house, half hotel. My suite gave me the
impression of being a waiting-room in the sky.

I presented myself at Ferrer's house the following day. He
greeted me with polite wariness. He was then at the height of
his film career, having won the Academy Award for his
performance as Cyrano a few years previously. He announced
that he wanted to start work on the script immediately and
then challenged me to a game of chess which he won with
ease. Like most of the Beverly Hills set he played games to win.
You 'killed' your opponent at tennis, or else you 'took him
apart' at golf: it was another extension of the rat race, there was
little or no real enjoyment in it and on most of the private
courts you could see the fashionable middle-aged lawyers,
agents and doctors hastening their inevitable coronaries with
set after set of gruelling competitive tennis.

Ferrer had offices on the Columbia lot on Gower Street, and
true to his word commenced demolishing the existing script
page by page the following morning.

I was back on familiar territory, albeit this time with a firm
contract, my name on an office door in the writers' block,
entitled to the statutory hired Cadillac for transport and one
anonymous secretary. The actual script conferences in Ferrer's
office were unfailingly boring. He usually spent the first hour
phoning all his cronies and comparing notes on various sexual
triumphs. The second hour would be occupied with a re-
capitulation of the previous day's efforts and by that time it was
time to break for lunch. We sometimes ate in the executive
dining-room where the legendary Harry Cohn held court in
front of a massive array of vitamin pills. It was considered a
rare privilege to be invited to these noonday seances. I went
in some trepidation the first time, but found the mixture of
fear and sycophancy slightly more nauseous than the actual
food and counted myself lucky that I wasn't a permanent
member of the charmed but charmless circle.

I can't pretend that in 1954 I was lionized by the hostesses
of Beverly Hills; I had to wait another decade before I was

accepted. My stay at the Sunset Tower was intensely lonely. I worked my way through two completely fresh drafts of the script which drifted farther and farther from the original conception in an effort to accommodate Ferrer in the central role.

Halfway through my stint I received a cable from Roger with the news that Nanette's mother had been taken to hospital for a major operation: she had terminal cancer of the stomach.

Knowing that Nanette was alone – her father being away on tour – I put in marathon spurts at the typewriter in an effort to finalize the script and return home. Before leaving London Irving had suggested that I write a role for myself as an actor, and I had constructed a showy, if minor, character that I felt suited my capabilities. For good luck I named the character Clarke. I chose my moment to mention Irving's suggestion to Jose Ferrer, and although his response was pleasant enough I must have unwittingly dropped my guard, for I failed to detect that there was nothing but ice behind his smile. We parted company on good terms and I caught the plane back to London.

I had spent every spare dollar from my allowance on exotic clothes for Nanette, but the joy of our reunion was clouded by her mother's condition, and most of the clothes I had bought her did not fit, for she had lost over a stone in weight from worry. She had been making the long journey to the hospital twice a day during the eight weeks I had been away, and the strain of watching her mother die like some object in a mad scientist's laboratory had proved almost unbearable.

Mrs Newman, having survived two major operations, lingered a few more days. She existed between clean sheets and had her recently whitened hair brushed every morning. All the niceties were observed with scrupulous devotion, every effort was taken to preserve the dying flame – only human dignity was disregarded. Nanette's nightly visits to her bedside became meaningless in human terms. It was like visiting a broken statue and for a long time after she died Nanette found it impossible to cry.

Naturally the tragedy of his wife's death brought Mr Newman back to England, and after the funeral we met for the first time. If he still harboured any suspicions about me, he concealed them well and from that moment until his own unexpected death less than a year after he buried his wife he accepted me. He was a darkly handsome man and bore a strong resemblance to Laurence Olivier. Basically lonely and chary of betraying any emotion, he dedicated himself to that now almost vanished world of vaudeville. When the variety theatres closed one by one he adapted his adagio act to cabaret and was much in demand for he was a polished and professional performer. Cabaret, as I know it, is a far cry from the glittering decadence of Bob Fosse's film of the same name. Indeed, I have always thought that cabaret artists should be recruited into the intelligence services, since they possess to a very high degree the ability to ignore humiliation and withstand physical and mental pain.

Now that we were free to meet as we chose, Nanette and I spent most of our spare time painting and furnishing the flat. I heard nothing from Irving regarding the fate of my script, and took a job as an actor in a prestige television production of *Crime and Punishment*. In my comparative innocence I allowed myself to believe that it was merely a question of marking time until *Cockleshell Heroes* went into production and covered me in glory. But Mr Ferrer had other ideas. He had arranged to have my last script completely rewritten by Richard Maibaum who in later years was to gain more public recognition on the scripts of many of the Bond films.

The role I had so carefully constructed for myself was given to Tony Newley, who went on to score a notable success in the film. Not surprisingly I was bitterly disappointed by this second betrayal. Bearding Irving in his office, I made out a passionate defence of my script, but to no avail. Irving wanted the quiet life. Ferrer was signed to direct the film, the start date had been agreed and Trevor Howard cast in the second starring role. Shortly afterwards the unit left for Portugal and my name was not even sharing the credit on the script they took with them.

With malice that I can still savour at this distance, I was delighted to be sent for a few weeks later. Irving confided that the revised script was not producing the comedy results he had expected. He asked me if I would consider rejoining the venture (without Ferrer's knowledge, of course) to work behind closed doors with Phil Samuels and attempt to put back into the film those ingredients so sadly lacking. I thought, why not? I certainly didn't owe Mr Ferrer any loyalties and there was something hideously attractive about Irving's blatant double-game.

It was my first practical introduction to film industry politics at Cabinet level. Phil and I reshot certain key scenes with a second crew behind locked doors while, on an adjacent stage, Mr Ferrer proceeded with his version in blissful ignorance. I was amazed that we got away with it as long as we did, but inevitably there came a day when one of the actors was inadvertently scheduled to appear in both versions and the cover was blown. A monumental shouting match took place between Irving and Ferrer, but Irving carried the day and Ferrer departed. The film was eventually finished and I was reinstated as co-author of the screenplay. It went on to become a modest artistic and commercial success.

Thirty-six

Long before *Cockleshell Heroes* was unveiled, rumour had it that I was a fast man with the pen and I was offered a succession of tawdry scripts requiring what is known in the vernacular as 'a quick polish'. I became for a time the fashionable script doctor, to be called in when the patient was faltering. It was badly paid, hack work and mercifully I received little credit for it, coming and going like some back-street abortionist.

One script I didn't work on was my own divorce court drama. I had taken the best legal advice and engaged counsel, for I was assured that, because of the niceties of English law my case was by no means open and shut. The onus was on me to establish beyond doubt the actual date of separation.

On the due date I presented myself at court, soberly dressed and suitably pale of face. My solicitor and counsel greeted me without enthusiasm. 'Not our lucky day, I'm afraid,' said counsel. 'The divorce judge has been taken ill and we've drawn Judge Leon.'

'That isn't good?'

'Difficult to say. Could be tricky. You're number fourteen on the lists, so it all depends what sort of lunch he has. Might be a good idea if you sat in court and had a look at some of the others ahead of you. Give you the feel of the thing.'

I was not called before lunch, but stepped into the witness box for the first hearing after lunch. My counsel duly began to take me through my statement. All went smoothly until we reached the passage where I gave formal evidence of adultery as substance to my plea for a divorce on grounds of desertion.

'Just a minute, Mr Moyihan,' the judge interrupted. He turned to me. 'How did you know your wife had committed adultery?'

'I asked her, sir, and she admitted it.'

'What did you say to her?'

'I said, did you have sexual intercourse with this man.'

'You said *what*?'

I repeated it.

'Do you always talk like that?'

'Well, naturally I expressed myself in more colloquial terms, my Lord.'

'That's what I'm asking you. What did you say?'

I appealed to counsel for help, but he was staring at his papers and did not meet my eye.

'I hesitate to use the exact words, my Lord.'

Counsel looked up. 'Oh, I think his Lordship's familiar with most of the Anglo-Saxon terms.'

'Yes, I don't want any time-wasting. Just tell the court what you said.'

I took a deep breath. The gentlemen of the Press had their pens poised.

'Well, my Lord, I said, did he fuck you?'

'Yes, fair enough. Carry on, Mr Moyihan.'

It is easy enough, twenty years after the event, with the offending word now partially sanctified by its inclusion in the pages of *The Times*, to dismiss my hesitancy as craven, but on the day, and in that witness box, playing to a packed house, I was humiliated.

My statement continued and in due course we came to the all-important passage concerning the date of desertion. Again Judge Leon halted the proceedings and turned his attentions to me.

'Did you ask her to come back to you on that date?'

'Yes, sir.'

'How did you do that?'

I took a much needed glass of water.

'I phoned her.'

'And what did you say to her?'

'I asked her if she was prepared to resume her marriage with me.'

'And what was her reply?'

'She said no.'

'And what did you say to that?'

'Nothing, sir.'

'Nothing?'

I had become somewhat bloody-minded by now, for I had been in the witness box for the best part of an hour.

'I was phoning long-distance, sir, and at one pound a minute there didn't seem much point in prolonging the conversation beyond that point.'

Judge Leon stared hard at me. I had visions of my case being thrown out of court and having to tell Nanette that she would have to wait at least another year. I later learnt that he was a stickler for establishing beyond any reasonable doubt that there was no collusion in the cases brought before him. Since 90 per cent of the average divorce cases of those days were collusive, Judge Leon's court was a court to avoid.

In later years he and I became firm friends and I reminded him of my experiences that day. He raised a gentle and surprised eyebrow and professed no memory of the case beyond my name. If he reads this perhaps he will forgive me for quoting him and take this memory of distant days as a tribute to his own brand of literary legal humour which I have always admired.

He accepted my answer that afternoon and in due course granted a decree nisi. With commendable reserve he declined to anticipate the permissive society in his judgement and thus the Press had little to report. They did, however, give us generous space a few days later when Nanette and I announced our engagement.

With some foresight we planned our marriage for 27 August. I had been signed to rewrite a new Rank film called *The Black Tent* which was to be shot in and around the Roman ruins at Sabratha in Libya. The producer was an amiable Irishman named William McQuitty and he generously agreed that I could have a double room in the location hotel. Nanette had never travelled abroad before and thus it seemed an ideal opportunity to get a cut-price luxury honeymoon.

The film was to be directed by Brian Desmond Hurst who enjoyed a fearsome reputation. In actual fact, although he had an acid tongue and a hedonistic approach to life and work, his bark was mostly blarney. He had obviously made up his mind in advance to dislike me. The original story for *The Black Tent* had been written by Robin Maugham, and because he is a fine craftsman it was very well constructed. For the cinema, however, it was somewhat literary and Bill McQuitty had engaged me to make the dialogue more colloquial. This had obviously offended Brian.

'Why have they given me a fifth-rate writer like you?' he said, declining to shake my hand.

I had been primed by Bill McQuitty and was ready for him.

'Possibly because you are regarded as a fifth-rate director,' I replied, and from that moment onwards we got on famously. The film had a distinguished cast which included Tony Steel, Donald Sinden, Andre Morell and Donald Pleasance. The only female role of substance was being played by an unknown Italian beauty called Anna Maria Sandri. Her English, alas, did not match her good looks, and when the film was finished Nanette revoiced her entire role.

We were married at Caxton Hall, with Roger as best man, and the following morning caught a plane to Tripoli.

It was late at night when we landed and Bill McQuitty, unfailingly courteous, was at the primitive airport to greet us. Exhausted as we were he insisted upon driving us on the longest possible route to the Waddan Hotel, claiming with typical Irishness that it was important for me to 'soak up the atmosphere' as quickly as possible. It was so dark I could see nothing whatsoever and the solid wall of kerosene-impregnated heat nearly obliterated us.

We had been given a pleasant double room with its own private bathroom and Bill had thoughtfully provided flowers and a bottle of champagne. Alas, the flowers were crawling with nameless insects and the champagne was on the boil and in fact exploded before we could uncork it.

It says much for Nanette that our marriage survived the honeymoon. She loves the heat, I am destroyed by it. My brain becomes totally addled and I become a slow-moving, inarticulate moron. Tripoli in August is very hot indeed. The fact that Nanette could sleep well and long in such conditions began to unhinge me. She swears that on one occasion she woke up to find me bending over her with a fixed, maniacal expression on my newly married face. According to her I said, 'I could easily go off you, you know, for sleeping in this heat.' Naturally

I remain convinced that the story is apocryphal, but the fact remains that few marriages can have been tested so severely. There was the nightly slaughter of the cockroaches in the bathroom; they exploded like rotten chestnuts when hit with the heel of a shoe. There was also the hazard of the evening meal for the same *plat du jour* had a disconcerting habit of appearing in different guises six days out of seven. One week, I remember, they wheeled in an enormous and anonymous white fish on the Monday night. By Friday it was fit only to serve to Burke and Hare and the legions of wild cats that haunted the veranda of the outdoor dining-room became ever bolder.

Reading the menu was perhaps the only constant pleasure, for in honour of the film unit it was painfully translated into English. Our all-time favourite was an item which stated: 'Our British guests can ate the salad with impunity. All the water-cress served in this hotel is grown in water passed by the Minister of Health.'

The film was being shot in the desert and one of the most dramatic sequences took place in the Roman city of Sabratha. I have always been fascinated by ruins (one of my favourite books is Rose Macaulay's *Pleasure of Ruins* and she quotes in it Thomas Whately's remark that 'a moment of antiquity is never seen with indifference').

Eventually the film progressed to the point where my services as an actor were required. I had one scene in which I repeated previous triumphs by playing a dying enemy soldier who is found and cared for by a brave British officer. In the script the soldier was German, but because we now had Anna Maria Sandri in the cast it was decided to duplicate the entire scene, with this time me playing the soldier as an Italian. Alas, keen students of the cinema were denied an opportunity to compare my two identical characterizations, for although Tony Steel and I sweated in each others' arms for the best part of three days, the sequence was cut from the final version. I have the cans of discarded film in my own vaults now, but I have never found the necessary masochistic courage to run them.

Thirty-seven

Immediately after our return Johnny Mills rang me to say that he had been asked to appear in a new film to which he was greatly attracted, but that he felt work needed to be done on the script. My initial reaction was tactfully cool, for I was depressed with patching-up other people's efforts. Johnny begged me to at least meet the producer/director Jay Lewis and, after some further persuasion, I agreed.

Jay had offices in Great Cumberland Place and the first time I presented myself at his address I collided with the broker's men in the doorway, for they were in the process of taking possession of most of his furniture. Jay was a total individualist, passionate about films, living from hand to mouth between productions, and unperturbed when the creditors threatened violence.

He greeted me sitting at a collapsible card-table on which was a portable typewriter, a bottle of whisky and an overflowing ashtray. I seem to remember that he offered the broker's men a drink before they departed and then turned to me for the more serious part of the proceedings. He was disarmingly frank. 'Whatever you do, I can't pay you,' he said, 'because I'm a bit pressed at the moment, as you can see. But don't let that worry you, because I'm going to make this film and we're all going to do well out of it.'

Squatting on the floor in that bare room he outlined the story he had in mind. It was an unashamed frolic built around a baby being inadvertently smuggled aboard a British cruiser. Jay had already collaborated with Commander Gilbert Hackforth Jones on a workmanlike script, but they had exhausted their invention and he was turning to me to inject more originality into the lower-deck characters, and in particular to create two contrasting star roles for Johnny Mills and Dickie Attenborough.

I had no formal contract, it was merely a gentleman's

256

agreement, but Jay had insisted that, as a return favour for my taking him on trust, I write myself a leading role. Despite recent experiences with Mr Ferrer, I was inclined to believe my luck this time.

Time was against us. Although he had no funds and had not signed the distribution agreement for the film, he was forging ahead in all directions and had already secured the co-operation of the Royal Navy.

Jay had marvellous ideas for comedy, and he could plot the progress of a running gag with pinpoint accuracy. More importantly to me, when my own ideas started to take shape, he proved a sympathetic and discerning sounding-board. Writing under pressure to a deadline has considerable disadvantages, for there is little room for experiment. The gods were with me on that occasion and I invented what proved to be a superb character for Johnny. I don't think I was so successful with the role I devised for Dickie who had to carry more of the straight plot than the comedy.

Right up until the eleventh hour Jay was alone in believing that he would raise the necessary money, but raise it he did, although he was forced to sign blood-letting personal guarantees. The technical crew was engaged, with veteran cameraman Harry Waxman heading it, and the first contingent flew to Malta to make the necessary preparations. It was there we were to pick up H.M.S. *Birmingham* before moving on to Naples for the other location sequences.

In due course Johnny, Dickie and I received our movement orders and caught a scheduled BEA flight direct to Malta. However, as soon as we were airborne the captain of the plane informed us that we were being diverted because of an air-controllers' strike in France. As a result of this first link in a strange chain of events, the plane put down for an unscheduled refuelling in Rome. Whilst we were on the ground sudden fog reduced visibility to nil and arrangements were hurriedly made for an overnight stay in a transit hotel.

I had never been in Rome before. Johnny, who knew it well, suggested that we have a night on the town and took us for a gourmet meal. The first person I saw as we walked into the restaurant was Connie.

I can't pretend that our chance meeting – the final sequence in an unbelievable series of coincidences – was anything but a profound shock. Connie came out of it the undisputed winner. We had to walk past her table to get to our own and she greeted me, after four years, with a fairly devastating remark. 'It's Bryan Forbes, isn't it?' she said. Not even Groucho could have followed that.

We landed safely at Malta the following morning and had the afternoon to ourselves. Dickie and I went for a stroll in Valetta and it was on this occasion that I coined a personal nickname for him that survives to this day. He stopped at the first confectioner's and came out with a bag containing six chocolate cream whirls. He offered me one and then, to my amazement, consumed the other five. 'My God, you're a Billy Bunter,' I said. He readily agreed with the justice of my description and Bunter he became and Bunter he has remained. Careful and diligent in all other matters, he is a slave to chocolate and has been known to steal his children's Easter eggs. When he is offered a dish of after-dinner mints it is like the day of the locusts. Cadbury's should put up a monument in his honour.

Thirty-eight

During the time *The Baby and the Battleship* was being shot at Shepperton, I was offered a long-term writing contract with the Rank Organization, largely through the good offices of Bill McQuitty. The starting money was respectable and rose, through annual options, to modestly important figures at the end of three years. I wrote five full-length original screenplays during the course of the contract, none of which ever saw the light of day, and what had started out with such great expectations degenerated into a weekly chore, for I landed back where I had started, merely doctoring other people's scripts.

Everybody at the Rank Organization couldn't have been nicer, especially the late Earl St John, that enigmatic quasi-Englishman who convinced most strangers that he was a distinguished member of the aristocracy, whereas his apparent title sprang from the same line as Duke Ellington and King Vidor. Earl was a survivor. Frequently out of favour with the higher echelons, he stepped into the wings on several occasions to allow more flashy luminaries to occupy the stage. And when they departed to scant applause, as depart they inevitably did, there was Earl, unruffled and word perfect, to resume a familiar role.

I certainly owe him more than one debt of gratitude, for in later years he gave me my first chance at direction. And when eventually I occupied a similar position at EMI, I often found myself thinking, how would Earl have handled this situation? He loved films, even bad films, and now when the industry is mostly in the control of men who treat films as just another commodity ('No different,' as Mr Nat Cohen remarked in an interview in *The Guardian* in 1973, 'from the manufacture of shoes, or any other product') one realizes what a giant Earl was.

I didn't survive to the end of my Rank writing contract, which was self-terminated at the end of the first year. Something in me instinctively revolts against security. I function better when I am alone and at bay. There have been many times in my life when I have willingly sacrificed enormous sums of money rather than surrender my artistic freedom. Looking back, I suppose I could be a rich man by now, but I don't think I would have been any happier. I like money, I get real enjoyment from spending it, but I am fortunate in that I have never lived in craven fear of not having any.

I took another acting job, going back to television to play opposite the American star June Havoc in Somerset Maugham's *Theatre*. The day after the transmission Nanette and I drew our remaining money out of the bank, which was all of a hundred pounds, and drove to the South of France to join Sheila and Bunter for our first real holiday together. We all stayed in a small family *pension* on the Plage de La Garoupe on Cap d'Antibes, that same little beach that Scott and Zelda created in the twenties, actually importing the sand. I remember that holiday as sheer enchantment. We paid our first visit to a casino and were immediately hooked. Having lost a few much needed pounds the first evening, we spent the following day devising what we fondly imagined was a fool-proof system to beat the house. I think, in retrospect, it was quite a brilliant system, but to operate it successfully required the resources of Onassis. We went back the following evening to risk another five, and because our stakes were so low the return was minuscule. We played all night with painstaking dedication to win twenty pounds. Remembering that return drive along the deserted coast road from Cannes to Cap d'Antibes, unsullied, in those days, by the hideous apartment buildings, I can so vividly recall our joyous intoxication. We had won, we had actually won. And the twenty pounds bought four extra days on the beach.

After the holiday I went back to my typewriter, this time to forge a screenplay from ex-actor Clifton James's true-life adventure *I Was Monty's Double*. I wrote this for Maxwell Setton, the producer of *Appointment in London*. He had signed Clifton James to recreate his wartime deception and the central theme seemed, after some research, to be less fascinating than the story of the actor himself. Clifton had sketched in his life prior to the escapade that brought him transient fame, and it was these authentic glimpses of the theatrical hinter-world – the seedy round of provincial theatres, digs and sleazy agents that I felt would give the film real substance. Alas, once again, I had little or no say in the final version that reached the screen. The director, John Guillerman, insisted that I tag on a totally fictitious last act which involved the false Montgomery being kidnapped by a German commando squad and his subsequent rescue by the hero (played by Johnny Mills). I wanted the story to follow what happened in real life. Here was an unknown actor who, by sheer chance, was plucked from obscurity and given a few days of total power (for of course during the period he was actually impersonating Montgomery the deception had to be absolute: anything less would have exposed the whole intricate scheme). Immediately following the deception he was more or less brushed aside. He received scant official recognition and in fact contracted tuberculosis from which he eventually died. It was a brilliantly conceived idea, brilliantly executed, and Clifton James, who was a gentle and kindly man, deserved a better fate. To me this was the real story to tell on the screen, something with a beginning, a middle and an end. The glossy, predictable fiction that Guillerman so willingly embraced reduced the film to just another *Boy's Own Paper* adventure.

Once again I was invited to play a part in the film, just a minor role of a young officer who helped in the rescue. I was broke at the time and foolishly accepted, for I failed to admit that I couldn't swim and the role called for me to kill two German commandos in the water.

The exterior sequences were shot off the Spanish coast and Nanette flew with me to the location. She was as terrified as I was when the day came for me to perform. It was early spring and the sea unbelievably cold, so cold in fact that Johnny and I consumed an entire bottle of Spanish brandy within the first two hours without any ill-effects whatsoever. I managed to get into the water and Johnny (who knew my guilty secret) kept me afloat for the necessary length of time without arousing the director's suspicions. But when I was required to swim alone and murder the German, the game was up. I either had to drown or else admit my deception. Through genuinely chattering teeth I stammered my apologies. John Guillerman took it very well in the circumstances, persuaded me to go back into the water for a few quick close shots and then used a double for the major part of the action. To have died by drowning playing a minor role in a sequence I abhorred would have been the supreme irony.

Thirty-nine

By the middle of 1957 I was convinced that my career was meaningless. Nothing I ever wrote reached the screen intact and I was never seriously considered for important acting roles. We had little or no savings, and inevitably, following long-established tradition in the theatrical profession, we had started to live beyond our means.

I think the real moment of truth came when I was sent for by a producer called Mario Zampi. My interview with him was like a parody of all those phoney films purporting to reveal what goes on behind the scenes in showbusiness.

To me it was just another casting interview. I had vaguely heard that it was to be a film starring Janette Scott for Associated British, but beyond that my information was scanty.

Having watched with familiar resignation a procession of other young actors troop in and out of the producer's office before me, I was curiously indifferent by the time my name was called.

Mario Zampi halted me in the open doorway.

'Stop there!' he said. 'Don't move!' He had a broken English accent which heightened the suspense.

Framing his fingers to simulate a camera viewfinder he advanced slowly towards me and examined me from all angles. Then he stepped back, as though from some hitherto undiscovered masterpiece.

'Our search is over,' he exclaimed. 'We have found the perfect face.'

He embraced me and planted two damp kisses on my cheeks.

'I am going to make you into a star,' he said. 'You are going to play the leading role opposite Janette Scott in my new film. It's a story about two young lovers who run away to Gretna Green to get married.'

'D'you think we ought to consider testing Mr Forbes?' the

casting director said. I immediately crossed him off my Christmas card list.

'Test, what for?'

'Well, you know, just to make sure.'

'There's no need to test, I am sure. Maybe a little make-up test, later, but this boy is a brilliant actor. And such a face. It is the face I have been searching for.'

He embraced me again. At any moment, I thought, he's going to ask me to run away with him to Gretna Green.

'You take the script. The part is yours.'

As soon as I arrived home Nanette and I sat down and read the script together. It became depressingly apparent to me after a few pages that the role and indeed the entire script was commonplace. Nanette said nothing, and we read on to the end.

'Well,' I said. 'It's not very good, is it?'

'It's not too bad, and I'm sure you'll bring something extra to it, darling.'

We indulged ourselves in this vein for half an hour, desperately grasping at non-existent straws.

Some instinct warned me not to shout the good news around town to our friends. A week went by. I heard nothing further from Mr Zampi or the studio, and whenever I phoned my agent, Olive Harding, she confessed that everybody was being a little circumspect.

Some ten days after a star was born in Mario Zampi's office the second assistant phoned me to say that I was required at the studio the following morning for a camera test. He gave me the time of my call, which was later than I was accustomed to, and this reassured me.

'It's obviously going to be all right,' I said to Nanette. 'They've obviously called a stand-in for the lighting and everything will be ready by the time I get there.'

I went to the expense of a chauffeur-driven hire car for the journey to Elstree. Nobody noticed this extravagance except a bored commissionaire in the entrance.

'Could you tell me where my dressing-room is?' I asked.

'What production?'

'The Mario Zampi film.'

'Oh, that. Look on the list.'

He pointed to the notice-board before going back to his football pools. I walked over and examined the Call Sheet. There was a list of some twenty juvenile actors called at intervals of twenty minutes throughout the day. My name appeared towards the end and I was scheduled to do my test later in the afternoon. I was sharing a dressing-room.

My first instinct was to turn and flee the building, but actors are nothing if not optimistic, and I convinced myself that I was still in there with a fighting chance.

I waited in my dressing-room and eventually, around four in the afternoon, I was called on to the set. The actual dialogue I had to speak in the test has mercifully been blotted from memory, but I remember that it was played on the battlements of a castle and ended with a kiss. I was introduced to Janette Scott, who had certainly earned her money that day. Mario Zampi greeted me with distant warmth and I got the impression that he wasn't sure quite who I was. With the minimum of rehearsal we plunged into a take on camera. It was mostly angled over my shoulder and on to Janette. As soon as it was finished, Mario Zampi said 'Print it,' and I said goodbye to Janette and goodbye to the cameraman and left the set as the next actor entered.

I went home in my chauffeur-driven car and went straight to bed. Nothing happened for about ten days and then I received a polite letter from the casting department, thanking me for giving the test but saying that, after mature consideration, it had been decided that Janette Scott could not receive her first screen kiss from a divorced man. They asked me to return the copy of the script.

That was my one and only experience of being a film star.

I remained totally out of work for the best part of three months and it became obvious that I had to rethink everything. Nanette and I discussed the situation from every angle, and although she constantly urged me to hold on, I felt that I couldn't just drift. That was not the destiny I had in mind all those years ago when I wrote to Lionel Gamlin.

Right out of the blue the owner of a local garage offered me a partnership. He was an elderly man and his only son wanted nothing to do with the motor trade. The father was bitterly resentful of this and put a generous proposition to me. If I took the position he would pay me £3000 a year and commissions and when he retired 50 per cent of the equity. It was certainly the most attractive offer I had received for many a year and I set about convincing myself that I could live outside my chosen profession without regret. Nanette tried to argue me out of it. We exhausted each other in endless discussions, and I can remember lying on the bed in that small apartment in East Sheen, drained and angry. The phone rang. It was a producer named Aubrey Baring, who had been Maxwell Setton's partner and was now working for Carl Foreman.

Was I free to accept a part in the new Carol Reed film *The Key*?

I dragged myself to a sitting position and forced my voice to sound normal.

It would be quite a long schedule, Aubrey said. He hadn't got the final breakdown and schedule in front of him, but he thought I would be required for the entire fifteen weeks. Beginning 17 July.

'July 17th?' I repeated.

'Yes. Are you free?'

I improvised brilliantly. Reaching down by the side of the bed I picked up a copy of the *Evening Standard*.

'I'll just check my diary,' I said. 'Excuse me just a moment.'

I waved Nanette to silence and rustled the pages of the newspaper close to the receiver.

'July 17th's a bit dodgy, I'm afraid. At the moment I'm committed up until the 19th.'

'Well, I mean, a day or two isn't going to make much difference,' Aubrey said. 'But you would be available beyond that, would you? because both Carol and Carl want you for the part.'

'Could I see a script, d'you think?'

Nanette was frantic by now, thinking that I was overplaying my meagre hand. But I had learnt to play poker from Raoul Walsh and I kept my cards very close to the chest.

'Yes, we'll send you a script and talk to your agent.'

We exchanged a few more pleasantries and then we hung up. I rolled off the bed and under the bed, totally delirious. Fifteen weeks in a Carol Reed film! It was like winning the Derby with your last pound at 100 to 1.

The script duly arrived and with it confirmation that terms had been speedily and generously agreed with Olive. I was disappointed when I read the script, because the part was small, but I was in no position to quarrel with that. I was to play the second officer on board a wartime seagoing tug, with William Holden as the captain of the tug. Trevor Howard, Kieron Moore and Oscar Homolka were the other male stars, and the female lead had gone to Sophia Loren. This was to be her first English-speaking role. The production had a large budget and was obviously destined to be an important film, for Carol Reed was at the peak of his fame.

Carl I had known first in Hollywood, during the time I was married to Connie. He had come to England during the McCarthy period and made his home here. This was to be his first independent production for his own company and *The Key*, taken from the Jan de Hartog novel *Stella* and an Eric Ambler script in the first instance (Carl subsequently rewrote it), represented a major change in his fortunes.

And as the time approached for the film to begin, our lives took another twist for we chanced upon a strange, ruined house that obsessed me like Manderly obsessed the heroine of *Rebecca*.

It was too large, it had been empty for five years and it was way beyond our means to purchase or sustain. But the moment I saw it I knew I had found my home, and although set down in print it seems Gothic and absurd, I was determined to let nothing stand in my way.

Forty

Seven Pines is a very ordinary name for an extraordinary structure masquerading as a house. It is situated in some eleven acres of land close to Virginia Water in Surrey – perversely situated, in fact, at just the wrong angle for the landscape. It was built in 1937 by an eccentric millionaire called Tommy Backhouse. Architecturally it is a mess from the outside and – the first time we saw it – looked a cross between a biscuit factory and an early Odeon cinema. But it had been placed in an unbelievably beautiful setting, perched high above a valley that contained a lake and an island. It was completely screened with rare trees and shrubs and although totally overgrown one could still discern the route of a magnificent beech walk, the original carriage drive of old Lady Wentworth. She must have crossed the lake in olden times for at the low water mark one can still see the rusting remains of the iron bridge supports, and if you follow the line of beeches beyond our boundaries they lead straight to Virginia Water church.

Although the exterior of the house has now been modified and softened, when we first parted the tall grass on the neglected drive it was pure red-brick horror. We had been taken to it by an estate agent friend called Timothy Tufnell. Somewhat dishonestly we had given him the impression that we were in the market for a house. He volunteered to show us a few neighbouring properties. He was either too polite to enquire or else he assumed me to be well heeled, for he took us round a succession of mansions, the cheapest of which was £40,000. We were too embarrassed to disillusion him, but were running out of plausible excuses when he suddenly suggested that, purely for amusement, we should inspect a derelict he had had on his books for years. He told us it was a complete white elephant, but he thought we would be amused by it.

The drive was completely blocked with self-seeded spruce and we left his car at the broken-down entrance gates and hacked our way through the undergrowth until the house came into view.

I have mentioned earlier that ruins have always held a particular fascination for me. Age and neglect seem to combine to induce in me a feeling of mystery I long to share. Seven Pines had this immediate effect.

All the locks had been broken by vagrants and we were able to wander inside the deserted shell. Timothy explained that it had once been the most luxurious home and that, although it was now but a shadow of its former self, it had been built regardless of cost at a time when materials were superb and labour was cheap. He told us that structurally it could not be faulted, although obviously the design was a matter of personal taste. He advanced the theory that Mr Backhouse had designed himself the perfect interior and then told his builders to 'brick it up.'

We spent an hour looking around the empty rooms. The dining-room divided into two by means of a substantial wall which could be made to rise from the cellars at the touch of a button. Apparently Mr Backhouse had enjoyed playing practical jokes on unsuspecting friends who came to dinner. The control button for the wall had been put in the floor by his chair, and when he judged his guests sufficiently off-guard he would activate the machinery in the cellar and then hugely enjoy the resulting amazement that the disappearing or emerging wall produced.

We went down into the cellars that first day, but they were under water and the massive electric motor that controlled the wall obviously beyond repair.

But if the house itself fascinated me, it was the land surrounding the house that destroyed my reason. It was like some enchanted garden that children carry with them into dreams after a bedtime story. Indifferent squirrels criss-crossed ahead of us as we struck out and explored in the direction of the lake. Blue Pacific pines dotted the slopes of the valley, standing dwarfed beside clipper masts of Scotch and Douglas firs. There were plantations of silver birch, and perfectly placed weeping willows along the banks of the lake. There was a log boat-house and a curved wooden bridge leading across to the island, a bridge of curious design and seemingly spanning the water without visible means of support. The once perfect lawns had reverted to reed grass that slashed at our ankles and faces, grass so tall that it could easily conceal a fully grown adult. There was mystery in the garden, it seemed totally isolated from the main road we had but recently left, and when we stood on the island and looked back at the house it seemed buried in greenery and vivid colour like some Xanadu.

The asking price was £29,000. I must have been mad because when Timothy said that any genuine would-be pur-chaser could get it at a slightly lower figure – say £27,000 – I apparently agreed it was worth every penny. And there, for the moment, we left it.

I could talk of nothing else. The need to own the house grew in my mind like some benign tumour. I returned to it time and time again and some weekends Norman and Nona would join us and we would picnic in the vast deserted living-room. I began to assume pride of ownership and talked of the house to strangers as if it was already mine. Unbeknown to Nanette I carried out investigations and discovered that the house was empty because of a bankruptcy sale. With a little more probing I learnt the identity of the foreclosing mortgagee. It happened to be Barclays Bank. I had a friend in Barclays Bank who was an area manager. I rang him, explained the problem and asked if he could give me any hope. He called me back a few days later and said that it would be totally unethical and more than his job was worth to part with confidential information, but he could say that the property had been on the bank's books for some years, they were heartily sick of it and that any reasonable cash offer would be seriously entertained.

What did he mean by 'any reasonable cash offer'?

He could not be more specific.

I had spent a great many hours doing intricate calculations, budgeting every item for months to come, and allowing for the payment of known debts I had decided that by the time I had finished *The Key* I would have a surplus of £1000.

That being so, I had the nerve to ask my friend whether Barclays would consider £1000 to come under the heading of 'reasonable'.

He didn't think so, somehow.

'Look,' he said, 'go away and think about it. Raise as much as you can and then come back to me. I promise that I'll get your offer considered, whatever the amount you finally manage to raise.'

I explored every usual avenue. I tried to borrow the money from a number of building societies. I went to my own bank and asked for an overdraft. I went cap-in-hand to less attractive moneylenders. But actors were not thought to be good risks and I made no progress.

Now my mania reached certifiable proportions. Nanette was resigned and guardedly critical, but since she was convinced that I had lost the day she was content to humour me. I was near total despair when I suddenly thought of Roger. I showed him the house and explained the situation. He thought about it overnight and then told me he was willing to sell certain securities and give me a private mortgage for £7000 at a fixed interest of 5 per cent secured by my one and only insurance policy. It was an act of faith and great generosity, but utterly typical of him, and I remember he almost apologized for asking for interest, as though he was somehow driving a hard bargain.

The auction took place at the old Station Hotel at Sunningdale. It seemed a curiously anonymous place in which to decide one's future home. Nanette and I took our places to one side at the back of the room and tried not to catch the eye of any of the professionals.

Timothy was quietly assured and the proceedings started very casually. I think he opened the bidding at £3000 and the price moved upwards in £250 jumps. I held Nanette's hand and hoped that we did not betray our mounting anxiety. The price moved to £5000, then to £5500, faltered around £5800 and then reached the figure at which it had been decided I should make my first bid. For one awful moment I thought Timothy had forgotten for it seemed to take an age before I could catch his eye.

'Seven thousand,' I said.

The room appeared to go very quiet, and one or two people looked in our direction for the first time.

'I have a bid of seven thousand at the back of the room,' Timothy intoned. 'Who will give me seven five?'

A voice said, 'Seven four.'

Timothy looked to me.

'Seven five,' I said.

Pause.

'Any advance on seven five?'

'Seven eight,' the same voice said.

Back to me. 'Eight thousand,' I said in a very small, still voice.

'I have eight thousand at the back of the room. Against you, sir.'

I couldn't see the man's face, but after another agonizing wait, he spoke again. 'Eight two fifty.'

Nanette's nails bit into the back of my hand.

'Eight four,' I said, unable to stop myself.

Timothy looked to my opponent. 'Against you, sir.'

The man took his time, but finally shook his head.

'Any advance on eight four? Going at eight four . . . Going at eight four, then . . . Sold to Mr Forbes.'

The mallet descended. And in the same stunned moment that I realized Seven Pines was publicly and legally mine, I began to comprehend that I had gone four hundred pounds beyond my resources.

As we were leaving the auction room a total stranger approached us.

'I wanted that,' he said. 'D'you want to resell?'

'I've only just bought it.'

'Yeah, I know that, but I wanted it, see. I came late. Here, I'll give you a quick profit.'

He produced a wad of soiled five-pound notes.

'Give you a thousand over the odds. That's fair, isn't it?'

Nanette clutched my arm again. It was very tempting, but I hesitated only a second.

'No,' I said. 'I've bought it and I want to keep it.'

We walked out into the daylight towards the real nightmare.

Forty-one

For eighteen months we lived with newspapers on the floor and for six of those eighteen we were without heat, light and toilet facilities. The entire contents of our little flat in East Sheen didn't furnish one room at Seven Pines. At times we felt like the peasant victors of some uprising camping out in the vast Imperial Palace.

Poor Nanette suffered most during those early months, because it fell to her to manage the move single-handed. By the time we had completed all the legal formalities I was in Weymouth on location for *The Key*, spending fourteen hours a day packed with sea-sickness tablets. I am not one of Nature's sailors at the best of times, and we were required to head for the Portland Race every morning where our small but ocean-going tug stood on its end in the roughest seas we could find. Carol was determined to make the film as authentic as possible, and since the story demanded that the tug seek out and find crippled merchant ships, much of the action was spectacular and highly dangerous. He was the worst sailor of all and seemed to have a mental block about the mechanics of operating a ship at sea. He was consumed with his own private visions, and once he had decided how he was going to shoot a particular sequence he couldn't understand why some of his instructions were impossible to carry out. He thought that if he shouted 'Stop' the real-life captain of the tug could apply disc-brakes. Yellow of face, chain-smoking and denying himself any solid sustenance, he stared without comprehension while those around him argued the impossibility of his suggestions.

There was one classic moment when we had secured the services of a Royal Navy submarine which was masquerading as a German U-Boat for the purposes of the film. Bill Holden and I were on the bridge and the submarine was surfaced and awaiting orders from Carol. The string having gone in his legs from a prolonged bout of sea-sickness, he clutched the rail with one hand, and held the camera-viewfinder to his eye in the best Nelson tradition.

'This is the shot, Ossie,' he said to our principal cameraman Oswald Morris. 'The U-Boat comes up there, and we pan across to hold Bill and Bryan in a tight two-shot as they stop the tug and open fire with the Bofors gun. That's it.'

Ossie knew enough by now not to offer any immediate doubts.

'Be a very good shot, Carol.'

'Yes, yes, marvellous. Give me the megaphone.'

He addressed himself to the commander of the submarine across the waters.

'You'll surface there, where you are, if you'll mark that, Captain.' Then he turned to the captain of the tug, a stoical individual who had developed a sense of humour as self-protection against the insane collection of people he had on board.

'And when that happens – we'll give you a cue, of course – you stop. Stop everything.'

In his excitement he forgot his sea-sickness and was smiling at everybody.

'I stop the tug, do I?'

'That's right. Marvellous shot.'

'What d'you think I am, the last tram-driver? I've told you before, sir, I can't stop this bloody thing to order.'

'But it's imperative to the shot,' Carol said. 'Otherwise it won't work.'

The captain left the bridge in disgust. Carol was perplexed but not alarmed at this stage. He turned back to the submarine and raised the loud-hailer again.

'You quite clear, are you, Captain?'

The answer came back across the water loud and clear.

'Are you some sort of berk, or what?'

'What's he say?' Carol enquired.

Bill and I shook our heads.

'I don't think he heard you, Carol,' Ossie volunteered.

'I said it plainly enough. You try.'

Ossie took the loud-hailer. 'Sir, Carol would like you to come to the surface where you are now . . .'

'Tell him to mark it, mark the spot,' Carol interjected.

'Yes, if you could spot that on your charts.'

We waited.

'Look!' the submarine commander replied. 'I don't know what sort of jokers you've got on board there, but if you think I can bring this up from the bottom on a sixpence, you've got another think coming. It'll be a bloody miracle if I get within half a mile of it.'

'What's he saying?' Carol asked.

'Not too happy about it, Carol.'

'Well, explain the shot to him.'

'I don't think he actually appreciates the subtleties of the shot. Perhaps we ought to give him a little more flexibility.'

'Ruin the shot,' Carol said. 'He'll understand. You go over it with him.'

Carol disappeared as nausea took priority. Bill and I exchanged anxious glances with the camera crew.

'Go on, Ossie,' Bill said. 'You explain it to them. You heard Carol, it's quite easy. The submarine comes up and stops there – have the chippies put down some camera tape to give him a mark. You pan, tight two of Bryan and me as I stop the tug on another mark, and the Bofors gun which has never fired since 1939 will then open fire and with any luck blow us all out of the water. Fantastic shot. Carol gets the Academy Award, we get a burial at sea with full honours, and Columbia go out of business. Meanwhile, I'm going below to have a cup of coffee.'

Very wisely, Ossie didn't attempt any further explanation but handed responsibility to the first assistant. With commendable devotion to duty, he made one further effort to convince the submarine commander, but without success.

A few well-chosen words whistled back across the waters and the submarine turned and headed home for Portland. Carol never got over it.

Meanwhile, back at Seven Pines things went from bad to worse. I had bought the house without a survey, taking Timothy's word for it that the structure was sound. He had not told a lie. The actual bricks and mortar were solid enough, but the interior was a shambles. No plans existed, for the original builder had gone out of business during the war and all records had been destroyed in the Blitz. The house had originally been heated by two massive gas boilers generating sufficient power to move the *Queen Mary* out of dock. They had been reduced to red-rust and the Gas Board immediately condemned them. Most of the bathroom fittings had been stripped out by thieves during the time the house had stood empty. There were no lights and the first electrician we contacted for an estimate told us that everything would have to be rewired and that the job would necessitate nearly four miles of cable. Between the time of the auction and the day we moved in, all the lead had been stripped from the roof. In fact the only thing that worked was the gas stove we had brought with us from East Sheen. This stood in solitary splendour in the middle of the enormous kitchen.

We made endless mistakes that first year. The only help we had in the house were a couple we had engaged before the event. We had never had permanent staff before and Mr and Mrs Miles had never been in service before. Alice Miles proved to be an extraordinary little lady, the possessor of truly hidden talents. She had had one lung removed as a result of tuberculosis but had true Cockney grit and was a stranger to self-pity.

Nothing went right at first, but I was too stubborn and proud to admit defeat. Every spare penny I had was ploughed back into the house. I accepted any writing job that was offered to me. Friends couldn't believe we were actually living in the house, though we rapidly became oblivious to the impoverished surroundings. We bought bits and pieces of furniture from junk shops and ate in the kitchen by candle-light. We even had the nerve to put a divan in one of the bedrooms and invite Roger to be a weekend guest. There were no carpets on the floor and water for bathing had to be boiled on the gas stove and carried upstairs by hand. But we placed a full bottle of whisky on Roger's makeshift bedside table and, taking into account that he was not looking out on to a road, he professed himself very comfortable.

In order to conserve my limited funds I gave the main contract to an engaging character called Len. He had some nice embossed visiting cards and I hired him under the impression that he was the managing director of a concern the size of Bovis. This was a major overestimate, for Len's building firm consisted of Len and a bovine youth who enjoyed the nickname of Gladys.

One thing I will say, nothing ever fazed Len. He was not a rogue, for he went bankrupt as a result of two and a half years' work at Seven Pines. He was just an incorrigible optimist and could never admit that any job was beyond his experience. Certain things he did superbly well and for the first few months we were prepared to believe that he was a genius. Gladys, on the other hand, left much to be desired and had, in the course of a tortured apprenticeship, developed only one talent – that of breaking everything he touched.

Perversely, against all the evidence, I enjoyed every minute of those early months. There were many times when I had no idea how I was going to meet some of the bills, for none of the work was straightforward, and it seemed that just when we had overcome one major problem another would be uncovered.

The great day finally arrived when the newly installed boiler was switched on and we enjoyed the bliss of unlimited if expensive hot water. This was, perhaps, Len's greatest triumph, for he had been working by guesswork and rule of thumb, the heating system plans having been destroyed. We still had no carpets, and the furniture was dotted about the main rooms as in a warehouse, but we had introduced some colour into the house. The cellar was pumped dry and Len made it a point of honour to get the disappearing wall to function again. The whole house was still a folly, but at least it was home.

We still survive. I write these words in the new study I built four years ago on part of the terrace which overlooks the lake and which is pierced by a two-hundred-year-old pine of enormous girth. Like everything associated with Seven Pines, this tree is a contradiction. Any builder will tell you that, by rights, a tree of this size should have fractured the very foundations by now. It is a standing joke that I am a frustrated landscape gardener – Capability Forbes, as Tessa Kennedy nicknamed me. I know exactly what I would do if I ever won the treble chance on the football pools. Having taken care of all my nearest and dearest, I would spend the rest with an easy conscience, summoning a veritable herd of bulldozers to shape and mould my vivid dream. I have a water garden in my mind's eye, starting at the head of the valley just below the most magnificent of my pines, which would descend in gentle stages to where the lake begins. I would install great pumps to re-circulate the lower water and build a flight of stone stairs from the terrace, flanked and guarded by romantic statues. I would have the whole lake drained and scrubbed and then restocked with fish that would never be caught. I would buy the best sea-turf and resurface much of the lawns, then keep them manicured; place Gothic dovecotes all about them, white against the lush green. I would spend every penny preparing vistas I would never live to enjoy in full and consider myself fortunate and privileged.

Forty-two

1958 was an auspicious year, for it marked the formation of Beaver Films, the company that publicly cemented my private friendship with Bunter. I think it was Nanette and Sheila who ended our search for a suitable name, saying that since we worked like beavers we might as well admit to the fact.

The need to have a professional partnership stemmed from a growing and shared dissatisfaction with the state of the film industry and our respective roles within the industry.

Having made the decision to become producers, we were at a loss to know what to produce.

The irony of it was that all the time we were searching for an original idea we rudely ignored a suggestion of Nanette's. She brought a newspaper to me one day and pointed to a small paragraph tucked away in the middle pages. It concerned a man who had been ostracized by his workmates – 'sent to Coventry' as it was then termed. I read it without enthusiasm and when Nanette insisted that this was the sort of story we ought to tackle, I was less than kind. Then I forgot about it. We spent some months trying to drum up finance for a film showing the evils of apartheid, but without success, for then, as now, the subject was considered too risky for the commercial cinema.

We struggled to make a living, Bunter taking another acting job in a film called *Sea of Sand*, directed by ex-cameraman Guy Green. His co-stars were John Gregson and Michael Craig. During the long hours spent waiting on location for the right weather, Bunter, Michael Craig and Guy Green compared notes as to the present discontent. It appeared that Michael Craig had written an original synopsis in collaboration with his brother (who, confusingly enough, was called Richard Gregson).

On his return home Bunter handed me this synopsis and said that if I liked it we could buy it. If we bought it Guy Green wanted to direct it.

The title of the synopsis was *The Man Who Was Sent to Coventry*.

I read it and became excited by the idea, which naturally led me to apologize to Nanette.

We had a formal meeting and agreed to purchase the film rights from Richard and Michael. I was somewhat wary of Richard at our first meeting, for he has qualities that immediately inspire respect. He was later to become the best agent in town in partnership with Gareth Wigan.

I immediately set to work in the bare dining-room at Seven Pines and produced the first draft within three weeks. I gave a reading of it after a dinner-party at Guy's house, after which it was carefully pulled to pieces. However, there was nothing for me to resent in the post-mortem because for the first time in my life I was working with fellow professionals and their criticisms were put forward in a genuine effort to arrive at something constructively superior. Bunter elected to be the salesman, correctly judging that his tolerance was greater than mine. But even his unflagging optimism wilted as he peddled *The Angry Silence* (which was the title I had given the script) up and down Wardour Street. We were not brutally rejected. In the majority of cases the script was returned with enthusiastic comments, but to a man the various potential financiers were scared of the subject. This wasn't some safe comedy about the British working class, nor was it that other standby of the British cinema, the quasi-*This Happy Breed*.

I am not saying that my script succeeded where others had failed. All it did was to break a few of the taboos, and in the language I used I perhaps got closer to colloquial working-class speech than some of my contemporaries writing directly for the cinema. That was the extent of my aims and the sum total of my achievement. The title passed into the language.

It took Bunter fourteen months to raise the necessary finance for the making of the film. Most of the pre-production comments suggested we tone down the content or else give it a happier and more conventional ending. We resisted both schools of thought and declined to compromise. My own enthusiasm waned. The real credit for the making of the film must go to Bunter, for with commendable cunning he finally achieved success by inverted moral blackmail. The directors of British Lion had been extravagant in their praise of the script but voted against giving a distribution guarantee because they felt the budget was too high. With a persistence I could admire but not emulate, Bunter went back to them and put the fifty-dollar question. If a price of £160,000 was too high, at what price would they give the go-ahead? Although doubtless the directors of British Lion could smell the bait in the trap, they felt confident in giving their answer. They would make it for £100,000.

When Bunter returned with this qualified approval the rest of us were inclined to write it off to experience. We had underestimated his tenacity. He used some moral blackmail on us in turn, and proved to us that it could be done on a co-operative basis. If Guy Green, Pier Angeli, Michael Craig, Bernard Lee and myself would agree to work for a standard flat fee of £1000, he would produce and star in the film for no salary whatsoever, merely taking a slightly larger proportion of the hypothetical profits. By this approach he was confident we could bring the film in at the magic figure of £100,000. We had no counterargument and he started to work on his sums. He admitted later that he put the proposition to us on the spur of the moment and that it was only later that he seriously considered the viability of his own case. I never underestimated him again.

The final audited cost of the film was £97,981, an unbelievably low figure even in those days for a full-length first feature film.

Much of his enthusiasm rubbed off, and by the time the unit assembled in Ipswich for the location sequences there was a shared feeling of being involved in something special, an experiment that could well revitalize the flagging film scene. The film was tightly budgeted and scheduled, with no safety margin for errors or acts of God. If it rained we had to shoot in rain. As it happened we started the longest exterior sequence in foul weather and then had an embarrassment of sun. Normally, when such a thing happens, you go back and reshoot the first day's work, but our budget did not allow of such conventional luxuries. Instead, Arthur Ibbetson, our gifted cameraman, constructed vast screens to blot out the sun, a device which doubtless convinced the Ipswich spectators that film people were totally mad.

It was a strange period for Bunter and me. Films take a long time to make, and the enthusiasm that sustains during the actual shooting period gets diluted during the cut and thrust of the editing period. We were fortunate in having Tony Harvey as our editor. We had chosen him against the competition of more mature and illustrious names because he was so obviously in love with film.

During the editing period we were often perilously near the bread-line. The other actors, of course, had long since departed and were earning their living in other films and plays. Bunter, on the other hand, was still a full-time unpaid producer with creditors at the door. But he was totally single-minded and refused to entertain outside offers. I was slightly more fortunate in that I could always write in the evenings, and for a time my earnings, such as they were, subsidized both of us. I don't want to give the impression that I was the affluent member of the partnership allowing Bunter to exist on charity. Our friendship was such that it was accepted without discussion that whoever had the money shared it. When times were hard for me, Bunter wrote the cheques, and when I was in funds I paid some of his bills. If Nanette and Sheila ever questioned us too closely we turned bland faces towards them and lied. There seemed no point in revealing the truth about our joint finances, for the two girls would only have worried to no good purpose. I remember it as one of the bleakest but happiest periods of my life.

The completed film was screened for numbers of opinion makers and Bunter and I were much encouraged by the response. Privately we had many reservations about it. As always happens during the editing period, there had been many minor shifts of emphasis. Certain actors were stronger than others and thus their performances had added weight where none had been intended. Guy had concealed some of the inadequacies of my script and perhaps highlighted others. We would all like to have our time over again, but the choice is never there. You have made a film, you have spent the money, and the moment arrives when you have to reveal the result to friends and foes alike.

The film opened at the old Plaza cinema, following a dignified press campaign. We had no flamboyant premiere, but British Lion gave us the circle seats and we invited all the crew and cast and their families, and anybody else who had shown faith in us.

'Win or lose,' I said to Nanette, 'let's wake up at the Ritz.' My flamboyant gesture carried with it echoes of Scott and Zelda; there was a conscious desire to emulate the Jazz Age on a very modest scale. I therefore scraped together enough money to book a double room at the Ritz for one night. We changed into evening clothes and made our way to the Plaza in a taxi, lacking the funds for the statutory limousine.

The cinema was crowded and there was an air of genuine excitement and goodwill. Looking at the photographs of the period, both Bunter and I seem absurdly young, our faces blobbed white by the flashlight guns and curiously devoid of any character, wiped clean of past fears and future hopes – one might be looking at two total strangers.

The film went well and received sustained applause at the end. Afterwards we took a taxi to Fleet Street to wait for the first editions. We read them on the pavement and found ourselves acclaimed in wildly extravagant terms. It seemed, at long last, a moment for celebration without regard to cost, and I therefore announced that we would return to the Ritz and drink champagne.

The night porter at the Ritz, totally unaware of our new fame, brought us swiftly to earth again. When I asked for the key to our room and for champagne to be provided, he stared past me at Sheila and Nanette.

'You can't take *them* upstairs,' he said.

It didn't register for a moment. I even glanced over my shoulder, thinking that we had been joined by outsiders. Bunter was also taken, momentarily, off guard. Then, as if rehearsed in some ancient double-act, we both spoke at once.

Bunter said, 'How dare you?' and I said, 'What d'you mean, *them*?'

'Them,' the porter repeated. 'Women aren't allowed in the rooms at this time of night.'

'Them – those women – that woman, happens to be my wife,' I said. I realized that it wasn't a very original line from England's newest and most brilliant screenwriter.

The porter merely snorted in disbelief. It was an astounding moment and Bunter and I were unequal to it.

We both became very angry and in the best tradition demanded to see the manager. The porter remained unimpressed and merely repeated once again that he had his orders and wasn't about to flout them. I seem to remember that the dialogue then took an ugly turn, certain foul oaths being exchanged. Bunter, casting aside his recent performance as the little man who rejected violence as the answer to mankind's dilemma, threatened to punch the porter. I was equally aggressive and introduced a note of comedy into the proceedings by asking the porter to note how we were dressed, as if that had any significance. I also produced the newspapers and found myself expostulating, 'You don't seem to realize who we are. We had our film open tonight and we got great notices.' But such is the power of the London critics that even this left him unmoved.

After fifteen minutes of unseemly slanging we grabbed the keys to the room and marched upstairs. Once there we rang room service and requested our champagne. The wine cellar was locked and in the end we had to settle for hot chocolate, which we drank sitting on the edge of the double bed. We recovered sufficiently to see the funny side of the episode, but it was a damp end to an otherwise memorable evening, and I have never felt the slightest inclination to stay at the Ritz again.

Forty-three

In order not to confuse the narrative, I deliberately confined the preceding chapter to the story of *The Angry Silence* from the original idea to the opening night. But now it is necessary to go back and pick up the other threads of my life during this period.

Seven Pines was still a half-finished monument to optimism. We had accumulated a few more pieces of furniture, mostly cheaply acquired in village junk shops and country auctions. Nanette and I weren't very successful at auctions, seldom consulted each other and on at least two occasions bid against each other in ignorance. I once returned home with a mammoth collection of tins, three broken deck-chairs, a prototype sewing machine and a stuffed bird, having spent the whole afternoon trying to acquire a second-hand pram.

We needed the pram because Nanette was happily pregnant. I find the subject of pregnancy difficult to write about with any originality. Nanette has always been beautiful in my eyes, but I was totally unprepared for the added quality that her pregnancy bestowed. She became mysterious and still, the sort of beauty that Coppard sketched in subtle tones in so many of his neglected stories. The setting of Seven Pines lent enchantment to our happiness. There was a sense of isolation, we seemed divorced from the rest of the world. It was a hot summer and the grass by the lake was tall and burnt. I can remember us walking through it, planning for the child she carried so easily, and I can remember being amazed by her serenity, for I was prey, as other males before me, to many fears.

Acting according to convention rather than conviction I bought Nanette a dog during the early months of her pregnancy – a Labrador of impeccable pedigree we named Sam. Impending parenthood made idiots of us both and Sam swiftly took advantage. He proved impossible to house-train and we were finally **driven** to admit **defeat** and solicit the aid of a kennels.

The owner of the kennels was confident of success. 'We have never had a failure,' he said proudly. 'In two weeks, when you come to take him home again, you will have a new dog. Obedient, completely house-trained and a model of behaviour.' Sam was put behind bars and did his impersonation of a prisoner in Colditz as we made a guilty retreat from the scene of our crime.

Nanette cried all the way back to Seven Pines.

At the end of the scheduled two weeks the proprietor telephoned us. 'Sam is a highly intelligent dog,' he said, 'and is possibly resisting our well-tried methods of instruction. If you have no objection, we should like to keep him in for a further week, just to make sure of complete success.' Board and lodgings cost eight guineas a week. We agreed to a third week.

Complete success eluded Sam for a further two weeks beyond the three, and at the end of five weeks a demented voice pleaded with us to come and collect him before he destroyed the morale of the rest of the school. Sam had learnt nothing. At the command 'Sit!' he jumped on to your shoulders. When you told him to 'Stay!' he bounded out of sight. He was a hopeless case. He was also an incorrigible thief and would eat anything left within reach.

Perhaps his most spectacular feat was to eat a three-pound box of chocolates complete with wrappings. This slowed him down and he retired to his basket with a reproachful expression, obviously blaming us for putting such temptation in his path.

He was still there a few hours later and this was sufficiently out of character to cause Nanette some concern. 'I don't think he's at all well,' she said, sympathy having replaced her earlier anger.

'You wouldn't be at all well,' I said, 'if you'd eaten three pounds of Black Magic at one session.'

Nanette examined him more closely.

'There's a lump on his shoulder.'

I looked. I felt. There was a lump.

'D'you think he's done something awful to himself?'

We called the vet. He gave Sam an emetic and assured us

that Nature assisted by the potion would put things to right.

Nothing happened. We phoned the vet at midnight. 'Listen,' he said, 'there's no way that dog can hold on to what he's got. I gave him a dose strong enough to make an elephant abort. It's just a matter of time.'

The following morning Sam was still in his basket, nothing had happened, but he appeared to be in a coma. It was then that Mrs Miles enquired the whereabouts of a skewered shish-kebab she had left in the larder. Nanette and I exchanged glances and I rushed to phone the vet again.

'The elephant,' I said, 'hasn't aborted. I think you'd better come round quickly.'

When he arrived we told him of the missing shish-kebab. He examined Sam again. 'Good God!' he said. 'I can feel it. He's swallowed the bloody lot, skewer and all.'

Sam was speedily transported to the Royal College of Veterinary Surgeons. There he underwent a lengthy and expensive operation at the hands of Professor Knight. The metal skewer had somehow found its way into his lower intestine, miraculously avoiding damage to any vital organs on the journey down. It was eight inches long and I have the X-ray to prove it.

When we collected him he was still dopey from the anaesthetic, but with the same remarkable fortitude that had been the despair of the kennel owner, returned to his usual ebullient self on the journey home, and the moment he entered the house devoured two steaks and a whole Hovis loaf from the kitchen table.

Being a glutton for punishment around about this time, I decided that I would supplement my income and improve my own breakfast table by becoming a chicken farmer. Nanette was understandably dubious. 'You don't know anything about chickens,' she said. I was outraged.

'I was brought up on a farm.'

'You told me you were evacuated there. You went to school in West Ham.'

'Well, anyway there's nothing to chickens. They look after themselves. They eat anything, just scraps from the table, and

287

all you have to do is collect the eggs. Lovely great fat brown eggs.'

I purchased two huts complete with nesting boxes and then had an acre of land fenced in. That set me back £150. I then wrote off for fifty Rhode Island Reds. They came with instructions that their diet should consist of best corn and grit. I worked out that they would have to lay at least 3600 eggs before I recovered my initial investment. These calculations were carefully concealed from Nanette.

I persevered for three years. No chickens ever lived better, but they were an ungrateful lot and repaid my kindness by refusing to lay when eggs were expensive in the shops but producing in abundance when you couldn't give them away. They led sheltered, healthy lives and of course none of them were ever killed for the table. However, one night the fox dispatched thirty-seven and I decided that the time had come to admit defeat. I had religiously kept a detailed set of accounts. After three years as possibly the most humane chicken farmer of all time I was left with Stalag Luft III standing as an ugly blot in the middle of the orchard and two useless and feather-less old hens that the local butcher declined to dispatch (they subsequently died of old age). As a final act of masochism I added up the balance sheet and proved that over the years the average cost per egg had been 7s. 6d. (37½ new pence).

Whilst failing as a poultry farmer I accepted a commission from Carl Foreman to write the screenplay from John Boland's excellent thriller *The League of Gentlemen*, and I would like to pay my respects to Mr Boland for providing me with the basic framework for what was to become one of my most admired screenplays.

I was in awe of Carl, perhaps, in the beginning, too much in awe of him, for he is a complex character who seldom makes conversation, as such, but tends to address you with definitive statements. I was grateful to him for such an interesting and important assignment, and delighted to be working for a fellow writer who would, I felt, be more sympathetic than the average producer.

I worked hard on the script and produced the first draft within six weeks. Carl tore it to pieces. He wanted the finished screenplay to be offered to Cary Grant and told me politely but firmly that I had a long way to go before it was good enough to submit to that gentleman. I did three complete versions before Carl allowed the manuscript to be passed to the typing agency. Our relationship was never quite the same after the event, but that is not to say he didn't do me a great deal of good. I think perhaps he was disappointed that I resisted being cast as his Trilby, for he is somebody who likes to have his own way and we were two of a kind.

The script came back from the agency and I called at the Jermyn Street office to collect my copy. I was somewhat surprised to find that my name was not on the title page. Carl was away and I asked the secretary whether there was any explanation. She told me that Carl had felt that Cary Grant would not be impressed by a screenplay from an unknown British writer and that the submission stood a better chance if it appeared in this anonymous form. I left the office in a sober mood.

While waiting for Mr Grant's reaction, I accepted another scripting job, this time from Sydney Box, a resilient and chameleon-like producer who had survived some savage infighting within the Rank Organization. He had suggested that I write an original story based around the D-Day landings. John Guillerman was to direct.

I agreed the terms of my contract for this enterprise on 21 May 1959, a date I can recall with ease for more lasting reasons. At 1.25 a.m. on 21 May Nanette was safely delivered of our first daughter, Sarah, in Queen Charlotte's Hospital. Bunter was there to hold my hand and light my cigarettes. I noted in my diary that 'it was a fine, calm, moonlit night. I saw Nanette at 3.10 a.m. She was incoherent but otherwise safe and sound. The baby was slightly marked by the delivery but cried lustily.'

I drove back to Seven Pines before daybreak, sending my shouts to the stars.

When Nanette and Sarah returned home I worked hard on my D-Day script, which I had titled *The Children Get Bored on Sundays* (this was the ultimate code sentence broadcast by the BBC over its London Calling Europe Network giving the signal to the Resistance Forces that the invasion was being launched). Then one day whilst visiting my agent John

Redway, his partner, Leslie Linder, chanced to say that he had heard a rumour that Basil Dearden had bought my script of *The League of Gentlemen*.

It was the first I had heard of it. Since delivering the script I had a couple of conversations with Carl and had learnt that Cary Grant and subsequently David Niven had both declined to appear in it, and the rest had been silence.

I didn't know Basil intimately. He had the reputation – quite false when one got to know him – of being abrupt to the point of rudeness, and was said to have a dictatorial manner on the studio floor. I knew him to be a superb technician with a long list of distinguished and highly individual films to his credit.

When I got home that night I discussed Leslie's news with Nanette. 'Why don't you ring Basil Dearden?' she said. 'Nothing to lose by it. If he's bought it, he must like it, so why shouldn't you ring him?'

I allowed myself to be persuaded, though with mixed feelings, for if the news was true I was somewhat perplexed at the mystery surrounding it. It seemed odd that Carl had never mentioned such a possibility in advance.

Basil *was* abrupt. He gave the impression that he didn't care to be rung after office hours, and I found myself stammering congratulations.

'Why should you congratulate me?' Basil said.

He sounded like a Labour Exchange manager dealing with a request for unemployment benefit.

'Well, because of the script.'

'What about the script?'

'I wrote it,' I said.

'You wrote what?'

'The script of *The League of Gentlemen*, which I understand you've just bought. Or so I was told. And I wanted to say how pleased I was.'

'I've just bought it from Carl Foreman. I paid a large sum of money for it.'

The voice sounded crosser than ever. I got the feeling that my news had somehow taken the gloss off the purchase.

'Can you prove you wrote it?'

'Well, I have my original manuscript here, and of course I had a contract to write it.'

'It hasn't got your name on it.'

'Well, nevertheless, Mr Dearden, I assure you I did write it and I was just ringing to say how delighted I am you want to make it.'

'It's a very good script. Not quite right, but very good. Jack Hawkins is going to do it. Does he know you wrote it?'

'I don't know,' I said. 'I've never discussed it with him.'

'I also want Dickie Attenborough to play in it.'

'Well, it all sounds marvellous.'

There was a pause. 'You'd better come and see me then. Talk about it.'

We arranged a meeting. I immediately rang Bunter and gave him the conversation verbatim. He was an old friend of Basil's and was able to establish beyond any doubt that I was the author.

As a result of my subsequent meeting with Basil and his partner Michael Relph, we then joined with Jack and Bunter to go and see Carl. The misunderstanding was corrected, and it was after that meeting that the idea of *Allied Film Makers* started to take shape. We recruited Guy Green to join us and we were fortunate in having as our company secretary Leslie Baker, who was the main architect in deciding how the enterprise should be structured. Towards the middle of June a series of negotiations took place with John Davis of the Rank Organization who readily embraced the basic idea of a production and sub-distribution organization working under the umbrella of his empire.

It was a co-operative effort from start to finish. The six founder-members put up £5000 each, and in return for distribution rights John Davis provided a revolving fund of £1,000,000. We had internal autonomy as to choice of subjects, and since we were such a small board we agreed that voting should be unanimous. Once the vote to give approval on script and budget had been cast, then the individuals or partnerships actually making the film had total artistic control. The finished product was then distributed by the Rank Organization at a fee of $27\frac{1}{2}$ per cent, $2\frac{1}{2}$ per cent of which was returned to Allied Film Makers. We also retained varying proportions of the profits of each film.

The move received widespread approval and was seen to be a constructive approach to the problems of the ever-faltering British film industry. Even the title of our first film seemed, to the Press, to be appropriate. Carl had received a handsome profit from the sale of my script and thus everybody was happy. I was happier than most, because Basil readily agreed to my playing one of the major roles: what had started out with a certain amount of mystery, not to say acrimony, became a beautifully rounded piece of poetic justice.

It was in the midst of these momentous events that Bunter finally got the necessary finance to launch Beaver Films with *The Angry Silence*, and we commenced principal photography on 1 September 1959. We finished shooting on 28 October, and my diary records that on that same date I completed the revisions Basil and Michael had requested for the final version of *The League of Gentlemen*. Studying my writing schedule for that year it would seem that I had the output and stamina of a Dickens, writing, as it were, at least four scripts at once. But when one is excited by future prospects, the sap rises fast and it was a good time to be alive. I had a ravishing new daughter, I had money to buy some carpets and curtains for Seven Pines, and the great good fortune to be involved with people I respected who were embarked with me to give life and substance to cherished dreams. For the first time in my career I had control of my own material. There was nobody to blame but myself if I failed.

Forty-four

Basil and Michael had assembled a superb cast, for in addition to Jack and Bunter we had Nigel Patrick, Roger Livesey, Kieron Moore, Terence Alexander and Robert Coote. But perhaps the piece of casting that gave me the most satisfaction was the inclusion of Norman as one of the 'gentlemen'. Basil took him on my recommendation, sight unseen. Nanette and Basil's wife Melissa Stribling also had smaller roles, both of us being happily able to ignore cries of nepotism!

I think we all sensed that we were making a good film. Far from being a dictator on the set, Basil almost went to the other extreme: never could actors have been treated with such respect, and the atmosphere was relaxed and carefree for most of the time. My qualification is deliberate, for unbeknown to most the tragedy of Jack's career was creeping ever nearer.

Several times during the shooting of the film he had apologized for being hoarse, and then came the moment when his voice failed altogether and he was forced to leave the film for a period. There is no need for me to elaborate on the outcome of that fateful leave of absence, for Jack and Doreen have documented their story with great courage and dignity in Jack's autobiography. We shot around him for a few days and then when he returned Basil, handling the situation with loving care, restaged some of the sequences in such a way that no suspicions were aroused. The actual moment is still there on film. I can pinpoint the scene, indeed the very close-up of Jack when he knew beyond any shadow of a doubt that his magnificent and distinctive voice was slipping away. It makes his performance all the more impressive. He was certainly one of the bravest men I have ever met. Many people are diminished by lesser tragedies, but faced with an actor's ultimate nightmare from which there can be no relief, Jack hurled self-pity into the wings and started to learn a new part.

We completed the film on schedule and for a cost of

£174,000, which was amazing even for those halcyon days. During the course of the shooting period my D-Day script had run into difficulties, for Darryl Zanuck had suddenly announced a rival production, this time based on a best-selling work by David Howarth, *Dawn of D-Day*. Although we were ahead at this point in the race, Zanuck was a ruthless opponent and driven by a personal ambition to make a spectacular comeback in his own right. The Press was bombarded with grandiose statements, designed, I was sure, to weaken Anglo-Amalgamated's resolve. I urged Sydney Box and Nat Cohen not to lose heart, for I was convinced that if we refused to be panicked we would win. My script was finished and it had the merit of being an original for the screen instead of a quasi-documentary culled from a published book.

The first thing that had caught my attention during the time I was researching my material was a small item which stated that 20,000 French people were killed *during the liberation*. This seemed to me a savage irony to be used for dramatic effect. I also discovered that amongst the first parachutists to be dropped was a medical team composed entirely of conscientious objectors. I seized upon these two little-publicized events and moulded my story around them, making one of the conscientious objectors my main character. The central theme concerned a small French girl who was severely injured during the first bombardment. Throughout the momentous happenings of D-Day, I kept cutting back to the child fighting for her life in a farmhouse a few miles inland from the beach-heads. This farmhouse was first liberated by the British forces, and the race to save her life begun. The building was subsequently retaken by the German Army only to be liberated once again as the Americans made their break-out. I took a certain amount of dramatic licence, but not much, to make my plot work, and at the end of the day the child was flown out to a hospital in England, her leg amputated but her life saved. The final words of my screenplay came from an unknown soldier who witnessed the scene. 'Poor little bleeder,' he was made to say, 'she'll remember being liberated.'

We lost the race. The original producers and director left the field. There was a period when my hopes revived, for the production was taken over by Peter Rogers and Gerry Thomas who are best known for their continuously successful *Carry On* series. They were genuinely excited at the prospect of widening their own horizons and for a time we looked like winning. But the financiers lost their nerve, seemingly over-impressed by Zanuck's steamroller tactics, and what should have been a major British production capable of attracting a world-wide audience was thrown away. Zanuck continued on course and the finished film proved to be one of the biggest box-office successes in his long and varied career.

I believed passionately in *The Children Always Get Bored on Sundays* and still feel that it represents some of my best, if unseen, work.

So I soldiered on in my fashion, rejecting a lucrative offer to rewrite *The Maltese Falcon* (I told the studio in question that I could in no way improve upon the original). I was also solicited by Cary Grant. Tending my garden at Seven Pines one day I was amazed to see an enormous Rolls-Royce ease its way up the drive. The chauffeur informed me that Mr Grant wanted an immediate audience. Mr Grant was on location in one of the stately homes of England and it was his wish, if not command, that I be driven to him to discuss a commission. The offer was sufficiently intriguing to make me accept. I was driven in some style to meet Mr Grant for the first time, half suspecting that the whole thing was some elaborate practical joke. It wasn't. Mr Grant had sent for me and Mr Grant received me. He was most complimentary. He said that he had admired my work in *The Angry Silence* and wanted me to write a script for him. He owned, in partnership with a producer called Robert Arthur, a short story that he felt could form the basis for an elegant comedy thriller. *The League of Gentlemen* was never mentioned and for all I know he never connected me with Carl Foreman's submission of that piece. I conversed with him for half an hour between takes and then the Rolls took me back to Seven Pines. The whole episode was totally unreal and in discussion with Nanette I was inclined to dismiss it.

At this point Bunter and I were searching for a suitable project with which to follow *The Angry Silence*. It was Bunter's idea that we should purchase the screen rights to Mary Hayley Bell's novel *Whistle Down the Wind*. Hayley Mills had just scored a notable success in her screen debut, acting alongside her father in *Tiger Bay*. Disney had signed her to a long-term (but not exclusive) contract and she had been to Hollywood to make *Pollyanna* and *The Parent Trap*. She had, of course, a very special quality, being a child star devoid of the usual nauseating precociousness, and audiences were flocking to see her. *Whistle Down the Wind* had, as its core, a fascinating premise, difficult to translate into a film, but sufficiently challenging to make us want to attempt it, and certainly capable of providing Hayley with a completely different star role.

Bunter went to work with his usual determination and flair, treading that thorny path between friendship and business. He commenced negotiations with the Mills' agent, Laurie Evans, and using the resources of Allied Film Makers was able to secure the rights. The next hurdle was to sign Miss Mills to a contract.

We had privately agreed that I should direct the next Beaver film, a decision for which the outside world was totally unprepared. When we mentioned our intentions to Laurie over lunch we failed to detect any change of expression in his mandarin eyes.

We were congratulating ourselves in our office an hour or so later when we received a hand-delivered letter from Laurie. In it he informed us that Hayley was such a valuable property that she could not be entrusted to an unknown quantity such as me. The Mills family reserved the right of director approval and with no malice aforethought they found themselves unable to approve me. A list of acceptable directors was appended, headed by David Lean as I recall, the majority of whom were way beyond our financial resources. Guy Green's name was listed amongst the chosen people and it was he we finally put forward for the benediction.

I suppose, at the time, it was the most crushing blow I had ever experienced. Looking back I can appreciate Johnny and Mary's concern for Hayley's professional future, but when one is convinced of one's own ability, however untested, the thunderbolt of disappointment splits the ego like some rotten oak. I was totally incapable of concealing my hurt and reacted with stupid, if understandable, anger. I announced that in the circumstances I wanted nothing whatsoever to do with the project. I declined to write the screenplay, thus further injuring myself. Bunter pleaded nobly but in vain. I was adamant. If I wasn't good enough in one category, then presumably I was inferior in all categories and the thing could go ahead without me. Willis Hall and Keith Waterhouse were contracted to write the screenplay, an inspired choice as it turned out for their invention could not have been bettered.

While *Whistle* was being prepared without my help, I allowed myself to be seduced by the surface glamour of working for a legend. I accepted the commission from Cary Grant, but the pleasure was momentary. I found myself working for a perfectionist in miniature who spoke in riddles. Cary's idea of a script conference was to put me through the hoop of self-analysis. He began by asking me what my relationship had been with my mother and went on to enquire whether I had any children. I told him I had a daughter. 'Let her go,' he said. I explained it would be rather difficult to let her go at the present moment without risking prosecution since she was only eighteen months old. He flashed a famous and somewhat forgiving smile and returned to the subject of my mother. 'When you're working on the script,' he said, 'imagine that it's your mother and work out all your inhibitions on her.' Now the story idea I had been handed concerned a Raffles-like crook who was trying to switch a priceless Chinese jade head, and the effort of interposing my mother seemed scarcely worth the candle. He continued in this vein for the best part of an hour to the point where I was seriously considering jumping out of his hotel window. He, on the other hand, appeared to get enormous benefit from the discussion and when, inevitably, the telephone rang and he was reminded of his next social engagement, congratulated us both on having such a valid and rewarding session. 'We're going to have a lot of laughs on this one,' he said. 'It's all going to be very jokey.' I did my best to look encouraged.

From this promising beginning things rapidly went from

bad to worse. He rang a few days later and said he'd like another script conference and suggested that I meet him at Heathrow. Trying to keep my voice normal, I said that was an interesting venue but wouldn't we be more comfortable at Seven Pines? 'No, we're flying to Santa Margherita,' he said. 'We can talk on the plane.' It all sounded so reasonable the way he put it. So I caught the plane and during the trip we talked some more about my mother, and then he told me that he wanted me to find a spot in the film where he could use spectacles that enabled the wearer to see round corners. Right at that moment I could have done with a pair myself.

Upon arrival in Italy we drove to a magnificent hotel on the coast where I was accommodated in great luxury. There I met Mr Arthur for the first time. He was then the Stanley Baldwin of Universal Studios and played the role with some finesse. He treated me with flattering consideration and I was amazed to be told that the script was going very well. Since I hadn't put pen to paper at that stage, congratulations were somewhat premature. The visit was extremely pleasant although short-lived, for Cary announced that he had business elsewhere and would meet me in Milan in a few days' time. I duly went to Milan and waited for him. He rang me there to say that further pressing engagements would prevent us resuming our discussions and that I should return home and await his next call. I caught a severe chill waiting around in Milan airport, and the moment I arrived back at Seven Pines took to my bed with a high temperature.

Six days later I was invited to fly to Rome and to bring Nanette with me. We arrived and were given an enormous suite and again treated very well, Mr and Mrs Arthur being especially solicitous. I did have one brief talk with Cary during this trip which took place on the back lot of Cine Cita. This time in addition to questioning me closely about my relationship with Nanette and Sarah, he indicated that he felt it would be a good idea if I managed to work in a sequence that allowed him to use a rope-ladder that folded into the size of a pocket handkerchief. He was tremendously enthused about this. We did some shopping and then came home. I never saw Cary again.

I slaved my way through the script and duly sent the top copy to Mr Arthur. After two weeks' silence I rang him.

'Oh, hallo, Bryan,' he said. There seemed to be a marked lack of enthusiasm in the greeting.

'Did you receive the script?' I asked.

There was a pause.

'Yes, I got it.'

Another pause.

'What did you think of it?'

A longer pause.

'We thought it was kinda dull.'

'D'you mean you found it *all* dull or just parts of it?'

'I guess we found it all kinda dull.'

'There wasn't one scene that . . .'

He was a long time answering and I gained the impression that, since he wasn't paying for the call, his mind was elsewhere.

'No, it was a pretty general opinion.'

'Cary thought the same, did he?'

'I guess he did.'

'So . . . what happens now?'

'I don't know. I'll have to think about that.'

In the end it became a matter for my agent to settle. The final negotiations dragged on a few more weeks and then I was offered 50 cents in the dollar on the money still owed to me to drop the whole matter. I agreed and in due course received a cheque. It was of unusual design and when I went to cash it the teller shared my curiosity. He made enquiries, then came back all smiles. 'It's quite all right,' he said. 'It's drawn on Mr Grant's own bank.'

Forty-five

We flew to a snowbound New York, together with Sheila and Bunter, for the American opening of *The Angry Silence*. The film had been bought by an amiable character called Sig Shore, a one-man band determinedly anxious to gain recognition as a distributor. Fortunately he was by nature a gambler, for we opened in a blizzard, the newspapers couldn't be printed and thus the reviews were never read. It would be satisfying to be able to report that we surmounted these hazards and went on to triumph but, alas, such happy endings are few and far between in the cut-throat world of the American cinema. The reviews, when they finally appeared, were eulogistic, but they came too late. Living on borrowed time and (I suspect) borrowed money, Sig cheerfully paid for us to journey on to Los Angeles for a repeat performance in the sunshine. Bunter was rightly feted for his performance, I received my quota of congratulations for the script, but the film did not attract the crowds. Sig never lost faith in the film, but even his loyalty had a limit. I was lucky enough to get an Academy Award Nomination and won the British Academy Award for that year.

We returned home four days before Christmas to face another crisis. Guy Green informed us that he had been offered the direction of a film starring Olivia de Havilland at a much enhanced fee and asked if we would release him from his contract for *Whistle Down the Wind*. There was no point in standing in his way and we wished him well, but it left us facing bankruptcy. By now Willis and Keith had finished the first draft of the screenplay, the key technicians had been engaged and were already at work preparing the location, but without an approved director we could not proceed.

My previous hurt having receded with the passing of time, I felt bold enough to suggest that we made another attempt with the Mills family to get them to accept me as director.

Bunter, as usual, was ahead of me. 'I've already prepared the ground,' he said. 'Let's go now.'

For some reason that I have forgotten we drove to Cowden in separate cars – perhaps we felt the arrival of two Bentleys would be more impressive for the occasion.

I have no clear recollection of our dialogue that evening. Only Johnny, Mary and Hayley were present and they listened while Bunter filibustered on my behalf. I am quite sure that he brilliantly exaggerated such talents as I then possessed. Indeed, it was the first of many occasions when I have felt that he has been sidetracked from his true vocation in life. Always the optimist where I am the pessimist, he would have made a superb politician.

Johnny and Mary reacted with typical generosity. Johnny eased the cork from a bottle of champagne and said, 'Sod it, Mary, we can't let the chums go to the wall and I'm sure Forbesey will make a smashing film.' We charged our glasses and drank to each other, all of us very emotional and conscious, being actors, that the scene had been worth playing. We finished that bottle and another before Bunter and I departed into the night.

We stopped our cars a few miles down the road and got out to discuss the dramatic change of events.

'Well, you're directing,' Bunter said.

'Yes.'

'D'you think you *can* direct?'

'God,' I said, 'it's a bit late to think about that. I suppose I'll bloody well have to.'

Forty-six

Given the eleventh-hour atmosphere, I have never ceased to be amazed at the ease with which the film went together. Most of the credit for the smoothness of the production must go to Bunter, for he left nothing to chance, and certainly no director embarking on his first film could have had more loyalty and co-operation from his crew. Arthur Ibbetson was again the cameraman and when, on an early location hunt, I confided that I was none too sure of myself, he immediately gave me the best technical advice I have ever had. 'There are no rules,' he said, 'or if there are, you can always break them.'

It was somehow fitting that the first actor I ever directed was Norman. I had cast him in the role of the farm labourer, and since we were shooting in strict continuity for the opening weeks of the schedule, he started the film.

I had done my homework as best I could and the night before shooting began I drove out to the bleak location and paced the next day's work. We were staying at the Keirby Hotel in Burnley. Bunter and I occupied one of two penthouse suites, named Chattox and Demdike after the Witches of Pendle Hill. The farmhouse location was close to Pendle and it took us some forty minutes to drive from the hotel to the location.

When the actual moment came on the first day I found that I had completely lost my voice and was unable to say 'Action.' Instead I tapped Norman on the shoulder (my opening shot allowed this for he made his appearance from behind camera). It was an emotional moment for both of us. He seemed to do it perfectly the first take, but I felt it might seem a little pushy if I settled for only one take on the first shot on my first day. I congratulated Norman and told him the reason I wanted to go again was to have an 'insurance' take. The second attempt was cut halfway for some technical reason and I therefore had to go a third time. Norman's performance hadn't varied so, finding my voice again, I said, 'Fine, print it,' and walked away in what was I hoped a confident manner to the location for the second shot.

Penny Daniels, my brilliant and devoted continuity girl, followed me and whispered discreetly: 'Which one?' I didn't grasp what she was talking about. 'You had three takes,' she said, 'and all you said was print it. Which take d'you want to print?' 'Oh, God,' I said, 'well, the second one was useless, better print the first and the last. Is that all right?' 'You're the boss,' she said, and I think that was the moment when I realized that the film was actually mine.

The date was 13 February.

The first rushes when I saw them disappointed me and I asked Bunter if I could reshoot the opening sequence. He had the courage to agree.

The children I had selected from local schools proved to be exceptionally receptive to direction. I had taken a calculated risk from the beginning and apart from Hayley none of them were ever given a script. I wanted to avoid the trap of them 'acting' what could have been a sentimental, not to say banal, story by having too much awareness of what they were saying and doing. I therefore kept rehearsals down to a minimum and tried to give the children parallel and more easily acceptable illustrations, bullying them in a light-hearted manner. They responded to authority, I found, as long as I kept them amused. Beyond a certain point they became bored, and one can understand why – at that age (and most of my cast were between eight and ten) making a film is not a matter of life and death. They enjoy it, of course, but the novelty soon wears off and they don't have any professional fears or discipline to sustain them.

I also found that the crew and I had to be ultra proficient in what we were doing – for the first reaction of a child is usually the truest, and if you aren't ready with lights and camera to capture that split second look or instinctive turn of the head, then subsequent attempts obey the law of diminishing returns.

For six days a week life consisted of sleep and hurried meals. As soon as we arrived back from the location I fell into a hot

303

bath, dressed hurriedly, snatched a meal, then went to the local Odeon where, after the normal performance ended, we screened the previous day's rushes. Then back to the hotel for a post-mortem and a planning session for the next day's work, the schedule constantly being rearranged and adapted to take into the account the changing mood of the elements.

Bunter, although beset with problems, could always blot them out the moment his head touched the pillow. We were like some dotty, querulous married couple in our penthouse, arguing as to who should shave first in the mornings (I relinquished the single basin to Bunter and grew a beard. It gave me an extra fifteen minutes in bed and helped keep out the cold) or who should turn out the lights. Bunter's ability to fall asleep within seconds filled me with an unreasonable anger. I could ask him an important question concerning the following day's work, he would get as far as framing the first words of his answer and then fall fast asleep in mid-sentence. We only had one serious difference of opinion that I can remember, an isolated shouting match about some relatively un-important detail which we conducted away from the crew, standing in a pig-sty up to our knees in pig shit. At the height of the row we both became conscious of our ludicrous sur-roundings and broke up, the quarrel dissolved by hysterical laughter.

The finished film had to stand or fall by Hayley's perform-ance. It is almost always a lie to say that people are untouched by their fame, but I must record that Hayley was the exception. Her appearances for Disney in Hollywood had provoked near hysteria and one cannot discount the fact that our film was financed on her name and her name alone. Bunter and I were respected, but we couldn't have conjured up £150,000 without Hayley's involvement. Beyond the financial considerations, it is also abundantly clear to any student of the cinema that Hayley came to the screen with inherent talents that were truly instinctive and remarkable. The little boy, Alan Barnes, being younger and being good copy, stole some of Hayley's thunder when the reviews came out, but without detracting in any way from his portrayal, or that of the little actress Diana Holgate who played the third member of the family, Hayley's perform-

Left My photograph of Nanette and the children taken a few weeks after Emma's birth. *Below* Members of the Royal Ballet during the making of *The Tales of Beatrix Potter*

Left Dame Edith Evans on location in Manchester for *The Whisperers*.
Below Kate Hepburn during the filming of *The Madwoman of Chaillot*

ance carried the whole film. Where all the others were concerned they were totally moulded by me, firstly on the set and afterwards in the cutting room. But with Hayley it was different. I am not being falsely modest, for I directed her with equal intensity (on one occasion forcing her to do no less than seventy takes of the same scene). I demanded more of her because she had more to give, and in scene after scene she would come fully equipped to amaze me. Lifting her head from a comic she would walk on to the set and immediately assume another identity. The moment I said 'Cut' she would relax back into her own indolent and delightful personality – a child caught between many stools. The daughter of famous parents, catapulted into world fame at the age of thirteen, subjected to the full Hollywood publicity machine, mobbed and feted in public, she might well have come a spoilt and arrogant little beast. She didn't. One can usually tell a child's true character when he or she is in the presence of other children: the real horrors soon assert themselves. By virtue of who she was, Hayley naturally had little or nothing in common with the village children I had recruited, nothing, that is, except the affinity of age. But she never lorded it over them, she never demanded privileges they could not be granted, and within a week when their awe had subsided she seemed to melt into the surroundings, adopting their attitudes, their way of speech and, indeed, their sense of humour. One must also remember that she had to assume a local accent for the purposes of the film: she had to strive for that authenticity, whereas they only had to be themselves.

Grafted on to all these problems she had the normal difficulties of adolescence, isolation for long stretches from her home and family, a hotel existence amongst adults, and the disciplines of her craft. That is what made her remarkable, not the press hand-outs. And in a sense my subsequent career as a director rested on her: had she not been able to deliver the goods the blame would have been mine. She never failed me once, and I hope that I never failed her.

Forty-seven

> Who can feel sure that he has ever
> been understood? We all die unknown.
> *Balzac*

James ('Jimmy') Woolf was never a public figure in our most public of industries: he enjoyed reading other people's press cuttings, never his own.

I worked with him on five different films, all within the space of six years. We first met in 1960 when he asked me to write the screenplay of Joseph Kessel's novel *The Lion* for Jack Clayton.

Jimmy was a midwife for talent and smacked many of us into life. He was fond of saying, 'It's more blessed to receive than to give,' smiling at his own words behind the inevitable cigar, hand always held to his mouth, anxious to conceal the blemish of a scarred lip that few noticed. He lived his life through others, operating mostly from hotel bedrooms ('It's always cheaper to live at the Ritz' was another of his maxims). When he ventured forth it was for a purpose. He had a memory that retained trivia as well as hard facts, a quick mind that panned gossip and found the nugget before other prospectors on the same trail had even arrived at the water's edge.

My first encounter with him ultimately proved abortive, for my script of *The Lion* was never made. Then he asked me to script *The L-Shaped Room*, again for Jack Clayton. My second collaboration with the elusive Jack proved as unrewarding as the first. Like the ghost in his own film *The Innocents*, I was never quite sure that Jack existed in real life. Sometimes I saw him, sometimes I didn't. Unfailingly courteous and pleasant to be with, stimulating about every subject but the one in hand, he never allowed me to get too close. We enjoyed each other's company, but progress was painfully slow and Jimmy became increasingly fretful.

In the end the script conferences petered out and I commenced the script without any clear idea of Jack's intentions. I also had the added weight of a best-seller around my neck. Although resolved to be faithful to the *content* of Lynne Reid Banks's intensely felt and personal novel, I was ever conscious that certain key passages in the book would not translate easily to the screen; attitudes which, on the printed page, one could accept without question, did not stand up to closer examination in filmic terms.

When I was halfway through my first draft Jimmy announced that he had cast Leslie Caron for the central role. This inevitably meant another change of direction, for in order to make full use of Leslie's unique qualities it was obvious that the role would have to be reconceived. After much thought I embraced the change with enthusiasm, for it lifted the film out of the parochial kitchen-sink rut. The problems of *au pair* girls living in our major cities at that time was frequently the subject of headlines.

Jack went cold on the whole idea and to the best of my knowledge didn't even consider my finished script. Nothing happened for a few weeks then, capitalizing on his unconcealed love of surprise, Jimmy offered the direction of the film to me. Bunter was recruited to co-produce with Jimmy, and I was over the all-important hurdle of finding my second film.

Our choice for the role of Toby, the other leading role, was a comparatively unknown young actor called Tom Bell. He had come into prominence at the Theatre Workshop and was very much the sort of actor I had always aspired to be. I did not test him for the part, having a deep loathing of such self-indulgent exercises. He and Leslie both gave very true performances, though it was inevitable that hers would to some extent overshadow his. She went on to win the British Academy Award and the New York Critics Award for the best actress in her year.

The film ran into difficulties after I had completed it. The censor, John Trevelyan, had asked for numerous cuts, amendments and alternatives when we first submitted the script;

indeed, his observations ran to four closely typed pages and in view of what is happening today in the cinema some of his comments have a historical value.

They did not prohibit the word 'arse' in an 'X' film, nor 'God', 'God Almighty' or 'My God' as expletives, but 'Christ' and 'Jesus wept' were unacceptable. They were not happy about references to contraceptives, but did not insist. Breast and thigh rubbing and copulatory dancing were totally out, as were all erotic visuals, and we were asked to substitute the word 'tart' for 'whore', and even a mild joke about 'getting a bird in the oven' was questioned.

When I screened the finished film for the British Board of Film Censors, it was felt that the scenes in which abortion was discussed (in very oblique terms, I might add) would have to go. We protested. Trevelyan came up with the suggestion that the film should be shown to an audience of women selected entirely at random. If the majority of that audience were disturbed by the abortion scenes, then the cuts would stand. If on the other hand the majority raised no objection, the scenes would be left in. The trial screening took place, nobody objected, and we won our point.

Following the censor we had to satisfy other Boards, for the film had been made under the auspices of British Lion Columbia, a joint company involving both British and American finance. Purely fortuitously, Mike Frankovitch saw the first cut of the film on behalf of Columbia ahead of the British Lion Board. He asked for the film to be shortened in length, and after argument and discussion we took out seven minutes. It was then the British Lion turn, with Roy Boulting as spokesman. He wrote a very long and considered letter to Jimmy to put their case, which was that further and extensive cuts should be made on the grounds of overlength. Roy had attended the first of many publicity screenings, and the audience on this particular occasion had numbered 120. He felt that we should delete certain scenes in their entirety. To support his argument he contended that 'an overwhelming majority' of the audience in question agreed that the film was 'far too long.' He also quoted the opinion of Peter King, an exhibitor, who had urged that the film be cut by at least twenty minutes.

Jimmy was incensed for Roy had selected all his favourite moments in the film as candidates for the guillotine. Within minutes of receiving Roy's letter he dictated a much-needed defence of the creative position. He thanked Roy for his long and comprehensive memorandum and hoped that Roy would not resent his answering with equal frankness. He began by stating that he felt that any film lasting more than two hours was open to the suggestion that it was too long and that this had been true in the case of *Ben Hur*, *Guns of Navarone*, *Bridge on the River Kwai*, and *Room at the Top*, all of which had been criticized privately and in print as being overlength. 'However,' Jimmy continued, 'they seem to have survived such criticism most successfully.

'As regards the showing the other night, I would like to point out that it was the fourth film most of those present had seen that day and for every one who found it too long I can bring another opinion to say they did not find it dragged at all. Without wishing to be contentious, I strongly doubt that any majority of the 120 people present passed any opinion at all and that the "overwhelming majority" referred to consisted at most of six people.

'Regarding Peter King, possibly pig-headedly and arrogantly, his opinion is of no interest to me. His prime concern, like most exhibitors, is probably how fast and how many times a day he can get his customers in and out of the theatres for which he books.'

He then dealt with Roy's points in detail, defending our version of the film with passion, and ended by saying, 'I wish the film to take its chance as it stands. I know you believe all independent producers should have complete freedom and should stand or fall by their own judgement, and I ask you not to make an exception in this case.'

I added my own comments in a further letter to Roy and could not resist pointing out that were we to act upon all the suggested cuts from all informed quarters we would end up with a film that was marginally below normal first feature length and that would bear no resemblance whatsoever to the script so enthusiastically approved a year or so before.

The film was shown as we wanted it.

Jimmy and I flew to Hollywood three days after the London premiere. As we waited in the Heathrow departure lounge for our flight to be called Jimmy suddenly became very agitated. It was a Sunday and he had just discovered that the Sunday flight did not go direct to Los Angeles, but instead put down at San Francisco first. For reasons that I could not comprehend, this news threw Jimmy into panic.

'We must change planes, Byron,' he said. (He insisted that Byron was my real name.) I looked at him in horror. I am very superstitious about such things.

'We can't change now, our luggage has gone through.'

'Byron, don't argue, it's quite impossible for me to arrive in San Francisco.'

'Why not? Give me a reason.'

'I'm not prepared to discuss it, Byron. Just get on to the man and change our tickets.'

At that moment an announcement was made that our flight was boarding.

'What's wrong with this flight, what d'you know, Jimmy?'

'I don't know the Customs in San Francisco,' Jimmy hissed.

'But you haven't got anything.'

Jimmy always travelled in the clothes he stood up in and bought enough for his needs on arrival. Whenever we travelled together my first act was always to purchase him an electric razor and toothbrush. He was totally indifferent to his appearance, maintaining that shopping for oneself was boring.

Irritated that I refused to act, he tackled the airline staff himself. They listened politely and explained that there was no direct flight to Los Angeles that day. By now the plane was being held for us and he was eventually persuaded to go through the barrier.

While we were fastening our seat-belts I questioned him again. What was the reason for his near-hysteria?

'I'm carrying something for a friend.'

'Oh, God,' I said. 'Not drugs?'

'Of course not. Just a gift for a friend.'

'What sort of gift?'

'An expensive gift, Byron, and I have an absolute aversion to paying duty. It's against the laws of Nature.'

'What is it?'

He opened his jacket and tapped the lining.

'A little bauble.'

I looked around the cabin, but fortunately nobody was paying us any attention and the whine of the jets preparing for take-off obliterated our dialogue.

'Is it jewellery?' He nodded. 'Jimmy, you can't smuggle in stuff like that.'

'Who says it's smuggling?'

'If something's sewn into the lining of your jacket, that's smuggling, Jimmy.'

'Nonsense, Byron, you have a very old-fashioned view of life.'

'So do the Customs.'

'Only the Customs at San Francisco. The ones at Los Angeles are much more civilized. I know them all there and they wouldn't dream of suspecting me. Nor should they. This is just a gift for an old friend, and as such it doesn't count.'

I was nervous enough about an eleven-hour flight without the added hazard of exposure in the Customs sheds the moment we landed. My usually vivid imagination worked overtime. I could see the headlines: *British film men held on grave charges*. The first night of *The L-Shaped Room* would obviously be cancelled and we would both spend Christmas in jail. Probably San Quentin. In Death Row. If we didn't crash, that was.

Although the flight was without incident, I never relaxed for a moment. When we landed I carefully avoided Jimmy in the Customs Hall, pretending that I didn't know him. My bags were searched inside-out and I was directly responsible for keeping the onward flight waiting. I found Jimmy relaxed and smiling.

'You obviously got through all right,' I said.

'Of course I got through. What on earth are you talking about, Byron?'

He took a pill and fell asleep for the rest of the journey.

Jimmy's pills were famous. He had one for every occasion and his bathroom cabinet looked like a minor branch of Boots. A story was told of him that he was once flying with the owner of a famous London club who had to arrive in New

York at a certain time in order to conclude a vital business deal. The man was apparently pathologically scared of flying and it was only the chance of making a small fortune that had got him on the plane. He sat next to Jimmy and immediately commenced a barrage of anxious questions about the air-worthiness of the particular model they were flying in, the safety record of the airline, how experienced was the pilot, and so on. Jimmy had no such qualms. He once said to me during another flight we took together that I could sit back and stop fidgeting because there was no question of him dying in an air crash. 'I shall die in my bed of cancer,' he said in what I am sure he thought was a comforting tone of voice.

Doubtless he was equally positive with the night club owner, and apparently gave him a pill to take, assuring the unfortunate man that it was merely a mild sedative which would make the trip a pleasure. The pills were so mild, Jimmy said, that he himself took two after lunch to enjoy a short nap. The night-club owner swallowed the pill and the next thing he knew he was being gently shaken by an air-hostess and told to fasten his seat-belt as they were just landing at Heathrow. As legend had it he had been asleep for forty-eight hours, had missed his all-important business appointment in New York, had, in fact, been taken off the plane on a stretcher and flown back to London on a subsequent flight. The story is probably apocry-phal but not, knowing Jimmy, beyond the bounds of possi-bility, and I am inclined to believe it.

Whatever his personal idiosyncrasies, Jimmy was a brilliant businessman and never more so than when he was acting for others. During the course of our three-week stay at the Beverly Hills Hotel that year he negotiated two contracts for me. He was to produce a second remake of Maugham's *Of Human Bondage* and quickly concluded a contract for me to write the screenplay and play the second leading role. He also arranged for me to write and direct one of the most ambitious projects in Paramount's line-up of future films: an epic production of the early life of Sir Winston Churchill. This was the brainchild of an English agent working in Hollywood, Hugh French, an old friend of Jimmy's.

'But how can I possibly do both?' I protested.

'It's all arranged, Byron, just leave these things to me, you don't understand business. You do the script of *Human Bondage* first, which won't take you long, and then come to Ireland.'

'Ireland?'

'Yes, we're making it in Dublin at Ardmore Studios. While you're there you'll have lots of peace and quiet and you can write the Churchill script.'

So armed with a new portable typewriter and seventeen suitcases full of Christmas presents, I boarded the *Super Chief* on 2 December 1962, having been persuaded by Nanette not to fly home. (There had been two major air crashes within a week.) Jimmy refused to make the overland trip with me and we arranged to meet in New York where we would take the S.S. *France* to Southampton. My Hollywood friends stared at me in disbelief when I announced I was taking the train. 'But it takes *three* days,' they said.

From the moment we arrived on board the *France*, Jimmy's behaviour continued to be more bizarre than any film script. We were shown to two adjoining first-class cabins and I immediately started to unpack. I found my cabin luxurious and was well content, but Jimmy appeared in the doorway and insisted that we would have to get off the boat.

'You're not smuggling something back now?'

'Of course not. It's just that the accommodation is quite unsuitable, Byron.'

'This cabin's fine. I'll swop if yours isn't so good.'

'They're both hovels, Byron. We can't possibly spend five days in such squalor. Come along.'

'Where?'

'I shall take you to see the purser and demand that we either be given more suitable cabins or else leave the boat.'

'I don't want to leave the boat. I'm very comfortable and I want to get home safely for Christmas.'

Jimmy ignored all this and swept me away in search of the purser. We found this worthy gentleman at the head of a long queue of passengers seeking to reserve the best tables in the first class dining-room. Jimmy went straight to the head of the queue and immediately launched into his complaint. Once again I pretended that I wasn't with him, but much to my amazement, after a short and one-sided exchange, the purser left the queue and bowed Jimmy to follow him. I accompanied them and we were taken to the sun deck and ushered into the *Province Suite*.

Compared to the average first class cabin this was something out of a Bond film, with an enormous living area, two vast double bedrooms, two bathrooms, bar and hallway, and had obviously been designed to accommodate Heads of State. Jimmy took one look and said, 'Yes, much more suitable. We'll take it. How much extra?'

One could almost hear the sound of the cash register clicking in the purser's head. The boat sailed within the hour and obviously if the *Province Suite* was still free it was unlikely to be booked prior to departure. He half turned away and made some lightning calculations on the back of a menu.

'It will be sixty hundred and thirty dollars per person extra, monsieur.'

'I'll give you two hundred dollars' cash,' Jimmy answered.

The purser didn't hesitate.

'I accept,' he said.

After profuse thanks and a promise to have all our luggage transferred immediately, he backed out of the room.

Jimmy lit a fresh cigar. 'Those grabby French,' he said, 'they're no match for a Jewish boy.'

The moment I was home I embarked on a marathon session at the typewriter and had finished a draft of *Of Human Bondage* by 21 December. The following day I commenced the first draft of *Seance on a Wet Afternoon*, an act of penance more than anything else for I had a guilty conscience at having neglected Beaver Films for so long. I completed it seven days later, and when Sheila and Bunter came to Seven Pines on 31 December I gave it to Bunter as a New Year gift. On 1 January 1963 I lunched with Mike Frankovitch, then the European head of Columbia, to discuss the scripting and direction of James Clavell's best-seller *King Rat*. I had never been more in demand, but not surprisingly I was written out and badly in need of a holiday. I booked a holiday in Switzerland and, encouraged by the prospect of a rest, somehow found the necessary energy needed to complete the various loose ends of my complicated life.

Of Human Bondage was not scheduled to start shooting in Dublin until March, and most of my time before that date had to be devoted to the preparation of the Churchill script. I began to buy works of reference on a heroic scale, scouring the dusty shelves of my antiquarian friends in Charing Cross Road. Hugh French arranged for me to meet Anthony Montague-Browne who was then Churchill's private secretary. He seemed perfectly cast for the role and explained in some detail the requirements of the Churchill family and their contractual rights in the matter. I was to be given reasonable access to private documents under supervision, and the treatment and finished script had to be submitted to the Churchill estate for approval. He thought it would be useful if I met with Randolph Churchill who was then in the throes of writing the first volume of his father's biography. It was heady stuff and I was suitably impressed.

It was a very cold January that year and we were snowed in at Seven Pines. I welcomed the isolation that snow always confers and used the time to set down my thoughts in some detail. I am a quick reader and I tore into a dozen volumes pertinent to the period, all touching upon Churchill's early youth. The first thing that struck me as being peculiar were the recorded circumstances of his birth, since nearly every account gave a different version, the most popular being that he was born in a small cloakroom at Marlborough during a ball on St Andrew's Day. I found it odd that the Marlboroughs would celebrate St Andrew's Day in this fashion and put a question mark against the legend. I have noticed in the course of a lifetime's filmgoing that pregnant ladies often swoon during The Ball. This factor alone made me want to find a different solution. My analysis of all the material I could find on the subject led me to suspect that Lady Randolph Churchill was following the guns on the day of Winston's birth.

True to his word, Montague-Browne arranged an early meeting with Randolph. We exchanged letters and then I spoke to him on the phone and he invited me to spend a weekend at Stour, East Bergholt. Randolph had requested sight of my notes prior to my visit since he felt that as we were strangers it would give him a written introduction to my character and my approach to the subject. I polished some forty-odd pages and posted them off to him in some trepidation.

My visit started disastrously. Mindful of Montague-Browne's blunt warning ('He'll probably insult you, but answer him back, give as good as you take and all will be sweetness and light. He's basically a nice character.') I paid a visit to Fortnum and Mason on my way to Liverpool Street Station and purchased a bunch of very expensive and out-of-season flowers and the best bottle of brandy on the premises.

It wasn't until the train was drawing into Manningtree for East Bergholt that I became conscious of my first social error. He had sent one of his many researchers to meet me, a pale young man who was nicknamed Duke for reasons I was never able to establish, and I detected a twitch of amazement as I stepped from the train clutching my bouquet. The flowers had, of course, been intended as a gracious offering to Mrs Randolph Churchill, but even as my foot slipped on the icy platform I realized that there was no Mrs Churchill incumbent. Half-forgotten news items flashed in Citizen Kane montages before my eyes: they were either separated or divorced.

I confessed all immediately and solicited advice as to what was best done with the flowers.

'Oh, give them to him, he likes flowers,' Duke said. He treated me with ill-concealed condescension as we drove to the house. 'He'll probably put them in the hall,' he said, managing to convey that, though just acceptable, they weren't likely to take prizes. He also told me that he had left his master 'brooding'.

There was a power-cut in progress when I arrived but the house had a lived-in look that was not unwelcoming. Being greeted by Randolph for the first time, I repeated my explanation for the flowers, having decided that the truth was less embarrassing than invention. Randolph took it in good part and did in fact ask a servant to put them in the hall. He led me into his study and told everybody that we were not to be disturbed until dinner-time.

He wasted no time on formalities, but immediately attacked

me. Did I not realize that he was currently engaged upon the definitive biography of his father? Did I not appreciate that the first volume was due to appear at any moment and that naturally it would deal with the circumstances of his father's birth? I did? Then I must also realize that he had a prior claim to all the material.

I agreed. Obviously what he said was true.

'Then how is it,' he said, reaching for my notes and flourishing them under my nose, 'how is it, Mr Forbes, you have stolen my first scoop? How is it that you, and you alone, have managed to discover that most of the previous accounts of my father's birth are not according to the facts – facts which, let it be said, only I have access to?'

'Well, surely you've answered yourself,' I said. 'We've never met before, therefore we've never discussed the matter, and quite obviously I've never been granted access to the family papers. It was pure guesswork on my part.'

'How so?'

I took him through my somewhat laboured detective work to which he listened without comment. I could not tell whether he was inclined to believe me or not, and when I had finished he questioned me further.

He still found it highly suspicious that I had chanced upon the near truth, but he would accept my word for it. I breathed again. He offered me a drink. We settled down on opposite sides of the open fireplace, separated by dogs, upbringing and a mutual distaste. He looked in the fading afternoon light like some ravaged Roman emperor. The voice was thickened by incessant smoking. His gestures were extravagant and at times I had the feeling that I was listening to a parody of his father.

He went through my material in some detail and left me in no doubt as to his own feelings about the project. I suspected that he did not welcome the idea of the film since, inevitably, it would steal some of the thunder from his biography. Such praise as he found possible to give was given grudgingly, and when he disliked something he was scathing, offensively so. I listened to this monologue in growing discomfort which eventually turned to anger. The climax came when he suddenly shouted: 'Stop tapping with your pen on my armchair. Put the pen away.'

'Mr Churchill,' I said, 'it's quite obvious that this meeting is going to be very unrewarding. You invited me down here to be your guest and you have attacked me from the moment I set foot inside your house. You suspect me – quite unjustly – of having plagiarized your own book. However, you have a perfect right to dislike me on sight, just as I have a perfect right to dislike you. You have a reputation for boorishness which you have not neglected this afternoon, so in order not to prolong the mutual agony why don't you ask one of your acolytes to look up the time of the next train to London and I'll leave you in peace.'

Randolph looked at me in shocked disbelief. 'But I don't dislike you,' he said. 'How dreadful you should have gained that impression. It's more important that you stay and feel welcome. Do you really think I'm boorish?'

'Well, yes, so far,' I said.

'But that's dreadful, quite dreadful. Let's have a drink.'

He poured two generous tots and raised his glass to me. 'To the success of your script and my book,' he said. 'And to the great man who makes both of them possible.'

From that extraordinary moment onwards he could not have been nicer. He was in great form over dinner, telling a variety of highly libellous anecdotes, enjoying, I think, a fresh audience and a receptive one. I found him endearing and in many ways somebody deserving of compassion, for he seemed to be searching for some lost meaning to his life. The early bombast appeared to have been a façade, ugly but self-protective.

After dinner we had readings from the work in progress. Duke doing the honours from a lectern while Randolph listened appreciatively, frequently interrupting to make amendments. Eventually satisfied, he dismissed Duke and asked me to stay up with him and talk.

I am not being scurrilous in revealing that he drank, on occasions, to excess. During the course of that evening I became quite adept at concealing my own glass, for I had no wish to emulate his own capacity. We sat in front of a blazing fire far into the night and he talked – oh, how he talked – of his father and his own life. I have always regretted that I kept no record of that conversation, but the flow of words was such that had I tried to retain whole passages I would have missed others. All I have retained is a vivid memory of a man who, in Noel Coward's definitive phrase, remained 'completely unspoilt by failure.'

Nothing that had gone before prepared me for the final act of our solitary drama. Beckoning me to follow his unsteady progress, he led the way through the house to the yard outside. We slithered our way to a large brick structure that closely resembled a street air-raid shelter. It was windowless and had heavy steel doors which Randolph unlocked with difficulty. He motioned me inside. My joy must have been akin to that felt by Howard Carter entering the tomb of Tutankhamen. There was no disordered gold inside Randolph's tomb, only filing cabinets and cupboards full of documents and books, for this was the secure repository of Sir Winston's private papers.

Although it was bitterly cold my amazement and excitement warmed me like a generous tot of rum. Randolph proceeded to open some of the filing cabinets and brought forth a series of documents that were never intended for public scrutiny. His behaviour bore no resemblance to the man who had greeted me the previous afternoon. The significance of his change of heart penetrated my mounting hysteria, for it was obvious that had he not been in his cups this bounty would have been withheld. I took what I hope was an honourable lightning decision. I thought, I won't deny myself this unique opportunity, but I will deny myself any advantage from it. This resolved, I studied the letters, papers and scrapbooks he placed before me – pure manna to anybody in my position. Randolph seemed consumed with a desire to please me and took time to explain details. Then the intense cold seemed to grip him, for he shook as though seized with a sudden fever, and I thought for a moment that he was going to collapse. But the tremors ceased as abruptly as they had began and his manner became formal, distant almost, as if I didn't exist. He stared at me, brooding as Duke had put it, then in a controlled and gentle voice excused himself, saying that he was going to retire, but would I please feel free to continue looking at the papers. He handed me the keys and asked me to be sure to lock up securely. Then he stepped out into the night.

I became even more uneasy after his departure, for it occurred to me that there was a strong possibility that he would be unable to corroborate my story if called upon to do so. I had no means of determining his normal powers of recovery, but the chances were that, if he remembered anything, he would not choose to recall the last episode. I turned back to the papers, but after a few more minutes I reluctantly replaced them in the files and closed the doors. I locked the steel security doors and retraced my steps across the glistening yard and into the silent house. Alone in my room, I lay on top of the bed fully clothed for a long time, pondering the extraordinary variations I had been witness to.

I was the first about the following morning and went down to the breakfast room to find an array of heated silver salvers containing kidneys, liver, scrambled eggs and bacon. Duke put in an appearance. Without further ado I related the salient facts to him. I think he was suitably impressed, though possibly inclined to the belief that I was exaggerating until I handed him the keys of the kingdom.

I wandered in the frozen garden until lunchtime, being left to my own devices. Randolph failed to put in an appearance and I was informed that it was extremely unlikely he would be seen that day. After consultation with Duke I felt it best if I departed after lunch, and that is how my visit ended.

Immediately I got home I took the precaution of writing a detailed but discreet account to Montague-Browne. He replied immediately and with some sympathy for all concerned, saying that he felt Randolph 'has great qualities and labours under many difficulties,' a verdict with which, even with my limited knowledge, I totally agreed. Randolph did ring me on a few occasions following my visit and sent me some pamphlets he had had privately printed – further instalments in his never-ending battle with Fleet Street. When eventually I lowered my head over the typewriter to write his father's story, I was often taken with the similarities: the relationship of Winston to

Left My mother and father at their Golden Wedding Anniversary.
Below George Courtney Ward's picture of Nanette the day I said goodbye to my staff at Elstree Studios

The family, summer 1974

Lord Randolph and Randolph to Winston had many things in common, though in the end one struggled free of his father's shadow to lift again the 'tattered flag' he found lying on a stricken field, whilst the other was ultimately denied proper opportunities to champion the causes he had inherited.

My own Churchill story is a story of the lunacies and petty intrigues that the film industry seemingly cannot live without, and ultimately it is a story of failure. I will come to the final chapters in due course, for like everything connected with Sir Winston there was always an unpredictable element and it would be bad scholarship to anticipate events.

Forty-eight

Commonsense prevailed at that point, and in company with Sheila and Bunter we went for a much needed holiday in St Moritz. I went suitably equipped as an Olympic class skier, for appearances' sake only, an earlier experience of that highly fashionable sport having cured me for all time of any dreams of glory on the slopes.

Two years previously, having been inspired by the glossy travel brochures, Nanette and I had taken off for the Austrian snows. With typical flamboyance, not to say conceit, I had kitted us out at Simpsons, Piccadilly, choosing only the finest clothing and equipment. My good friend Jack Creed who had risen from the sales floor of that elegant establishment to become a member of the Board, tried to dissuade me from being too ambitious. I refused to be persuaded and selected the most expensive gear in the shop.

We got to Austria roughly forty-eight hours before the snows melted. True, we did have one morning on the nursery slopes and availed ourselves of the services of an impossibly dashing ski instructor. It took me an embarrassingly long hour to crab my way to the top of a very gentle incline, my tortuous progress made all the more humiliating by the presence of five-year-olds whizzing past with consummate ease.

I was close to a coronary by the time I gained the summit and badly in need of an oxygen mask. The superior young ski instructor only had eyes for Nanette and since she had trained as a ballet dancer her grasp of the essentials of the balance needed put me to immediate shame.

Eventually finding the courage to look down the route I had just climbed I became convinced that I was on the North face of Everest. The instructor explained everything to me a third time then took off with Nanette. She reached the bottom without mishap and it was then my turn.

Ignoring the multi-lingual jeers of the assorted infants swooping around me like seagulls dipped in paint, I became increasingly aware that I could not delay forever. I had long since ceased worrying about my dignity: it was merely a question of survival. I started to bring my skis into line as I had been told, but the moment I lifted the first an inch off the ground I was in motion.

Before I had covered ten yards I was on my back, totally demented and criss-crossed by an accompanying posse of little horrors. I went past Nanette and the instructor like a Toulouse Lautrec impersonator who had suddenly found himself in a Keystone Kops movie, eyes tightly closed, arse burning from the friction and heading straight for a wooden tea-hut. The final humiliation came when my headlong flight was arrested by the waiting children and the moment they had stopped me they made off again, climbing the impossible slope as though on invisible wires.

Near hysteria replaced the relief on Nanette's face. I struggled to my feet and kicked the rented skis loose. 'That's it!' I said. 'That's the last time I ever set foot on any bloody slope. The whole thing is impossible and absurd.'

We spent the next two days inside the hotel while it poured with rain, our only diversion being a growing disbelief in the gargantuan appetites of our fellow guests, all of whom closely resembled Oliver Hardy dressed as a yodeller.

'Look,' I said, 'why don't we go on to Paris. At least Paris is civilized and we know it.' We went to Paris. When we arrived at the hotel (a three-star recommendation from the Bunters who must have been drunk at the time) I was greatly concerned that our luggage was taken from us by an old lady. I was shocked at the thought of her carrying our heavy cases up to our rooms, and she was shocked by the thought that I was attempting to rob her of a tip. We had a somewhat farcical wrestling match in the lobby of the hotel, watched by an assortment of amazed fellow guests and staff. The old lady proved to be as strong as an ox and I lost the best of three falls. In the confusion I omitted to count the number of cases and when we eventually reached our room (which contained a double bed so large that it touched three of the four walls) I suddenly discovered that the one containing my entire wardrobe was missing.

I dashed downstairs again but the taxi had disappeared. It was the beginning of a three-day nightmare worthy of Kafka. I went to the police who sent me to the Ministry of Transport, who directed me back to the police. I spent hours filling in forms only to find that I had made out an application to *import* suitcases. Before this mistake had been pointed out I wasted a further afternoon with Customs officials. Never tell me that the French haven't got a sense of humour. When they read my completed form they behaved as though Fernandel had given them a command performance.

After the laughter and heavy wit, more advice accompanied by dramatic gestures. Another form and directions to the taxi-drivers' lost property office. It was on the other side of Paris. I went there, only to find it closed – not only closed but to all intents derelict.

Back to the hotel and our hideous room. The act of getting undressed for bed had much in common with the Marx Brothers' ship's cabin scene in *A Night At The Opera*. That portion of the room not filled with the enormous bed was occupied by the bidet and a small shower stall. Use of the bidet carried with it the certain risk of castration and the shower head, corroded solid, was at such an angle that it flooded the foot of the bed.

I suspect that at one time the room had been a broom cupboard, for it was cramped between the lift-shaft and a toilet apparently directly connected to the Paris Metro. When you pulled the chain the water appeared to drop into a bottomless pit and then a short time afterwards was forced back with an angry roar accompanied by a chill wind. The lift was hand-operated by the old crone and was in use throughout the night. Since everybody in the hotel appeared to be sleeping on our floor and in constant need to relieve themselves, our slumbers were, to say the least, fretful.

By the end of the third day I had become, in Nanette's memorable phrase, 'a one-man Marat Sade' intent upon mass murder. It was a holiday to remember.

Fortunately, there was no repetition in St Moritz and having recharged my batteries in the hot house luxury of Suvretta House I came back to finalize my plans for the trip to Dublin.

Montague-Browne had kindly arranged for me to have a short meeting with Sir Winston on the day before my departure, so on the afternoon of 25 February I presented myself at No. 28 Hyde Park Gate. Sir Winston was sitting beside the fire in one of the downstairs rooms. He was wearing his dark blue siren suit and greeted me gravely as though I had come on an important mission. After making the necessary introductions Montague-Brown left us alone, though he had previously warned me that Sir Winston tired easily and therefore my visit would have to be a short one.

I sat on the opposite side of the fire immediately aware that I was unequal to the occasion. A sense of awe overwhelmed me and drove most of my pre-rehearsed dialogue clean out of my head. We exchanged a few pleasantries, and then he said, 'You must lead a very interesting life, Mr Forbes.' I felt compelled to deny that my life had any interest worth talking about.

He stared at me for a long time.

'Would you like a whisky?'

'Thank you, sir, yes.' It was about three-thirty in the afternoon and I was already drunk with nerves.

'Pour me one, too, while you're about it.' He gestured to the decanter by his side. If I showed any hesitation as to the correct amount to pour, he dismissed it with another gesture. I handed him half a tumbler full and took a slightly less generous measure for myself. He then offered me a cigar, which I accepted but could not light.

'Anthony's told me about the script you're writing. Tell me more.'

I explained that I was having difficulties locating authentic material, material that I could trust, for surprisingly enough his early life was not very well documented at that time. Choosing something at random, I asked him if he could remember what horse he had ridden at the Battle of Omdurman. He thought for a long time.

'It was a Grey,' he said. 'A Windsor Grey.'

Did he also remember the name of the horse? He stared past

me. His glass was empty and he motioned me to refill it. 'And you,' he said.

I topped up my own glass. The whisky, combined with the heat of the fire, was already conspiring to render me even more stupid than I already felt. I noticed that his cigar had gone out and I struck a match for him and he rested his hand on mine while I held the flame steady.

'I know quite a bit about you, Mr Forbes,' he said out of the blue. 'I think you'll write a very good script about me . . .' The words trailed off again. Trying to judge my moment, I broke the silence and attempted to draw him on the subject of his father. Again he stared at me. It was as if his mind was like a lighthouse: sometimes the beam came round and illuminated the past, and then revolved again and all was blackness.

'I didn't know my father,' he said. 'Not at the time. Not at the time.'

Then he returned to his original and devastating opening remark. 'You have a very interesting life, Mr Forbes.' For the second time I could find no rejoinder to it. So we just sat and looked into the fire. He seemed very tired and it took him a long time to raise the glass to his lips, though once it was there he dispatched its contents expertly. He allowed me to replenish it a third time before Montague-Browne returned and silently indicated that the audience was at an end. I took my farewells and walked unsteadily out of the room.

I realized that I was totally drunk and in no condition to drive away from the house. So I confessed all to Montague-Browne who put me in the secretaries' office where I was provided with bread and butter and a cup of tea. After a decent interval I felt confident enough to face the mundane world again then suddenly remembered that I had brought with me a first edition of Sir Winston's biography of his father in the hope that he would sign the two volumes for me. Montague-Browne took them but warned that his boss was very reluctant to sign anything those days. He did sign them though and I have them still. They are possibly amongst the last he ever so honoured.

I was still in a daze when I boarded my flight for Dublin the following morning. Prior to my departure I had engaged a chauffeur cum valet who had worked on several of my films as a unit driver. His name was Reg Howell – The Great Reg as he came to be known, for he stayed in my employment until his retirement in 1973. Reg followed in my white Bentley, taking the land-sea route and carried with him some hundred volumes that I required for my further research on the Churchill script.

Jimmy had taken the penthouse suite in the Gresham Hotel for us to share for the duration of the film and immediately upon arrival I moved a plain trestle table into my bedroom, hired an electric typewriter and went to work. It was an ideal arrangement, for I had the necessary isolation coupled with the day and night hotel service. I could thus work any hours I chose without worrying about meals or the necessity to dress. I frequently wrote through the night when the script was going well, the Great Reg fending off all unwelcome calls and attending to my basic needs – an endless supply of coffee and cigarettes.

Gradually the rest of the cast assembled. Kim Novak and Larry Harvey were playing the Bette Davis and Leslie Howard roles. Henry Hathaway, the director, had wanted the main cast in Ireland ahead of time for rehearsals and we mostly drove out to Kim's hotel for these sessions. She had chosen to stay put outside Dublin in a hotel that had once been the home of John McCormack, a large mansion standing in its own wind-swept grounds and overlooking a lake. The arrival of the film company and especially the arrival of Kim, who was then a major sex symbol, had evoked considerable local interest and she felt the need to be unavailable to the Press.

I liked her very much and felt sorry for her because she and Hathaway never hit it off from day one. Larry was always the supreme professional and never allowed his private feelings to intrude upon his work. Affable, very funny, unfailingly polite, he was too battle-scarred to want to get involved in a personality war. Contrary to the image he liked to foster in the Press, he was not a difficult man to work with, though he had a contempt for anything sham and never concealed his true feelings if pushed too far.

Because of my own involvement with the Churchill script Nanette had reluctantly agreed to a certain degree of separation.

Hathaway had cast her for the secondary female role, but she was not required until later in the schedule and I had persuaded her that it would be better if I broke the back of my assignment before she arrived.

The studios at Ardmore were being picketed by the local technicians' union when we started shooting. It was a very Irish strike, since they greeted us with much affection whenever we drove through their ranks and were easily persuaded to put down their placards and join us for a few jars. The studio itself had a pleasant rural atmosphere. The pace of things swiftly reddened Henry Hathaway's neck and he chewed his cigars at a faster rate. He had considerable reservations about the suitability of Kim in the leading role. She, I felt, wanted to be wanted, but that was not Hathaway's style. The film plodded up to the starting post in an atmosphere of suspicion.

To understand Kim Novak one has to have some appreciation of her background. She was the product of a particular era in Hollywood, and of a particular studio regime during that era. She confided to me that early in her career she had been told 'All you are is a piece of meat in a butcher's shop.' I am certain that she was quoting verbatim, for the people who were then in control had perfected a grossness of language and behaviour towards the contracted talent that defies exaggeration.

'*The Story of a Bitch*' screamed the first trade advertisements, and since film publicity men never throw away the first mould they think of, it was inevitable that Kim be cast as a bitch heroine in real life as well as in the celluloid fiction.

Hathaway had made considerable revisions to my script and some of the dialogue was a little heavy-handed. He had also decided that medical students who drank tea were not his idea of masculinity, so the tea rooms where Maugham's crippled hero first meets the waitress, Mildred, had been transformed at his insistence into a cross between a Western Pool parlour and an Irish beer house. Poor John Box, the art director, wandered around despondently, telling everybody willing to listen that he had it in mind to resign. 'The fucking hero's got a club foot,' Hathaway said, 'you want him to lose his balls as well?'

Resignations were in the air from day one. Larry was never a selfish actor and did his best to help Kim in her scenes, but she was so scared of Hathaway that she could hardly think straight. It was embarrassing to be present when he directed her, for he was blunt to the point of crudeness. It was quite obvious that the explosion had to come sooner or later. The only way to get a performance from Kim was by kindness and kindness was a luxury on our set.

Possibly because of my reputation with Leslie Caron on *The L-Shaped Room* Kim became convinced that I was her only hope of salvation. She asked me to dinner at her hotel. When I arrived I found she had arranged for the meal to be served in her room. It was a wild and romantic night with an impossibly bright moon shining through John McCormack's Georgian windows. Warning bells sounded loud and clear as I stepped over the threshold. I listened to her closely reasoned and not unflattering case, but refused to be drawn into any sort of commitment. I had enough experience to know that the film was locked into a disaster course and that although I might be given a hero's welcome at the outset, there was nothing but a firing squad at the end of the road. I liked Kim and wanted to help her, but the moment was not propitious. When I drove back to the Gresham that night I knew it could only be a matter of time, that a showdown was inevitable.

Ray Stark of Seven Arts, the American company responsible for the financing of the film, flew in from New York. His major contribution was to send everybody enormous bunches of flowers with false greeting cards attached. Thus Kim got a bouquet from Hathaway and Hathaway got one from Jimmy and I got one from Larry, the only beneficiary being the local florist.

It was decided to stop shooting on Kim while they shopped around for a replacement. This news was concealed from Kim but effectively leaked to everybody else. Within a matter of hours it had become front-page news and a fresh batch of journalists flew in to lay siege. Larry and I continued to work spasmodically, acting as it were in a vacuum, and Hathaway concentrated on the exterior scenes which did not involve Kim.

Hathaway finally resigned from the film and flew out the same day. I got the expected phone call from Kim, during which she invited me to take his place. When I declined, she flew to London and went to ground. The Press had a field day and shooting came to a complete halt.

It was now Ray Stark's turn to invite me to step into the breach as director. He said that the alternative was abandonment. In the end I agreed to take over the direction until such time as a permanent replacement could be found. I said that I would not, under any circumstances, direct Kim because I felt that she was confused enough. Instead I would concentrate on one important sequence which was mainly concerned with the sub-plot between Siobhan McKenna and Larry. It was a sequence which could be taken in isolation and left the new director, whoever he turned out to be, free to structure the bulk of the film according to his own conception of it.

I began work the following morning while negotiations started with Ken Hughes to replace me. It says much for Larry that he accepted my changed role without protest. We obtained some usable footage which I believe was included in the final version of the film.

I finished my stint and Ken Hughes arrived to take over the reins. I had no quarrel with his desire to rewrite the script himself and indeed welcomed it, since my original had long since been abandoned. There were further rumours that Elizabeth Taylor was going to replace Kim, but they were the dying embers of a story that had become a bore.

It seems incredible now that I ever found time to work on my Churchill script, but of course the drama has been condensed in this account and there were long periods when I was not required on the film. My part in the saga took the best part of two months and by that time my acting contract had run out. I arrived at the studio one morning expecting to resume work only to be told at third hand that my role had been taken over by Jack Hedley. My dressing-room had already been stripped and my name removed from the door. I was handed my personal possessions in a brown paper parcel. I was angered at the method, but not unrelieved. Jimmy was back in London, so I occupied the penthouse suite alone and used the peace and quiet to complete my script. I have seldom written with such enthusiasm.

I became so immersed in Churchill's early life that, borrowing from Sir Winston's own account of his father and suiting his words to my own purposes I tried to show that 'it is not by soft touches of a picture, but in hard mosaic or tessellated pavement, that a man's life and fortunes must be presented in all their reality and romance'. I adopted an unconventional method of telling the story, unconventional in that many of the more accepted practices for screen biographies were consciously flouted.

I felt that the end of Churchill's story had obscured all the beginnings and in studying the great mass of material charting the middle and later years I was struck by the selectivity of his biographers. They appeared to live in the shadow of a common literary Whip, duly filing out at Division time to record the same vote with too much favour and not enough fear. In my frequent letters to Marty Rackin, then the supervising Head of Production for Paramount, I emphasized my belief that one should never handle history, even in the making, with too much reverence. He appeared to trust my judgement: as I sent him instalments of work in progress his letters became more and more enthusiastic.

On 4 April he wrote to say that he had received the first half of the film and that 'it is a fine job . . . you have brought the characters to life . . . Take your time, we are not contractual ogres . . . you are getting into the meat of the story. You have now set up the cause and I assume Part 11 is the effect.'

I had somehow to marry the present with the past, visually and economically. I achieved this by the device of starting the film in the deserted House of Commons and stated in my stage directions: 'We are intruding – that is the feeling I want. It is night and there is no sound. We search out the empty Government benches, then gradually become aware of a sound from afar. The sound resolves itself, it becomes the sound of the House in session, but without identity.

'We can just make out the blurred voice of a Member making a speech, and all this time my camera is creeping forward, panning off to take in the empty Opposition benches.

Then my camera pans back to the Government benches and now, dramatically, they are peopled. The year is 1874. Lord Randolph Churchill is on his feet addressing the House. He is twenty-five years old and gives the impression that he would be more at home in the stalls of the Gaiety Theatre than the Houses of Parliament.

'Again we do not hear his words as he makes his maiden speech, but we photograph him from all angles, utilizing television techniques that allow us to have three or more images on the screen at once, overlapping each other so that the multiple portrait of one man gives us an immediate and lasting impression of character in the shortest possible time.

'This multiple image is, in turn, suddenly and ruthlessly replaced by the horrifying spectacle of an H-bomb explosion. We watch the mushroom blossom silently, enormously, seeing through it the staring faces of Disraeli's Opposition.'

I took the year 1874 as the present, whilst using the device of intercutting a series of dramatic pictures that flashed backwards from 1963 to the constant starting point of Lord Randolph's maiden speech. In this way I hoped to convey a sense of historical perspective which would place the early life of Winston Churchill firmly in context in the minds of my future audiences.

This opening sequence (during which I intended to superimpose my credit titles) was not to be judged in isolation: it was the key to my whole structure. The dramatic framework I had chosen surrounded two events of note: starting with Lord Randolph's maiden speech in 1874 and ending with Winston's speech to the House in 1901. I employed the same device of cross-cutting stock newsreel footage with normal recreated footage during Winston's 1901 speech as I had during his father's, but with this difference: when it came to Winston's turn I reversed the procedure, going *forward* in time to the morning of 11 May 1941. The last image would show Churchill the war-leader, then aged sixty-seven, standing in hat and coat amid the ruins of the Chamber which the German bombers of the night before had reduced to rubble.

I ended my 400-page script with these words:

'I would have him stand there a long time – long enough for

us to roll up our end titles – contemplating the desolate scene, grinding his stick in the charred wreckage; for this was his home, not Blenheim, and if there were tears on his face that May morning I would photograph them, for they were tears for the "old talking shop" and they came from his heart.'

I finished writing those words in the Gresham at three o'clock on the morning of 14 April having worked non-stop from 11 a.m. the previous day and completing a last stint of fifty pages. My diary emotionally records: 'I cried as I wrote the last paragraph. Home to England!'

The finished script was sent to Montague-Browne and Paramount on 19 April and by that time I was back in my beloved Seven Pines. Picking up the threads with Bunter I discovered that our plans for *Seance on a Wet Afternoon* had reached stalemate. Simone Signoret had been approached to play the role of the medium, but had turned it down because she shared Nanette's and Sheila's aversion to the central theme of kidnapping a child. For a variety of reasons every other leading actress we thought of was unavailable and it seemed highly probable that we would have to shelve the whole project.

I began again, completely rewriting the script as a vehicle for two men with the idea of submitting the revised version to Sir Alec Guinness and Tom Courtenay. Without in any way denigrating the eventual performances of Kim Stanley and Bunter, I still think that had my idea worked it would have made an incredible film, bizarre in the extreme and years ahead of its time.

The rewrite was completed by 2 May and dispatched to Sir Alec and Tom. While waiting for their reactions I received word from Montague-Browne that the Churchill Estate liked my script and would give their unofficial approval to it. He explained that he wasn't in a position to go further at the moment because, legally, the submission of the script had to come from Paramount and they had not yet made any indication of their feelings. I was further encouraged by a wildly enthusiastic cable from Hugh French and a letter from my esteemed American agent, Evarts Ziegler, who said 'If Churchill and Paramount don't like it I will throw up, give up and go into the shoe business.' He is still my agent and has so far not challenged Dolcis, but Paramount in an abrupt about face decided that they didn't like it.

TREATMENT DISAPPOINTING FROM OUR POINT OF VIEW STOP FEEL LACKING IN PERSONAL DRAMA STOP REGARDS RACKIN was the cable I received. Nothing else. That was all.

After the first shock I sublimated my anger and disgust in work, but like the *herpes simplex* virus it lay just beneath the surface of my ego. From time to time I received vague rumblings on the grapevine that the project was being reconsidered, but nobody communicated with me direct. I was a plague carrier. The usual game of executive musical chairs was played out at Paramount and both Rackin and his superior, Jacob H. Karp, departed. Then, by chance, I learnt that Columbia were on the point of purchasing the rights for Carl Foreman. With the help of Bud Ornstein of United Artists I rushed in with a counter bid, but I was too late, my own house, as it were, was sold over my head.

The London Press was not slow to solicit my reaction to this development since the Churchill project had always commanded space. I expressed my disappointment at being 'pipped at the post'. For reasons I never fully comprehended this innocuous phrase offended Carl and he issued a characteristically portentous statement under the heading 'These are the facts' to the effect that far from being 'pipped at the post' my treatment had been unacceptable to Sir Winston. Further, a spokesman in Carl's publicity office claimed to one newspaper that my efforts had been rejected by the Churchill family. The paper published this defamatory untruth.

A decade after the event it all seems so squalid and unimportant, but at the time I felt utterly crushed and was persuaded to take legal advice. The newspaper subsequently published a retraction and paid costs. I approached Montague-Browne for corroboration of my version, but although he wrote back most sympathetically his position was such that his feelings had to remain private. The new arrangement with Carl and Columbia was financially advantageous to Sir Winston's estate and there was nothing further to be said or done.

I had my script bound in full Morocco, an expensive conceit

perhaps, and placed it on my shelves alongside those other unsung efforts I alone thought worthy of preservation.

Carl wrote his own script and years later asked me to direct it. I felt at the time that his gesture, however well-intentioned, betrayed a certain lack of sophistication (or too much sophistication, depending on your point of view). I had a legitimate reason for declining his offer and the eventual honour fell to Bunter. I have never seen the film he made from Carl's script, which is disloyal of me, but there are some places you never want to return to.

Forty-nine

Sir Alec Guinness wrote a gracious and flatteringly-phrased letter, but declined to appear in *Seance*. The script was now in ruins, having undergone so many changes that it resembled a literary abbatoir. I had no idea what to do next and it seemed likely that we would have to abandon it. Then Richard Gregson made a suggestion. He felt that a fellow screenwriter might find a way of releasing me from my mental block and arranged for Ken Taylor, another of his clients, and somebody whose work I had admired, to visit me at Seven Pines. Ken sat down one Sunday morning and read the various versions. At the end of this marathon, he said: 'Try something very simple, but revolutionary. Go back to the woman and instead of having her communicate with an *imaginary* child, make it her own child, a child who died at birth.' It was a brilliantly simple solution and I embraced him for it and later sent him a crate of champagne, he having refused any form of financial reward. I wrote 110 new pages in under a week and that was the script I shot.

Our eventual choice of actress for the leading role was Kim Stanley. I had recalled her extraordinary performance in a little-known film, *The Goddess*, flew to New York, located her, persuaded her and signed her.

How can I describe Kim? A brilliant actress, instinctive and inventive, but her own worst enemy. A delightful person, but haunted by self-doubt. No temperament whatsoever in the ordinary boring theatrical sense, but often maddening to work with. Bunter was amazing with her, for the film had to stand or fall by their intricate relationship and I had deliberately written dialogue where the cues frequently bore no relation to what had gone before. It was like a monster crossword being solved by two people at once, each consulting a different set of clues. Kim found the technicalities of film-making alien and frightening. She was a fervent disciple of the New York

Method School of acting and Bunter's ability (learnt from necessity) to switch from actor to producer and back to actor again throughout the working day, disconcerted her.

It was often an agonizingly difficult film to make, though never an unhappy one. Once again I was directing a small child, this time a girl called Judith Donner I had discovered in a local Weybridge school. Gerry Turpin was lighting camera-man for me and Derek Yorke my editor, three of the *Saturday Night* team reunited after a long absence. There is no single shot in the film that does not owe something to Gerry's invention. He gave a remarkable look to the film without which it would have failed. Derek brought that total dedica-tion to the editing bench that has always been his hallmark, considering every frame with the stooped concentration of a Biblical scholar on the shores of the Dead Sea.

Many times during the shooting period I became convinced that we were on a disaster course and that the finished result would be dismissed out of hand. (In retrospect I find I have conveniently disregarded the agonies of the actual making of all my films, yet when I come to consult the pertinent diaries I find that day after day the entries record nothing but despair. It's like childbirth, I suppose – the pain and the fears are lost in the delight of the eventual delivery.)

There were some incidents to lighten the daily struggle. One particular night stands out. We were scheduled to shoot a number of unrelated sequences which, in order to save money, were lumped together. The night's call began as soon as the light had faded and we assembled in Great Portland Street. It is never easy to film in the streets of London, for the authorities don't bend over backwards to grant facilities. On the night in question we began with a scene involving Bunter catching and riding a London Transport double-decker bus. Jack Rix, my production manager, had hired a bus complete with authentic driver and conductor, though we intended to substitute our own actor-conductor for the actual shoot-ing.

He was a West Indian I had used on previous occasions called Frank Singuinea, and for some reason the costumiers had given him a uniform that made him look as though he was working for Wells Fargo. It was quite hopeless and there was no way of changing it. I therefore approached the real-life conductor and asked if he would be kind enough to lend us portions of his uniform, namely the cap, jacket and badge. I suspect he was an Alf Garnett, for he eyed Frank with unconcealed distaste but, lacking the courage of his dubious convictions, produced a quite ludicrous excuse. 'This is my personal licence to conduct,' he said, 'and it is not allowed to leave my person.'

'Well, we don't want to keep it,' I said. 'We just want to borrow it for a few minutes. You can have it back between shots.'

'I have to inform you that such procedure is outside my jurisdiction. It is clearly laid down that a personal licence cannot be passed to any other party. At all times, it must remain on my body.'

He sounded like a character out of the Goon show, but I didn't have time to prolong the argument. My prop man, Georgie Ball, quickly fashioned a make-shift badge out of a cigarette packet and Gerry said he could get away with it in the available light. I tacked something else on to the fake cap and we were ready for shooting. It was an easy shot on paper and merely required Bunter to jump on the moving bus. I rehearsed the extras and in an effort to placate the real conductor told him that he still remained in charge and could give the necessary signals to his driver. The driver was instructed to circle the block and come back to the starting point as soon as possible.

We turned the cameras, Bunter jumped on board and the bus went a few yards and then stopped. Bunter got off and ran back to me. 'He's a maniac,' he said. 'The moment I got on he asked me for my fare. I told him I hadn't got any money on me and that it didn't matter, but he insisted that it was against the law for anybody to travel without a fare.'

I had a further discussion with the conductor, explaining that we had hired the bus for the night and therefore it was ours to do as we wished with it. I explained it very patiently in words of two syllables. Mr Attenborough, I told him, was an actor. He was *acting* getting on a bus. He would *pretend* to give the money. It was all in order and we were not breaking the law.

'Right,' the man said. 'Just as long as I have made my own position clear. I have registered the complaint and what you do from now onwards is your own responsibility.'

We did the shot again and this time the bus moved out of sight without mishap. But it didn't reappear. After ten minutes I sent all the assistants to look for it and it was eventually found at a Request stop where a near-demented Bunter, complete with false nose, was attempting to convince half a dozen real passengers that the bus was not in service. The conductor, apparently, had been prepared to take them on board.

Having sorted that out, I removed some of the seats on the upper deck for I had a dialogue sequence to get with Bunter and Frank with the bus in motion. We therefore had to use a blimped Mitchell camera, which is a bulky piece of equipment. The moment my carpenters started to remove a few seats the real conductor went berserk. We decided to ignore him and I concentrated on instructing the real-life driver. He proved to be another from the same mould.

'When we get going,' I said, 'just keep driving. Make for Trafalgar Square.'

'Where's Trafalgar Square?' he said.

'You don't know where Trafalgar Square is?'

'Never driven in London before. We're from Uxbridge.'

We patiently gave him the route, calmed the conductor again and took on board some twenty extras to fill out the scene. I was directing them downstairs and told the driver to move off. He had only gone a few yards when our friend the conductor pressed the bell for him to stop. 'Now what's happened?' I said.

'You are smoking downstairs. Smoking is only allowed on top deck. I must therefore ask you to either stop smoking or get off the bus.'

'I am the director,' I said. 'It is my bus. I have paid for it. I have paid for you and your driver. I am allowed to do what I like during the period of hire.'

'Not while I am in charge,' he said.

I flung my cigarette out into the night.

'Furthermore,' he said, 'I must point out to you that the Sambo impersonating a London Transport conductor is improperly dressed.'

'I *know* he's improperly dressed. I explained that to you when I asked if we might borrow your cap and badge.'

'He looks a typical Sambo.'

'Don't call him Sambo,' I said. 'His name is Mr Singuinea and he is a member of Equity.' My own dialogue was becoming as absurd as his, and I went upstairs before I lost all control and threw him into the gutter. We somehow managed to shoot the sequence without more delays, although the bus, as unpredictable as its crew, finally gave out altogether in Oxford Street.

Perhaps the most extraordinary event of our location shooting in London took place in Soho. The script called for Bunter to make certain purchases at a street trader's stall in Berwick Market before the kidnapping. Having been moved on several times by the police I realized that any attempt to set up my camera in such a crowded thoroughfare would immediately invite confiscation. I therefore told Jack to try and find me a first floor room above one of the neighbouring shops that I could rent for a short period. Bunter was fitted with a radio microphone and it was my intention to shoot the sequence from above and afar with a telephoto lens.

Jack came back and reported that he had done a deal with the owner of a betting shop who was prepared to grant us facilities at an exorbitant price. Rather than waste time in argument I agreed the terms and we prepared to move a small unit into the building. The owner preceded us up the stairs and produced a large bunch of keys. There were three separate locks on the door he opened for us, which I thought odd, but nothing had prepared us for the sight which greeted us inside the room.

It was bare of all furniture, squalid in the extreme and crouched in one corner were three Chinamen in their underwear. The stench was such that Penny, my continuity girl, was unable to remain in the room.

'Don't mind them,' the owner said. 'They won't give you any trouble, but keep the door locked.'

We hastily set up the Arriflex camera in the window, an

action which caused obvious alarm to the Chinese and it occurred to me that they possibly thought the camera was a machine gun. It was necessary for us to work with handkerchiefs over our mouths, since the unfortunate inmates of the room had used one corner as a loo. I have no idea what they made of the whole thing, for they remained in the corner throughout and although I felt compelled to give them a smile as I exited, their expressions never changed.

The owner of the shop was waiting outside and relocked the door.

'What's happening in there?' I asked him. 'Why are those men locked in without clothes?'

'You paid me for the use of the room, not for information.'

I told Bunter the details and we both resolved to get to the bottom of the matter. After some enquiries amongst the costermongers in the neighbourhood we learnt that there was a flourishing trade in smuggling Chinese into the country without visas or passports. They were kept minus their clothes until such time as their friends could produce enough money to buy a forged passport, after which they were released to vanish into Soho and find employment as waiters and laundrymen. A sad and sordid trade.

I wanted to reach Kim as a woman as well as an actress, but I got the impression that her genuine emotions were exclusively reserved for her work, and of course that is the yellow-brick road to self-destruction. I had this transient intimacy with her, a sort of love affair through the lens that is often characteristic of the relationship between a director and his leading lady, but when the time came for us to say goodbye, I scarcely knew her as a person. She had this distaste for anything that smacked of conventional stardom. I tried to convince her that star performances cannot be avoided. They are the flashes of lightning that illuminate the dramatist's darkness. The theatre was never intended to be a temple where all the high priests look and sound alike (which seemed to me to be the end result of the Strasberg Method). The Theatre needs mysticism, occasional blasphemy, rituals that are larger than life, disciples who are not afraid to risk damnation. Kim remained unconvinced.

She was undoubtedly one of the most naturally gifted actresses of her generation, with the intelligence to recognize what was good for her, but sometimes ignoring that intelligence. Sadly, she now acts less and less. She once told me that she despised the trappings of success, so perhaps her withdrawal is deliberate.

She never told me what she thought about her finished performance on the screen, or indeed what she thought about the film as a whole. It was as if she wished to wipe the slate clean. I thought it a great performance, and my judgement was confirmed by the New York film critics who awarded her their accolade: it was the second time in a row that I had guided my leading lady towards that coveted honour.

It is always lonely out there on the studio floor, for we practise our craft at ungodly hours. Kim was lonelier than most, for she never stopped trying to come to terms with truth – her truth. And that is more than can be said for most of us.

Fifty

John Trevelyan, the censor, was not impressed with *Seance on a Wet Afternoon* and I recorded his verdict, warts and all, in my diary for 2 January 1964. Granted the need for a film censor, a question open to continuing debate, it is doubtful whether anybody could have done the job better than John. Chain-smoking his way through porn and pleasure, his lean and hungry look gave no indication of his true character. In the early days my relationship with him was purely formal but as he eased into his emperor's clothing he made a genuine effort to remove most of the mystique and was at some pains to earn the confidence of responsible film-makers. That is not to say that John dispensed one law for us and another for the out and out carpetbagger. We all had to abide by the same rules, but he used his vast experience of the worst of human nature, to which, within the confines of Wardour Street he was no stranger, to judge whether we had introduced violence or sex for purely spurious effect or whether our intentions had been dramatically honourable. To this extent he was primarily responsible for the growing maturity of British films during the Sixties. There are some who blame John in part for the present permissive society, failing to recognize that change was inevitable. What he did – all he could do – was to give a lead, guiding film-makers and audiences alike in deliberate, easy stages. Emotionally I am opposed to all and any form of censorship, but I am cynically aware of the commercial profitability of violence and perverted sex and there is no doubt in my mind that had we not had John's restraining hand the flood gates of filth would have opened wide a decade ago. And I do not think it is difficult for men of reason and intelligence to define filth. I think it is dishonest to postulate that there should be no restrictions put upon those responsible for the manufacture and public exhibition of mass 'entertainment'. I believe passionately in the cinema as a means of enlightenment, but I cannot embrace the idea that the calculated exploitation of violence or degrading sexual acts has any place of honour in a civilized society. I have often wondered whether the defenders of total permissiveness draw the line at public execution. Films are made for commercial gain. They are made to be shown to the widest possible audience. It is not difficult to make a film that degrades both the participants and the participators. If you doubt this truism pay your money and buy a ticket for one of the fringe cinemas in New York. There, in 1974, in colour, on the wide screen, the first show starting at 10 a.m., you could have seen an infinite variety of photographed illustrations from the more depressing pages of Kraft-Ebbing.

Naturally, being a person of intelligence and sophistication, you would have left the cinema uplifted, with a greater understanding of the human spirit. The sight of all those pathetic creatures struggling to maintain some semblance of dignity whilst performing their sad acts would have enhanced the quality of your life and made you a better person. You would not have been corrupted in any way, any more than you would have been corrupted by viewing documentary footage of Belsen for pleasure. After all, a working knowledge of multiple rape is all part of life's rich pageant. You are not only being entertained, you are supporting the arts, widening your horizons, keeping up with trends, and you are much too sensible for it to have any lasting effect – only *them*, other people, are capable of being diminished by such experiences. Anonymous in the darkness, you can sit back and enjoy the edifying spectacle of an 'actress' masturbating, or an 'actor' pulping a woman's face during an act of sexual degradation. Then, as your experience widens, and your spiritual needs increase, you can move on to greater pleasures, confident in the certain knowledge that there is no limit to human invention. Perhaps the trailer for next week will reveal *glimpses of a more artistic* teasing nature – who knows? Perhaps one of the gifted purveyors of mass entertainment is planning a musical comedy version of the Moors Murders. You need never fear that you will become bored by repetition, for as long as there is money to be made somebody, somewhere, somehow will satisfy your needs.

Do I anticipate with exaggeration? I doubt it. By the time this book has appeared in print, some part of what I have written above will be in mass circulation, much of it will be old hat. Perhaps Miss Linda Lovelace will be preparing to give us a nude version of *French Without Tears*. After all, Mr Brando has already invited his leading lady to become an amateur proctologist for our edification. He has also promised her a glimpse of a sexual *Animal Farm*, adding a scatological experience which Orwell, in his artistry, declined to predict. This, we have already been assured on high authority, is great art, so we can go to see it with a clear conscience.

1972 was the year of *Last Tango in Paris*, the 'most liberating movie ever made' in the words of Miss Paulene Kael, but her words were out of date even as she wrote them. I am not engaged in the noble art of film criticism, but *Last Tango* could fill the columns of *Private Eye*'s Pseuds Corner for many an issue. Although Brando improvised some of the most banal passages of dialogue, I noted that he failed to improvise revealing his genitals. It was left to the delectable Miss Schneider to realize the masturbatory fantasies of her male audiences – the poor women who paid the same increased price of admission (you always know when you are seeing real art in the cinema, because the exhibitors charge you more) were cheated of their ration of male flesh. The fact that the film was beautifully photographed, had Francis Bacon backgrounds for the titles, a clean sound track and – wonder of wonders – a supremely phoney film within a film, convinced many of the critics that they were in the presence of The Second Celluloid Coming. But technical excellence should not conceal the fact that the plot came out of the ark and that denuded of its four-letter words and butter scene it was a barren offering. Brando is a superb actor and Miss Schneider no hardship to behold in the bath, but did it tell us as much about the human condition as, say, *La Fin du Jour* made thirty years previously, the negative of which was burnt in order that Hollywood could perpetrate a stale remake?

What *Last Tango in Paris* did was to make buggery acceptable as art to those who prefer buggery to Renoir. In two years' time or even less it will look like *Mary Poppins* in the cultural sexual revolution, because the real victory was won at the box office.

Perhaps we shall soon reach that sublime state when, in the words of Norman Mailer, 'the sexual organs show more character than the actors' faces'. As somebody who cares about the film I hope that day comes sooner than later, because then perhaps total boredom will have set in with our audiences and we can set about creating stories that will once again concern themselves with human dignity rather than human degradation.

The question of the human spirit occupied my thoughts when I sat down to write the script of *King Rat* in April 1964. Clavell's stunning novel was drawn from his own experiences as a Japanese prisoner of war in Singapore's Changi Jail. Faced with the task of condensing its 400 pages into screenplay form, I stripped away those portions of the novel I did not wholeheartedly admire (mostly the introduction of native girls which, though possibly authentic, belonged to the realm of Dorothy Lamour) and posed one single question: how did men survive under such conditions? It is my most complex screenplay, with little action and mostly concerned with the interplay of character.

As soon as I had finished the first draft, we made plans to move to Los Angeles. Mike Frankovitch, then production head of Columbia, was anxious to placate the Hollywood craft unions by halting what were termed 'runaway' productions. He decided that two of his first films, my own and William Wyler's *The Collector* which previously would have been shot in Singapore and England, should be made from the Gower Street Columbia studios.

We rented a modestly luxurious house on Laurel Way, high in the Beverly Hills canyons and complete with pool – the first we had ever enjoyed. Our passages were booked on the *Queen Mary* and we were taking the Great Reg with us and a sweet Irish girl called Alice we had engaged as a nanny for Sarah. With my usual morbid turn of mind I convinced myself that I would never see my parents again. The year before I had moved them from Newbury Park to a bungalow much nearer Seven Pines. My father was delighted to have a much larger garden, but found the effort of getting to know his new neighbours posed problems. He became concerned with one family who lived at the far end of his land. 'I can't decide what they are,' he said mysteriously. 'They're either Turks . . . or Canadians.' His choice has always fascinated me.

I suppose I never take a trip abroad without one last walk round my own garden and I am always filled with forebodings. I look at a particular tree I have planted and say to myself, well, you'll never see that grow to maturity. I also have a habit of remaking my Will on the eve of departure and have on two occasions had the new Will witnessed at London Airport, sometimes using the staff at the check-in counter as witnesses, a sight which can hardly inspire confidence in my fellow-passengers. It is also a sad fact of my life that most location films seem to start in spring and thus year after year I have been abroad when the garden at Seven Pines was perfection, returning inevitably to the tail-ends of bleak, wind-swept summers when everything is dank and the roses mottled with black spot.

I missed my garden that summer in Hollywood before the film started and, perversely, I also missed the English weather. The rented house was comfortable, we swam in the heated pool at midnight, we made many friends, lived on cheesecake, and yet we were unsettled. There were many problems during the preparatory stages of the film, mostly concerned with casting. From the beginning I had wanted a then almost unknown young actor called George Segal. I was determined to avoid the more obvious star names who I felt would get between the story and the audience. This conception did not find immediate sympathy with the studio and I had to sweat it out. I think they finally gave in to me out of boredom and once George had been signed I was able to forge ahead, assembling one of the best casts I have ever worked with. It included a number of old friends imported from England, chosen as much for their physical appearance as their acting ability since it was vital that they looked under-nourished. When the film came out some critics complained that the cast failed to look as though they were near starvation, but real efforts were made – John Standing in particular dieting to the point where he fainted from malnutrition. The same stipulation had to be made in respect of the 800 extras needed throughout the story.

I was on less sure ground when it came to selecting my first Hollywood crew, for of course I was a complete stranger and had to rely on my own instincts when interviewing personnel. I selected Burney Guffey as my cameraman and the choice dismayed the studio departmental heads. Although his distinguished career ranged from being John Ford's operator on *The Informer* to an Academy Award for *From Here to Eternity*, he was not at that time fashionable and Hollywood is a place where success is measured by your last credit.

He came to see me in my office, a quietly spoken man wearing a wide-brimmed hat, explaining that he was allergic to the sun. We discussed the style of photography I wanted for the film (it was one of the last major films to be made in black and white) and then I hired him. He knew what the talk was about him, and said, 'Well, don't feel too badly if they don't let you have me.'

'If I direct the picture,' I said, 'you'll photograph it. The only thing I can't answer for is if they fire *me*!'

I picked Raoul's brains for the rest of my crew and he led me to my first assistant, Russ Saunders and Freddie Zinnerman's editor, Walter Thompson. They were all much older men than I had been used to, and indeed the average age of my entire crew must have been fifty – my focus puller was in his sixties!

The next problem was to find a suitable location. My art director, Bob Smith, eventually took me to a ranch at Thousand Oaks in the San Fernando Valley, mid-way between Los Angeles and the Malibu coast. He had discovered a dried-up river bed surrounded on all sides by dusty hills which looked as much like Changi in 1943 as Hampstead Garden suburb. Bob convinced me that it would work and retired to his drawing board.

Jimmy Clavell has since told me of his emotions when he visited the simulated Changi at Thousand Oaks for the first time. Bob had performed miracles in an amazingly short space of time. Bulldozers had moved in to clear some twenty-five acres preparatory to building the largest man-made set in the history of Columbia Pictures. I know that it is standard practice for film companies to talk in superlatives, but the undoctored statistics were impressive. There were two main areas in the set. Bob had placed an exact replica of the main prison on an escarpment overlooking the river bed. This was set inside a thirty feet high concrete wall running well over two hundred yards. Below this he positioned the actual camp, building some fifty-two bamboo shacks, some sixty feet long, and with either thatched or tin roofs. Most of these were wired for electricity and contained workable plumbing (such utilities being mostly there for the actual process of making the film rather than historical accuracy). The hillsides around the entire area were sprayed green and hundreds of fake palm trees were planted on their slopes. Enclosing the entire compound was an eight-foot high bamboo and barbed wire fence. In all some half a million square feet of timber, six miles of barbed wire, forty-five thousand feet of straw matting and ten thousand gallons of paint were used by two hundred and fifty skilled craftsmen working round the clock. The entire operation was completed in seven weeks.

In addition, of course, the property department at the studio had to manufacture and then 'age' literally thousands of small items, consulting Clavell and other survivors to discover and then master the ingenuities of that past and horrific age. But the greatest problem we had to solve was to ensure a constant supply of live rats. Braver men than I visited the Los Angeles dock area and came back with a dozen pairs for mating. These were taken direct to the location and housed in cages below the main hut, where eventually they formed part of the action of the film. I learnt a great deal about the mating habits of rats during the making of the film. The female, for instance, can have up to twelve litters a year with anything up to fourteen per litter, the young being born blind and helpless twenty-two days after fertilization. These alarming statistics meant that we had to take stringent precautions and exercise a strict moral code! The actor cast as keeper of the rats became immersed in his role and spent all of his spare time under the hut with his charges.

I well remember the first day of shooting. Reg and I drove

from Laurel Way before first light and I arrived on the location slightly ahead of the main crew. Looking around the vast set all my intricate preparations seemed inadequate. The first shot involved a large crowd and I had planned a little bravura with a complicated camera movement on the crane. I should perhaps mention that in a supreme effort of self-discipline I had managed to forgo cigarettes for the best part of four months, feeling that if I could survive the test of shooting my first film in Hollywood I would be cured once and for all.

It is vital for a director, like a military commander, to establish his authority as quickly as possible and I was therefore anxious for the first day to go smoothly. Russ and the other assistants began to get the extras and cast into position. Fires had to be lit and every man directed in a specific task. During all this I mounted the crane beside Burney and the camera crew and was taken aloft to survey the battlefield. Below me close on a thousand men were awaiting my instructions. I stared at them through my viewfinder. The set went very quiet. Seconds and then minutes ticked away and I became more and more conscious that I hadn't got a thought in my head. I might have been staring down at a crowd of holiday makers on a beach. Panic filled my mouth with bile. Nobody offered any advice, nobody asked me to hurry – the ball, as they say, was in my court. I looked through my viewfinder again, feeling the reverse of Nelson, but inspiration never came. With what I hoped was a normal expression and in what I prayed would come out as a normal voice, I turned to my camera operator, Andy, and said: 'Do you have a fag by any chance?' He stared at me and seemed confused. Then I remembered that the word 'fag' had an entirely different connotation in Hollywood, being then slang for a homosexual. 'Do you have a cigarette?' I stuttered. He produced one. I put it in my mouth and he lit it for me. I drew deeply, saturating my lungs with all that injurious tar and toxins: it was like resuming an old love affair. Without making any medical pronouncements, I can only report that the fog in my brain cleared and that I was galvanized into coherent action. I gave the set-up to Burney, snapped a few instructions to Russ below and ten minutes later we had the first shot in the can. I got through two packs of cigarettes that day and never looked back. There must be a moral there somewhere, but I don't want to be told it.

Day by day descriptions of the making of a film must perforce be boring to outsiders, and are best excluded in a narrative of this kind. Yet I must honour many debts, for the making of *King Rat* was a watershed in my professional life, a unique experience I am unlikely to repeat. I was being paid to create something I passionately believed in with the absolute minimum of interference and the maximum loyalty and co-operation of studio, cast and crew alike. I learnt a great deal from that American crew and however fortunate I am in the future, the situation will never be quite as perfect again. It was a hard, physical film to make, not without its moments of despair and indeed desperation, but at the end of the sixty-two shooting days I was so affected I could scarcely talk for fear of breaking down. I had a rage to live on amongst those tumble-down huts in that barren area we had transformed for an all-too-brief spell of make-believe.

Now, ten years later, the river bed has been flooded to form an artificial lake where my imitation Changi once stood. The ranch at Thousand Oaks has become a fashionable housing estate with a country club and a golf course. I see my bamboo town as some Atlantis below the waters, buried, like a Hollywood that will never return, with some of my yesterdays.

Fifty-one

Emma was conceived in Hollywood, in that rented house high above the Los Angeles smog. It was a wretched pregnancy for Nanette, for she found the heat tiresome and was sick for most of the time I was making the film.

We returned to England just before Christmas 1964 and the baby moved for the first time on New Year's Day. Perhaps it was the return to her native climate, perhaps women carrying feel a primal need to be by their own fireside, but certainly Nanette blossomed when we got home. It therefore seemed the more unthinkable when we were told that all was not well with our unborn child.

She had naturally consulted a gynaecologist in Beverly Hills and once we were home she attempted to make an appointment with Tim Flew, that excellent man who had delivered Sarah. Alas he had been taken seriously ill and was no longer practising. We were recommended to a Mr Braith-waite-Rickford. Although totally different in personality from Tim Flew, he exuded the same confidence. After an examination he told us that one of the reasons Nanette had been so unwell during the early months was that the baby was in a strange position. He took Nanette into hospital for a few days in order to carry out a more detailed examination under anaesthetic, and during this operation he attempted to manipulate the baby into the correct position. The baby resisted all attempts and we were told that this left only two alternatives: it could either be a breech birth or a Caesarian. In the gentlest of layman's language Braithwaite-Rickford told me that a breech delivery held no particular dangers for the mother, but that it was always possible that the head of the child, coming last instead of first, might suffer some damage. With a Caesarian, he explained, there was little or no risk to the child but, although the procedure had become commonplace, it was still a major operation and as such carried with it an element of danger to the mother. The decision, having heard the evidence, had to be mine.

I can recall to this day, when happily it is all far behind us, the night we made the choice – or rather Nanette made the choice. Her calmness humbled me and despite all my inconclusive arguments she would not entertain any risk to the child. She was carrying it and she intended to have it and if a Caesarian was the right choice for the child, then she would have the Caesarian. She picked up the phone and fixed the date – 14 May.

In the midst of all these private agonies I was forced to fly back to Hollywood with John Barry in order to record the music for the film. It was a successful trip and in our curious industry success breeds success. I was much in demand. The Mirisch Brothers offered me virtually a blank cheque to write, produce and direct three films for them. They immediately purchased the screen rights of Kingsley Amis' novel *The Egyptogolists* which, it was intended, I should develop as a vehicle for Peter Sellers.

Seance had proved a triumph in America and during this visit I was honoured by a special screening at the Directors Guild Theatre. After the performance I received the most gracious compliment that has ever come my way. Leslie Caron had brought Jean Renoir as her guest. She introduced me to him in the aisle after the lights went up. I thanked him for the honour he had done me and said that I had admired him for twenty years. 'Then we are equal,' Renoir said, 'for I have just admired you for two hours.'

My future was mapped out for years to come, only the uncertainty about our unborn child clouded the horizon. I flew back immediately we finished recording the music and plunged myself into work. In addition to the Mirisch contract I was involved in discussions to do a further picture for Columbia, an adaptation of Robert Louis Stevenson's *The Wrong Box* which had been scripted by the phenomenally successful writing team of Larry Gelbart and Burt Shevelove.

Every day seemed to bring new offers, the majority of which I declined to entertain. There was one notable exception. Late one night I was sitting at my desk when I received a call from

Los Angeles. It was from a complete stranger who gave his name as Ronald Shedlo. He was breathlessly frank and told me that he was unknown and without any influence. He said that he had recently formed a partnership with another young hopeful named Michael Laughlin and that together they had purchased the screen rights of a novel by Robert Nicolson called *The Whisperers*. I was their first choice to direct it. 'And if you turn us down,' Mr Shedlo said, 'my next call will be to Ingmar Bergman.'

Such flattery was impossible to resist and after a further exchange of information I told him to send me a copy of the novel and said that I would consider it.

I was also being romanced – for there is no other word – by the late Charlie Feldman. Charlie had been one of the great Hollywood agents. He was now an independent producer, listing amongst his successes *A Streetcar Named Desire*. He was almost the last of the Great Spenders and when he desired something or somebody the price tag was immaterial.

He laid siege to me to direct *Casino Royale*, the only one of the Bond novels that was not owned by Harry Saltzman and Cubby Broccoli. (And here perhaps I should tell a fateful story against myself. Nanette and I were dining one night in the White Elephant and on our way to the table I was stopped by Cubby who asked whether I would be interested in directing a new film he was involved in. 'It's a sort of thriller,' he said. 'Lots of action, shooting and pretty girls. It's called *Dr No*.' I was feeling rather grand in those days and the Fleming novels had not yet become a cult. I gave Cubby some suitably bland reply, saying that I was heavily committed elsewhere, and joined Nanette at our table. When she asked me what the conversation with Cubby had been about, I was very condescending. 'Oh, it was nothing important,' I said, 'he wanted me to direct some thriller called *Dr No*.' I wonder whether, several hundred million dollars later, Cubby has ever recalled that conversation? I certainly have. It haunts me still.)

By the time Charlie approached me with his request the Bond films were well on their way to becoming legends, and Charlie never took no for an answer. He started the bidding by

offering me $300,000 plus other substantial fringe benefits. I
could have all the artistic controls I wanted, in writing, guaranteed. He would fight all my battles for me. At the very least, he
said, would I do him the favour of re-reading the novel? I
re-read it. Although I could enjoy it as a work of fiction it
seemed totally removed from what I wanted to put on film
and I therefore told Charlie that I would have to refuse his
generous offer. Charlie's reaction was to increase the offer to
$500,000 and 25 per cent of the profits. I tried to explain that
the money wasn't the stumbling block, that I didn't feel com-
petent to do justice to this type of material. 'Come to the South
of France and we'll talk it out,' Charlie said. 'There's nothing
like a spell at Eden Roc to get rid of doubts.'

I explained that Nanette was just about to have a baby and
that there were added complications. 'Fine, I'll wait,' Charlie
said. 'Let Nanette have the baby and then move the whole
family down to Eden Roc. Do her good.'

The complications of my life became increasingly hideous
and yet they were the complications of success not failure. I
commenced writing the script of *The Egyptologists* while
Nanette and I counted the days to 14 May. The night before
that date I drove her to Queen Charlotte's once again. The
operation was due to take place at 8 a.m. and my ever-active
imagination ran riot during that sleepless night. I could not
think beyond the first incision of the surgeon's knife. I drove
back to the hospital early in the morning. Nanette's room was
empty when I arrived for she had already gone down to the
operating theatre. On her bedside table I found a letter from
her and in it she said what our marriage had been worth to her.
It was a letter from somebody who had premonitions of death
and it destroyed me. I became convinced that I would never
see her alive again. The trials and tribulations of the film
industry seemed but dross and I regretted all the days we had
spent apart.

The story, of course, has a happy ending. Emma was born
unmarked, perfect, serene, as most Caesarian babies are, for
they do not have to fight their way into the world, but are
lifted out. My darling wife was the one given the gift of pain,
for a Caesarian is the only operation that produces a new life

and perhaps that is what gives women the courage to endure it. When Nanette, unconscious, was wheeled back to her room, she seemed like a beautiful wounded stranger, somebody from another planet, totally removed from my experience.

Amongst the many gifts, telegrams and flowers that arrived at the hospital to congratulate Nanette was a note from Charlie Feldman telling her to choose the colour of a Rolls-Royce convertible. This was Charlie's none too subtle way of soliciting Nanette's vote for the *Casino Royale* project. She did not take him up on the offer.

The climax came just a month after the birth of the baby. I was due to fly back to Hollywood yet again for the sneak previews of *King Rat* and there was a Godfather-like confrontation at London airport half an hour before my departure. Charlie turned up with a group of business associates and representatives from Columbia Pictures who were to be the financiers for *Casino Royale*. With Nanette post-natal-tearful in one corner of the departure lounge, I listened while Charlie put his arguments again and again. By now he had increased his offer to an unbelievable sum of money – $800,000 in all for me to produce, write and direct. He had somehow persuaded Columbia to his way of thinking and their representatives also pressed me to accept. In the end I finally stopped protesting and said yes a few seconds before kissing Nanette goodbye and boarding my plane.

Contemplating my navel in the bathroom of my Beverly Hills hotel suite the following day, I faced the realities of the situation. I knew I would enjoy earning and spending what was left of $800,000 after tax and could see myself writing the script in the South of France with Nanette driving past in her new Rolls-Royce, but I couldn't see myself actually directing the film. You need a particular temperament to embark upon a James Bond fantasy, and I didn't have it.

The moment the offices opened in New York I placed a call to Leo Jaffe the vice-president of Columbia and said that I had thought it over very seriously and despite their more than generous offer had come to the conclusion that I would have to change my mind. His reaction was interesting. He behaved as though I had robbed them of $800,000 and accused me of playing a double-game. Having made the decision I stuck to it, though the recriminations continued for nearly a week. *Casino Royale* was eventually made with three directors contributing, I believe, among them John Huston, and I am sure a good time was had by all. Poor Charlie died a few years later. He alone bore me no grudge and whenever we met would crack a joke about my artistic purity, but never with malice.

I busied myself with other absurdities, notably the sneak previews for *King Rat* which took place in Long Beach. Some unsung genius in the exploitation department had devised a new electronic method of measuring the audience reaction and a selected number of customers were wired to a machine that charted the valleys and peaks of their enthusiasms. Naturally the thing didn't work because when the graph was compared to the script of the film it appeared to give the maximum reading in exactly the wrong places. Subsequently it was discovered that many of the guinea-pigs had deliberately switched the wires, and there were one or two spectacular results from couples necking in the back row who had paid no attention to the film at all.

In due course I was shown prototypes of the posters. It appeared that I had remade *King Kong* for there was George Segal standing on top of a mountain of human bodies, arms outstretched like the beast of yesterday. THE SWINGING, FIGHTING STORY OF THE MEN OF FIVE NATIONS was the legend alongside the art work. I pointed out that the only piece of physical violence in the whole film was a single scene where George slapped Willie Fox's face during a hysterical outburst. Wouldn't, I enquired, the public feel somewhat cheated if they came in expecting to see a John Wayne style action drama and were given something totally different? 'Look,' they said, 'you know your side of the business and we know ours.'

The final advertisements were only slightly less appalling. 'Somehow they survived and raged and roared and cheated and clashed and dreamed and even hoped . . . And none fell lower or felt better . . . than the king of the pack at Changi camp . . .'

I know that every film-maker has excuses for his failures – and, alas, *King Rat* made little or no impression in America, although it was given long and impressive reviews by the top-line critics – but I remain convinced that whatever chance it had was thrown away by run-of-the-mill and basically dishonest exploitation. Now it has become a cult film on the university campuses, but in 1965 when it was first shown Vietnam was still a *clean* war, and the American mass audiences were unlikely to take kindly to such a cynical view of human behaviour. It had no happy or heroic ending and said some unpopular things about the American dream. The real audience, the audience for whom it was intended, stayed away.

After making my protests I packed my bags and prepared to journey home. Before I left I was persuaded to meet an elder statesman who let it be known that he was prepared to favour me with a project of immense and unique importance. He refused to discuss the subject matter in advance and I was duly summoned to the throne room. This was a parody of everything one imagines a Hollywood producer's office to be. I walked what seemed like a hundred yards to the great desk. The elderly producer had his back to the light. The surface of the desk was bare except for what looked like a copy of the New York telephone directory. After a suitable pause for effect and the obligatory offer of an unspeakably bad cigar, he picked up the tome and clasped it to his bosom.

'Mr Ford,' he said, 'I have here what is probably the greatest human story ever told. It is the story of your own very gracious Lord Baden-Powell and I have called it *The Sun Never Sets*. I would like you to consider it, for I think you would bestow a privilege upon what is already a privileged enterprise. Take it home and read it and let me know your views.'

I could hardly lift it, but I managed to thank him and staggered back across the acres of wall to wall carpet producing, by the time I reached the door, enough static to illuminate a small town. His voice called me from a long way away.

'Oh, Mr Ford, just one thing. You'll notice when you read it that we've played down the Boy Scout angle.'

Fifty-two

Knowing that I needed actors of the highest calibre to play the stylized black comedy of *The Wrong Box*, I approached Ralph Richardson to play one of the two eccentric uncles. He was then in Spain, finishing *Dr Zhivago*. He replied immediately with a hand-written letter. 'Dear Forbes, although I was greatly taken with the script and would like to attempt the role of Uncle Joseph, I must point out one glaring error. Corridor trains were not in general service at the time indicated in your piece and unless this is corrected I might be precluded from accepting your offer.'

I replied thanking him for his perspicacity, acknowledged the truth of his observation about corridor trains but pointed out that were we to remove this small error there would be no plot and the role of Uncle Joseph would disappear. I asked if, in the circumstances, he could see his way to overlooking this lack of authentic period detail in the interests of dramatic licence.

His second letter arrived by return. He could accept my argument and the role. There was, however, one small request. He felt very comfortable in the jacket he was wearing for *Dr Zhivago* and since both stories were more or less of the same period, would I object to him wearing the same jacket in *The Wrong Box*?

Students of the cinema who can arrange to see both films in the same programme can check Sir Ralph's wardrobe: his costume is identical in both. Throughout the film he addressed me as Professor and when once I apologized for keeping him waiting (we needed sun and the skies over Bath were dark with storm clouds) he replied: 'My dear Professor, you forget, I have just been working for David Lean. Compared to him you are the speed of light.'

I was fortunate in all my casting and had an embarrassment of riches. I had Wilfred Lawson, that under-estimated, unreliable, uninsurable and supremely gifted actor. I had Johnny Mills, Michael Caine, Peter Cook, Dudley Moore, Cecily Courtenidge, Thorley Walters, Avis Bunnage, Hilton Edwards, Leonard Rossiter, Irene Handl and Peter Graves, to name but a few, for the featured cast numbered seventy. I also had Tony Hancock, surely with Sid Fields one of the two great comedians of our time. And of course I had Peter Sellers giving the quintessence of his talents in the minor role of Doctor Pratt.

Perhaps I can be forgiven for admitting that the greatest pleasure of all was the opportunity of directing my beloved Nanette in a part that finally allowed her to shine. Julie Harris had designed her a wardrobe of superb Victorian elegance which she wore to perfection. Just in case our detractors accuse me of nauseating bias, let me add that her performance was judged by the company she kept and accorded accolades by such respected critics as Mr Bosley Crowther, Mr Alexander Walker, Mr John Coleman and those more-often-than-not fearsome gentlemen who write anonymously for *Time* and *Newsweek*.

Willie Lawson and Tony Hancock gave their last performances on film for me. Each in his way was unique, and they both had an element of tragedy in their personal lives. Both were diffident about their talents and beset with self-doubts, the classic clown's mask hiding the private torment. Tony once said to me: 'You're the only director who ever told me I wasn't being funny. Most of them were afraid, they always felt I knew best, and you see, I never knew. I always wanted to be told, and now I've left it too late.'

I love actors, and *The Wrong Box* was an actors' picture. I loved Tony and Willie more than most. Being a comedian is the loneliest of occupations for the public demands so much, and when the laughter stops – or worse still when you think it might stop – then for some, like Tony, there is only the last act in some impersonal hotel room a long way from home, free at last from the ravening crowd.

Fifty-three

Immediately after I had finished shooting *The Wrong Box* I started writing *The Whisperers*, completing this script in eight days: it seemed to set itself down on the page and the first version was the last save for such small revisions as I made on the studio floor. I had long wanted to do a film about loneliness and old age and Robert Nicolson's beautifully written novella was constructed in such a way that my task of translating it for the screen was made easy.

Nicolson and I were fortunate in that Dame Edith Evans was around to play his Mrs Ross and from start to finish my film was conceived and dedicated to her. I took it upon myself to feel outraged on her behalf that she had been so neglected by the British film industry. Apart from Emlyn Williams' *The Last Days of Dolwyn* and Thorold Dickinson's *The Queen of Spades* many years before, nobody it seemed to me had ever used her truly unique qualities on film. I except the Korda version of *Lady Windermere* because here she was merely recording her definitive stage performance of Lady Bracknell. It seemed a tragic waste that nobody had really written a film to make full use of her extraordinary talents.

She took me entirely on trust. I sent her the Nicolson novella and discussed my thoughts for the film and she agreed to play the part before I had written a word of the script. It is fashionable to suppose that great actors and actresses are difficult people to direct, yet it has always been my experience that the greater the talent the smaller the problems. Those with minuscule abilities usually coast along for a few years on the strength of a single performance and obviously feel the need to bolster their basic inadequacies with a fine show of temperament, the object being, I am sure, to disguise their transparent fears.

There was an incident after the film had finished shooting which epitomises Edith's remarkable character. We were

361

engaged in what is technically known as 'post-synching', a process whereby one replaces faulty or indistinct location sound. During the session I was called to the phone to hear a tearful Mrs Miles explain that our central heating boiler had blown up and flooded the kitchen with a hundred gallons of hot and rusty water. It was coming up to winter and obviously an emergency that had to be dealt with on the spot. I asked everybody in the recording studio to have a cup of coffee while I made a series of phone calls to the manufacturers. The original boiler had cost me nearly a thousand pounds to install some seven years previously and I had fondly imagined that it would perform for the rest of my lifetime. I was therefore amazed when a bland spokesman for the boiler company informed me that seven years was the average lifespan of such an object. 'That particular boiler is obsolete now, of course, so there's no question of spare parts. It'll mean a completely new installation.' 'All right,' I said, 'I won't argue about it, though it seems totally unbelievable – when can you supply and fit a new boiler?'

'What is it now?' the spokesman said. 'October. Well, I can't promise anything, but the earliest we could do it would be January.'

I asked him how he thought I was going to survive without any form of heating or hot water until January. 'Yes, I can see your problem, sir, but that's the situation. There's only one other alternative. You could try a firm of Japanese welders over at Greenwich. Can't vouch for them, but I'm told they handle temporary repairs.' He gave me their number.

When I came off the phone I naturally discussed the disaster with Dame Edith and the others. They all commiserated with me, and then we went back to work. When I was leaving the studio later in the day John Hargreaves, my indispensable colleague over many years, approached me. 'Dame Edith asked me to give you something,' he said. 'But first of all she made me promise that I would get you to accept.'

'Accept what?'

'You have to give me your word first.'

I refused, being totally baffled by the conversation and eventually, without any prior undertaking on my part, Johnny handed me a cheque. It was signed by Dame Edith and the amount was £500.

'She said she has nobody to leave her money to and she was worried about the children going cold. She told me that if you refused to keep it she would never forgive you.'

That night I wrote her a letter. In it I said that although I would not cash her cheque I would not return it and to this day it remains under the glass top of my dressing table, a constant reminder of a very dear and generous woman.

The saga of the boiler had a happy ending. With nothing to lose I rang the Greenwich number and sure enough a Japanese voice answered. Yes, they did weld boilers but only at one price, forty pounds. Yes, they did guarantee the job. They could come that same day. They came. They did the job most expertly and the boiler has performed ever since. And that is how the great age ended.

Fifty-four

The entry in my visitors' book reads: 'Help!' There are two signatures after it – Henry T. Weinstein and Ely Landau. The date is 26 January 1968.

Their unannounced arrival at my door was impressive, for they are both gentlemen of Falstaffian proportions. Henry I knew by repute as a theatrical producer in New York and the man who had been in charge of the last and ill-fated Marilyn Monroe film in Hollywood. Ely, an ex-truck driver who had bought himself a New York television station and then launched into independent film production, was the man behind Sidney Lumet's distinguished *The Pawnbroker*. Their combined credentials, like their girths, were therefore not to be dismissed.

They came on a mission of great urgency. Would I be prepared at alarmingly short notice to take over the direction of *The Madwoman of Chaillot* from John Huston? The film was virtually cast, the main set half finished. The script by Edward Anhalt required further work done on it and for various convoluted contractual reasons the start of the film could not be delayed beyond 28 February. If I agreed in principle they would tell me the other conditions.

Having satisfied myself that the situation with my fellow director John Huston was capable of being resolved honourably, I sat down and read the script. I had only a hazy recollection of Giraudoux's play from the stage production starring Martita Hunt many years before. Anhalt had up-dated the theme and introduced a variety of fashionable attitudes in an effort to give the film a modern validity. I was intrigued but not over-impressed by the possibilities his script offered. I told Henry and Ely of my immediate reaction in fairly blunt terms since they had made it obvious that there was no time for subtleties. Ely was adamant that the script could and would be improved and indicated that Anhalt would make himself available for such rewrites as I deemed necessary.

It appeared there was one major condition and if that could be solved they were confident that the others would be mere formalities. Miss Katharine Hepburn had the right to approve the director. Mr Huston was of course a very old friend of Miss Hepburn.

Was Miss Hepburn aware that they were in London discussing a replacement for Mr Huston? She was aware, but my name had not yet been put to her. I would have to fly to Arles immediately where she was currently making *The Lion in Winter* and convince her that I was a suitable alternative. If I gave the word they would phone ahead and alert her.

He would be a foolish man indeed who turned down the chance to direct Miss Hepburn. Plane bookings were made for us all to fly to Marseilles the following morning on the only available flight. Mr Weinstein and Mr Landau scribbled their message in my visitor's book and departed. I was left with the distinct impression that they were figments of somebody's inspired imagination and that the whole episode was an elaborate hoax.

The plane that took me to Marseilles the following morning lurched and hesitated on the final approach as though sharing my own mixed feelings as to what lay beneath the dark clouds.

One of the most consistent disappointments of public life is that public people seldom live up to private expectations. The famous novelist who writes so vividly of perfect physical love has blackheads by the side of his nostrils and tells smutty jokes. The politician who spellbinds the masses with his rhetoric is oafish without his teleprompter.

So, as the hired Rolls-Royce took me from Marseilles to Arles, I stared with disbelief at the winter-burnt picture-postcard countryside and wondered how long the myth would resist dissolving. Rather as certain murderers put the chopped remains of their victims into baths of acid, I jumbled my preconceptions of Miss Hepburn and dropped them into the sulphur of my experience. What, I wondered, would be left an hour after my arrival? Partially-fleshed bones or merely the gold fillings from her teeth?

We met for the first time in her small hotel room. She greeted me looking like a ravishingly attractive member of the Foreign Legion and within the space of thirty minutes had dazzled, bewitched and flattered me into signing on for the duration of the war. Sunlight, that cruellest of arc-lamps, appeared as if on cue, striking across that remarkable face with an intensity that could utterly destroy the cosmetic industry. Miss Hepburn moved her chair to get more of it. She wore no make-up. I won't say that her face looked wholesome, because that would invite her to dismiss this entire book with her favourite expletive 'Oh shoot,' a form of swearing she has perfected to give the maximum impact with the minimum of offensiveness. In any event 'wholesome' is a word that conjures up a certain bovine quality, and bovine Miss Hepburn certainly is not. It is a face that could give employment to a whole generation of ship-builders.

She gave me a cup of coffee, immediately assuming the multiple role she was to play throughout the entire shooting of the film, that of keeper, nurse, masseuse, assistant director, dietician and analyst. She picked up a copy of the *play* of *Madwoman of Chaillot*, not the screenplay, and from where I sat it looked as though she had studied it for a degree in literature: every margin was covered in notes. She read one of her big scenes to me, uninvited – not to impress (although I was impressed) but merely, I am sure, to share her enthusiasm with the newcomer. Without waiting for any comment from me she then launched into a short speech about John Huston. She wasn't going to be disloyal and she didn't see much point in digging up the recent past. End of that conversation. She steered me into talking too much, telling anecdotes which she laughed at and seduced me while managing to look utterly vulnerable herself. I gave in fact a two-hour audition without knowing it.

We had lunch downstairs in the modest hotel restaurant amid the locals in their Sunday best. It takes a lot, as you know, to divert the French from their stained napkins but Miss Hepburn's appearance, although obviously not unexpected, made everybody appear like characters in a Bateman cartoon. It was a riveting and curious experience, an audience rather than a conversation and yet an audience devoid of pomp. When it was over I was really no wiser as to my own chances, but Ely assured me all was well. 'She liked you all right. She would have said so there and then if she hadn't.'

In Nice the following day I met and addressed Huston's dispirited troops. Taking a leaf from Kate's new-found book, I made a short speech telling his hand-picked crew that loyalty was something I admired and that therefore I would be entirely sympathetic if they felt they could not work with me. If they decided to follow Mr Huston I promised to get them a proper and honourable settlement, but that I wanted a quick answer and no post mortems after their decision had been reached.

Giving them time to think about it I inspected the partially finished set on the back lot of the Studios de la Victorine. The studio at Nice is set back half a mile from and parallel to the sea and the single runway of Nice airport. It is a relaxed and informal little community and like much of the French film industry has an engaging air of unreality about it – as though it is a film set of a film studio rather than the real thing. Those who have seen Truffaut's *Day for Night* will have gained a two-fold impression of what I mean, for that film within a film was shot at Victorine and utilized the remnants of my *Chaillot* Paris. I questioned the decision to build the set in that particular location and asked whether any allowance had been made for aircraft noise. This was greeted as mild heresy. Mr Huston had taken the decision in his wisdom and I must inherit his philosophy. I paid renewed respects to the departed Mr Huston but gave notice that things would now be done my way or not at all. The basic construction of the huge outdoor setting was too advanced for me to change its position, but I halted all further work until I had had an opportunity of establishing priorities.

I was shown the other facilities of the studio and then met Huston's crew again. Three of them had decided to resign and they were thanked for their honesty and paid off. Over a bottle of wine in the studio cafe we then held a council of war to determine how to proceed. It became increasingly obvious that time was against me and that in many areas the production was in a state of disarray. None of the costumes had been agreed, few of the other locations had been chosen, and many of the roles remained uncast. I derived little encouragement from the meeting but did my best to conceal my mounting fears. The only positive factor came from my immediate liking for the great French cameraman Claude Renoir, who gave deliberate professional answers to my many enquiries and who seemed to have a firm grasp of the situation without any illusions.

I flew back to London the next day in order to pack sufficient clothes to last six months and make the necessary domestic arrangements. I had asked Ely to track down Edward Anhalt for at that juncture I had three separate versions of the script – Anhalt's original, Huston's partially finished version and a third collection of papers that took into account Ely's own conception as discussed with Kate. I received word back that Anhalt could not make himself available for any further work on the script. There was no time to think of alternatives and after consultation with Ely it was agreed that I would have to assume the added responsibility of producing a final blueprint. This was a necessary chore rather than a welcome honour and something thrust upon me. At a later date Anhalt (who had resisted sharing any credit with me for the final screenplay) sought to share the blame for the reception it had been accorded at the hands of the critics. He chose to ignore that he had already taken considerable liberties with Giraudoux's text, long before I came on the scene and gave a published interview in which he berated me for daring to tamper with his inventions. Claiming a perception after the event he declined to acknowledge previously, he stated that although *The Madwoman of Chaillot* is a fantasy and satire, fantasy and satire simply don't work on the screen. He may well be right, in which case one wonders why he took the assignment in the first place.

The majority of the star roles had been agreed before I made my appearance, and the list of names read like *Who's Who in the Cinema*. It says a great deal for Ely and Henry that they managed to assemble such a cast, for I inherited with pleasure and expectation Charles Boyer, Yul Brynner, John Gavin, Paul Henreid, Danny Kaye, Oscar Homolka, Margaret Leighton, Giulietta Masina and Donald Pleasance. I was responsible for adding Richard Chamberlain, Claude Dauphin, Dame Edith, Fernand Gravet, Gordon Heath, Nanette and Gerald Sim, together with a host of superb French character actors.

I had no opportunity to get to know my exalted cast before I started shooting, since their necessarily complicated contracts did not allow of such luxuries. I was scheduled to begin shooting on an outside location, an empty hotel on the Promenade des Anglais which was condemned and awaiting demolition. In the fragmented and episodic opening sequence that Anhalt had devised each of the main characters was given a vignette introduction. Paul Henreid came first and he arrived in Nice the night before the first day. I had never met him before and as it turned out I was not to meet him until he made his appearance on the set. This was the pattern of the first two weeks and I began to get the impression that I was hosting a guest celebrity show rather than directing a very expensive film.

The main hazard was the siting of the huge composite setting. When Huston made the original decision nobody had pointed out the proximity to a busy airport. It is my belief that he chose the site in the off-peak season, but of course the moment the tourist hordes returned we were subjected to at least forty take-offs and landings a day and as a consequence suffered inordinate delays. There was no question of not shooting real sound, for the first third of the film consisted of a long scene with all the conspirators seated around a table in front of the Café Francis, talking their heads off. At certain times of the day it was impossible for me to hear what the actors were saying in rehearsal let alone on an actual take. Mainly because of this we slipped further and further behind.

It was of course 1968, the year of the near-Revolution. At first the disturbances were mostly confined to Paris and the larger provincial cities, but within a short time the rumours became realities on our doorstep. Uncollected refuse started to rot on street corners, petrol and food disappeared from the garages and shops, the planes stopped flying as the last of the alarmed tourists made their exit. We were grateful for the bounty of silence but became more and more conscious of our isolation. As a general strike took its grip of the country we discovered that we were the only film unit still working. We were visited by union officials from Paris and our own crew had huddled consultations between shots. Finally a deputation came to me and with the utmost politeness informed me that they had been instructed to join the strike. In the best traditions of French comedy they had arrived at what they hoped was an acceptable compromise. Being at some pains to assure me that their actions were in no way directed at me personally, they said they would honour the call from their union by striking during their lunch hour. This enchanting solution might have come from Giraudoux's own pen, but it was, alas, doomed to failure. The moment the union learnt what was happening more pressure was applied and the production was finally brought to a standstill by a complete withdrawal of labour.

It was during this momentous period in recent French history that Dame Edith arrived, coming via Milan and thence by car to Nice. She appeared dressed as for the Royal Enclosure at Ascot, seemingly unaware of current events, but full of praise for the kindness of the BEA Captain of her flight who had apparently gone below normal operating heights to give his passengers a scenic view of the Italian coastline. Edith and Kate had never met before and it fell to me to make the introduction. I took Edith to Kate's rented villa which was a short distance from our own. There was Edith in a Hardy Amies creation of the palest lemon silk, complete with hat and white gloves, and there was Kate looking like a freshly scrubbed Dead End kid. We sat on the veranda overlooking the calm waters of the Bay and sipped iced tea. I was content to be an unobtrusive witness. They conversed about mutual friends and then Kate offered her hospitality. 'Listen Edith,' she said. 'Please feel free to treat this place as your own. I know how boring it is to stare at the walls of a hotel bedroom after you've been working all day. You can come and go here as you want. Come and have dinner, or else if you want somebody to go over your lines with you Phyllis will always help out, because she's used to doing it for me. This is open house. The only thing I have to tell you is that I go to bed early every night. I get up early and as soon as I've had dinner I go to bed. I'm usually in bed by half past seven, but apart from that the place is yours.'

There was a beautifully timed pause while Edith looked out to sea. 'That's very generous of you,' she said, 'but what do people do who *don't* go to bed at half past seven?'

As a result of the delays I had to lose Claude Renoir who was committed to join another film. To replace a cameraman of his calibre two thirds of the way through a film is not easy. I placed a call to Burney Guffey in Los Angeles. I had no idea of his availability, for since our *King Rat* days his career had happily prospered and he had just won an Academy Award for his colour photography on *Bonnie and Clyde*. It was therefore fairly certain that he was in great demand and the job I could offer was hardly a plum. I explained the situation to him and he told me that he was considering two or three other offers. Then he said, 'But I'll catch the next plane.' It was an act of friendship I shall never forget.

The priorities of our situation demanded that I break off shooting in Nice for a period and journey to Paris where we had to shoot in and around the Palace of Chaillot. I was looking for the Madwoman's house and concentrated my search in the Chaillot district. It seemed that the Chaillot of my dreams no longer existed and I was just about to look elsewhere when I chanced upon a derelict house in the Rue Scheffer half-hidden behind a high wall. The wall itself was decorated with obscene graffiti directed at de Gaulle and the gates to the house barred. I walked over to a garage on the opposite side of the road and enquired as to the ownership of the house. The proprietor made an extravagant gesture of despair. 'It belongs to a mad-woman,' he said. 'She refuses to sell.' He pointed to the two modern blocks sandwiching the tiny house. 'But maybe she's not so mad, maybe she's holding out for more money.'

I could hardly believe my good fortune. Ray Simon, my Art Director, made urgent enquiries and discovered the where-abouts of the owner. Using powers of persuasion known only to film companies, he obtained limited permission for us to shoot in the house and garden.

It was unbearably humid in Paris that week and lacking any form of police protection or co-operation, the logistics of moving a film circus around the streets were formidable. Above all, when we did shoot, we immediately attracted a vast crowd, for even in the middle of a revolution the citizens of Paris were not to be denied the spectacle of Hepburn as La Folle. She stopped traffic whenever she appeared.

Our relationship suffered its only set-back during this Paris period. Infatuated by the atmosphere at the Madwoman's derelict house Kate insisted that she use one of its rooms as her dressing-room. This meant that she was often a considerable distance from our constantly changing shooting area. On the morning in question I was trying to finish a sequence involving Richard Chamberlain at the Palais de Chaillot, and since Richard was the second biggest sightseer's attraction, a large and excited crowd had collected. When I reached the last shot but one on Richard I dispatched a unit car to fetch Kate, but by the time she arrived, costumed and anxious to work, the sun had disappeared and Burney told me he was unable to shoot. Understandably this caused Kate no little annoyance, for her costume and make-up were elaborate and took some time to prepare. She remonstrated with me and I replied in kind before we left in separate cars for our hotel.

I was soaking myself in the bath when the telephone rang. It was Kate. 'Listen,' she said. 'It's ridiculous for you and me to quarrel. Come on over to my room and let's talk it out.'

We kissed and made up over a bottle of Dom Perignon. 'Why don't you break the habits of a near-lifetime,' I said, 'put on a dress and come out to dinner with me tonight?'

'I never go out to a restaurant. The last time I went out to a restaurant I fainted from claustrophobia. Besides, I don't have anything to wear.'

'You travel,' I said, 'with a ton of Louis Vitton luggage. They can't all contain torn trousers and tennis sneakers.'

'No, it's no good asking me.'

'I tell you what I'm going to do,' I said. 'I'm going back to my room to finish changing. I shall make a reservation . . .'

'Where?' she interrupted.

'That's up to me, I'm taking you out and I'm paying. Now, if you'll let me finish. I shall come back here in thirty minutes.

I want you to put your hair up, put on a dress, shoes and a spot of lipstick. If you're not ready when I knock on the door, the love affair is over.'

'Oh, shoot,' she said. 'Son of a bitch, what sort of invitation is that?'

'The best one you're going to get tonight.'

I left. Half an hour later I knocked at her door. I gave my arm to a very stunning lady, dressed as I had requested, and together we went downstairs to the waiting car.

I suppose that to dine alone in Paris with Katharine Hepburn during a French revolution, in a private room in the hotel where Oscar Wilde died, must rate three stars in any personal Michelin.

Kate and I sat on a sofa for two in one of the basement rooms. A fire burnt in the grate beside our private table and after coffee had been served the curtains were drawn and the waiters stayed away. It was rather like the setting for a Victorian seduction and in a sense I was seduced again that evening. A different Kate, a totally relaxed Kate, a Kate devoid of mannerism beguiled the hours away.

It was a strange time to be in Paris, to exist in deserted hotels at reduced rates, without benefit of American voices endlessly demanding Evian water to brush their teeth with, to be a paid spectator, to be directing a film, to have one's cake and Miss Hepburn too.

The ranks were thinning: most of my main cast had departed, but I had several major sequences still to shoot and by now I was under daily pressure from the financiers to finish as soon as possible. Revolutions, jet aircraft, and sundry acts of God notwithstanding, the ultimate responsibility rests with the director. I had been working non-stop for twenty-three weeks and felt totally drained and exhausted, yet as we planned and executed the last few days' work it was not relief I felt so much as that old enemy, sadness. I had worked with so many gifted people, most of them household names, staring through my viewfinder in disbelief on many occasions, finding in the glass an assembly of talents such as few directors are ever blessed with. When the film finally appeared it was fashionable to deride my all-star cast, as though there was something shameful in collecting together so much lustre under one roof. It is a line of argument I find hard to follow.

The last shot was made on 4 July. We had an emotional end-of-picture party for those who still remained, dancing under festooned lime trees, exchanging gifts and letting off fireworks. It was a farewell to so many things. I sensed my life was once again going to change direction, and I am not a creature who enjoys change. I confided in one of my greatest friends, Leslie Bricusse, for while he envies me the settled haven of Seven Pines, I envy him his ability to enjoy the wanderlust. He constantly plans to come home to roost and never does. I plan to travel for sheer pleasure and never do. But you cannot borrow a way of life even from your dearest friends. In searching for the meaning of our past actions we arrive at the present truth: namely that there is no sweet mystery of life, only a continuation of our many imperfections.

The reaction of the previous six months had taken a greater toll of my energies than was at first obvious. I became progressively more disenchanted with the state of the industry which seemed to lurch from one crisis to another. Perhaps what distressed me most was the emphasis being placed on violence in the films being made. Every producer I came in contact with seemed determined to find instant success by outdoing his nearest rival in the violence stakes. Many of the films I saw sickened me and I became openly critical of the way in which the industry seemed to be galloping down a cul de sac. The same old parrot cry of 'give the public what it wants' totally ignored the fact that audiences were still declining every year. What was actually meant was 'give a particular section of the public what *it* wants and ignore the rest'. The poverty of the industry could not be blamed on television and the bingo halls – for in many cases those who bemoaned the existence of the competition had large stakes in the continued expansion of that competition: Judas as it were betraying Judas and collecting twice. To many of us it was a time of growing despair and even the occasional success brought no lasting satisfaction, for in a a way it seemed morally wrong to succeed when so many colleagues were denied the right to attempt success.

Fifty-five

I sat on the beach and watched a deformed dog urinate on yesterday's sandcastles. The dog graphically illustrated my feelings at that moment. It was Easter 1971 and I had just been relieved of all further responsibility as Head of Production for EMI-MGM Studios at Elstree, a position I had held for two years.

Fame, or what passes for fame in this most instant of all ages, can be likened to the pursuit of a holiday sun tan: one works hard to achieve it and suffers in the process. Then, once it has been achieved, one looks in the mirror and wonders if the effort has been worth the candle. It will fade. No question, it will fade. It fades and then the next time around we commit ourselves to the burning sun again, starting the whole ageing process anew. The ultimate reward is a skin like the last croco-dile bag in Asprey's, and underneath a soul parched and devoid of energy.

The story of my term of trial at Elstree was first docu-mented with over-much acclaim, then questioned, probed and criticized, and finally exhaustively explored in obituary. I have not yet reached that sublime state of objectivity, untainted by bitterness, apology or regret, which will allow me to write the full story as I would wish to tell it. I promise all in due course. The time is not yet ripe. Whatever is exaggerated has no value, as Tallyrand said, and my act of contrition, when it appears, will satisfy friends and enemies alike, for I have no intention of depriving the former of necessary pleasures or the latter of summary justice.

In 1971 I sat on a near-deserted beach in Barbados, a stranger to my family, contemplating what remained of my navel. I felt spent, rather like an athlete who has over-trained for the big event, been widely tipped to win and then with-drawn by the coach with inadequate explanation. My health, which had never failed me before, was suddenly in doubt. I had pushed myself very hard for two years, seeking some emotional Camelot I could share with others, shunning all things inferior to my own taste, alienating the exponents of the Age of Compromise and in the end the bold experiment of my appointment had been allowed to fail. It had become convenient for it to fail. That was the impression received and the impression given. It had been put about that I had wanted too much power, yet the truth was I never had enough to carry through my plans in their entirety for the revitalization of an industry that has never lacked spokesmen but consistently lacked statesmen. It had been put about that I hankered after too much personal publicity, a strange accusation from an industry that invented publicity as we know it. It had even been said that I was personally responsible for the depressed price of EMI shares on the stock market, for the purveyors of lies only stab by proxy. Nothing, I learnt, recedes like success.

I went with much sadness from a place I had loved and took my leave of many good people, too many to acknowledge here. I had time during the holiday that followed to ponder the truth of 'After such knowledge, what forgiveness?' Rather like a painter sitting down to study himself in preparation for a self-portrait, I spent long hours out of the sun staring at myself in the mirror of our hotel bedroom. I began a Journal again, I fasted, I made valiant attempts to give up smoking, since there is often a need to inflict self-punishment on such occasions. I felt more and more that, professionally, my life had been blighted by a morality that few others understood or shared.

Nothing one writes is wholly original – only the arrangement of words sometimes makes it appear so. I have tried in this book to describe myself through my actions and if it is an inadequate portrait then the blame must go to the writer in me who, ignoring Connolly's dictum, went astray to explore a world sown with alien corn.

I write this final chapter on a kitchen table in a rented house in Westport, Connecticut. Outside the dogwood has yet to blossom. I am once more hostage to a celluloid fortune. Despite all previous experience I am about to embark on yet another 'grandiose excursion'. I need a little more more madness to survive. My ashtray is full and my conceits intact.

Am I Nobby Clarke masquerading still as Bryan Forbes, or am I Bryan Forbes struggling to return to Nobby Clarke?

Would it be better to revert to an old trick that once served me well and resurrect 'John Seton' of transient *Picturegoer* fame, allowing him to have the last word? What would that ghostly journalist pen now? After all, he knew me better than most.

John Seton writes: 'When asked how much of himself he put into his work, Forbes invariably replied that he had only been concerned with 'aspects of love'. His first volume of autobiography, published somewhat boldly before the age of fifty, contained some indications that this was true. Certainly in his fiction and the films he wrote and directed, he seemed to be reaching out to explain the direction of his own life. He was a man not wholly at ease with success, who could embrace honourable failure with more pleasure than he could endure fame that needed to be bought at any price. He gave the impression that his best was yet to come.

'The aspects of his love were most readily explained by the company he kept and the company he could without pain avoid; those aspects which were ever reflected in his love of his friends, his books, his home, his two daughters and, most especially, of his wife, Nanette.'

Index